Risk Thinking
for Cloud-Based
Application Services

Risk Thinking for Cloud-Based Application Services

Eric Bauer

CRC Press
Taylor & Francis Group
Boca Raton London New York

CRC Press is an imprint of the
Taylor & Francis Group, an **informa** business
AN AUERBACH BOOK

CRC Press
Taylor & Francis Group
6000 Broken Sound Parkway NW, Suite 300
Boca Raton, FL 33487-2742

First issued in paperback 2020

© 2017 by Taylor & Francis Group, LLC
CRC Press is an imprint of Taylor & Francis Group, an Informa business

No claim to original U.S. Government works

Version Date: 20161206

ISBN 13: 978-0-367-65808-3 (pbk)
ISBN 13: 978-1-138-03524-9 (hbk)

This book contains information obtained from authentic and highly regarded sources. Reasonable efforts have been made to publish reliable data and information, but the author and publisher cannot assume responsibility for the validity of all materials or the consequences of their use. The authors and publishers have attempted to trace the copyright holders of all material reproduced in this publication and apologize to copyright holders if permission to publish in this form has not been obtained. If any copyright material has not been acknowledged please write and let us know so we may rectify in any future reprint.

Except as permitted under U.S. Copyright Law, no part of this book may be reprinted, reproduced, transmitted, or utilized in any form by any electronic, mechanical, or other means, now known or hereafter invented, including photocopying, microfilming, and recording, or in any information storage or retrieval system, without written permission from the publishers.

For permission to photocopy or use material electronically from this work, please access www.copyright.com (http://www.copyright.com/) or contact the Copyright Clearance Center, Inc. (CCC), 222 Rosewood Drive, Danvers, MA 01923, 978-750-8400. CCC is a not-for-profit organization that provides licenses and registration for a variety of users. For organizations that have been granted a photocopy license by the CCC, a separate system of payment has been arranged.

Trademark Notice: Product or corporate names may be trademarks or registered trademarks, and are used only for identification and explanation without intent to infringe.

Library of Congress Cataloging-in-Publication Data

Names: Bauer, Eric, author.
Title: Risk thinking for cloud-based application services / author, Eric Bauer.
Description: Boca Raton : Taylor & Francis, a CRC title, part of the Taylor & Francis imprint, a member of the Taylor & Francis Group, the academic division of T&F Informa, plc, [2017] | Includes bibliographical references and index.
Identifiers: LCCN 2016045236| ISBN 9781138035249 (hb : alk. paper) | ISBN 9781315268835 (e)
Subjects: LCSH: Cloud computing--Risk assessment. | Business enterprises--Computer networks.
Classification: LCC QA76.585 .B3943 2017 | DDC 004.67/82--dc23
LC record available at https://lccn.loc.gov/2016045236

Visit the Taylor & Francis Web site at
http://www.taylorandfrancis.com

and the CRC Press Web site at
http://www.crcpress.com

Contents

SECTION II ANALYZING THE CLOUD SERVICE CUSTOMER'S PROBLEM

SECTION III   CLOUD SERVICE QUALITY RISK INVENTORY

SECTION IV   CLOUD SERVICE QUALITY RISK ASSESSMENT AND MANAGEMENT

Author

Eric Bauer is a Bell Labs Fellow in Nokia's Applications and Analytics business group where he focuses on quality, reliability, availability, and efficiency of cloud-based services. Mr. Bauer has authored three books on cloud computing: *Reliability and Availability of Cloud Computing* (2012), *Service Quality of Cloud-Based Applications* (2013), and *Lean Computing for the Cloud* (2016). Mr. Bauer also wrote *ETSI NFV Quality Accountability Framework* (ETSI, 2016-01), *ETSI NFV Service Quality Metrics* (ETSI, 2014-12), and *Quality Measurements of Automated Lifecycle Management Actions* (QuEST Forum, 2015-08). Before focusing on the cloud, he worked on reliability of software, systems, and network-based solutions and wrote three general reliability engineering books: *Practical System Reliability* (2009), *Design for Reliability: Information and Computer-Based Systems* (2010), and *Beyond Redundancy: How Geographic Redundancy Can Improve Service Availability and Reliability of Computer-Based Systems* (2011). Earlier in his career, Mr. Bauer spent two decades designing and developing embedded firmware, networked operating systems, IP PBXs, Internet platforms, and optical transmission systems. He has been awarded more than twenty US patents and has published several papers in the *Bell Labs Technical Journal*. Mr. Bauer earned a BS in electrical engineering from Cornell University and an MS in electrical engineering from Purdue University. Mr. Bauer lives in Freehold, New Jersey.

Abbreviations and Acronyms

ALARP	as low as reasonably practicable
ASP	application service provider
BAU	business as usual
CAS	Casualty Actuarial Society
CFO	chief financial officer
COSO	Committee of Sponsoring Organizations of the Treadway Commission
CRO	chief risk officer
CSC	cloud service customer
CSP	cloud service provider
DOA	dead on arrival
DSPR	Dam Safety Priority Ratings
EBITDA	earnings before interest, dividends, taxes, depreciation, and amortization
ERM	enterprise risk management
ETA	event tree analysis
ETSI	European Telecommunications Standards Institute
FG	forwarding graph
FMEA	failure mode effect analysis
FMECA	failure mode effect and criticality analysis
FMO	future mode of operation
FTA	fault tree analysis
HACCP	hazard analysis and critical control points
HAZOP	hazard and operability studies
HRA	human reliability assessment
IEC	International Electrotechnical Commission
IEEE	Institute of Electrical and Electronic Engineers
ISO	International Organization for Standardization
IT	information technology
ITIL	Information Technology Infrastructure Library

ITSCM	information technology service continuity management
ITSM	information technology service management
KRI	key risk indicator
KPI	key performance indicator
KQI	key quality indicator
LOPA	layers-of-protection analysis
MANO	management and orchestration
MCDA	multicriteria decision analysis
MOP	method of procedure
MOS	mean opinion score
NDI	nondevelopmental item
NE	network element
NFV	network function virtualization
NOAEL	no-observable-adverse-effect level
NOEL	no-observable-effect level
OLA	operations-level agreement
PDCA	plan–do–check–act
PHA	preliminary hazard analysis
PMO	present mode of operation
PNF	physical network function
QMS	quality management system
RACI	responsible–accountable–consulted–informed
RCA	root cause analysis
RCM	reliability-centered maintenance
RFP	request for proposal
ROE	return on equity
RPO	recovery point objective
RTO	recovery time objective
RTP	real-time transport protocol
SLA	service-level agreement
SLO	service-level objective
SLS	service-level specification
SMS	service management system
SO	service outage
SPOF	single point of failure
TCP	transmission control protocol
VL	virtual link
VNF	virtualized network function (e.g., a software-only application that runs on cloud/NFV)

Introduction

Enterprises take risks, like developing new product/service offerings and expanding into new markets and sales channels, in pursuit of reward. Many enterprises are moving their applications and information technology (IT) services to the cloud in order to deliver new services and value faster and to improve their operational efficiency without compromising user service quality. Better risk management results in fewer operational surprises and failures, greater stakeholder confidence, and reduced regulatory concerns; in essence, proactive risk management maximizes the likelihood that an enterprise's objectives will be achieved, thereby enabling organizational success. This work methodically considers the risks and opportunities that an enterprise taking their applications or services onto the cloud must consider to obtain the cost reductions and service velocity improvements they desire without suffering the consequences of unacceptable user service quality. The better the risk management that an enterprise has in place, the more risk the organization can take in pursuit of returns.

Target Audience of This Book

This book is intended for readers from diverse backgrounds:

- **Operations and maintenance professionals** who are responsible for service management of cloud-based applications
- **Service integration professionals** who integrate applications, infrastructure, management, orchestration, and functional components into compelling services for end users
- **Product and solution engineers** who develop cloud-based applications and services
- **Strategy professionals** and consultants who plan an organization's evolution from the present mode of traditional operation to the future mode of cloud-based operation
- **Business professionals** who assure that cloud-based service offerings meet the organization's business objectives
- **Quality professionals** who are responsible for the quality management systems supporting cloud-based service offerings

Given this diverse target audience, the book assumes only basic knowledge of cloud computing and expects no prior knowledge of either risk management or quality management. Development, integration, operations, and maintenance professionals will benefit from the entire work. Readers with limited time can start with Chapter 32, "Connecting the Dots," to see the arc of the cloud risk management story, and then follow cross-references back into earlier sections of the book that are most relevant to them. Strategy and business professionals will find Chapter 31, "Cloud and Creative Destruction," particularly interesting.

A Story Told in Five Sections

This cloud risk management story is told in five sections:

- Section I, "Framing the Cloud Service Customer's Problem"—Chapter 1, "Cloud Computing Fundamentals," lays out the standard definition of cloud computing, highlighting the roles of both the cloud service customer, who operates cloud-based applications and user-facing services, and the cloud service provider, who offers infrastructure, management, orchestration, and service components as-a-service to cloud service customers. This work focuses on the cloud service customer organization's risks. Chapter 2, "Desired Cloud Service Customer Benefits," derives the three canonical business goals for a cloud service customer's investment in the cloud:
  1. Deliver new service and value faster
  2. Improve operational efficiency
  3. Deliver acceptable service quality to users

  Chapter 3 introduces risk and risk management, and Chapter 4 discusses cloud service qualities. Note that cloud security risks are not considered in this work.
- Section II, "Analyzing the Cloud Service Customer's Problem," considers the changes that a cloud service customer must make to sustainably improve their operating efficiency and accelerate their pace of service innovation to deliver new services and value faster. The IT service life cycle model is used to frame the Section II analysis. Chapter 5, "Application Service Life Cycle" considers exactly what can change in the application service life cycle to reduce operating expenses and accelerate the pace of service innovation. Chapter 6, "Lean Application Capacity Management," considers how the key cloud characteristic of rapid elasticity and scalability (Section 1.4.5) can reduce the cloud service customer's opex and accelerate their pace of service innovation. Chapter 7,

"Testing Cloud-Based Application Services," considers how application and service testing changes in the cloud, especially automated validation testing. Chapter 8, "Service Design, Transition, and Operations Processes," considers how the key characteristics of cloud computing enable streamlining of service design, transition, and operations processes to improve operational efficiencies. Chapter 9, "Continual Service Improvement," interlocks the plan–do–check–act cycles of IT service management, quality management, risk management, and lean computing. Chapter 10 considers improving operational efficiency of cloud-based applications. Chapter 11, "Service Strategy," considers how a cloud service customer's service strategy can evolve to accelerate and maximize the benefits of improvements in the service design, transition, operation, and continual service improvement processes.

■ Section III, "Cloud Service Quality Risk Inventory," methodically considers risks that must be managed, controlled, and treated by cloud service customers to assure that acceptable service reliability, service latency, service quality, and service outage downtime is delivered to users. These risks are organized into 14 vectors; each risk vector is considered in a separate chapter (Figure 0.1).

■ Section IV, "Cloud Service Quality Risk Assessment and Management," applies ISO 31000 risk management to the risk causes detailed in Section III, "Cloud Service Quality Risk Inventory," that confront cloud service customers.

■ Section V, "Discussion"—Chapter 31, "Cloud and Creative Destruction," considers how cloud technology will fundamentally disrupt the application service business by dramatically lowering the cost and increasing the flexibility of the computing resources that application services rely upon. Chapter 32, "Connecting the Dots," reviews a holistic risk management framework and recommendations for cloud service customers to reduce the uncertainty that the organization achieves the cost reduction and acceleration in the pace of service innovation that they desire without delivering unacceptable service quality to users.

Extensive cross-references are used, and each section is relatively self-contained, so readers can dive directly into whatever section interests them most.

Standard, Authoritative Concepts and Terminology

This book uses industry standard terminology and concepts to bypass minor inconsistencies across the industry, such as the definition of cloud computing or the differences between test, verify, and validate. Specifically, this work builds on

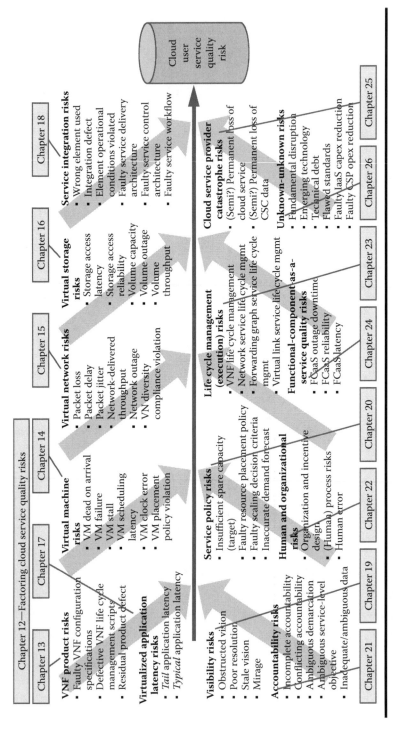

Figure 0.1 Organization of Section III, "Cloud Service Quality Risk Inventory." CSC, cloud service customer; CSP, cloud service provider; FCaaS, functional-component-as-a-service; IaaS, infrastructure-as-a-service; VM, virtual machine; VN, virtual network; VNF, virtualized network function.

the most authoritative references available,* especially the following international standards from the International Organization for Standardization (ISO) and the International Electrotechnical Commission (IEC):

- ISO/IEC 17788, *Cloud Computing Vocabulary and Concepts*
- ISO/IEC 17789, *Cloud Computing Reference Architecture*
- ISO 31000 family of risk management standards
- ISO/IEC 20000 family of IT service management standards
- ISO 9000 family of quality management standards
- ISO/IEC 25000 family of software and system quality standards
- ISO/IEC/IEEE 15288, *System Life Cycle Processes*
- ISO/IEC/IEEE 29119 family of software and system testing standards
- ISO/IEC/IEEE 24765, *Systems and Software Engineering Vocabulary*

As ISO/IEC 17789, *Cloud Computing Reference Architecture*, is not detailed enough to permit rigorous analysis, this work leverages the authoritative European Telecommunications Standardization Institute's (ETSI's) Network Functions Virtualization (NFV, http://www.etsi.org/technologies-clusters/technologies/nfv) suite of standards as a target cloud computing architecture. The book also leverages the IT Infrastructure Library (ITIL®), ISACA (isaca.org) Risk IT, TM Forum (tmforum .org) service-level agreement (SLA) management principles, and QuEST Forum (tl9000.org) quality measurements.

Reliability, Availability, Capacity Management, and Risk of Cloud-Based Application Services

Industry experts were initially concerned that cloud infrastructure would not be a suitable platform for hosting highly available "five 9s" applications. *Reliability and Availability of Cloud Computing* (Bauer and Adams, 2012) argued that traditional high availability and georedundancy mechanisms should satisfactorily mitigate likely cloud infrastructure failure modes. *Service Quality of Cloud-Based Applications*

---

* Officially sanctioned international standards development organizations like the International Organization for Standardization (ISO, http://www.iso.org) and International Electrotechnical Commission (IEC, http://www.iec.ch) are deemed the most authoritative references available. References from industry bodies like the Institute for Electrical and Electronic Engineers (IEEE, http://www.ieee.org), Telemanagement Forum (TM Forum, http://www.tmforum .org), and Quality Excellence for Suppliers of Telecommunications Forum (QuEST Forum, http://www.tl9000.org) are authoritative, but less authoritative than officially sanctioned international standards development organizations. References from a national government like the US National Institute for Standards and Technology, the US Department of Defense, or the US Federal Aviation Administration are also authoritative. Peer-reviewed scholarly works are less authoritative because of less rigorous review and approval prior to publication.

(Bauer and Adams, 2013) methodically considered how subcritical and critical failures of cloud infrastructure, management, and orchestration were likely to impact the user service reliability and latency of cloud-based applications. Key insights of that work were captured in ETSI's *NFV Service Quality Metrics* (ETSI, 2014-12), QuEST Forum's *Quality Measurement of Automated Lifecycle Management Actions* (QuEST Forum, 2015-08), and *ETSI NFV Quality Accountability Framework* (ETSI, 2016-01), which your author developed.

Lean Computing for the Cloud (Bauer, 2016) methodically considers how application capacity management can fully leverage the key cloud characteristic of rapid elasticity and scalability. However, as cloud service customers operate their application services leaner to reduce excessive online application capacity, they increase the risk that insufficient online capacity will be available to serve user demand with acceptable service quality. This book, *Risk Thinking for Cloud-Based Application Services*, methodically considers how cloud service customers manage the risk of achieving their objective of delivering new services and value faster and with improved operational efficiency against the downside consequences of failing to serve all user demand with acceptable service quality.

Acknowledgments

The author gratefully acknowledges Mark Clougherty and Randee Adams for their frequent reviews and insightful feedback. Don Fendrick, Brian McCann, Gary McElvany, Barry Hill, Chris Miller, and Dan Johnson provided invaluable support for the work. Renee Miller, Bob Domino, Jean-Marie Calmel, Narayan Raman, and Enrique Hernandez-Valencia provided business and practical insights into the topic. The book benefited greatly from keen feedback provided by Tim Coote, Steve Woodward, Dave Milham, and Paul Franklin.

FRAMING THE CLOUD SERVICE CUSTOMER'S PROBLEM

I

The focus of this work is on reducing the uncertainty (i.e., risk) of a cloud service customer achieving their goals of reduced operating expense, accelerated pace of service innovation, and acceptable user service quality. Figure I.1 visualizes how this part explains this focus in the following chapters.

- **Cloud Computing Fundamentals** (Chapter 1)—reviews cloud computing basics, roles in cloud computing, input–output model of cloud computing, key characteristics of cloud computing, and cloud service management fundamentals
- **Desired Cloud Service Customer Benefits** (Chapter 2)—reviews cloud infrastructure service provider business models, cloud service customer business model, factoring benefits of cloud/virtualized network function (NFV), information technology (IT) service management objectives, and the focus of this work
- **Risk and Risk Management** (Chapter 3)—considers risk, simplified risk impact model, risk treatment options, risk appetite, risk management methodologies, and cloud service customer risk management
- **Cloud Service Qualities** (Chapter 4)—considers fundamental quality concepts; user service quality; ISO/IEC 25010 product quality; ISO/IEC 25012 data quality; data, information, knowledge and wisdom; and quality model for cloud-based applications

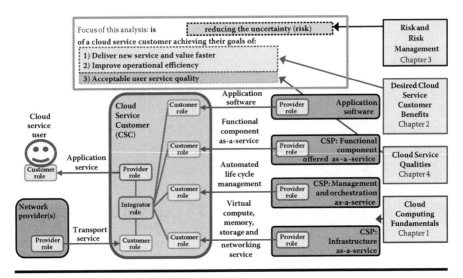

Figure I.1 How Section I frames the cloud service customer's problem.

Chapter 1

Cloud Computing Fundamentals

This section reviews key terminology and concepts that are used in this analysis via the following sections:

- Cloud computing basics (Section 1.1)
- Roles in cloud computing (Section 1.2)
- Input–output model of cloud computing (Section 1.3)
- Key characteristics of cloud computing (Section 1.4)
- Cloud service management fundamentals (Section 1.5)

1.1 Cloud Computing Basics

The standard* definition of cloud computing is a "paradigm for enabling network access to a scalable and elastic pool of shareable physical or virtual resources with self-service provisioning and administration on-demand" (ISO/IEC, 2014-10-15). As the standard ISO/IEC 17789 (ISO/IEC, 2014-10-15) cloud computing reference architecture is not detailed enough to support the rigorous analysis of Section II, "Analyzing the Cloud Service Customer's Problem," and Section III, "Cloud Service Quality Risk Inventory," this work considers the network function

---

* The most authoritative reference on cloud computing is ISO/IEC 17788:2014, *Cloud Computing Overview and Vocabulary* (ISO/IEC, 2014-10-15). The ISO/IEC reference is inspired by the seminal US Government National Institute of Standards and Technology's (NIST's) *NIST Definition of Cloud Computing* (Mell & Grance, September 2011).

virtualization (NFV) cloud architecture. The NFV suite of cloud standards* was developed by the world's leading telecommunications service providers and suppliers via the European Telecommunications Standards Institute (ETSI) as the standard framework for deploying risk communications applications onto cloud computing platforms.

Figure 1.1 gives a high-level architecture framework for cloud-based services to enable users (called *cloud service users*) to access *applications* executing on shared, *virtualized infrastructure* via *access and wide area networking services*. *Management and orchestration systems*, driven by configuration and policy data, automate application and resource life cycle management functions to enable greater service agility with lower operating expenses. Consider each major architectural component separately:

- **Virtualized infrastructure** (or network function virtualization infrastructure, NFVI)—A cloud infrastructure service provider organization makes virtualized compute, storage, and networking resources available to organizations [called *cloud service customers (CSCs)*] to host their application software instances. This architectural component is primarily responsible for fulfilling two key cloud computing characteristics: multitenancy (Section 1.4.3) and resource pooling (Section 1.4.6). Virtualized infrastructure is considered further in Section 1.1.1, "Shared Cloud Infrastructure."
- **Applications**—Application services are implemented as service chains of software components, application instances, and functional components (e.g., database) offered as-a-service. Software applications that execute on cloud infrastructure are called virtualized network functions (VNFs), and cloud-based application services are often composed of multiple VNFs along with functional components offered as-a-service (e.g., database-as-a-service, load-balancing-as-a-service), which together offer valuable services to cloud service users. VNFs are contrasted with physical network functions (PNFs), for which application software is bundled with dedicated physical compute, memory, and storage.
- **Management and orchestration**, along with operations support systems (OSSs), business support systems (BSSs), and management systems together with descriptors and other information elements, enable many aspects of service life cycle management to be automated to shorten fulfillment times, improve quality, and reduce operating expenses. Together, these components are primarily responsible for fulfilling two key cloud computing characteristics: on-demand

---

* ETSI network function virtualization is reviewed at http://www.etsi.org/technologies-clusters /technologies/nfv. Documents most relevant to this work:
  · Introductory NFV white paper (ETSI, 2012-10-22)
  · Updated NFV white paper (ETSI, 2012-10-22)
  · NFV-MAN 001, *Management and Orchestration* (ETSI, 2014-12)
  · NFV-INF 010, *Service Quality Metrics* (ETSI, 2014-12)
  · NFV-REL 005, *Report on Quality Accountability Framework* (ETSI, 2016-01)

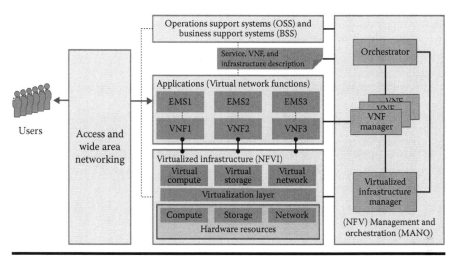

Figure 1.1 Canonical cloud architectural framework. EMS, element manage-ment system. (Based on ETSI, *NFV-MAN 001 Management and Orchestration.* **Sophia Antipolis, France: European Telecommunications Standardization Institute: http://www.etsi.org/deliver/etsi_gs/NFV-MAN/001_099/001/01.01.01_60/gs_NFV -MAN001v010101p.pdf, 2014-12.)**

self service (Section 1.4.4) and rapid elasticity and scalability (Section 1.4.5). Automated life cycle management is discussed further in Section 1.1.2.

■ **Access and wide area networking**—Wireless and wireline networking carries internet protocol (IP) packets from the user's smartphone, tablet, laptop, or other device across access and wide area networks to the cloud service provider's (CSP's) data center where the virtual infrastructure hosting the application soft-ware instance serving the user is located. This architectural component fulfills the key cloud computing characteristic of broad network access (Section 1.4.1).

Two aspects of the canonical cloud architectural framework of Figure 1.1 are particularly important to this analysis:

■ Shared cloud infrastructure (Section 1.1.1)
■ Automated life cycle management (Section 1.1.2)

1.1.1 Shared Cloud Infrastructure

Resource utilization and operational efficiency are improved via resource pooling (Section 1.4.6) and multitenancy (Section 1.4.3), both of which are implemented via virtualization of shared cloud infrastructure equipment. Virtual compute, mem-ory, storage, and networking can be offered by infrastructure service providers to application service providers via technologies such as hypervisors, Linux containers, and other virtualization mechanisms. For convenience, this book will refer simply to virtual machines (VMs) as the primary unit of infrastructure capacity, so this should be understood to cover Linux containers and other implementation options as well.

Virtualized infrastructure operated by CSPs has three logical layers:

- **Hardware resources**—physical compute and storage servers, Ethernet switches, along with cabling, power, cooling, and supporting equipment
- **Virtualization layer**—hypervisors and other software that enables multitenancy so multiple application software instances can efficiently and effectively share hardware resources
- **Virtual compute, storage, and network service layer** that provides virtual compute, storage, and networking service as resources to application instances operated by CSCs.

1.1.2 Automated Life Cycle Management

CSP management and orchestration systems, driven by configuration data provided by a CSC, can automate execution of service life cycle management actions. For instance, automated life cycle management actions can include the following:

- Check VNF instantiation feasibility
- Instantiate VNF
- Update or upgrade VNF software
- Modify VNF software
- Terminate VNF instance
- Scale VNF software instance up/out or down/in
- Heal a VNF instance

Management or orchestration systems monitoring application, system, or infrastructure performance; fault and alarms status; demand patterns; and other factors can even automatically apply business logic to trigger appropriate automated life cycle management actions, further reducing the need for manual actions.

1.2 Roles in Cloud Computing

Figure 1.2 offers one mapping of standard, primary roles onto the canonical cloud architectural framework of Figure 1.1.

- **Cloud service user** is defined as "natural person, or entity acting on their behalf, associated with a CSC that uses cloud services" (ISO/IEC, 2014-10-15). In other words, a cloud service user is an end user, or an application operating

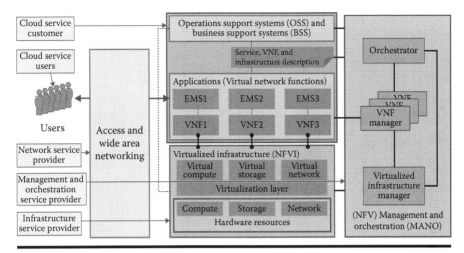

Figure 1.2   Generic cloud computing roles on the canonical cloud architectural framework.

on his/her behalf, who enjoys cloud-based application services such as social networking applications or watching streaming movies.

■ **Cloud service customers (CSCs)** are organizations that operate cloud services for cloud service users, such as an organization that offers streaming entertainment or real-time communications services to end users via cloud-based applications. For example, a company that offers streaming movie services to end users by deploying their application software onto some other organization's infrastructure-as-a-service offering is a CSC. Application services offered to cloud service users are composed from a chain of application software instances (VNFs) hosted by virtual compute, memory, and storage instances offered by an infrastructure CSP and zero or more functional components offered as-a-service by some CSP. A management and orchestration CSP provides automated life cycle management for the service chain and included service components.

■ **Cloud service provider (CSP)** is broadly defined as a "party which makes cloud services available" (ISO/IEC, 2014-10-15). In this work, we focus on three fundamental types of CSPs:

  – Infrastructure CSPs (aka infrastructure-as-a-service providers)— Organizations that offer virtual compute, memory, and storage services to CSCs.

  – Management and orchestration CSPs—Organizations that offer automated life cycle management services to CSCs.

  – Functional component CSPs—*Functional component* is defined as "a functional building block needed to engage in an activity, backed by an implementation" (ISO/IEC, 2014-10-15); some CSPs will offer functional components such as databases or load balancers to consumers via platform-as-a-service offerings. While there is some disagreement across the industry regarding exactly what functionality offered as-a-service should be classified as platform-as-a-service versus software-as-a-service (or even infrastructure-as-a-service), the exact taxonomy is unimportant for this analysis.

Note that a single CSP organization can offer infrastructure, management and orchestration, and functional components as-a-service. Likewise, a particular CSC organization can elect to buy all of their cloud services from a single organization, like their organization's private CSP or a public CSP, or they can stitch together a service from cloud service offerings from several different providers. CSCs may elect to operate the VNF managers that directly support their VNFs, or they may allow the CSP's generic VNF managers to perform that service. Some customers will select a single CSP organization for simplicity, business considerations, or other reasons; other CSCs will select different CSPs based on pricing, performance, functionality, or other considerations.

- **Network provider**—at the highest level, there are two classes of networking beyond the cloud data center:
  - **User access networking**—for access and wide area networking to carry traffic between cloud service users' service access devices and the point of presence for the CSC's infrastructure-as-a-service provider
  - **Intraservice networking**—formally defined as the CSP network provider role that "may provide network connectivity between systems within the cloud service provider's data centre, or provide network connectivity between the cloud service provider's systems and systems outside the provider's data centre, for example, cloud service customer systems or systems belonging to other cloud service providers" (ISO/IEC, 2014-10-15)

This work does not explicitly consider the differences between (wide area) intraservice networking provided by a CSP network provider and (local area) intraservice networking provided by the infrastructure-as-a-service provider; the CSP network provider role will not be explicitly considered in this work. Instead, the general network provider role will be used to capture network providers who both carry traffic between cloud data centers in the service delivery chain as well as haul traffic to and from cloud service users.

Two other roles relevant to our analysis are as follows:

- **VNF software supplier**—organizations that supply applications and component software to CSCs
- **Service integrator**—organizations that integrate application and component software with functional components offered as-a-service and management information to create offerings that deliver value to cloud service users

Real services offered by CSCs will rely on the offerings of several different software suppliers, integrators, and service providers, as well as CSC staff. Section III, "Cloud Service Quality Risk Inventory," in general, and Chapter 21, Accountability Risks, in particular, considers risks associated with complex cloud service delivery chains.

Figure 1.3 illustrates these cloud computing roles in a useful accountability framework (ETSI, 2016-01). Note that the accountability framework highlights the following:

1. Which party is the provider
2. Which party is the customer
3. What product or service is offered by the provider to the customer

For example, infrastructure-as-a-service CSPs are providers of virtual compute, memory, storage, and networking service to CSCs. The framework of Figure 1.3 will be used throughout this book.

Two fundamental points regarding accountability from the framework of Figure 1.3 are highlighted in Figure 1.4:

1. Cloud service users hold CSCs primarily accountable for delivering valuable services with acceptable quality.
2. CSCs have accountability for arranging, managing, and integrating the set of software suppliers, CSPs, service integrators, and others who directly and indirectly support the CSC's service delivery chain.

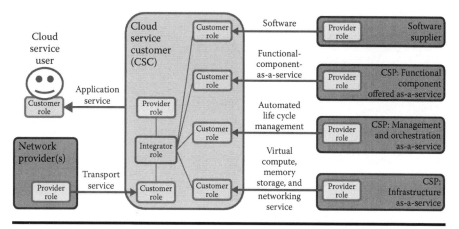

Figure 1.3 Canonical cloud accountability framework.

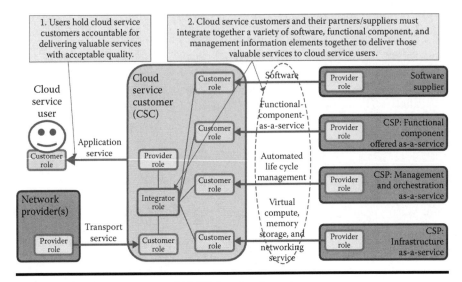

Figure 1.4 Primary accountabilities for cloud service.

1.3 Input–Output Model of Cloud Computing

Cloud service delivery can usefully be viewed as the input–output model shown in Figure 1.5. Fundamentally, cloud service users consume application services from various CSC organizations, and those CSC organizations rely primarily on both CSP organizations and software suppliers. The CSPs rely primarily on both electricity providers and infrastructure hardware and software suppliers. Cash flows

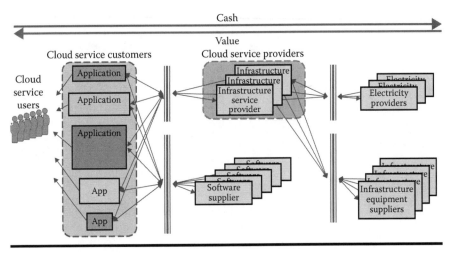

Figure 1.5 Input–output model of cloud computing (general view).

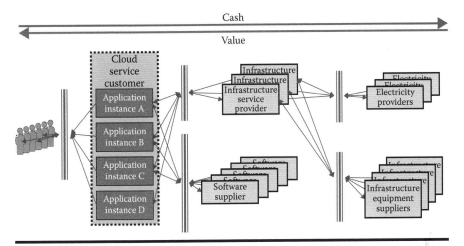

Figure 1.6   Input–output model of cloud computing (cloud service customer view).

from left (cloud service users) to right (hardware, software, and electricity suppliers), and value increases from right to left (e.g., suppliers to CSPs to CSCs).

As this analysis focuses on the CSC, the CSC's view of the input–output model shown in Figure 1.6 is useful. A single CSC will often have application instances deployed on CSP infrastructure in several geographic regions, which gives the CSC flexibility to

1. Place an individual user's workload onto a particular application instance based on the user's location, workload patterns, application performance characteristics, maintenance schedules, and myriad other factors
2. Scale application capacity in different infrastructures based on resource pricing and other considerations
3. Rapidly mitigate service impact of disaster scenarios that impact a single cloud data center or region

1.4 Key Characteristics of Cloud Computing

ISO/IEC (ISO/IEC, 2014-10-15) stipulates that cloud computing has six key characteristics*:

■ Broad network access (Section 1.4.1)
■ Measured service (Section 1.4.2)

---

* The six (ISO/IEC, 2014-10-15) key characteristics of cloud computing are fundamentally the five essential characteristics of cloud computing offered by NIST in Mell and Grance (September 2011) plus *multitenancy* (Section 1.4.3).

- Multitenancy (Section 1.4.3)
- On-demand self-service (Section 1.4.4)
- Rapid elasticity and scalability (Section 1.4.5)
- Resource pooling (Section 1.4.6)

1.4.1 Broad Network Access

Broad network access is defined as "a feature where the physical and virtual resources are available over a network and accessed through standard mechanisms that promote use by heterogeneous client platforms. The focus of this key characteristic is that cloud computing offers an increased level of convenience in that *users can access physical and virtual resources from wherever they need to work*, as long as it is network accessible, using a wide variety of clients including devices such as mobile phones, tablets, laptops, and workstations" (ISO/IEC, 2014-10-15). Operationally, this means that end users can access cloud-based application services via generally available wireless and wireline IP networks.

1.4.2 Measured Service

Measured service is defined as "a feature where the metered delivery of cloud services is such that usage can be monitored, controlled, reported, and billed…. The focus of this key characteristic is that *the customer may only pay for the resources that they use*. From the customers' perspective, cloud computing offers the users value by enabling a switch from a low efficiency and asset utilization business model to a high efficiency one" (ISO/IEC, 2014-10-15). When CSCs pay only for resources that are used, application services that are engineered so cloud resource usage tracks with application service usage, which tracks with application revenue, can reduce business risk by better linking the application service provider's costs with application service revenues.

1.4.3 Multitenancy

Multitenancy is defined as "a feature where physical or virtual resources are allocated in such a way that multiple tenants and their computations and data are isolated from and inaccessible to one another" (ISO/IEC, 2014-10-15). Multitenancy enables CSPs to share virtualized resources across many applications with different patterns of demand and boost the utilization of their physical infrastructure equipment.

1.4.4 On-Demand Self-Service

On-demand self-service is defined as "a feature where a cloud service customer can provision computing capabilities, as needed, automatically or with minimal interaction with the cloud service provider. The focus of this key characteristic is that *cloud computing offers users a relative reduction in costs, time, and effort needed to take an action, since it grants the user the ability to do what they need, when they need it, without requiring additional human user interactions or overhead*" (ISO/IEC, 2014-10-15). This means that CSCs (or automated systems working on their behalf) can install, configure, and provision cloud resources to serve their applications in real time. On-demand self-service of capacity planning and fulfillment actions, coupled with rapid elasticity, enables significant reductions in fulfillment times for capacity change actions compared to traditional deployments.

1.4.5 *Rapid Elasticity and Scalability*

Rapid elasticity and scalability is defined as "a feature where physical or virtual resources can be rapidly and elastically adjusted, in some cases automatically, to quickly increase or decrease resources. For the cloud service customer, the physical or virtual resources available for provisioning often appear to be unlimited and can be purchased in any quantity at any time automatically, subject to constraints of service agreements. Therefore, the focus of this key characteristic is that cloud computing means that the *customers no longer need to worry about limited resources and might not need to worry about capacity planning*" (ISO/IEC, 2014-10-15). Application service providers (or automated systems working on their behalf) can allocate and release infrastructure resources on the fly, thereby enabling application service providers to transform from allocating and configuring capacity based on peak forecast demand (which may never even be approached) to just-in-time, demand-driven capacity configuration.

1.4.6 *Resource Pooling*

Resource pooling is defined as "a feature where a cloud service provider's physical or virtual resources can be aggregated in order to serve one or more cloud service customers.... From the customer's perspective, all they know is that the service works, while they generally have no control or knowledge over how the resources are being provided or where the resources are located. This offloads some of the customer's original workload, such as maintenance requirements, to the provider" (ISO/IEC, 2014-10-15). Resource pooling, coupled with multitenancy, enables CSPs to leverage economies of scale to boost operational efficiencies beyond what has traditionally been feasible.

1.5 Cloud Service Management Fundamentals

CSCs are fundamentally executing information technology (IT) service management processes to support the design, transition, delivery, and improvement of some

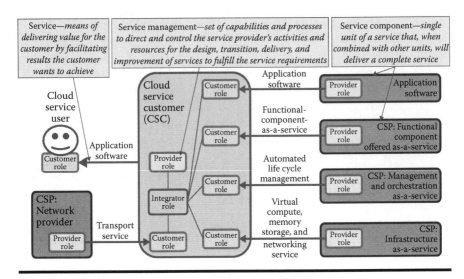

Figure 1.7   Fundamental IT service management concepts.

information technology service offered to cloud service users. The ISO/IEC 20000 family of standards is the most authoritative reference for IT service management* for the design, transition, delivery, and improvement of information technology services. Figure 1.7 overlays standard IT service management concepts relevant to cloud user service quality onto the canonical cloud accountability framework of Figure 1.5. A CSC delivers an application *service* to end users that is produced by a chain of *service components*. The CSC's IT *service management* processes support the design, transition, delivery, and improvement of that service.

ISO/IEC 20000-1, *IT Service Management System Requirements* (ISO/IEC, 2011-04-15), formally defines the concepts of Figure 1.7 as follows:

> **Service**—means of delivering value for the customer by facilitating results the customer wants to achieve

---

* The ISO/IEC 20000 series of IT service management standards includes the following:
  · ISO/IEC 20000-1:2011, *Service Management System Requirements*
  · ISO/IEC 20000-2:2012, *Guidance on the Application of Service Management Systems*
  · ISO/IEC 20000-3:2012, *Guidance on Scope Definition and Applicability of ISO/IEC 20000-1*
  · ISO/IEC Technical Report 20000-4:2010, *Process Reference Model*
  · ISO/IEC Technical Report 20000-5:2013, *Exemplar Implementation Plan for ISO/IEC 20000-1*
  · ISO/IEC Technical Report 20000-9:2015, *Guidance on the Application of ISO/IEC 20000-1 to Cloud Services*
  · ISO/IEC Technical Report 20000-10:2015, *Concepts and Terminology*
  · ISO/IEC Technical Report 20000-11:2015, *Guidance on the Relationship Between ISO/IEC 20000-1:2011 and Service Management Frameworks: ITIL®.*

Service management—set of capabilities and processes to direct and control the service provider's activities and resources for the design, transition, delivery and improvement of services to fulfill the service requirements

Service component—single unit of a service that when combined with other units will deliver a complete service

EXAMPLE: hardware, software, tools, applications, documentation, information, processes or supporting services.

Chapter 2

Desired Cloud Service Customer Benefits

Cloud computing is a disruptive technology that can unlock business value for organizations that effectively exploit it. Cloud service providers (CSPs) offer shared, elastic resources on demand in a pay-as-you-go business model to cloud service customer (CSC) organizations. CSC organizations leverage the elastic, on-demand resources via agile techniques to build application services and value faster than with traditional deployment models. In addition, CSCs can offer service to users with materially lower business risk because the pay-as-you-go resource pricing dramatically lowers the cost of an unsuccessful (think "fail fast, fail cheap") service offering; elastic scalability coupled with pay-as-you-go resource pricing enables the CSC to efficiently cover the upside of surging user demand.

Section 2.1 reviews the standard Cloud Infrastructure Service Provider Business Models, and Section 2.2 considers the Cloud Service Customer Business Model. Section 2.3, "Factoring Benefits of Cloud/Network Functions Virtualization," considers how the canonical benefits of cloud computing are likely to accrue to both CSPs and customers. Section 2.4 reviews the standard IT Service Management Objectives, and Section 2.5 reviews the Focus of this Work, including what topics are out of scope.

2.1 Cloud Infrastructure Service Provider Business Models

Sustainable business models that enable both CSPs and CSCs to thrive are materially different from traditional business models. In particular, cloud infrastructure service provider organizations take on the capital expense of physical compute, memory, storage, and network infrastructure equipment, as well as physical data centers to house the equipment, along with providing electric power, operations, administration, maintenance, and support to offer on-demand resources to CSC organizations. No successful business would invest to build and offer cloud infrastructure without a clear model for obtaining a business value for both the up-front capital investment and the ongoing costs of operating the physical equipment to deliver infrastructure-as-a-service.

The commercial (aka public) CSP business model is fairly straightforward: the aspiring cloud infrastructure service provider organization constructs a business model that covers the capital costs of the equipping and operating their cloud data centers, and then recovers their costs plus a return via fees paid by their CSCs for usage of their elastic, on-demand cloud infrastructure resources. To survive, the public CSP strives to maximize the service revenue returned on their infrastructure investment while minimizing their operating expenses. The business model is not unlike that of a commercial airline: having sunk a large investment in aircraft capacity, the enterprise strives to maximizes return on that investment by filling their service capacity at the highest price the market will bear. As readers are undoubtedly well aware, clever pricing (aka yield management) of airline tickets, hotel rooms, and myriad other services is a best practice for managing (aka shaping) service demand to maximize a service provider's return on finite physical assets. Fundamentally, charging CSCs on a fee-for-service basis simplifies the CSP's business model because of the virtuous cycle in which increasing service demand leads to greater revenues, which justify greater investments in service delivery capacity.

The CSP has to solve two fundamental business problems:

1. Deploy the right amount of physical infrastructure capacity in the right geographies to serve CSC demand. The right amount of physical infrastructure capacity for a CSP is driven by their CSCs' needs, business model, capital resources, appetite for risk, and other factors.
2. Shape CSC demand for virtual resource services to maximize the CSP's operational efficiencies so the business case works. For example, resource pricing might vary based on the following: time of day; grade of service such as whether resource service can be curtailed or preempted; whether capacity was reserved or purchased on the spot market; and so on.

Intelligent pricing models for infrastructure service enable CSCs to shape their individual infrastructure demand so that the aggregate infrastructure demand that the CSP serves is high enough to maximize the CSP's operational efficiencies. For instance, applications with high resource demands during the day (e.g., when their human users are awake) should be financially incented to release excess resources in off-peak periods, and applications that can run anytime (e.g., remote software updates) should be financially incented to shift their demand to off-peak periods to level the CSP's workload by increasing usage in less popular periods. Proper resource pricing is a win for all stakeholders:

- CSCs are charged a fair pay-as-you-go price that permits them to acquire resources on demand and to release those resources when they are no longer needed to reduce their costs.
- CSCs further reduce their costs by shaping their cloud service demand to increase the CSP's operational efficiencies (e.g., discounts for off-peak periods, discounts for accepting voluntary demand management actions by the CSP).
- CSPs invest and deploy sufficient physical capacity to serve all demand, shape demand to maximize utilization and operational efficiencies of their finite physical capacity, and share enough of the savings with their customers that both the CSP and their CSCs win.

There are four standard deployment models for cloud infrastructure:

- **Public cloud**—"cloud services are potentially available to any cloud service customer and resources are controlled by the cloud service provider..." (ISO/IEC, 2014-10-15)
- **Private cloud**—"cloud services are used exclusively by a single cloud service customer and resources are controlled by that cloud service customer..." (ISO/IEC, 2014-10-15)
- **Community cloud**—"cloud services exclusively support and are shared by a specific collection of cloud service customers who have shared requirements and a relationship with one another, and where resources are controlled by at least one member of this collection..." (ISO/IEC, 2014-10-15)
- **Hybrid cloud**—"Cloud deployment model using at least two different cloud deployment models..." (ISO/IEC, 2014-10-15)

Public cloud infrastructure-as-a-service providers will use the aforementioned market-based pricing model for balancing CSP infrastructure capacity supply with aggregate CSC infrastructure service demand. Some private cloud, community cloud, and hybrid cloud infrastructure-as-a-service providers will also use market-based pricing of virtual resources to optimally address their two fundamental business problems of deploying the right amount of physical infrastructure and shaping demand to maximize their operational efficiencies.

Private and community cloud infrastructure-as-a-service provider arrangements that do *not* rely on market-based pricing of virtualized infrastructure resources must find some other mechanism (e.g., centralized planning) to solve the fundamental problems of deploying sufficient capacity to serve aggregate CSC demand with acceptable quality and with sufficient efficiency that operating expenses are controlled. The history of centralized planning in the last century does not suggest that a utopian model of planned resource allocation will work as well (Hayek, 1944) for private, community, or hybrid clouds as market-based pricing mechanisms might; this work focuses on the CSC's business. Fortunately, bursting CSC demand that exceeds a private or community CSP's capacity to an appropriate public CSP (along with appropriate demand management techniques) may provide a practical alternative to the traditional capacity management practice of deploying materially more hardware capacity than is necessary to serve the peak forecast demand several years into the future.

2.2 Cloud Service Customer Business Model

CSCs have three fundamental business problems:

- **Develop and deploy compelling application services to users faster than competitors**—Delivering new services and value to users faster than one's competitors is a significant business advantage. The essential cloud characteristic of broad network access (Section 1.4.1) means that cloud service users can be served by myriad CSC organizations, rather than merely CSC organizations in the same city, state, or region as the user. Successful CSCs must bring compelling services to market faster than their competitors to gain critical mass and market share. Thus, velocity of service innovation and agility are critical success factors for CSCs.
- **Scale up capacity for successful services on a pay-as-you-go basis**—It is fundamentally difficult to predict if and when application services will become popular (e.g., go viral). The essential cloud characteristics of rapid elasticity and scalability (Section 1.4.5) coupled with measured service (Section 1.4.2) and usage-based pricing enable CSCs to deploy modest online application capacity initially with modest pay-as-you-go costs and rapidly scale capacity with user demand. Thus, more of the CSC's operating expenses—and hopefully revenue—track with actual service demand. Coupling more of the CSC's operating expenses for pay-as-you-go virtual resources with actual application service demand derisks the CSC's application business case by reducing frontend costs that must be sunk regardless of whether the application is successful or not.
- **Retire unsuccessful services quickly and inexpensively (aka fail fast, fail cheap)**—Inevitably, many service prototypes, trials and deployments will not be commercially successful, so they should be retired expeditiously to control costs. On-demand self-service (Section 1.4.4), Rapid elasticity and scalability (Section 1.4.5), and measured service (Section 1.4.2) enable the CSC to expeditiously retire unsuccessful or obsolete services and immediately stop paying for them, thereby *failing fast* and *failing cheap*.

Solving these three fundamental CSC business problems enables organizations to rapidly and inexpensively prototype and trial services until they hit upon the right offering that becomes popular with users.

2.3 Factoring Benefits of Cloud/Network Functions Virtualization

Cloud computing offers a range of exciting benefits; however, the upside rewards and downside risks are not evenly distributed to CSPs and CSCs. This section considers how the nine "benefits of network functions virtualisation" expected by the world's largest telecommunications service providers for their massive planned investment in cloud/network functions virtualization (NFV) in the European Telecommunications Standards Institute (ETSI) NFV white paper (ETSI, 2012-10-22) apply to both CSCs and cloud infrastructure service providers. Benefits of cloud computing suggested by other sources are broadly similar to these benefits. None of the nine benefits in the white paper are specific to the telecommunications industry; enterprises in other businesses are likely to be seeking most or all of these benefits when they invest in cloud. Section 2.3.10 gives a Benefit Summary.

2.3.1 Reduced Equipment Costs

The first benefit given in the NFV white paper (ETSI, 2012-10-22) is as follows:

> Reduced equipment costs and reduced power consumption through consolidating equipment and exploiting the economies of scale of the IT industry.

The primary implications of this benefit:

- Suppliers of open, commodity compute, memory, storage, and networking infrastructure for the Information Technology (IT) industry are in fierce competition to maximize throughput and power efficiency.
- CSP organizations who purchase this infrastructure equipment directly enjoy the benefits of this competition among suppliers.

The benefit of reduced equipment costs is captured by infrastructure-as-a-service cloud providers who own and operate infrastructure equipment. The CSP may, or may not, decide to pass along some of those cost savings to their CSCs. There is a small faulty infrastructure capex reduction risk (Table 26.5) to user service quality in that some infrastructure equipment cost reduction feature may compromise compatibility in a way that creates user service impact.

2.3.2 Increased Velocity of Time to Market

The second benefit given in the NFV white paper (ETSI, 2012-10-22) is as follows:

> Increased velocity of Time to Market by minimising the typical network operator cycle of innovation. Economies of scale required to cover investments in hardware-based functionalities are no longer applicable for software-based development, making feasible other modes of feature evolution.

This enables the following benefits for CSCs:

■ **Leverage software-, platform-, and infrastructure-as-a-service** to both derisk development (because offered services are demonstrated to be stable and mature) and shorten time to market (by selecting only as-a-service offerings that are generally available).

■ **Leverage the open and diverse ecosystem** of software and integration suppliers. Rather than having to develop all software from scratch, CSCs can source application components from industry and open-source projects. Suppliers with expertise in integration, testing, and other specialties can be contracted to further accelerate time to market.

■ **Apply modern development practices** like Agile and DevOps. While Agile and DevOps can be applied to applications hosted on traditional hardware platforms, the cloud characteristics of rapid elasticity and scalability (Section 1.4.5) and on-demand self-service (Section 1.4.4) make it easier to fully apply Agile and DevOps principles and practices.

■ **Leverage rapid elasticity and scalability** to shorten test intervals by executing more test cases in parallel on elastically scaled test-bed capacity.

CSPs can also accelerate their pace of innovation compared to traditional deployments. Shortening a CSC's service design and transition intervals to increase velocity inevitably carries a modest risk that flawed process and tool changes will allow user service–impacting defects to escape into the service operation phase.

2.3.3 Reduced Development Costs and Intervals

The third benefit given in the NFV white paper (ETSI, 2012-10-22) is as follows:

> The possibility of running production, test and reference facilities on the same infrastructure provides much more efficient test and integration, reducing development costs and time to market.

The fulfillment steps described in Section 2.3.2 largely apply to reduced development costs and intervals as well. In addition,

- Leveraging off-the-shelf functional components offered as-a-service by CSPs or software from commercial suppliers or open-source projects is generally faster and cheaper than developing bespoke service components.
- Leveraging standardized interfaces and automated life cycle management mechanisms can accelerate service integration activities.
- Leveraging on-demand resource capacity can eliminate bottlenecks associated with scheduling development, integration, and testing activities onto a finite pool of target compute, memory, storage, and networking resources. For instance, as cloud capacity is elastic and scalable, CSCs can order sufficient test-bed capacity to potentially execute all tests in parallel to shorten test pass intervals rather than having to serialize test case execution across a limited number of test beds.
- Improving test effectiveness by reducing the difference between test configurations and production configurations is enabled by cloud. In addition, organizations can use on-demand elastic resource capacity to create huge test configurations that are exercised by huge fleets of test clients to verify at-scale performance that traditionally was impractical or infeasible.

Infrastructure CSPs are likely to remain somewhat constrained by hardware, but functional component as-a-service and management and orchestration CSPs can potentially reduce their development costs and intervals as CSCs can.

Shortening a CSC's service design and transition intervals to increase velocity inevitably carries a modest risk that flawed process and tool changes will allow user service–impacting defects to escape into the service operation phase.

2.3.4 Targeted Service Introduction and Rapid Scaling

The fourth benefit given in the NFV white paper (ETSI, 2012-10-22) is as follows:

> Targeted service introduction based on geography or customer sets is possible. Services can be rapidly scaled up/down as required. In addition, service velocity is improved by provisioning remotely in software without any site visits required to install new hardware.

CSCs leverage rapid elasticity and scalability (Section 1.4.5) and on-demand self-service (Section 1.4.4) to scale online application capacity ahead of demand so that the CSC's opex tracks closer to application demand, which hopefully is tied to revenue or business value; Chapter 6, "Lean Application Capacity Management" considers this topic in detail. For instance, a new service can be deployed with limited capacity (and hence modest cost) and promoted to a limited target market; if the service proves popular, then the CSC can rapidly scale online application to serve that rising demand.

Functional component as-a-service and management and orchestration CSPs can also capture benefits of targeted service introduction and rapid scaling. Note that infrastructure service is fundamentally tied to actual capacity of the underlying physical infrastructure equipment, which is not subject to rapid scaling, and thus, infrastructure CSPs cannot fully capture the benefits of rapid scaling.

Targeted service introduction and rapid scaling inherently carry user service quality risk because if online capacity is not correctly scaled ahead of user demand, then at least some users will not receive acceptable service quality. Specific user service quality risks associated with rapid scaling include the following:

- Faulty scaling decision criteria risk (Table 20.3)
- Inaccurate demand forecast risk (Table 20.4)
- Life cycle management (Execution) risks (Chapter 23)
- Visibility risks (Chapter 19)
- Faulty resource placement policy risk (Table 20.2)

2.3.5 Open and Diverse Ecosystem

The fifth benefit given in the NFV white paper (ETSI, 2012-10-22) is as follows:

> Enabling a wide variety of eco-systems and encouraging openness. It opens the virtual appliance market to pure software entrants, small players and academia, encouraging more innovation to bring new services and new revenue streams quickly at much lower risk.

This benefit is primarily captured by CSCs who have ready access to a wide range of VNFs, open-source projects, and functional components to source service components from. As many of these service components will be offered off the shelf from some supplier or service provider's catalog, they will be available faster, cheaper, and probably with higher service quality than bespoke service components.

Software-as-a-service and platform-as-a-service providers who offer functional components can also leverage diverse software products from across the ecosystem. Infrastructure CSPs have less ability to leverage diverse players across the ecosystem because their drive for operational efficiency may push them to aggressively drive commonality and eliminate complexity from their operational environment.

While new suppliers of key service components can bring benefits to CSCs, they also raise risks to user service quality, especially the following:

- VNF product risks (Chapter 13)—Unfamiliar software suppliers, especially start-ups, may have weak development processes, which allow more residual defects to escape into production resulting in VNFs that may be less reliable than those from best-in-class software suppliers.

- Service integration risks (Chapter 18)—Unfamiliar software suppliers, especially start-ups, may have different integration requirements and assumptions compared to familiar and best-in-class software suppliers, thereby increasing the risk of a service integration defect being introduced and escaping into the service operation phase.
- Visibility risks (Chapter 19)—Unfamiliar software suppliers, especially start-ups, may not provide sufficient visibility into operation of their component to enable rapid and reliable localization and root cause analysis of service quality impairments.
- Service policy risks (Chapter 20)—Unfamiliar software suppliers, especially start-ups, may have unusual, and perhaps unstated, operational policy needs for optimal performance.
- Accountability risks (Chapter 21)—Unfamiliar software suppliers, especially start-ups, may not have consistently and clearly articulated their roles, responsibilities, and demarcation points.

Appropriate supplier qualification diligence can treat these risks.

2.3.6 *Optimized Capacity and Workload Placement*

The sixth benefit given in the NFV white paper (ETSI, 2012-10-22) is as follows:

> Optimizing network configuration and/or topology in near real time based on the actual traffic/mobility patterns and service demand. For example, optimisation of the location & assignment of resources to network functions automatically...

CSCs can leverage rapid elasticity and scalability (Section 1.4.5) and on-demand self-service (Section 1.4.4) to optimally place online application capacity near cloud service users to assure the best quality of user experience. Serving user demand from application instances hosted in a local cloud data center should both reduce transport latency (because photons or electrons don't travel so far) and improve networking quality (because fewer intermediate systems and facilities are in the service delivery path to introduce network impairments). Likewise, software-as-a-service and platform-as-a-service providers can colocate online service capacity with the CSC application instances to optimize service latency, reliability, and availability.

Note that optimized capacity and workload placement has a completely different view from the infrastructure CSP, as their goal is likely to be driving up utilization of their physical infrastructure equipment to maximize their operational efficiency. For example, CSPs can maximize their operational efficiency by placing CSC workloads onto their physical infrastructure equipment to smooth and optimize aggregate demand for their cloud services.

Faulty capacity optimization or workload placement risks delivering unacceptable service quality to some cloud service users.

2.3.7 Multitenancy Support

The seventh benefit given in the NFV white paper (ETSI, 2012-10-22) is as follows:

> Supporting multi-tenancy thereby allowing network operators to provide tailored services and connectivity for multiple users, applications or internal systems or other network operators, all co-existing on the same hardware with appropriate secure separation of administrative domains.

Having multiple CSCs all coexisting on the same hardware (i.e., multitenancy [Section 1.4.3]) fundamentally benefits CSPs as it leverages resource pooling (Section 1.4.6) and permits the infrastructure service providers to increase utilization of their physical resources and drive operational efficiency improvements. However, multitenancy support increases the CSC's application user service quality risk due to virtual machine risks (Chapter 14), virtual networking risks (Chapter 15), virtual storage risks (Chapter 16), and virtualized application latency risks (Chapter 17) ultimately caused by resource-sharing policies and multitenancy operations.

2.3.8 Reduced Power Consumption

The eighth benefit given in the NFV white paper (ETSI, 2012-10-22) is as follows:

> Reduced energy consumption by exploiting power management features in standard servers and storage, as well as workload consolidation and location optimisation. For example, relying on virtualisation techniques it would be possible to concentrate the workload on a smaller number of servers during off-peak hours (e.g., overnight) so that all the other servers can be switched off or put into an energy saving mode.

Infrastructure CSPs pay for the electricity that powers physical infrastructure equipment and the data centers that house that equipment, so cost savings due to reduced power consumption are captured by the CSP.

How the CSP balances their desire for reduced power consumption against consistently high-quality delivery of virtual infrastructure services to their CSCs determines the level of user service quality risk. For example, "live" virtual machine migration enables a CSP to consolidate workloads so they can power off infrastructure equipment offering capacity that is not needed during low-usage periods to reduce power consumption, but the virtual machine migration event may cause transient impact to user service quality. Uncoordinated power management actions by CSPs risk compromising the user service quality delivered to CSC users being served by service components hosted in the virtual resources being manipulated. Thus, it is essential that CSPs and CSCs agree on what level of virtual resource service impact is acceptable and what coordination/orchestration will be provided to minimize the risk of user service impact.

2.3.9 *Improved Operational Efficiency*

The ninth benefit given in the NFV white paper (ETSI, 2012-10-22) is as follows:

Improved operational efficiency by taking advantage of the higher uniformity of the physical network platform and its homogeneity to other support platforms:

- IT orchestration mechanisms provide automated installation, scaling-up and scaling out of capacity, and re-use of Virtual Machine (VM) builds.
- Eliminating the need for application-specific hardware. The skills base across the industry for operating standard high volume IT servers is much larger and less fragmented than for today's telecom-specific network equipment.
- Reduction in variety of equipment for planning & provisioning. Assuming tools are developed for automation and to deal with the increased software complexity of virtualisation.
- Option to temporarily repair failures by automated re-configuration and moving network workloads onto spare capacity using IT orchestration mechanisms. This could be used to reduce the cost of 24/7 operations by mitigating failures automatically.
- The potential to gain more efficiency between IT and Network Operations.
- The potential to support in-service software upgrade (ISSU) with easy reversion by installing the new version of a Virtualised Network Appliance (VNA) as a new Virtual Machine (VM). Assuming traffic can be transferred from the old VM to the new VM without interrupting service. For some applications it may be necessary to synchronise the state of the new VM with the old VM.

The improved operational efficiency scenarios listed associated with *taking advantage of the higher uniformity of the physical network platform and its homogeneity* will primarily be captured by the CSPs who own and operate the uniform and homogeneous physical network platforms. However, some of the automated life

Purported NFV benefit from first ETSI White Paper (ETSI, 2012-10-22)	Directly Benefits Cloud Infrastructure Service *Provider*	Directly Benefits Cloud Service *Customer*	Risk to User Service Quality
Reduced equipment costs	✓✓✓	No	💧*
Increased velocity of time to market	No	✓✓✓	💧*
Reduced development costs and intervals	No	✓✓	💧*
Targeted service introduction and rapid scaling	No	✓✓✓	💧*💧*💧*💧*
Open and diverse ecosystem	No	✓✓	💧*💧*
Optimized capacity and workload placement	No	✓✓	💧*💧*
Multitenancy support	✓✓✓	No	💧*💧*💧*💧*
Reduced power consumption	✓✓	No	💧*💧*
Improved operational efficiency	✓✓✓	✓✓	💧*💧*

Figure 2.1   Summary of NFV benefits by role.

cycle management mechanisms like automated self-healing of failed service components enable CSCs to improve their operational efficiency as well.

Changes to operational policies, processes, procedures, and tools to improve operational efficiency inevitably carry some risk that service-impacting defects will escape into the service operation phase, but robust quality management processes can treat those risks.

2.3.10 Benefit Summary

Figure 2.1 shows the risk to user quality of a cloud-based application service offered by a CSC organization associated with each of the canonical NFV benefits.

2.4 IT Service Management Objectives

As Section 1.5, "Cloud Service Management Fundamentals" suggested, IT service management (i.e., the support the design, transition, delivery, improvement, and retirement of some information technology service) is at the heart of CSCs' value add. Clause 4.1.1.4, "Service Management Objectives," of ISO/IEC 20000-2, *Guidance on the Application of Service Management Systems* (ISO/IEC, 2012-02-15), offers four generic objectives for IT service management:

1. Enable increased business agility through faster delivery of new or changed services
2. Reduce unplanned non-availability for business critical services

3. Optimize the cost of the services delivered through operational efficiency
4. Increase quality of services while reducing risk

Cloud deployment offers CSC organizations an opportunity to materially improve performance against each of those standard IT service management objectives:

1. "Enable increased business agility through faster delivery of new or changed services." An open and diverse ecosystem (Section 2.3.5) furnishes cloud service customers with myriad software applications, components, functional components offered as-a-service, and more service components available off the shelf for immediate inclusion in new services. Increased velocity of time to market (Section 2.3.2) reduces time to first service trial, and targeted service introduction and rapid scaling (Section 2.3.4) enable cloud service customers to rapidly scale up service capacity on success, or experience (initial) market failure fast and cheap so the offering can quickly iterate to success.
2. "Reduce unplanned non-availability for business critical services." Reducing service outage downtime due to both routine and catastrophic failures is considered in this work.
3. "Optimize the cost of the services delivered through operational efficiency." The open and diverse ecosystem (Section 2.3.5) should enable more attractive pricing of service components. Pay-as-you-go pricing for virtual resources, especially from competitive infrastructure service providers, should yield attractive pricing for the compute, memory, storage, and networking resources that host cloud-based applications. Cloud management and orchestration automate life cycle management actions to enable improved operational efficiency (Section 2.3.9) by sustainably removing waste from the cloud service delivery chain.
4. "Increase quality of services while reducing risk." Reducing uncertainty of consistently fulfilling a cloud service customer's user service quality objectives is the focus of this work.

2.5 Focus of This Work

Combining the insights of Section 2.3, "Factoring Benefits of Cloud/Network Functions Virtualization," and Section 2.4, "IT Service Management Objectives," one sees that organizations are likely to invest in developing and deploying cloud-based applications in pursuit of three business goals:

1. Accelerated pace of service innovation
2. Reduced operating expenses
3. Delivering acceptable service quality to users

The focus of this book is reducing the uncertainty (risk) of a CSC achieving their goals of

- Delivering new service and value faster
- Improving operational efficiency
- Acceptable user service quality

The following topics are beyond the scope of this work:

- Functional capabilities and requirements on products and services.
- Access and wide area networking considerations.
- Service usability characteristics, like simplicity.
- Project management risks, like schedule and budget.
- Security-related risks, such as ISO/IEC 27005, *Information Security Risk Management*.
- Supply chain risk management, defined by ISO/IEC 20243 as "the identification, assessment, prioritization, and mitigation of business, technical, and physical risks as they pertain to the manufacturing process including the use of third-party components and services in addition to the delivery of the product to the end user"(ISO/IEC, 2015-09-15).
- Regulatory concerns, such as how to locate data containing personally identifiable information to minimize risk of breaching privacy laws.

Chapter 3

Risk and Risk Management

Businesses take risks to earn returns. Best practice is for organizations to *ensure that risks to services are assessed and managed*.* This chapter lays the foundation for rigorous risk assessment and management of user service quality risk based on ISO 31000, *Risk Management Principles and Guidelines* (ISO/IEC, 2009-11), via the following sections:

- Risk (Section 3.1)
- Simplified risk impact model (Section 3.2)
- Risk treatment options (Section 3.3)
- Risk appetite (Section 3.4)
- Risk management methodologies (Section 3.5)
- Cloud service customer risk management (Section 3.6)

---

* From clause 4.1.1, "Management Commitment," of ISO 20000, *IT Service Management System Requirements* (ISO/IEC, 2011-04-15).

3.1 Risk

The primary definition of *risk* in Merriam-Webster's dictionary is "possibility of loss or injury."* This work will use the more technical ISO Guide 73, *Risk Management Vocabulary* (ISO, 2009), definition of risk as follows:

> effect of uncertainty on objectives
>
> > NOTE 1 An effect is a deviation from the expected—positive and/or negative.
> > NOTE 2 Objectives can have different aspects (such as financial, health and safety, and environmental goals) and can apply at different levels (such as strategic, organization-wide, project, product and process).
> > NOTE 3 Risk is often characterized by reference to potential events and consequences, or a combination of these.
> > NOTE 4 Risk is often expressed in terms of a combination of the consequences of an event (including changes in circumstances) and the associated likelihood of occurrence.
> > NOTE 5 Uncertainty is the state, even partial, of deficiency of information related to, understanding or knowledge of an event, its consequence, or likelihood.

Uncertainty can be broadly factored into two types:

- **Knowledge-based (or epistemic) uncertainty** is variability due to inadequate knowledge. For example, residual defects remain in application software precisely because the software supplier did not have sufficient knowledge of their existence to debug and correct them.
- **Stochastic (or aleatoric) uncertainty** is variability due to the nature of physical phenomena such as random queue lengths and waiting times. For example, the latency and loss characteristics of Internet Protocol (IP) packets traversing a virtual network are subject to stochastic uncertainty due to congestion and queuing. Stochastic uncertainty covers chaotic aspects (aka butterfly effect) of complex systems in which tiny changes in initial conditions produce nonlinear impact on outputs.

The uncertainty-oriented definition of risk is best understood by considering two categories of risk:

- Safety risk (Section 3.1.1)
- Enterprise risk (Section 3.1.2)

---

* http://www.merriam-webster.com/dictionary/risk, retrieved 2/12/16.

3.1.1 Safety Risk

The standard safety-oriented definition of *risk* is given in ISO Guide 51, *Safety Aspects—Guidelines for Their Inclusion in Standards* (ISO/IEC, 2014-04-01), as follows:

> combination of the probability of occurrence of *harm* and the severity of that harm
>
>> Note 1 to entry: The probability of occurrence includes the exposure to a hazardous situation, the occurrence of a hazardous event and the possibility to avoid or limit the harm.

ISO Guide 51 (ISO/IEC, 2014-04-01) defines *harm* as follows:

> injury or damage to the health of people, or damage to property or the environment

The US Department of Defense (2012-05-11) takes a more pragmatic view of safety risk in MIL-STD-882E:

> *Risk.* A combination of the severity of the mishap and the probability that the mishap will occur.
> *Mishap.* An event or series of events resulting in unintentional death, injury, occupational illness, damage to or loss of equipment or property, or damage to the environment. For the purposes of this Standard, the term "mishap" includes negative environmental impacts from planned events.
> *Probability.* An expression of the likelihood of occurrence of a mishap.

Cloud-based applications are rarely safety or human-life critical, so the adverse consequences of poor user service quality often result in a loss of customer satisfaction rather than injury or damage to the health of people, or damage to property or the environment.

3.1.2 Enterprise Risk

Enterprises achieve a return by taking risk, like developing a new product, changing product pricing, moving into a new market, or executing other business decisions. The dynamic and volatile markets that enterprises inhabit are drenched in uncertainty. The Enterprise Risk Management Committee (2003) suggests the following four categories of enterprise risk:

1. **Financial risks**, such as swings in prices of enterprise inputs or foreign exchange rates, liquidity or credit risks, inflation, and so on. Common financial risks include
   a. Poor financial strategy
   b. Asset losses
   c. Goodwill and amortization
   d. Liquidity crises
   e. High debt and interest rates
2. **Operational risks** include risks related to business operations. Operational risks are often quantified via performance metrics like variance, standard deviation, or below-target risk (BTR). Common operational risks include
   a. Earnings shortfall
   b. Cost overruns
   c. Poor operating controls
   d. Accounting problems
   e. Capacity problems
   f. Supply chain issues, including late delivery, poor quality, and fraud
   g. Employee issues and fraud
   h. Noncompliance
   i. High input costs
   j. Information Technology (IT) security
3. **Strategic risks** include risks from reputational damage, competition, changes in patterns of customer demand, market conditions, regulatory changes, technology innovations, and so on. Strategic risks may be quantified via solvency-related measures such as probability of ruin or value at risk (VaR). Common strategic risks include
   a. Demand shortfalls
   b. Customer losses/problems
   c. Merger and acquisition problems
   d. Pricing pressure
   e. Product/services competition
   f. Product problems
   g. Regulation
   h. Research and development
   i. Management change
   j. Corporate governance
   k. Miscommunication/false guidance

4. **Hazard risks**, such as fires, floods, and force majeure events that damage an enterprise's plant and equipment. A broader set of external risks may also be considered as well, including
   a. Declining commodity prices
   b. Rating impacts
   c. Industry crises
   d. Legal risks
   e. Country or foreign economic issues
   f. Weather losses
   g. Partner losses
   h. Political issues
   i. Terrorism

User service quality risks can cascade into the following enterprise risks:

1. **Operational risk**—Failing to meet user service quality objectives represents an operational risk to the organization.
2. **Financial risk**—Failing to meet user service quality targets that were contractually committed in service-level agreements with customers creates a derivative* financial risk of penalty liabilities.
3. **Strategic risk**—Chronic failure to meet user service quality objectives can result in customer dissatisfaction and churn, which raises a reputational risk for the cloud service customer (CSC) organization. One or more high visibility service outages or worse performance on published quality surveys (e.g., J.D. Power Wireless Network Quality survey, Consumer Reports rankings) compared to competitors also create reputational risks. However, this reputational risk is fundamentally a *derivative* quality objective because the market's threshold between acceptable and unacceptable performance is heavily influenced by competitors' performance, and market, regulatory, and other factors.

---

* The US Department of Treasury (http://www.occ.gov/topics/capital-markets/financial-markets/trading/derivatives/index-derivatives.html retrieved 11/15/15) defines *derivative* as follows:

> A *derivative* is a financial contract whose value is derived from the performance of underlying market factors, such as interest rates, currency exchange rates, and commodity, credit, and equity prices.

> We shall call "performance of the underlying...factors" a *primary objective*, and performance of a "value...derived from performance of the [primary] underlying...factors" a *derivative objective*.

3.2 Simplified Risk Impact Model

Figure 3.1 gives a simplified risk impact model. Risk events, like virtual machine failures, occur with some probability across time (i.e., frequency), and risk control mechanisms attempt to limit the adverse impact of those events. Some of those risk events are successfully controlled, so there is little or no user service impact. Risk events that are not successfully controlled produce greater user service impact. Thus, the frequency of risk events, the probability of successful control of a risk event, and the likely user impact of both successfully and unsuccessfully controlled events all contribute to the overall user service impact of any particular risk type.

This simplified risk impact model of 3.1 can be roughly captured as Equation 3.1:

$$Risk_{Event} \approx Likelihood_{Event} \times Consequence_{Event} \qquad (3.1)$$

Event is defined by the International Organization for Standardization (ISO, 2009) as "occurrence or change of a particular set of circumstances." For instance, activation of a residual software defect into a service-impacting failure is an event.

Likelihood is defined by the ISO (2009) as "chance of something happening."

Consequence is defined by the ISO (2009) as "outcome of an event affecting objectives."

Conceptually, risks combine together as shown in Equation 3.2. Note that rare, correlated risks (aka black swans) may produce overall impact materially greater than the sum of the impact of the individual risk events.

$$Risk_{Overall} \approx \sum_{All\ Events} Risk_{Event} \qquad (3.2)$$

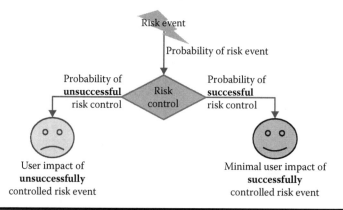

Figure 3.1   Simplified risk event impact model.

3.3 Risk Treatment Options

Organizations, including CSCs, have a handful of basic risk treatment options that can be considered:

1. Replace or remove the risk source (Section 3.3.1)
2. Change the risk likelihood (Section 3.3.2)
3. Change the risk consequences (Section 3.3.3)
4. Share the risk with external party (Section 3.3.4)
5. Retain the risk (Section 3.3.5)
6. Reject accountability (Section 3.3.6)
7. Avoid the risk (Section 3.3.7)

Note that not all options are appropriate or feasible for all risks and some treatments address multiple risk types. CSCs will often apply multiple treatments to high-likelihood and high-impact risks, such as deploying treatments to both reduce the likelihood of a risk as well as taking steps to limit the consequences of risk events that do occur.

3.3.1 Replace or Remove the Risk Source

Organizations implicitly or explicitly make build-versus-buy decisions for every component in their service solution. Every decision to source a component from a particular supplier or to build it with internal resources is a risk treatment decision. For example, if an acceptably low-risk virtualized network function (VNF) implementation is not available to buy and impractical to build, then the CSC might opt for a physical network function (PNF) implementation, or rearchitect their service to eliminate the need for the high-risk service component.

Obviously, it is far cheaper to select the right sourcing option the first time than replacing a component that is found to be unsatisfactory once the service is built, tested, and deployed.

3.3.2 Change the Risk Likelihood

Once a risk source is included in the service solution, actions can be taken to reduce the likelihood of adverse events occurring. For example, better training can reduce the risk of some human errors, and more testing can reduce the risk of residual defects that might be activated in commercial service.

3.3.3 Change the Risk Consequences

Steps can be taken to reduce undesirable consequences resulting from an event occurrence. For example, highly available systems rapidly detect failures and automatically recover user service to redundant elements to minimize the user service impact of inevitable failure events.

3.3.4 Share the Risk with External Party

Service-level agreements are a common way to share risk with a service provider. As will be explained in Section 4.1.4, "Service-Level Objectives, Specifications, and Agreements," a service-level agreement includes both a service-level specification (SLS) and consequences or remedies if the SLS is violated. Broadly speaking, there are two classes of risk-sharing remedies.

- An **in-kind risk-sharing arrangement** focuses on minimizing service consequences of a risk event, like respond/restore/resolve maintenance services and corrective actions following root cause analysis of adverse events.
- A **monetized risk-sharing arrangement** focuses directly on monetary rewards or penalties based on actual performance (i.e., results). Life insurance is a simple monetized risk-sharing arrangement: it doesn't alter the likelihood or consequences of death to the insured party; instead it simply compensates some third-party beneficiary if the insured party dies during the term of insurance.

Practically, in-kind risk-sharing arrangements often help directly improve service quality performance, while monetized risk-sharing arrangements either incentivize suppliers to improve performance or hedge financial risks.

3.3.5 Retain the Risk

Businesses fundamentally retain the risk of offering some product or service in the hope that sufficient customer demand exists at an adequate price point for the organization's business case to work. Along with that overarching business risk, organizations will likely accept some level of business-as-usual risk around their core competences. For example, the risk of executing a flawed or inoperable business plan is typically retained by the target organization. Organizations will opt to retain most ordinary risks as a normal part of doing business.

3.3.6 Reject Accountability

Some risks are beyond the expectations of reasonable customers and thus can be rejected by an organization. For example, if a user's application service session is abruptly terminated due to battery exhaustion of the user's device, then the CSC can generally reject accountability for the service impact because keeping the user's wireless device adequately charged is not the CSC's responsibility. Some extreme or extraordinary risks that are beyond the CSC's reasonable accountability might also be rejected; for example, acts of war may have different accountability compared with ordinary failures. Practically, service providers may explicitly descope some risks by partially or totally placing them outside of their accountability, like how property insurance companies routinely cover damage due to wind or rain, but damage due to storm water flooding may require a special flood insurance rider.

3.3.7 Avoid the Risk

Some risks simply exceed an organization's risk appetite, so an appropriate treatment is to temporarily delay or permanently decline to offer a product or service until the risk landscape materially changes. For example, successful organizations carefully time their entry into a market so they avoid both the myriad uncertainties and risk of entering a new/emerging market too early, as well as the difficult competitive risks of entering a maturing market too late.

While successful organizations are unlikely to permanently decline to use cloud technology, they will each make careful business decisions about the timing and rollout plans of the cloud to avoid using the technology when it is too risky for them…but not wait so long that they are at a competitive disadvantage.

3.4 Risk Appetite

ISO Guide 73 (ISO, 2009) defines *risk appetite* as the "amount and type of risk that an organization is willing to pursue or retain." Organizations typically have different risk appetites for different types of risk. For example, a particular organization may have

- ■ **No risk appetite** for willful breach of laws or regulations
- ■ **Low risk appetite** for financial risk like swings in exchange and interest rates
- ■ **Moderate risk appetite** for cost reductions to their existing product and service offerings
- ■ **High risk appetite** for trialing new technologies, products, and service offerings

Figure 3.2 shows the well-known product adoption life cycle curve, in which innovators adopt a new technology or product first, followed by early adopters, early majority, late majority, and finally laggards. A key factor behind this adoption curve is the risk appetite of the adopting organizations. Innovators embrace the risks associated with being the first adopter of a new product or technology. Innovators know that the particular state-of-the-art product or technology that they choose might not live up to the breathless claims made by suppliers and analysts, and might completely fail as a product or technology; they accept high risk

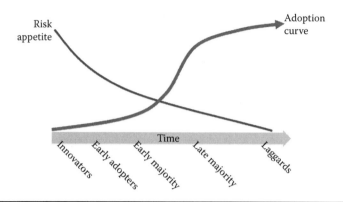

Figure 3.2 Risk appetite across the product adoption curve.

as a trade-off for being first into a market or to achieve some other material business advantage. Early adopters and early majority organizations have less appetite for risk and thus want to see how the innovators fare so they can avoid some of their mistakes. Late majority organizations wait until a product or technology is mature and well understood so risk associated with the product or technology is low. Laggards often have a very low appetite for risk and perhaps wait until they are forced to adopt a product or technology only when it becomes the lowest-risk choice of the alternatives offered at the time.

Note that as successful enterprises have a finite overall risk appetite, they will likely have a higher risk appetite for items supporting their enterprise's differentiated value to improve their position in the market, and take a more conservative risk posture on noncore operations. For example, a retailer inevitably has some appetite for occasional stock-out events that may disappoint customers and has no appetite at all for death or permanent disability due to health and safety risks.

When an objective and quantitative risk criteria statement is impractical or infeasible, one should characterize the amount and type of user service quality risk that the organization will tolerate in pursuit of their overall objectives. One practical methodology is to map a range of general risk statements into risk appetite categories for the target CSC organization. For example,

- **High appetite** for risk…typically in pursuit of positive benefits
    - Innovative service offerings and "failing fast"
    - Being first to market and gaining market share
    - Agility of services offered to end users
    - New technologies and new (sourced) products
    - Early adoption of open-source software and open standards
    - Opex reduction, including staff reductions enabled by automation of service life cycle management and operations
    - Capex reduction

- **Medium appetite** for risk…typically in pursuit of positive benefits
  - Service quality, reliability, availability, or latency impairments impacting small numbers of users
  - Occasional episodes of degraded user service quality for moderate numbers of users
- **Low appetite** for risk…typically avoiding negative consequences
  - "Severity 0" service outages that trigger regulatory scrutiny, make the news, and/or impact stock price
  - Chronic user service quality problems that produce churn
  - Financial risk, like swings in exchange and interest rates
- **No appetite** for risk…typically avoiding negative consequences
  - Willful breach of laws or regulations
  - Death, permanent disability, or time lost because of insufficient safety protocols

Different organizations offering different services to different customers will inevitably have somewhat different risk appetites.

Risk appetite is often visualized as a map across frequency (*x*-axis) and magnitude (*y*-axis) of events, as shown in Figure 3.3:

- The *unacceptable* region covers space beyond the organization's tolerability to bear risk after treatment
- The *tolerable* region covers space that the organization will tolerate after risk treatment
- The *acceptable* region covers normal operational risks with regular policies, processes, and procedures without any exceptional risk treatment
- The *opportunity* region covers very-low-risk space from which the organization can launch cost saving or other valuable activities (e.g., releasing some resources to pursue other business opportunities) and still maintain an acceptable risk profile

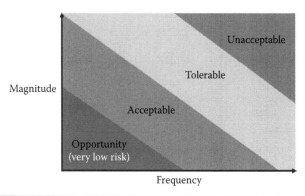

Figure 3.3   Canonical risk map.

Risk tolerance is an organization's readiness to bear a risk after treatment in order to achieve its objectives. For example, organizations inevitably want their IT projects to be completed on schedule and without exceeding their budget, but they typically tolerate modest overruns (perhaps 10% budget overrun and 2-week schedule slip).

Risk threshold is a related concept introduced by ISO/IEC/IEEE 16085:2006, *Systems and Software Engineering Risk Management* (ISO/IEC/IEEE, 2006-12-15), which is defined as follows:

> a condition that triggers some stakeholder action

Clause 5.1.2.2 of the standard goes on to explain the following:

> Risk thresholds are the maximum levels of measured risk criteria that are acceptable without explicit review by the stakeholders. Risk thresholds shall be defined for individual risks or combinations of risks. A risk threshold for the project as a whole should be defined. Risk thresholds should be derived for system and software from the system integrity levels in accordance with the provisions of ISO/IEC 15026:1998. Risk thresholds may also be defined for cost, schedule, technical, and other relevant consequences or exposure values. (ISO/IEC/IEEE, 2006-12-15)

Performance or quality thresholds that prompt notifications, escalations, or management reviews are often practical manifestations of the limit of risk tolerance. For example, the threshold at which a problem must be reported to regulatory authorities or government bodies is often in the *unacceptable* risk tolerance region.

3.5 Risk Management Methodologies

The ISO (2009) defines *risk management* as "coordinated activities to direct and control an organization with regard to risk." Information Technology Infrastructure Library (ITIL®) offers the following about risk management:

> The process responsible for identifying, assessing and controlling risks. Risk management is also sometimes used to refer to the second part of the overall process after risks have been identified and assessed, as in 'risk assessment and management'. This process is not described in detail within the core ITIL publications. (Axelos Limited, 2011)

Risk management is best understood by considering several examples:

■ Safety risk management (Section 3.5.1)
■ Enterprise risk management (Section 3.5.2)

- Risk IT (Section 3.5.3)
- ISO 31000 risk management (Section 3.5.4)

3.5.1 Safety Risk Management

Figure 3.4 visualizes a simple yet effective safety risk management model from the Dam Safety Office, (2011). Periodically, dam failure modes and their probabilities are analyzed; the failure risk is evaluated (often via F–N curves; Section 29.4.4); a risk treatment decision is made; and appropriate corrective actions are taken.

Figure 3.5 illustrates the MIL-STD-882E (Department of Defense, 2012-05-11) system safety process for managing safety risk.

3.5.2 Enterprise Risk Management

Two popular enterprise risk management models are the following:

- **Casualty Actuarial Society (CAS) Enterprise Risk Management** (Enterprise Risk Management Committee, 2003) is illustrated in Figure 3.6, defined by the Casualty Actuarial Society as follows:

  …the discipline by which an organization in any industry assesses, controls, exploits, finances, and monitors risks from all sources for the purpose of increasing the organization's short- and long-term value to its stakeholders. (Enterprise Risk Management Committee, 2003)

- The **Committee of Sponsoring Organizations of the Treadway Commission (COSO) Enterprise Risk Management Integrated Framework** is illustrated in Figure 3.7.

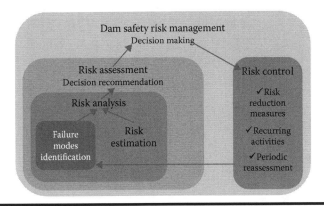

Figure 3.4   Dam safety risk management concepts. (From Dam Safety Office, *Interim Dam Safety Public Protection Guidelines—A Risk Framework to Support Dam Safety Decision-Making,* Denver, Colorado: US Department of the Interior, 2011.)

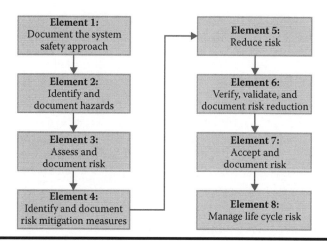

Figure 3.5 MIL-STD-882E system safety process. (From Figure 4 of Department of Defense, *MIL-STD-882E System Safety,* Wright-Patterson Air Force Base: US Department of Defense, 2012-05-11.)

Figure 3.6 Casualty Actuarial Society Enterprise Risk Management.

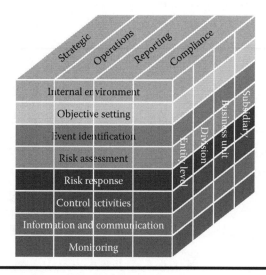

Figure 3.7 COSO Enterprise Risk Management Integrated Framework.

3.5.3 Risk IT

ISACA Risk IT (ISACA, 2009) is a framework (rather than a standard) for the control and governance of business-driven IT-based solutions and services that interlocks with both ISACA's COBIT and Val IT frameworks. The Risk IT framework is based on six principles:

1. Connect to business objectives.
2. Align IT risk management with enterprise risk management.
3. Balance the costs and benefits of risk management.
4. Promote fair and open communication about risk.
5. Establish the right tone at the top of the organization and enforce accountability.
6. Risk management is a continuous and ongoing process.

Risk IT considers IT risk scenarios for events that can impact the organization's business. As shown in Figure 3.8, each IT risk scenario has five attributes: actor, threat type, event, asset/resource, and time.

This work focuses on managing the risk of unacceptable user service quality delivered by cloud-based applications when organizations pursue reduced operating expenses and a brisker pace of service innovation. Security-related threats and general business threats (e.g., omitted external requirements, regulatory risks) are out of scope. The specific actor and time attributes are relevant in practice but are not considered deeply in this work.

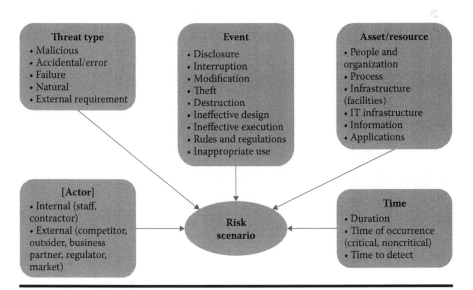

Figure 3.8 Risk IT scenario components. (From Figure 14 of ISACA, *The Risk IT Framework*, Rolling Meadows, Illinois: ISACA (http://www.isaca.org), 2009.)

The Risk IT framework factors the risk management problem into three domains (Figure 3.9):

■ **Risk governance** (RG) assures that risk management is appropriately integrated with enterprise processes, via the following processes:
  – Establish and maintain a common risk view (RG1)
  – Integrate with enterprise risk management (ERM) (RG2)
  – Make risk-aware business decisions (RG3)
    Risk governance is discussed in this work but it is not a primary focus.
■ **Risk evaluation** (RE) assures that IT risks and opportunities are identified, analyzed, and presented in business terms, via the following processes:
  – Collect data (RE1)
  – Analyze risk (RE2)
  – Maintain risk profile (RE3)
    Risk evaluation is a focus of this work.
■ **Risk response** (RR) assures that IT risks, issues, and events are addressed cost-effectively via the following processes:
  – Articulate risk (RR1)
  – Manage risk (RR2)
  – React to events (RR3)
    Risk response is a focus of this work.

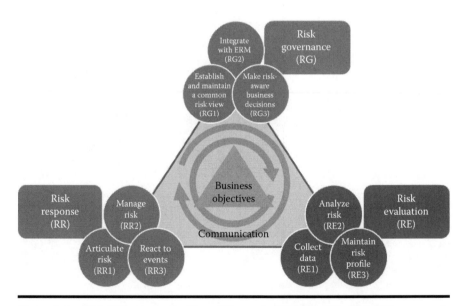

Figure 3.9 Risk IT framework. (From Figure 6 of ISACA, *The Risk IT Framework*, Rolling Meadows, Illinois: ISACA (http://www.isaca.org), 2009.)

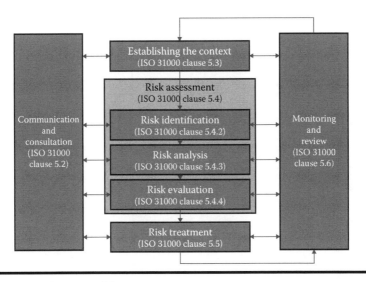

Figure 3.10   ISO 31000 risk management process.

Note that the Risk IT framework was developed before ISO 31000 was published, so Risk IT is not tightly aligned with ISO 31000. This book considers the principles and guidance of Risk IT but aligns with ISO 31000 risk management.

3.5.4 ISO 31000 Risk Management

ISO 31000, *Risk Management—Principles and Guidelines* (ISO, 2009-11-15), is the world's most authoritative reference on risk management and opens with the following:

> The generic approach described in [ISO 31000] provides the principles and guidelines for managing any form of risk in a systematic, transparent and credible manner and within any scope and context.

The ISO 31000 risk management process is visualized in Figure 3.10.

ISO 31000 can be applied to a wide range of disciplines, such as ISO 27005, *Information Security Risk Management* (ISO/IEC, 2011), which applies ISO 31000: 2009 risk management principles to the ISO 27000 family of information security standards.

3.6 Cloud Service Customer Risk Management

Fundamentally, organizations expect that cloud deployment will enable reduced opex and accelerated service innovation while maintaining acceptable user service

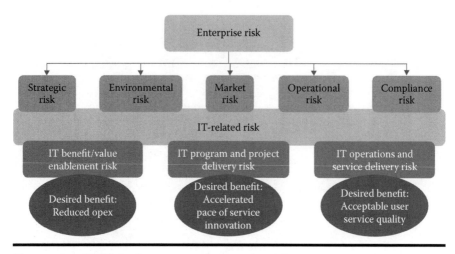

Figure 3.11   IT risk in the context of enterprise risk.

quality. Figure 3.11 shows how the three primary CSC goals for cloud deployment relate to their enterprise risks.

■ The flip side of *reduced operating expenses* is *IT benefit/value enablement risk*; an IT project can fail to deliver the promised or potential value, which compromises the enterprise's position relative to its internal objectives, and perhaps relative to competitors who are successful in adopting a technology. This work considers the expected IT benefit/value to CSCs of reduced operating expense and accelerating the pace of service innovation by deploying applications on cloud technology.

■ The flip side of *accelerated pace of service innovation* is *IT program and project delivery risk*; poor program/project management can doom an IT project to failure. This work considers the expected IT program delivery benefit to CSCs of accelerating the pace of service innovation by deploying applications on cloud technology.

Figure 3.12   Cloud risk management.

■ The flip side of *delivering acceptable service quality to users* is *IT operations and service delivery risk*; failing to delivery acceptable service quality to end users can doom a project. The risk of unacceptable user service quality is considered in this work.

As shown in Figure 3.12, the CSC's fundamental risk management problem is reducing the uncertainty that their cloud-based application delivers new service and value fast with improved operational efficiency yet without unacceptably impaired user service quality, reliability, latency, or availability.

Chapter 4

Cloud Service Qualities

Figure 4.1 visualizes products and services from the cloud service customer's (CSC's) perspective. CSCs operate software products to deliver valuable service to cloud service users. Those software products rely on virtualized compute, memory, storage, and networking service delivered by an infrastructure-as-a-service provider organization. Automated life cycle management services are delivered by a management and orchestration service provider organization based on data.

This chapter applies standard concepts from ISO/IEC 25010, *Product Quality Model*, ISO/IEC 25012, *Data Quality Model*, and other authoritative quality references to consider service qualities in the following sections:

- "Fundamental Quality Concepts" (Section 4.1) introduces *quality* (Section 4.1.1); defects, errors, failures, and incidents (Section 4.1.2); service quality (Section 4.1.3); and service-level objectives, specifications, and agreements (Section 4.1.4).
- User service quality (Section 4.2) delivered by the CSC to their cloud service users.
- ISO/IEC 25010 product quality (Section 4.3) of software products, as well as cloud service provider service products, used by the CSC.
- ISO/IEC 25012 data quality (Section 4.4) of machine-readable artifacts that drive automated life cycle management actions.
- "Data, Information, Knowledge, and Wisdom" (Section 4.5) explains how a CSC's policies and plans translate into data that is processed by management and orchestration systems to automate life cycle management actions.
- "Quality Model for Cloud-Based Applications" (Section 4.6) offers an integrated quality model for CSCs.

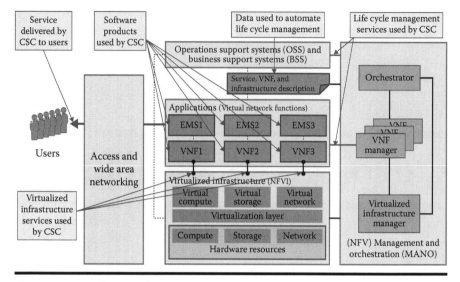

Figure 4.1   Products and services in the cloud service customer's context. EMS, element management system.

4.1 Fundamental Quality Concepts

The following fundamental concepts are considered in this section:

- Quality (Section 4.1.1)
- Defects, errors, failures, and incidents (Section 4.1.2)
- Service quality (Section 4.1.3)
- Service-level objectives, specifications, and agreements (Section 4.1.4)

4.1.1 Quality

ISO 9000 (ISO, 2015-09-15) defines *quality* as "degree to which a set of inherent characteristics of an object fulfills requirements." ISO/IEC 25010 offers a more a practical definition of quality in clause 3.1 that is more useful for our purpose:

> The quality of a system is the degree to which the system satisfies the stated and implied needs of its various stakeholders, and thus provides value.

After all, a flawless implementation of faulty or incomplete requirements is unlikely to yield outstanding quality in use for end users.

4.1.2 Defects, Errors, Failures, and Incidents

Figure 4.2 visualizes the general failure cascade: some *defect* is activated to become an *error*, which produces a *failure*, which may ultimately cascade into a service-impacting *incident*.

Figure 4.3 visualizes a typical software failure cascade: some *human error* produces a *design fault*, which is activated as an error in software (called a *fault*), which produces a *failure*, which cascades into a service-impacting *incident*.

The commonsense notion of a *human error* is formally defined in the context of information and communications technology (ICT) systems by TL 9000 as *procedural error*:

> An error that is the direct result of human intervention or error. Contributing factors can include but are not limited to
>
> a) deviations from accepted practices or documentation,
> b) inadequate training,

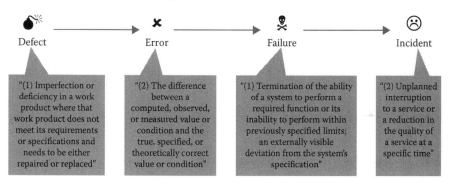

Definitions from ISO/IEC/IEEE 25765:2010, *Systems and Software Engineering Vocabulary*

Figure 4.2 General failure cascade.

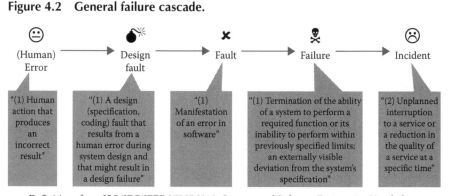

Definitions from ISO/IEC/IEEE 25765:2010, *Systems and Software Engineering Vocabulary*

Figure 4.3 Typical software failure cascade.

c) unclear, incorrect, or out-of-date documentation,
d) inadequate or unclear displays, messages, or signals,
e) inadequate or unclear hardware labeling,
f) miscommunication,
g) non-standard configurations,
h) insufficient supervision or control, or
i) user characteristics such as mental attention, physical health, physical fatigue, mental health, and substance abuse.

Examples of a Procedural Error include but are not limited to
...

c) unauthorized work,
d) not following Methods of Procedures (MOPs)
e) not following the steps of the documentation,
f) using the wrong documentation,
g) using incorrect or outdated documentation,
h) insufficient documentation,
...
j) user panic response to problems,
k) entering incorrect commands,
l) entering a command without understanding the impact, or
m) inappropriate response to a Network Element alarm.

4.1.3 Service Quality

The primary definition of *service* is as follows (ISO/IEC/IEEE, 2010-12-15):

> means of delivering value for the customer by facilitating results the customer wants to achieve

Service quality is usefully considered via the canonical service delivery model of Figure 4.4 (TM Forum, 2012-11): a service provider delivers some service product to a service customer across some defined reference point (aka a service demarcation point). The service provider and customer agree on objective and quantitative service-level objectives (SLOs), which can be captured in a service-level specification (SLS).

Three key responsibilities in the canonical service delivery model of Figure 4.4 are as follows:

■ The service provider is responsible for controlling service quality risks to minimize the likelihood that delivered service fails to meet SLOs.

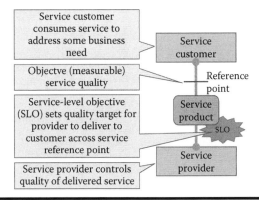

Figure 4.4   Canonical service delivery model.

- The service customer engineers their service architecture and operational policies to both
  - Minimize the sensitivity of their customer-facing service quality to episodes of poor delivered service quality from their service provider
  - Minimize adverse user service consequences of unacceptable service quality delivered by their service provider
- Delivered service quality is monitored across the reference point to determine if/when delivered service quality fails to meet objectives. Failure to meet quality objectives typically triggers root cause analysis and corrective actions to enable continuous quality improvement.

4.1.4 Service-Level Objectives, Specifications, and Agreements

As shown in Figure 4.5, service customers and service providers align their quality expectations via SLSs and occasionally formalize that alignment via a service-level agreement (SLA) or operational-level agreement (OLA). Let's consider that roll-up one level at a time.

According to TM Forum (2012–11), an SLS fundamentally has four components:

1. **Key quality indicator**, which defines a service quality measurement that is relevant to the service customer, like service outage downtime or service reliability.
2. **Estimator**, or **measurement procedure**, for exactly how the service quality measurement will be made. Mature quality metric specifications, like *product*

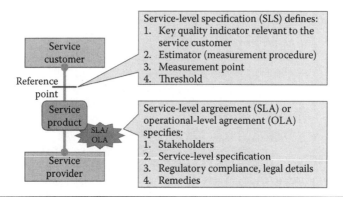

Figure 4.5   Service-level specifications and agreements.

attributable service outage downtime (measurement SO4 [QuEST Forum, 2012-12-31]), are good estimators.

3. **Measurement point** defines where the service quality measurement is to be taken. Ideally, this is the demarcation point between the service provider or supplier's accountability and the customer's accountability, but the decomposed and virtualized nature of cloud-based applications and services makes specification of measurement points far more challenging than with traditional, physical equipment.

4. **Threshold** specifies the minimum acceptable level of measured service quality. Note that threshold in an SLS is neither the engineered performance target nor the best estimate of likely performance but, rather, the limit (i.e., minimum level) of acceptability agreed on by the service customer and service provider.

SLSs can then be incorporated into agreements that stipulate remedies if delivered service quality fails to meet the agreed-upon threshold. These agreements are commonly called service-level agreements (SLAs) when the customer and provider are from different organizations or operational-level agreements (OLAs) if the customer and provider are from the same commercial organization. These agreements typically include the following:

1. **Stakeholders**—Service provider and customer organizations are explicitly identified, along with the roles and responsibilities of each party.

2. **SLS**—Giving measurement details and a minimum acceptable service level for one or more key quality indicators.

3. **Remedy**—If actual service quality breaches the threshold of minimum acceptable service quality stipulated in the SLS. Typically, the remedy details the service provider's response to unacceptable service quality, such as how quickly they will respond and resolve the problem, what (if any) root cause analysis will be performed by the service provider and shared with the customer, and how quickly corrective actions will be deployed to prevent reoccurrence of the service quality impairment. In extreme cases, remedies include the right of the customer to prematurely terminate the contract with the service provider and/or be liable for liquidated damages.
4. **Regulatory compliance and legal details**—As appropriate.

Note that SLAs can be faulty, such as incompletely specifying a measurement procedure or measurement point, or setting the wrong threshold, so regular SLA reviews can be conducted, and appropriate SLA refinements agreed on, to assure reasonable outcomes for both service providers and service customers.

4.2 User Service Quality

The focus of this analysis is the risk of service quality impairments experienced by users of application services offered by CSCs. This analysis considers the following indicators detailed in Section 4.2.1, "User Service Qualities to be Considered":

■ Service Reliability (Section 4.2.1.1)
■ Service Latency (Section 4.2.1.2)
■ Service Quality (Section 4.2.1.3)
■ Service Outage Downtime (Section 4.2.1.4)

The suitability of these four generic service quality indicators is demonstrated by mapping them against two authoritative quality-in-use standards:

1. International telecommunications union quality of service (Section 4.2.2)
2. ISO/IEC 25010 quality in use (Section 4.2.3)

As shown in Figure 4.6, user service quality can fundamentally be measured either at or near the point of use (e.g., the user's smartphone) or at the edge of the CSC's accountability perimeter (e.g., the demarcation point between the CSC's infrastructure service provider and the appropriate network service provider). As this work does not explicitly consider access and wide area networking impairments, we will consider user service quality risks measurable at the infrastructure provider's point of presence.

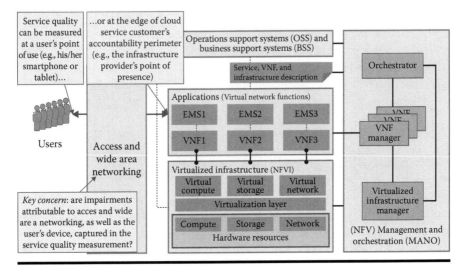

Figure 4.6 Logical measurement points for user service quality.

4.2.1 User Service Qualities to Be Considered

There are four broad and generally applicable user service quality characteristics to consider for key indicators:

1. Service reliability (Section 4.2.1.1)
2. Service latency (Section 4.2.1.2)
3. Service quality (Section 4.2.1.3)
4. Service outage downtime (Section 4.2.1.4)

Various application-specific user service qualities, like lip sync, may be appropriate for specific applications, but application-specific quality objectives are beyond the scope of this work.

4.2.1.1 Service Reliability

Service reliability is the probability that an application or system correctly responds to input within the maximum acceptable response time. Service reliability of transaction-oriented applications is the probability that a user request will be correctly served within the maximum acceptable time. Session-oriented services—like streaming media, interactive, communications and gaming—often have two high-level service reliability metrics:

1. **Service accessibility**—characterizes the ability of a user to establish a service session, such as the ability of a user to establish a service session, stream a video, or establish a call

2. **Service retainability**—characterizes the likelihood that a successfully established session delivers acceptable service until orderly session release, such as the likelihood that a streaming video, voice/video call, or gaming session continues until normal session termination

4.2.1.2 Service Latency

Application response time or service latency strongly impacts an end user's quality of experience. Unacceptably long service latency will prompt users to abandon a pending request, thereby deprecating the operation into a service reliability impairment. Postdial delay is a widely known service latency measurement; the interval between pressing *play* and when video rendering begins (aka video access time) is another well-known service latency measurement.

4.2.1.3 Service Quality

Different applications have different sensitivities to delivery impairments of bearer traffic. The user-visible impact of service delivery impairments like lost or late packets depends on the type of traffic (e.g., voice versus video), the nature and duration of the delivery impairment, the lost packet compensation implementation of the end point, and even exactly what traffic was impacted (e.g., video I-frame versus P-frame). Whether or not an episode of lost or late packets is transparent to an end user or intolerable is directly impacted by all of these factors. Service quality measurements are generally application specific, like video freeze rate, video freeze time ratio, and video quality for streaming video services.

4.2.1.4 Service Outage Downtime

Outage (but not downtime) is formally defined by TL 9000 as follows:

> incident that causes the unavailability of service or functionality (QuEST Forum, 2012-12-31)

Downtime (but not outage) is formally defined by Information Technology Infrastructure Library (ITIL®) as follows:

> The time when an IT service or other configuration item is not available during its agreed service time. The availability of an IT service is often calculated from agreed service time and downtime. (Axelos Limited, 2011)

Service outage downtime is usefully considered along two dimensions:

1. **Outage downtime** because every minute of outage downtime potentially impacts a system or service users. Ideally, outage downtime measurements prorate the impact of partial capacity loss and partial functionality loss events; for

example, an event that impacted all functionality for half of a service's users for 60 minutes would be counted as 30 minutes of service outage downtime (i.e., 50% capacity loss of a 60-minute outage). TL 9000 "Service Impact All Causes Outage Downtime" per unit per year (SO2 [QuEST Forum, 2012-12-31]) or "Service Impact Product-Attributable Outage Downtime" per unit per year (SO4 [QuEST Forum, 2012-12-31]) are best-practice measurements of outage downtime.

2. **Outage event frequency** because each event creates incremental maintenance work for the service provider themselves, and perhaps forces users to waste their time working around the outage event. TL 9000 "Service Impact All Causes Outage Frequency" per unit per year (SO1 [QuEST Forum, 2012-12-31]) and Service Impact Product-Attributable Outage Frequency per unit per year (SO3 [QuEST Forum, 2012-12-31]) are best-practice measurements of outage event frequency.

4.2.2 *International Telecommunications Union Quality of Service*

The International Telecommunications Union (ITU) defines quality of service (QoS) as the "totality of characteristics of a telecommunications service that bear on its ability to satisfy stated and implied needs of the user of the service" (ITU-T, 2008-09). Clause 3.1.1.5 of (ITU-T, 2008-09) defines six service quality characteristics:

1. **Speed**—*Performance criterion that describes the time interval that is used to perform the function or the rate at which the function is performed. (The function may or may not be performed with the desired accuracy.)* This characteristic will be measured via service latency (Section 4.2.1.2), which is the mathematical reciprocal of speed. As each operation has a completion latency, it is useful to aggregate myriad individual measurements into a cumulative distribution function and consider the speed of a particular point on that distribution, such as the 90th percentile latency, 99th percentile latency, etc.

2. **Accuracy**—*Performance criterion that describes the degree of correctness with which the function is performed. (The function may or may not be performed with the desired speed.)* This characteristic will be captured via service reliability (Section 4.2.1.1).

3. **Dependability**—*Performance criterion that describes the degree of certainty (or surety) with which the function is performed regardless of speed or accuracy, but within a given observation interval.* This characteristic is indirectly measured via service reliability (Section 4.2.1.1).

4. **Availability**—*Availability of an item to be in a state to perform a required function at a given instant of time or at any instant of time within a given time*

interval, assuming that the external resources, if required, are provided. This characteristic is measured via service outage downtime (Section 4.2.1.4), which is mathematically related to availability via Equation 4.1.

$$Availability = \frac{total\_time - service\_outage\_downtime}{total\_time} \qquad (4.1)$$

5. **Reliability**—*The probability that an item can perform a required function under stated conditions for a given time interval.* This characteristic is captured via service reliability (Section 4.2.1.1).
6. **Simplicity**—*Ease and lack of complexity in the benefit to the user of a function of the service.* Usability characteristics are not considered in this book.

4.2.3 ISO/IEC 25010 Quality in Use

ISO/IEC 25010 (ISO/IEC/IEEE, 2010-12-15) clause 4.1 begins as follows:

> Quality in use is the degree to which a product or system can be used by specific users to meet their needs to achieve goals with effectiveness, efficiency, freedom from risk and satisfaction in specific contexts of use.

For this analysis, quality in use is the degree to which an application can be used by cloud service users to meet their needs to achieve specific goals with effectiveness, efficiency, freedom from risk, and satisfaction in specific contexts of use.

ISO/IEC 25010 formally defines quality in use by five characteristics and a handful of subcharacteristics. Table 4.1 gives both the formal definition of each quality-in-use characteristic and subcharacteristic, as well as its applicability to this analysis.

4.3 ISO/IEC 25010 Product Quality

The primary definitions of *product* are (ISO/IEC/IEEE, 2010-12-15) as follows:

1. an artifact that is produced, is quantifiable, and can be either an end item in itself or a component item
2. complete set of computer programs, procedures, and associated documentation designed for delivery to a user

ISO/IEC 25041 (ISO/IEC, 2012) defines *product quality* as follows:
degree to which the product satisfies stated and implied needs when used under specified conditions

Table 4.1 ISO/IEC 25010 Quality-in-Use Model Applied to Cloud User Service Quality

Quality-in-Use Characteristics and Subcharacteristics	Definitions (ISO/IEC, 2011-03-01)	Applicability to Cloud User Service Quality Risk Management
Effectiveness	"Accuracy and completeness with which users achieve specified goals"	Addressed via service reliability (Section 4.2.1.1)
Efficiency	"Resources expended in relation to the accuracy and completeness with which users achieve goals"	Considered in Chapter 10, "Improving Operational Efficiency of Cloud-Based Applications"
Satisfaction	"Degree to which user needs are satisfied when a product or system is used in a specified context of use"	Addressed via service quality (Section 4.2.1.3)
Usefulness	"Degree to which a user is satisfied with their perceived achievement of pragmatic goals, including the results of use and the consequences of use"	Out of scope
Trust	"Degree to which a user or other stakeholder has confidence that a product or system will behave as intended"	Trust in a service is earned with consistent performance across time. Rigorous demonstrations can improve trust
Pleasure	"Degree to which a user obtains pleasure from fulfilling their personal needs"	Out of scope
Comfort	"Degree to which the user is satisfied with physical comfort"	Out of scope
Freedom from risk	"Degree to which a product or system mitigates the potential risk to economic status, human life, health, or the environment"	Partially addressed via service outage downtime (Section 4.2.1.4)

(Continued)

Table 4.1 (Continued)   ISO/IEC 25010 Quality-in-Use Model Applied to Cloud User Service Quality

Quality-in-Use Characteristics and Subcharacteristics	Definitions (ISO/IEC, 2011-03-01)	Applicability to Cloud User Service Quality Risk Management
Economic risk mitigation	"Degree to which a product or system mitigates the potential risk to financial status, efficient operation, commercial property, reputation, or other resources in the intended contexts of use"	Out of scope
Health and safety risk mitigation	"Degree to which a product or system mitigates the potential risk to people in the intended contexts of use"	Out of scope
Environmental risk mitigation	"Degree to which a product or system mitigates the potential risk to property or the environment in the intended contexts of use"	Out of scope
Context coverage	"Degree to which a product or system can be used with effectiveness, efficiency, freedom from risk, and satisfaction in both specified contexts of use and in contexts beyond those initially explicitly identified"	Partially addressed via service outage downtime (Section 4.2.1.4) and service reliability (Section 4.2.1.1)
Context completeness	"Degree to which a product or system can be used with effectiveness, efficiency, freedom from risk, and satisfaction in all the specified contexts of use"	Partially addressed via service outage downtime (Section 4.2.1.4) and service reliability (Section 4.2.1.1)
Flexibility	"Degree to which a product or system can be used with effectiveness, efficiency, freedom from risk, and satisfaction in contexts beyond those initially specified in the requirements"	Out of scope

The industry broadly factors requirements and product (or service) qualities as either of the following:

■ **Functional qualities**—Functional qualities characterize the implementation of functional requirements, which are defined as "what a product or process must accomplish to produce required behavior and/or results" (ISO/IEC/IEEE, 2010-12-15). The ease with which a CSC, integrator, or software supplier can configure preexisting and new virtual network functions and functional components offered as-a-service into services that are highly valuable to target user community (or perhaps even individual) creates business opportunities. As discussed in Section 2.5, "Focus of This Work," functional qualities are beyond the scope of this work.

■ **Nonfunctional qualities**—ISO/IEC/IEEE 24765, *Systems and Software Engineering Vocabulary* (ISO/IEC/IEEE, 2010-12-15) defines, *nonfunctional requirement* as follows:

> a software requirement that describes not what the software will do but how the software will do it.
> EXAMPLE software performance requirements, software external interface requirements, software design constraints, and *software quality attributes.* Nonfunctional requirements are sometimes difficult to test, so they are usually evaluated subjectively

ISO/IEC 25010, *System and Software Quality Model* (ISO/IEC, 2011-03-01), clause 4.2 defines a system/software product quality model based on eight nonfunctional characteristics and various subcharacteristics. Clause 1 of ISO/IEC 25010 stipulates the following:

> Although the scope of the product quality model is intended to be software and computer systems, *many of the characteristics are also relevant to wider systems and services.*

Table 4.2 indicates applicability to a CSC of each product quality characteristic and subcharacteristic for both user service quality and CSC operational efficiency.

4.4 ISO/IEC 25012 Data Quality

ISO/IEC 25012, *Data Quality Model* (ISO/IEC, 2008-12-15), defines *data* as follows:

> reinterpretable representation of information in a formalized manner suitable for communication, interpretation, or processing
> NOTE 1 Data can be processed by humans or by automatic means.

Table 4.2   Applicability of Product Qualities to User Service Quality and CSC Operational Efficiency

Product Quality Characteristics and Subcharacteristics	ISO/IEC 25010 Product Quality Definitions	Applicable to User Service Quality	Applicable to CSC Operational Efficiency
Functional suitability	"Degree to which a product or system provides functions that meet stated and implied needs when used under specified conditions"	–	–
Functional completeness	"Degree to which the set of functions covers all the specified tasks and user objectives"	–	–
Functional correctness	"Degree to which a product or system provides the correct results with the needed degree of precision"	–	–
Functional appropriateness	"Degree to which the functions facilitate the accomplishment of specified tasks and objectives"	–	–
Performance efficiency	"Performance relative to the amount of resources used under stated conditions"	–	✓
Time behavior	"Degree to which the response and processing times and throughput rates of a product or system, when performing its functions, meet requirements"	✓	✓
Resource utilization	"Degree to which the amounts and types of resources used by a product or system, when performing its functions, meet requirements"	–	✓
Capacity	"Degree to which the maximum limits of a product or system parameter meet requirements"	–	✓

(Continued)

Table 4.2 (Continued)   Applicability of Product Qualities to User Service Quality and CSC Operational Efficiency

Product Quality Characteristics and Subcharacteristics	ISO/IEC 25010 Product Quality Definitions	Applicable to User Service Quality	Applicable to CSC Operational Efficiency
Compatibility	"Degree to which a product, system, or component can exchange information with other products, systems, or components, and/or perform its required functions, while sharing the same hardware or software environment"	–	–
Coexistence	"Degree to which a product can perform its required functions efficiently while sharing a common environment and resources with other products, without detrimental impact on any other product"	–	✓
Interoperability	"Degree to which two or more systems, products, or components can exchange information and use the information that has been exchanged"	–	–
Usability	"Degree to which a product or system can be used by specified users to achieve specified goals with effectiveness, efficiency, and satisfaction in a specified context of use"	–	–
Appropriateness recognizability	"Degree to which users can recognize whether a product or system is appropriate for their needs"	–	–
Learnability	"Degree to which a product or system can be used by specified users to achieve specified goals of learning to use the product or system with effectiveness, efficiency, freedom from risk, and satisfaction in a specified context of use"	–	–

(Continued)

Table 4.2 (Continued)   Applicability of Product Qualities to User Service Quality and CSC Operational Efficiency

Product Quality Characteristics and Subcharacteristics	ISO/IEC 25010 Product Quality Definitions	Applicable to User Service Quality	Applicable to CSC Operational Efficiency
Operability	"Degree to which a product or system has attributes that make it easy to operate and control"	–	–
User error protection	"Degree to which a system protects users against making errors"	✓	✓
User interface aesthetics	"Degree to which a user interface enables pleasing and satisfying interaction for the user"	–	–
Accessibility	"Degree to which a product or system can be used by people with the widest range of characteristics and capabilities to achieve a specified goal in a specified context of use"	–	–
Reliability	"Degree to which a system, product, or component performs specified functions under specified conditions for a specified period of time"	✓	✓
Maturity	"Degree to which a system, product, or component meets needs for reliability under normal operation"	✓	✓
Availability	"Degree to which a system, product, or component is operational and accessible when required for use"	✓	✓
Fault tolerance	"Degree to which a system, product, or component operates as intended despite the presence of hardware or software faults"	✓	✓
Recoverability	"Degree to which, in the event of an interruption or a failure, a product or system can recover the data directly affected and reestablish the desired state of the system"	✓	✓

(Continued)

Table 4.2 (Continued)   Applicability of Product Qualities to User Service Quality and CSC Operational Efficiency

Product Quality Characteristics and Subcharacteristics	ISO/IEC 25010 Product Quality Definitions	Applicable to User Service Quality	Applicable to CSC Operational Efficiency
Security	"Degree to which a product or system protects information and data so that persons or other products or systems have the degree of data access appropriate to their types and levels of authorization"		
Confidentiality	"Degree to which a product or system ensures that data are accessible only to those authorized to have access"		
Integrity	"Degree to which a system, product, or component prevents unauthorized access to, or modification of, computer programs or data"	Security topics are out of scope for this book	
Nonrepudiation	"Degree to which actions or events can be proven to have taken place, so that the events or actions cannot be repudiated later"		
Accountability	"Degree to which the actions of an entity can be traced uniquely to the entity"		
Authenticity	"Degree to which the identity of a subject or resource can be proved to be the one claimed"		
Maintainability	"Degree of effectiveness and efficiency with which a product or system can be modified by the intended maintainers"	–	✓
Modularity	"Degree to which a system or computer program is composed of discrete components such that a change to one component has minimal impact on other components"	–	✓
Reusability	"Degree to which an asset can be used in more than one system, or in building other assets"	–	✓

(Continued)

Table 4.2 (Continued) Applicability of Product Qualities to User Service Quality and CSC Operational Efficiency

Product Quality Characteristics and Subcharacteristics	*ISO/IEC 25010 Product Quality Definitions*	*Applicable to User Service Quality*	*Applicable to CSC Operational Efficiency*
Analyzability	"Degree of effectiveness and efficiency with which it is possible to assess the impact on a product or system of an intended change to one or more of its parts, or to diagnose a product for deficiencies or causes of failures, or to identify parts to be modified"	—	✓
Modifiability	"Degree to which a product or system can be effectively and efficiently modified without introducing defects or degrading existing product quality"	—	✓
Testability	"Degree of effectiveness and efficiency with which test criteria can be established for a system, product, or component and tests can be performed to determine whether those criteria have been met"	—	✓
Portability	"Degree of effectiveness and efficiency with which a system, product, or component can be transferred from one hardware, software or other operational or usage environment to another"	—	✓
Adaptability	"Degree to which a product or system can effectively and efficiently be adapted for different or evolving hardware, software, or other operational or usage environments"	—	✓
Installability	"Degree of effectiveness and efficiency with which a product or system can be successfully installed and/or uninstalled in a specified environment"	—	✓
Replaceability	"Degree to which a product can replace another specified software product for the same purpose in the same environment"	—	✓

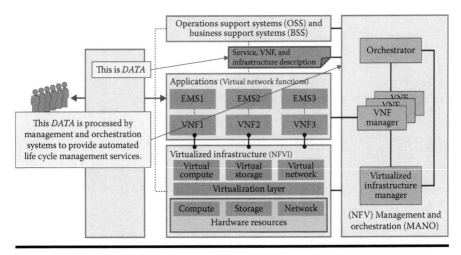

Figure 4.7 Data and automated life cycle management in cloud.

As shown in Figure 4.7, service, virtualized network function (VNF), and infrastructure description files that are used by management and orchestration systems to automate life cycle management actions are data. Data relevant to user service quality of cloud-based applications include the following:

■ Management and orchestration information elements, such as VNF descriptors (VNFDs), which "describe a VNF in terms of its deployment and operational behaviour requirements. The VNFD also contains connectivity, interface and KPIs requirements that can be used by NFV-MANO functional blocks to establish appropriate Virtual Links within the NFVI between VNFC instances, or between a VNF instance and the end point interface to other Network Functions" (ETSI, 2014-12).
■ CSC's methods of procedure (MOPs).
■ Application user data.
■ Alarms and fault management data.
■ Performance management data.

ISO/IEC 25012 defines *data quality* as follows:
    degree to which the characteristics of data satisfy stated and implied
    needs when used under specified conditions
Poor data quality impacts the following user service quality risks:

■ Faulty VNF configuration specification risk (Table 13.1)
■ Residual defect in VNF life cycle management script risk (Table 13.2)

- Faulty service workflow risk (Table 18.6)
- Life cycle management (execution risks) (Chapter 23)
- Human process risk (Table 22.3)—Impacted by faulty MOPs.
- Service policy risks (Chapter 20)—Faulty policies include the following:
  - Insufficient space capacity (target) risk (Table 20.1)
  - Faulty resource placement policy risk (Table 20.2)
  - Faulty scaling decision criteria risk (Table 20.3)
  - Inaccurate demand forecast risk (Table 20.4)
- Visibility risks (Chapter 19)—Poor-quality performance, fault, alarm, or configuration information creates the following risks:
  - Obstructed vision risk (Table 19.1)
  - Blurred vision risk (Table 19.2)
  - Stale vision risk (Table 19.3)
  - Mirage risk (Table 19.4)

Table 4.3 gives definitions and applicability of the 15 data quality characteristics to both user service quality and CSC operational efficiency.

4.5 Data, Information, Knowledge, and Wisdom

Figure 4.8 visualizes the data–information–knowledge–wisdom (or DIKW) hierarchy, and Table 4.4 offers more complete definitions of the four hierarchy levels. This hierarchy reflects common usage:

- We're drowning in *data* (e.g., files).
- Data are analyzed to extract *information* like *who*, *what*, *when*, and *where*.
- Information helps build useful *knowledge* to explain *how*.
- Knowledge is distilled into *wisdom* to explain *why*.

As an illustration, let's apply the DIKW hierarchy to the hypothetical task of managing a stock portfolio as shown in Figure 4.9:

- **Wisdom**—Stock markets are so efficient that experts rarely outperform broad market indexes mutual funds by enough to cover their fees.
- **Knowledge**—The Standard & Poor's (S&P) 500 index approximates the stock market for large companies in the United States.
- **Information**—The companies are in the S&P 500 index.
- **Data**—Stock market symbols and prices for companies in the S&P 500 index.
- **Stock trading systems**—Select and execute trades necessary to create a stock portfolio matching the S&P 500 index.

Table 4.3   Applicability of ISO/IEC 25012 Data Quality Model to User Service Quality Risks

Data Quality Characteristics	Definitions (ISO/IEC, 2008-12-15)	Applicable to User Service Quality	Applicable to CSC Operational Efficiency
Accuracy	"The degree to which data have attributes that correctly represent the true value of the intended attributes of a concept or event in a specific context of use. It has two main aspects"	✓	✓
Syntactic	"Syntactic accuracy is defined as the closeness of the data values to a set of values defined in a domain considered syntactically correct." Example: capturing "Marj" instead of "Mary."	✓	✓
Semantic	"Semantic accuracy is defined as the closeness of the data values to a set of values defined in a domain considered semantically correct." Example: capturing "John" instead of "George."	✓	✓
Completeness	"The degree to which subject data associated with an entity has values for all expected attributes and related entity instances in a specific context of use."	✓	✓

(Continued)

Table 4.3 (Continued)   Applicability of ISO/IEC 25012 Data Quality Model to User Service Quality Risks

Data Quality Characteristics	Definitions (ISO/IEC, 2008-12-15)	Applicable to User Service Quality	Applicable to CSC Operational Efficiency
Consistency	"The degree to which data have attributes that are free from contradiction and are coherent with other data in a specific context of use. It can be either or both among data regarding one entity and across similar data for comparable entities."	✓	✓
Credibility	"The degree to which data have attributes that are regarded as true and believable by users in a specific context of use."	–	✓
Currentness	"The degree to which data have attributes that are of the right age in a specific context of use."	✓	✓
Accessibility	"The degree to which data can be accessed in a specific context of use, particularly by people who need supporting technology or special configuration because of some disability."	–	✓
Compliance	"The degree to which data have attributes that adhere to standards, conventions, or regulations in force and similar rules relating to data quality in a specific context of use."	–	–
Confidentiality	"The degree to which data have attributes that ensure that it is only accessible and interpretable by authorized users in a specific context of use."	–	–

(Continued)

Table 4.3 (Continued)   Applicability of ISO/IEC 25012 Data Quality Model to User Service Quality Risks

Data Quality Characteristics	Definitions (ISO/IEC, 2008-12-15)	Applicable to User Service Quality	Applicable to CSC Operational Efficiency
Efficiency	"The degree to which data have attributes that can be processed and provide the expected levels of performance by using the appropriate amounts and types of resources in a specific context of use."	–	✔
Precision	"The degree to which data have attributes that are exact or that provide discrimination in a specific context of use."	✔	✔
Traceability	"The degree to which data have attributes that provide an audit trail of access to the data and of any changes made to the data in a specific context of use."	–	–
Understandability	"The degree to which data have attributes that enable it to be read and interpreted by users, and are expressed in appropriate languages, symbols and units in a specific context of use."	–	–
Availability	"The degree to which data have attributes that enable it to be retrieved by authorized users and/or applications in a specific context of use."	–	✔
Portability	"The degree to which data have attributes that enable it to be installed, replaced or moved from one system to another preserving the existing quality in a specific context of use."	–	✔
Recoverability	"The degree to which data have attributes that enable it to maintain and preserve a specified level of operations and quality, even in the event of failure, in a specific context of use."	✔	✔

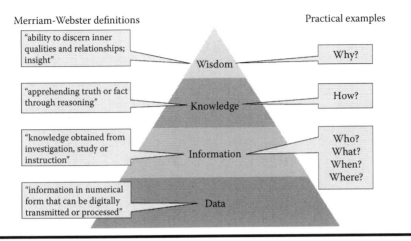

Figure 4.8   The knowledge hierarchy.

The stock portfolio produced via Figure 4.9 might not actually produce the outcome desired for reasons including the following:

1. Stock trading systems failed to execute correct trade due to product/system quality problems.
2. Portfolio of stocks might not accurately match the S&P 500 because the stock symbols and price data used as input to the stock trading systems were faulty.
3. The wisdom, knowledge, or information that drove the investing strategy was faulty (e.g., due to some human error) or was overtaken by external factors.

This same hierarchy can be used to model automated life cycle management actions. Figure 4.10 illustrates how the knowledge hierarchy can usefully be applied to the automated application capacity management problem, often called "autoscaling." Consider each layer in the autoscaling knowledge hierarchy of Figure 4.8, from the top down (left to right in Figure 4.10):

- **Wisdom**—Organizations adopt lean cloud capacity management (Chapter 6, "Lean Application Capacity Management") to minimize resource consumption, and hence operating expenses, by maintaining the leanest application capacity that is consistent with the organization's risk appetite and service quality objectives.
- **Knowledge**—Maintain enough online capacity to cover working demand plus sufficient spare capacity to cover random variations and nonforecast demand, as well as failures and demand in the capacity growth lead time interval.

Table 4.4 Definitions of Data, Information, Knowledge, and Wisdom

Term	Merriam-Webster's Definition[1]	ISO/IEC 25012 Definition
Data	"1: factual information (as measurements or statistics) used as a basis for reasoning, discussion, or calculation … … *3: information in numerical form that can be digitally transmitted or processed"*	Reinterpretable representation of information in a formalized manner suitable for communication, interpretation, or processing[2]
Information	"… 2(a)1: *the knowledge obtained from investigation, study, or instruction* …"	Knowledge concerning objects, such as facts, events, things, processes, or ideas, including concepts, that within a certain context have a particular meaning
Knowledge	"a(1): the fact or condition of knowing something with familiarity gained through experience or association … c: the circumstance or condition of *apprehending truth or fact through reasoning*: cognition …"	Not defined
Wisdom	"… b: *ability to discern inner qualities and relationships: insight* …"	Not defined

[1] Retrieved from http://www.meriam-webster.com/dictionary on March 7, 2016.
[2] ISO/IEC/IEEE 24765, *Systems and Software Engineering Vocabulary* (ISO/IEC/IEEE, 2010-12-15), defines *data* as "a representation of facts, concepts, or instructions in a manner suitable for communication, interpretation, or processing by humans or by automatic means." ISO/IEC 15939, *Systems and Software Engineering Measurement Process* (ISO/IEC, 2009-10-01), defines *data* as "collection of values assigned to base measures, derived measures and/or indicators."

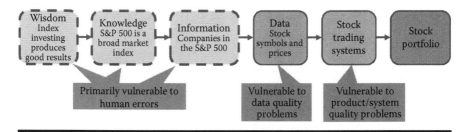

Figure 4.9   A knowledge hierarchy example: investing.

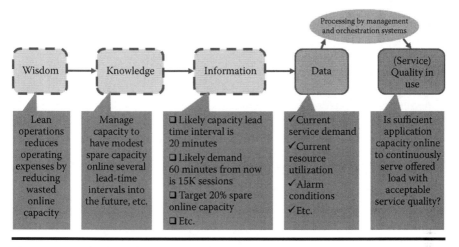

Figure 4.10   The knowledge hierarchy and cloud autoscaling.

- **Information**—Forecast demand, capacity change lead times, spare capacity targets, and so on are information that determines the CSC's optimal application capacity change decision criteria.
- **Data**—Current service demand, resource utilization and performance, alarm conditions, and so on are the data that are compared to the application's current capacity change decision thresholds to drive autoscaling decisions.
- **Processing by management and orchestration systems**—Automated systems gather, process, and compare data with capacity management policy information and decision criteria to decide exactly what capacity change fulfillment actions are appropriate to execute when.
- **Outcome: service quality in use**—Life cycle management data are directly processed by cloud management and orchestration systems, and indirectly processed by infrastructure, application, and functional component elements; the ultimate result is the level of instantaneously available online application capacity to serve user demand. Minimizing the portion of users experiencing unacceptable or poor service quality in use is typically the desired outcome.

4.6 Quality Model for Cloud-Based Applications

This chapter has methodically applied ISO/IEC product, data, and in-use quality models to cloud-based applications to enable deeper consideration of the requirements and evaluation of those qualities to enable more effective risk assessment and management. The result is the highest-level quality model visualized in Figure 4.11, which broadly covers the risks of Section III, "Cloud Service Quality Risk Inventory."

Figure 4.11 illustrates the flow of information through the cloud quality model; consider stages from right to left (i.e., by causality, rather than by effect):

- **Service quality in use**—The quality of experience for application users is primarily driven by the product quality of the systems, software, components, and resources in the user service delivery path. If insufficient application capacity is online to serve aggregate offered workload, then the service may queue requests (thereby increasing service latency) and/or reject user requests (thereby impacting service reliability).

- **Systems**—Overload/congestion control mechanisms to queue or shed traffic when offered workload exceeds online capacity is a system feature, not a bug. Thus, service latency or service reliability impairments attributed to correct operation of overload/congestion controls are not quality problems to be attributed to those products. While quality problems in management and orchestration systems themselves (rather than the scripts, descriptors, and other information elements provided to those systems) can cause autoscaling actions to fail, failure of autoscaling does not cause user service to be directly impacted.

- **Data**—Autoscaling is driven by cloud management and orchestration systems, which are driven scripts, descriptors, input parameters, and other information elements. Autoscaling-related data used by cloud management and orchestration systems are inherently vulnerable to data quality problems,

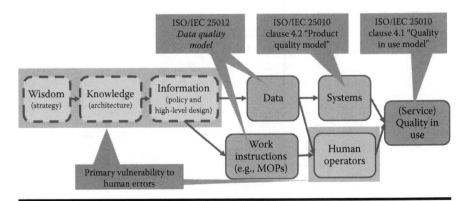

Figure 4.11   Quality model for cloud-based applications.

which can cause autoscaling to fail outright, or to fail to complete the necessary reconfiguration of service capacity and/or to take longer than necessary. Autoscaling information elements are particularly vulnerable to the following data quality impairments from Section 4.4:

- − Semantic and syntactic accuracy
- − Completeness
- − Consistency
- − Currentness
- − Efficiency
- − Precision

■ **Information** (policy and high-level design)—Autoscaling is driven by capacity decision and planning policies that are automatically evaluated and executed. Autoscaling policies likely consider the following:

- − Minimum spare online capacity target (e.g., at least 30% online capacity above current actual demand)
- − Maximum spare online capacity target (e.g., no more than 100% online capacity above current actual demand)

Cloud management and orchestration elements compare autoscaling policies to information (in the form of data) about the state of the target service, such as the following:

- − Current application configuration
- − Current fault/alarm status
- − Current workload
- − Current resource utilization
- − Current capacity change lead time
- − (Short-term) user demand forecast
- − Planned maintenance schedule

TL 9000 (QuEST Forum, 2012-12-31) offers several examples of poor-quality human policies relevant to cloud-based applications:

    b)   inadequate training,

      ...

    d)   inadequate or unclear displays, messages, or signals,

      ...

    g)   non-standard configurations,
    h)   insufficient supervision or control

Accurately representing faulty information or policy as data does not morph the true root cause into a data quality problem…just like one can't blame the printer for accurately rendering a poorly written document. Thus, service latency or reliability impairments attributed to faulty autoscaling policies should not be attributed either to data artifacts faithfully representing those faulty policies or to management and orchestration systems properly processing those data artifacts.

■ **Human operators**—Human operators on the CSC's engineering staff monitor alarms, fault notifications, and performance of production services to assure proper operation. For example, when capacity-related alarms are presented to operations staff, those operators should promptly execute appropriate work instructions to reconfigure the application so users are served with minimal quality impact (e.g., manually ordering capacity change actions, directing some or all offered load to another online application instance). TL 9000 (QuEST Forum, 2012-12-31) offers several examples of human procedural errors relevant to cloud-based applications:

    a)   deviations from accepted practices or documentation,
       ...
    c)   unauthorized work,
    d)   not following Methods of Procedures (MOPs),
    e)   not following the steps of the documentation,
    f)   using the wrong documentation,
       ...
    j)   user panic response to problems,
    k)   entering incorrect commands,
    l)   entering a command without understanding the impact, or
    m)   inappropriate response to a Network Element alarm.

■ **Work instructions** (e.g., MOPs)—Human operators take specific actions based on work instructions and MOPs. Human work instructions are vulnerable to data quality impairments such as semantic and syntactic accuracy, completeness, consistency, and currentness. TL 9000 (QuEST Forum, 2012-12-31) offers several examples of poor-quality work instructions relevant to cloud-based applications:

       ...
    g)   using incorrect or outdated documentation,
    h)   insufficient documentation,
    i)   translation errors

■ **Knowledge** (architecture)—The architecture frames an implementation model for an organization's strategy; practically, the architecture also defines what the service will *not* be able to do very well. Architectural flaws often manifest as chronic performance or quality problems because inadequate risk treatments are deployed to robustly control service operation.

■ **Wisdom** (strategy)—CSCs select a strategy to drive their architecture, policy, design, implementation, and operations. This strategy materially impacts the likely benefits and consequences of an organization's investment. As an example, consider two strategic options:

- **Lean capacity management**, i.e., minimize online application capacity to reduce operating expenses by keeping the smallest application capacity online that serves users with acceptable service quality and adequately mitigates inevitable failures and other unforeseen events.
- **Traditional capacity management**, i.e., minimize the absolute number of configuration changes made to production systems to minimize the risk of user service impairment.

  Each of these strategic options leads to vastly different rates of scaling actions and operating expense profiles. While one doesn't generally think of the quality of a strategy, one can consider the quality of a strategy as the degree to which the strategy satisfies the stated and implied needs of the organization, and thus provides value.

A well-known engineering mantra is "garbage in equals garbage out," and that applies directly to the quality model of Figure 4.11. Failing to properly localize and treat the true root cause of risk at the source wastes resources and thus is less efficient for all parties concerned. Thus, care should be taken to clarify roles and responsibilities across the service creation and delivery chain to minimize the risks to user service quality.

ANALYZING THE CLOUD SERVICE CUSTOMER'S PROBLEM

II

As discussed in Chapter 2, "Desired Cloud Service Customer Benefits," enterprises deploy services on the cloud in pursuit of two overarching goals:

- Deliver new service and value faster
- Improve operational efficiency

A simple "lift and shift" of existing applications and current operational processes and practices will not deliver the full potential of cloud computing. This section focuses on how an organization's service design, transition, and operations processes and practices change to increase the likelihood of achieving their goals.

The information technology (IT) service framework visualization of Figure II.1 is a useful foundation when considering exactly how time and effort can be squeezed out of a cloud service customer's (CSC's) operations to achieve the faster, cheaper application service with acceptable service quality. The IT service life cycle of Figure II.1 factors IT service management as the IT Infrastructure Library (ITIL®) does:

- The **service design** phase captures and analyzes requirements, architects and designs a service solution, and then develops/integrates and verifies a service implementation.
- The **service transition** phase deploys service implementation instances into production.
- **Service operation** manages user service delivery and eventual retirement.

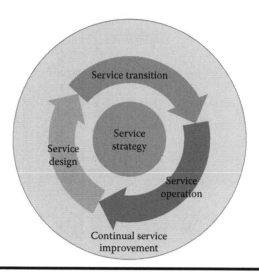

Figure II.1   Traditional IT (ITIL) service life cycle.

- **Continual service improvement** processes operate across all phases to improve operational performance to improve outcomes for stakeholders.
- **Service strategy** frames the context, nature, implementation, and deployment model of services that an organization will offer to users.

Figure II.2 illustrates how Section II, "Analyzing the Cloud Service Customer's Problem," considers the changes necessary to achieve the CSC's goals of faster service innovation with lower expenses and acceptable service quality.

- **Application Service Life Cycle** (Chapter 5) considers how the key characteristics of cloud computing change application design, transition, and operations activities to achieve the CSC's goals.
- **Lean Application Capacity Management** (Chapter 6) considers how application capacity management optimally leverage the key cloud characteristic of rapid elasticity and scalability (Section 1.4.5).
- **Testing Cloud-Based Application Services** (Chapter 7) considers how testing evolves for cloud-based applications.
- **Service Design, Transition, and Operations Processes** (Chapter 8) considers how the key characteristics of cloud computing change IT service design, transition, and operations processes.
- **Continual Service Improvement** (Chapter 9) considers how continual service improvement activities support cost, cycle time, and quality improvement actions.

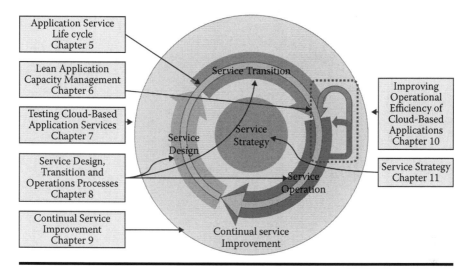

Figure II.2 Organization of Section II, "Analyzing the Cloud Service Customer's Problem."

- **Improving Operational Efficiency of Cloud-Based Applications** (Chapter 10) considers how lean thinking applies to operations of cloud-based applications.
- **Service Strategy** (Chapter 11) considers how CSCs' service strategies can leverage cloud computing to minimize the uncertainty of achieving their goals of faster service innovation at lower cost with acceptable service quality.

Chapter 5

Application Service Life Cycle

To achieve the business objectives of reduced operating expense and increased pace of service innovation, cloud service customers (CSCs) streamline the service design, transition, and operation phases of the application service life cycle (Figure 5.1). In particular, the service design and service transition phases must execute faster to accelerate the pace of service innovation, and costs must be squeezed out of service operations—as well as service design and service transition—to reduce operating expenses. As CSCs accelerate their pace of innovation, and especially as they adopt Agile and DevOps methods, these phases will overlap more and more. This chapter considers how the development/deployment cycle time can be accelerated by the cloud and how operational efficiencies can be improved in the application service life cycle for cloud-based application services.

Section 5.1 considers *cloud changes enabling application service life cycle improvements*, and Section 5.2, "Standard System Life Cycle Processes," considers how those changes map onto standard system life cycle activities. Section 5.3, "Summary of Likely Application Life Cycle Changes," consolidates insights of previous sections in tabular form as well as visualizing application life cycle processes likely to accelerate the pace of service innovation via cloud computing (Figure 5.4) and application life cycle processes likely to improve operational efficiency via cloud computing (Figure 5.5).

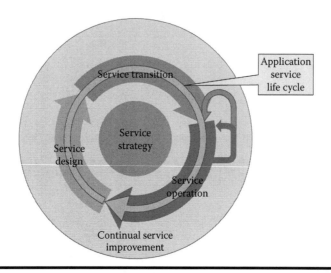

Figure 5.1   Application service life cycle.

5.1 Cloud Changes Enabling Application Service Life Cycle Improvements

Before considering exactly how the application service life cycle is likely to change for cloud-based applications, let us review the features that enable material improvements:

■ **Just-in-time, pay-as-you-go resource capacity**—On-demand self-service (Section 1.4.4), rapid elasticity and scalability (Section 1.4.5), and measured service (Section 1.4.2) mean that availability of compute, memory, storage, and networking resources is no longer a limiting factor. Developers and testers have nominally instantaneous access to arbitrarily large pools of resources to simulate, develop, integrate, and test service architectures, designs, and implementations. For instance, as cloud capacity is elastic and scalable, CSCs can order sufficient test-bed capacity to theoretically execute all tests in parallel to shorten test pass intervals rather than having to serialize test case execution across a limited number of test beds. Operations or development staff can rapidly transition new software builds into service to trial and scale up capacity ahead of rising demand...and easily retire resource capacity when appropriate. For instance, new services with cloud-friendly architectures can be deployed with limited capacity (and hence modest cost) to a limited target market; if the service proves popular—or goes viral—then the CSC can rapidly scale online application to serve that rising demand. Leveraging on-demand resource capacity can eliminate bottlenecks associated with scheduling development, integration, and testing activities onto a finite pool of target compute, memory, storage, and networking resources. This is considered in Chapter 7, "Testing Cloud-Based Application Services," and Chapter 11, "Service Strategy," especially Section 11.2, "Agile Thinking about Service Strategy," and Section 11.3, "DevOps Thinking about Service Strategy."

■ **Automated life cycle management**—Cloud infrastructure, management, and orchestration enable application life cycle management actions to be automated so that humans are no longer in the loop for many service transition and operation actions. Automation of application and service life cycle management actions shortens execution times for automated actions and reduces both the risk of human errors and operating expense.

■ **Off-the-shelf functional components offered as-a-service**—Platform- and software-as-a-service providers will offer myriad off-the-shelf service components like database-as-a-service and load-balancing-as-a-service that can be integrated into application service offerings. Leveraging stable functional components offered as-a-service is generally faster and cheaper than developing bespoke service components.

■ **Off-the-shelf service component software**—Off-the-shelf (i.e., preexisting) software components available from commercial suppliers or open-source projects are generally faster and cheaper for CSCs than developing bespoke software components.

■ **Standardized ecosystem**—Numerous standards development organizations and open-source projects are driving standardized interfaces between key architectural components that CSCs will rely upon. Leveraging components and services with standardized interfaces can reduce vendor lock-in.

■ **Rich, diverse tools and services**—As the market expands, it becomes profitable for suppliers to develop powerful tools (e.g., formal method verification tools, Monte Carlo simulation tools) and niche services, which offer greater value to CSCs than would be generally available for boutique, proprietary, and/or less successful ecosystems.

■ **Commonality**—Widespread use of a suite of open-source products and commercial products drives a level of implementation and operational commonality across the industry that simplifies design, transition, and operation of cloud-based applications.

■ **Competition**—Standardization, commonality, and widespread adoption will entice a more players to offer products and services into the ecosystem, resulting in competition, which accelerates innovation, improves service quality, and drives down costs.

5.2 Standard System Life Cycle Processes

ISO/IEC/IEEE 15288:2015, *System Life Cycle Processes*, is the most authoritative reference on system life cycle processes. The standard defines *system* as a "combination of interacting elements organized to achieve one or more stated purposes." This work considers a system that is a combination of interacting service components (especially virtualized network functions [VNFs] and functional components offered as-a-service) organized to achieve the purpose of delivering application service to users.

As shown in Figure 5.2, the standard details 14 *technical processes* in the application service life cycle agreement processes, which we will consider. Figure 5.3 illustrates how those 14 standard technical processes map onto the traditional application service life cycle of Figure II.1. The standard also discusses agreement processes, organizational project-enabling processes, and technical management processes, which we will not consider.

Likely process changes to accelerate application service innovation and agility and reduce the CSC's operating expenses, as well as associated changes to user service quality risks, are considered separately for each process:

- Business or mission analysis process (Section 5.2.1)
- Stakeholder needs and requirements definition process (Section 5.2.2)
- System requirements definition process (Section 5.2.3)
- Architecture definition process (Section 5.2.4)

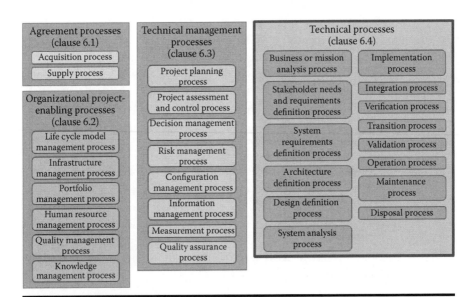

Figure 5.2 ISO/IEC/IEEE 15288, *System Life Cycle Processes*. (From Figure 4 of ISO/IEC/IEEE, *15288—Systems and Software Engineering—System Life Cycle Processes*, Geneva: International Organization for Standardization et al., 2015-05-15.)

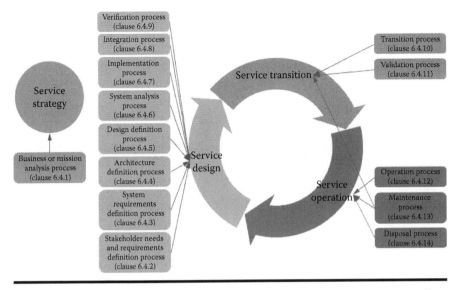

Figure 5.3   Mapping standard system life cycle technical processes onto application service life cycle.

- Design definition process (Section 5.2.5)
- System analysis process (Section 5.2.6)
- Implementation process (Section 5.2.7)
- Integration process (Section 5.2.8)
- Verification process (Section 5.2.9)
- Transition process (Section 5.2.10)
- Validation process (Section 5.2.11)
- Operation process (Section 5.2.12)
- Maintenance process (Section 5.2.13)
- Disposal process (Section 5.2.14)

Each section considers the following:

- Overview of technical process. We focus on changes enabled by cloud computing rather than on process optimizations that can apply equally well to either cloud-based or traditionally deployed applications. For example, all of the ISO/IEC/IEEE 15288 technical processes begin with "(a) prepare for X" activity, and most conclude with a "manage X" activity, but those general project management activities will not be considered.
- Likely process changes to accelerate service innovation and agility.
- Likely process changes to reduce operating expenses.
- Likely risks to user service quality.

5.2.1 Business or Mission Analysis Process

Clause 6.4.1 of ISO/IEC/IEEE 15299 considers the business or mission analysis process, which includes the following primary activities:

> "b) Define the problem or opportunity space
> c) Characterize the solution space
> d) Evaluate alternative solution classes"

None of these activities are fundamentally different for a cloud-based application service compared to a traditionally deployed application service. However, organizations that materially accelerate their pace of service innovation and reduce their cost structure can successfully address a broader range of market opportunities, so their service strategy (Chapter 11) may evolve, but the business or mission analysis process need not materially change.

5.2.2 Stakeholder Needs and Requirements Definition Process

Clause 6.4.2 of ISO/IEC/IEEE 15299 considers the stakeholder needs and requirements definition process, which includes the following primary activities:

> "b) Define stakeholder needs…
> c) Develop the operational concept and other life cycle concepts…
> d) Transform stakeholder needs into stakeholder requirements…
> e) Analyze stakeholder requirements…"

While a CSC's stakeholders will likely change to include one or more cloud service providers (CSPs), the stakeholder needs and requirements definition process need not materially change.

5.2.3 System Requirements Definition Process

Clause 6.4.3 of ISO/IEC/IEEE 15288 considers the system requirements definition process, which includes the following primary activities:

> "b) Define system requirements
>   1) Define each function that the system is required to perform.
>   2) Define necessary implementation constraints.
>   3) Identify system requirements that relate to risks, criticality of the system, or critical quality characteristics.
>   4) Define system requirements and rationale.
> c) Analyze system requirements tasks
>   1) Analyze the complete set of system requirements.
>   2) Define critical performance measures that enable the assessment of technical achievement.

3) Feed back the analyzed requirements to applicable stakeholders for review.
4) Resolve system requirements issues."

While none of the key characteristics of cloud computing (Section 1.4) directly
drive changes in the system requirements definition process, Agile software development (Section 11.2) and DevOps (Section 11.3) will fundamentally change an
organization's system requirements process compared to traditional development
models. In particular, incremental development and continuous delivery enable the
second Agile principle:

Welcome changing requirements, even late in development. Agile processes harness change for the customer's competitive advantage. (Beck
et al.)

Thus, various practical aspects of an organization's requirements process are
likely to change to support agile system requirements.

5.2.4 Architecture Definition Process

Clause 6.4.4 of ISO/IEC/IEEE 15288 considers the architecture definition process,
which includes the following primary activities:

"b) Develop architecture viewpoints…
c) Develop models and views of candidate architectures…
d) Relate the architecture to design…
e) Assess architecture candidates…"

Targeting an application for cloud deployment does not inherently change the
architecture definition processes. However, availability of both off-the-shelf functional components offered as-a-service and software components as well as "standard"
templates for service architectures and workflows can accelerate the architecture definition process by leveraging mature and presumably well-documented architectural
elements, especially the following:

"c) Develop models and views of candidate architectures"
"1. Define the system context and boundaries in terms of interfaces and interactions with external entities.
2. Identify architectural entities and relationships between entities that address key stakeholder concerns and critical system
requirements."
Cloud standards and functional components offered as-a-service
offer service interfaces that must be considered in service architectures for cloud-based applications. These service boundaries
and relationships may be fundamentally different from those of
traditional application deployments.

"d) Relate the architecture to design"
> "1. Identify system elements that relate to architectural entities and the nature of these relationships."

Available functional components offered as-a-service and off-the-shelf software components may simplify identification and selection of service components.
> "2. Define the interfaces and interactions between the system elements and with external entities."

Service interfaces to functional components offered as-a-service and off-the-shelf software components will be well specified, thereby eliminating the need to invest time and effort creating new interface specifications.

5.2.5 Design Definition Process

Clause 6.4.5 of ISO/IEC/IEEE 15288 considers the design definition process, which includes the following primary activities:

> "b) Establish design characteristics and design enablers related to each system element…
> c) Assess alternatives for obtaining system elements…"

None of these activities are fundamentally different for a cloud-based application service compared to a traditionally deployed application service. While cloud deployment is likely to offer a broader array of off-the-shelf VNFs and functional-component-as-a-service offerings to consider than are generally available with traditional deployments, the make-versus-buy decision process is fundamentally the same. Leveraging off-the-shelf functional components offered as-a-service and software components in mature service architectures and workflows can accelerate the design definition process.

5.2.6 System Analysis Process

Clause 6.4.6 of ISO/IEC/IEEE 15288 considers the system analysis process and stipulates the following:

> [System analysis] can provide confidence in the utility and integrity of system requirements, architecture, and design. System analysis covers a wide range of differing analytic functions, levels of complexity, and levels of rigor. It includes mathematical analysis, modeling, simulation, experimentation, and other techniques to analyze technical performance, system behavior, feasibility, affordability, critical quality

characteristics, technical risks, life cycle costs, and to perform sensitivity analysis of the potential range of values for parameters across all life cycle stages. It is used for a wide range of analytical needs concerning operational concepts, determination of requirement values, resolution of requirements conflicts, assessment of alternative architectures or system elements, and evaluation of engineering strategies (integration, verification, validation, and maintenance). (ISO/IEC/IEEE, 2015-05-15)

Cloud deployment changes many aspects of the deployment and operational context of a target service. The following factors can materially impact system analysis of cloud-based applications:

- **Standards and commonality around cloud-based applications can reduce, bound, or constrain uncertainties** that might exist with one-of and proprietary deployments
- **Availability of advanced system analysis tools**—Standards, commonality, and a vibrant ecosystem are likely to encourage development of powerful system modeling and analysis tools that produce better results faster than would otherwise be possible.
- **More professional and consulting services options for system analysis**—A standard, vibrant ecosystem can support a wide range of professional and consulting services providers who offer diverse and competitive outsourced system analysis options.

5.2.7 *Implementation Process*

Clause 6.4.7 of ISO/IEC/IEEE 15288 considers the implementation process and stipulates the following:

> This process results in a system element that satisfies specified system requirements (including allocated and derived requirements), architecture, and design. (ISO/IEC/IEEE, 2015-05-15)

Cloud deployment impacts the standard "(b) perform implementation" activities stipulated by the following:

1. "Realize or adapt system elements, according to the strategy, constraints, and defined implementation procedures."
   A wide range of generally available functional components offered as-a-service as well as VNFs available from the ecosystem reduce the volume of

bespoke service components that the CSC must procure. Cloud management and orchestration standards and systems enable a rich set of service creation, verification, and implementation tools, which can shorten cycle times.

2. "Package and store the system element."
   All of the artifacts for cloud-based services are virtual/software-based so they can be efficiently packaged, stored, and version-controlled. Having no physical artifacts to package, store, version-control, and so on significantly simplifies CSC service design activities and reduces costs.

5.2.8 Integration Process

Clause 6.4.8 of ISO/IEC/IEEE 15288 considers the integration process, which "synthesizes a set of system elements into a realized system (product or service) that satisfies system requirements, architecture, and design." Off-the-shelf functional components offered as-a-service and software components, coupled with standardized interfaces and on-demand resource capacity supported with automated allocation and configuration of resources, applications, and services, enable materially faster and cheaper integration processes. Cloud deployment impacts the standard "(b) perform integration—successively integrate system element configurations until the complete system is synthesized" activities:

1. "Obtain implemented system elements in accordance with agreed schedules." Stable functional components offered as-a-service are likely to be immediately available for CSCs to incorporate into application services, along with a variety of application and other service components from the cloud ecosystem. Generally available VNFs and applications can be quickly downloaded for integration into application services, rather than having to arrange for physical delivery of traditional (hardware-based) service components.

2. "Assemble the implemented system elements."
   "Assembling" cloud-based application services involves instantiating and configuring necessary service components, and appropriately chaining those components together to implement the required functionality. All of those assembly steps are performed automatically, so there are no required manual actions to slow the assembly process.

3. "Perform check of the interfaces, selected functions, and critical quality characteristics."
   Integration testing, like verification testing, is completed with on-demand resource capacity, so multiple integration tests can potentially be executed in parallel to shorten the integration testing interval.

5.2.9 Verification Process

Clause 6.4.9 of ISO/IEC/IEEE 15288 considers the verification process and stipulates the following:

> The Verification process identifies the anomalies (errors, defects, or faults) in any information item (e.g., system requirements or architecture description), implemented system elements, or life cycle processes using appropriate methods, techniques, standards or rules. (ISO/IEC/IEEE, 2015-05-15)

Just-in-time, pay-as-you-go resource capacity theoretically enables all or most verification test cases to run in parallel rather than having being forced to serialize execution of test cases because of finite test beds for test case execution. Cloud management and orchestration also enables greater automation in testing, such as allocating and configuring test beds prior to test execution, and releasing resources after test execution. Chapter 7, "Testing Cloud-Based Application Services," considers verification of cloud-based application services in detail.

5.2.10 Transition Process

Clause 6.4.10 of ISO/IEC/IEEE 15288 describes the transition process as follows:

> This process moves the system in an orderly, planned manner into the operational status, such that the system is functional, operable and compatible with other operational systems. It installs a verified system, together with relevant enabling systems, e.g., planning system, support system, operator training system, user training system, as defined in agreements. This process is used at each level in the system structure and in each stage to complete the criteria established for exiting the stage... (ISO/IEC/IEEE, 2015-05-15)

Traditionally, all of these transitions were performed manually; cloud management and orchestration systems, supported by on-demand self-service (Section 1.4.4) and rapid elasticity and scalability (Section 1.4.5), enable all of these transitions to be automated. The primary service transitions for cloud-based applications are as follows:

- **Onboarding**—Deploying an application into the production environment so it can be brought online.
- **Instantiating**—Bringing an application instance online and into service. Note that this can happen both immediately following successful onboarding

and at a later time when an additional application instance is brought online to increase service capacity.

■ **Scaling**—Increasing or decreasing the online capacity of a preexisting application instance.

■ **Terminating** (aka retiring)—Taking an application instance offline and deallocating associated resources. Note that removing (e.g., deleting) an application that has been onboarded is covered by the disposal process (Section 5.2.14).

■ **Release change**—Changing (e.g., patch, update, upgrade) the software release of an onboarded application.

Automated life cycle management, coupled with just-in-time, pay-as-you-go resources, enables service transitions to be completed automatically so human operators are no longer *in the loop* but, rather, *on the loop* in a supervisory capacity. This enables service transitions to be completed faster with less risk of human error. Costs are reduced because *on the loop* takes less human effort than *in the loop*. Note that Chapter 6, "Lean Application Capacity Management," considers primarily scaling service transition to increase or decrease the online capacity of preexisting application instances, and secondarily, instantiating and terminating service transitions to bring applications instance online and offline as appropriate.

5.2.11 Validation Process

Clause 6.4.11 of ISO/IEC/IEEE 15288 considers the validation process, which has the purpose "to provide objective evidence that the system, when in use, fulfills its business or mission objectives and stakeholder requirements, achieving its intended use in its intended operational environment." Essentially, the validation process assures that a particular application instance is "right as built" or a service transaction is "right first time." Automated life cycle management, coupled with just-in-time, pay-as-you-go resources, enables validation testing to be aggressively automated for cloud-based applications to shorten cycle times. Chapter 7, "Testing Cloud-Based Application Services" considers validation of cloud-based application services in detail.

5.2.12 Operation Process

Clause 6.4.12 of ISO/IEC/IEEE 15288 stipulates, "the purpose of the Operation process is to use the system to deliver its services." The standard defines two primary activities:

"b) Perform operation, including:
  1) Use the system in its intended operational environment, and
  2) Apply materials and other resources, as required, to operate the system and sustain its services—these are baseline assumptions for both traditional and cloud-based application services.

3) Monitor system operation,
4) Identify and record when system service performance is not within acceptable parameters, and
5) Perform system contingency operations, if necessary—cloud management and orchestration systems which monitor and enforce policies and configurations, will automatically trigger self healing and other corrective actions as appropriate. Automatic monitoring, impairment detection and execution of appropriate corrective actions both shortens the duration of service impairment episodes and reduces the workload for human operations staff.

d) Support the customer, including:
1) Provide assistance and consultation to the customers as requested—on-demand self service by cloud service customers enables cloud service users to tailor their service configuration to improve their quality of experience.
2) Record and monitor requests and subsequent actions for support, and
3) Determine the degree to which delivered system services satisfy the needs of the customers—these are baseline assumptions for both traditional and cloud-based application services."

Automated life cycle management, especially self-healing, coupled with on-demand self service by end users should reduce costs associated with operation processes.

5.2.13 Maintenance Process

Clause 6.4.13 of ISO/IEC/IEEE 15288 stipulates, "the purpose of the Maintenance process is to sustain the capability of the system to provide a service" (ISO/IEC/IEEE, 2015-05-15). Automated life cycle management, especially self-healing, automatically detects service quality degradation and failure events and automatically initiates appropriate corrective actions, thereby minimizing user service impact and reducing the need for some human maintenance actions. Automated life cycle maintenance and aggressive continual service improvement (Chapter 9) can reduce costs for maintenance processes.

5.2.14 Disposal Process

Clause 6.4.14 of ISO/IEC/IEEE 15288 stipulates

The purpose of the Disposal process is to end the existence of a system element or system for a specified intended use, appropriately handle replaced or retired elements, and to properly attend to identified critical disposal needs (e.g., per an agreement, per organizational policy, or for environmental, legal, safety, security aspects). (ISO/IEC/IEEE, 2015-05-15)

The primary activities stipulated by the standard for this process are as follows:

"b) Perform disposal, including:

1) Deactivate the system or system element to prepare it for removal

2) Remove the system, system element, or waste material from use or production for appropriate disposition and action

3) Withdraw impacted operating staff from the system or system element and record relevant operating knowledge

4) Disassemble the system or system element into manageable elements to facilitate its removal for reuse, recycling, reconditioning, overhaul, archiving or destruction

5) Handle system elements and their parts that are not intended for reuse in a manner that will assure they do not get back into the supply chain.

6) Conduct destruction of the system elements, as necessary, to reduce the amount of waste treatment or to make the waste easier to handle.

c) Finalize the disposal, including:

1) Confirm that no detrimental health, safety, security and environmental factors exist following disposal.

2) Return the environment to its original state or to a state that specified by agreement.

3) Archive information gathered through the lifetime of the system to permit audits and reviews in the event of long-term hazards to health, safety, security and the environment, and to permit future system creators and users to build a knowledge base from past experiences."

Disposing of a software-only application is largely automated, enabling faster and cheaper execution. Disposal (i.e., reallocation) of resources that had supported the cloud-based application is entirely managed by CSPs. Traditionally, many organizations were reluctant to retire nonprofitable offerings from service. While the cloud lowers the direct costs of disposing of a service, the organization's business processes may need to change to promptly decide to dispose of nonprofitable, obsolete, or otherwise unsuccessful service rather than continuing to squander resources with little or no hope of profitable business returns. Note that while the CSC organization is not responsible for most activities tied to disposing of resources when a cloud-based application is withdrawn from service, CSP organizations may charge the CSC fees associated with the release (deallocation) of cloud resources to recover some of their costs.

5.3 Summary of Likely Application Life Cycle Changes

Table 5.1 consolidates the likely benefits to both accelerating the pace of service innovation and reducing the CSC's operating expenses for each process activity in four columns:

- *ISO/IEC/IEEE 15288 Business or Mission Analysis Process Activity*—Technical process and major activities, from Section 5.2, "Standard System Life Cycle Processes."
- *Accelerates innovation*—Captures whether cloud-related changes are likely to accelerate the pace of CSC service innovation or otherwise increase the CSC's service agility. Options:
  No change
  ✓—slight acceleration in pace of service innovation or agility
  ✓✓—moderate improvement in pace of service innovation or agility
  ✓✓✓—substantial improvement in pace of service innovation or agility
- *Reduces CSC costs*—Captures whether cloud-related changes are likely to reduce the CSC operating expenses compared to traditional deployment. Options:
  No change
  ✓—modest reduction in CSC workload or costs for task
  ✓✓—significant reduction in CSC workload or costs for task
  ✓✓✓—complete elimination or dramatic reduction in CSC effort and/or costs for task
- *Quality risk*—Captures how the risk of user service quality impairment for cloud-based deployment compares to traditional application deployment. Options:
  No change
  ☺—Quality risk is lower (i.e., better) for cloud-based application deployment.

Figure 5.4 visualizes the likely service innovation acceleration by process.

Figure 5.5 visualizes the likely opex reduction by process. Note that opex improvement of lower software licensing/usage fees due to increased competition across a vibrant open-source and commercial ecosystem is not shown in Figure 5.5.

Delivering new services and value faster in general, and continuous delivery models in particular, mean that the service design/transition/operation cycle time shrinks from months to weeks and perhaps to days. So operational efficiency—especially for service design, transition, and disposal—becomes even more important than for traditional deployments.

Table 5.1 Summary of Business or Mission Analysis Process Changes for Cloud Service Customers

ISO/IEC/IEEE 15288 Business or Mission Analysis Process Activity	*Accelerates Innovation*	*Reduces CSC Costs*	*Quality Risk*
Business or mission analysis process (Section 5.2.1)	**No change**	**No change**	**No change**
B: Define the problem or opportunity space	No change	No change	No change
C: Characterize the solution space	No change	No change	No change
D: Evaluate alternative solution classes	No change	No change	No change
Deployment on cloud does not inherently change an organization's business or mission analysis process. However, greater service agility and lower costs enable CSC to profitably pursue more business opportunities.			
Stakeholder needs and requirements definition process (Section 5.2.2)	**No change**	**No change**	**No change**
B: Define stakeholder needs	No change	No change	No change
C: Develop the operational concept and other life cycles	No change	No change	No change
D: Transform stakeholder needs into stakeholder requirements	No change	No change	No change
E: Analyze stakeholder requirements	No change	No change	No change
Deployment on cloud does not inherently change an organization's stakeholder needs and requirements definition process.			
System requirements definition process (Section 5.2.3)	✓	**No change**	**No change**
B: Define system requirements	✓	No change	No change
C: Analyze system requirements	✓	No change	No change
Agile development with continuous integration and continuous deployment provides timely user feedback to support agile definition and analysis of system requirements.			

(*Continued*)

Table 5.1 (Continued)   Summary of Business or Mission Analysis Process Changes for Cloud Service Customers

ISO/IEC/IEEE 15288 Business or Mission Analysis Process Activity	Accelerates Innovation	Reduces CSC Costs	Quality Risk
Architecture definition process (Section 5.2.4)	✓	✓	☺
B: Develop architecture viewpoints	✓	✓	☺
C: Develop models and views of candidate architectures	✓	✓	☺
D: Relate the architecture to design	✓	✓	☺
E: Assess architecture candidates	No change	No change	No change
Greater standardization of interfaces, functionality, assumptions, and so on across the cloud ecosystem creates a foundation for somewhat faster, cheaper architecture definition activities.			
Design definition process (Section 5.2.5)	✓	**No change**	**No change**
B: Establish design characteristics and design enablers related to each system element	✓	No change	No change
C: Assess alternatives for obtaining system elements	✓	No change	No change
More (commercial) off-the-shelf service components such as functional components offered as-a-service and VNFs featuring standardized interfaces are likely to be available for consideration, along with standard service architecture and workflow templates, which accelerates service design.			
System analysis process (Section 5.2.6)	✓	✓	**No change**
B: Perform system analysis	✓	✓	☺
System analysis results are likely to get better and faster as advanced analysis tools (e.g., formal method checkers, Monte Carlo simulators, etc.) become available for popular cloud environments.			
Implementation process (Section 5.2.7)	✓✓	✓✓	**No change**
B: Perform operation	✓✓	✓✓	No change

(Continued)

Table 5.1 (Continued)   Summary of Business or Mission Analysis Process Changes for Cloud Service Customers

ISO/IEC/IEEE 15288 Business or Mission Analysis Process Activity	Accelerates Innovation	Reduces CSC Costs	Quality Risk
Standardized interfaces and off-the-shelf service components, as well as standard service architecture and workflow templates, simplify implementation.			
Integration process (Section 5.2.8)	✓✓✓	✓✓	☺
B: Perform integration— successively integrate system element configurations until the complete system is synthesized	✓✓✓	✓✓	☺
Off-the-shelf functional components offered as-a-service and software components, coupled with standardized interfaces and on-demand resource capacity supported with automated allocation and configuration of resources, applications, and services, enable faster and cheaper integration processes.			
Verification process (Section 5.2.9)	✓✓✓	✓✓✓	**No change**
B: Perform verification	✓✓✓	✓✓✓	No change
Large test beds can be created on demand to automate parallel execution of test cases.			
Transition process (Section 5.2.10)	✓✓✓	✓✓✓	☺
B: Perform the transition	✓✓✓	✓✓✓	☺
Automated life cycle management enables faster service transitions and reduces costs.			
Validation process (Section 5.2.11)	✓✓✓	✓✓✓	☺
B: Perform operation	✓✓✓	✓✓✓	☺
Automated validation testing enables faster service transitions and reduces costs.			
Operation process (Section 5.2.12)	No change	✓✓✓	☺
B: Perform operation	No change	✓✓✓	☺
D: Support the customer	No change	✓✓✓	☺

(Continued)

Table 5.1 (Continued)   Summary of Business or Mission Analysis Process Changes for Cloud Service Customers

ISO/IEC/IEEE 15288 Business or Mission Analysis Process Activity	*Accelerates Innovation*	*Reduces CSC Costs*	*Quality Risk*
Cloud management and orchestration enables powerful service monitoring and analytics to automate and improve operations activities. On-demand self-care enables users to tailor and improve their quality of experience while lowering the CSC's operating expenses.			
Maintenance process (Section 5.2.13)	✓	✓ ✓ ✓	☺
B: Perform maintenance	✓	✓ ✓	☺
C: Perform logistics support	✓	✓ ✓ ✓	☺
Cloud management and orchestration permits life cycle management actions to be automated so that human operators are mostly *on* the maintenance process loop rather than *in* the maintenance process loop.			
Disposal process (Section 5.2.14)	✓ ✓ ✓	✓ ✓ ✓	**No change**
B: Perform disposal	✓ ✓ ✓	✓ ✓ ✓	No change
C: Finalize the disposal	✓ ✓ ✓	✓ ✓ ✓	No change
Retiring or disposing of prior—or perhaps unsuccessful—releases of cloud-based application services is much faster and simpler than for traditionally deployed application services. These differences underpin support for "failing fast, failing cheap." Note that organizations may have to change their processes and practices to promptly decide to retire unprofitable, obsolete, or otherwise unsuccessful services rather than carrying expenses based on unrealistic dreams of eventual profitability.			

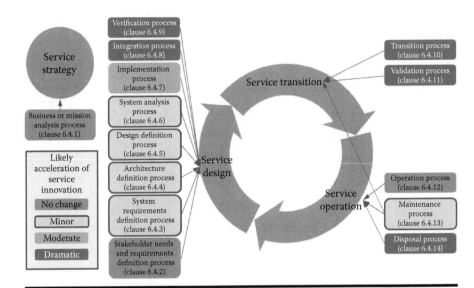

Figure 5.4 Likely *acceleration in pace of service innovation* via process changes with cloud.

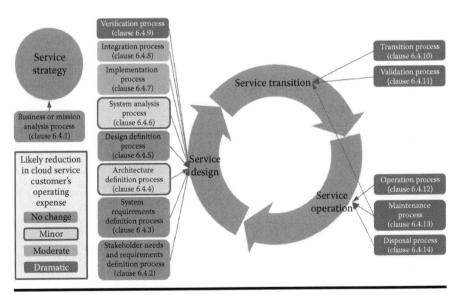

Figure 5.5 Likely *reduction in operating expenses* via process changes with cloud.

Chapter 6

Lean Application Capacity Management

Figure 6.1 visualizes lean application capacity management in which capacity decision processes continuously monitor application and resource usage along with other characteristics, and automatically transition online application capacity into service ahead of rising user demand and retire application capacity behind falling demand. The goal is *just enough* online capacity available *just in time* to continuously serve offered user workload with acceptable service quality while holding sufficient reserve capacity to cover inevitable failure events and unforecast demand surges without wasting resources on excessive capacity.

This chapter is organized as follows:

- Capacity management basics (Section 6.1)
- Simplified capacity management model (Section 6.2)
- Understanding application demand and demand management (Section 6.3)
- Understanding online application capacity (Section 6.4)
- Canonical application capacity management model (Section 6.5)
- Lean application capacity management strategy (Section 6.6)
- Managing capacity emergencies (Section 6.7)
- Perfect capacity management (Section 6.8)

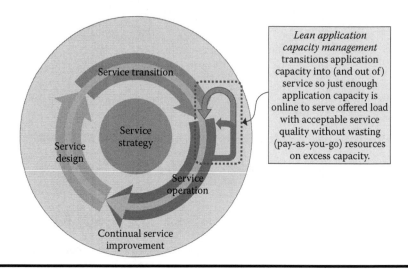

Figure 6.1 Lean application capacity management.

6.1 Capacity Management Basics

Two basic concepts are used throughout this discussion:

1. Capacity management processes (Section 6.1.1) frame capacity management in the context of IT service management.
2. Fast start-up and slow start-up capacity (Section 6.1.2) factor capacity change fulfillment actions into two broad types.

6.1.1 Capacity Management Processes

Capacity management considers the resources required to deliver an IT service capacity and performance to serve the needs of the business. IT Infrastructure Library (ITIL®) capacity management factors into three subprocesses:

1. **Component capacity management**—Cloud service provider (CSP) organizations have primary responsibility for making virtualized compute, memory, storage, and networking resources rapidly available to cloud service customers (CSCs) [i.e., rapid elasticity and scalability (Section 1.4.5)] via on-demand self-service (Section 1.4.4) mechanisms. Thus, CSC organizations largely outsource the component capacity management problem to the CSP organization, which delivers component service on demand.
2. **Service capacity management**—Manages online application capacity. The key cloud characteristics of rapid elasticity and scalability (Section 1.4.5) and on-demand self-service (Section 1.4.4) enable a fundamental

transformation of service capacity management for cloud-based applications. For example, on-demand rapid elasticity and scalability of virtualized component capacity—coupled with usage-based charging of component/resource capacity—enables CSCs to inexpensively deploy small trial applications, which can be scaled up with user demand, retired when a newer version is available, or simply terminated if the trial is unsuccessful. Figure 6.2 overlays the simplified application capacity management model of Figure 6.4 onto the traditional IT (ITIL) service life cycle of Figure II.1. Capacity management decisions are regularly evaluated by automated mechanisms throughout the service operation phase; as necessary, capacity change orders are requested and fulfilled via appropriate service transition activities.

3. **Business capacity management**—Increased service agility will enable successful CSCs to rethink their business capacity management mechanisms and processes. In particular, automated on-demand self-service (Section 1.4.4) enables CSCs to automate customer care of their end users, and automated self-care mechanisms can scale more cost effectively with growing and shrinking user service demand than traditional customer care arrangements.

The primary user service quality uncertainties associated with CSC capacity management are as follows:

1. Faulty service capacity management policies, decisions, or fulfillment actions maintain insufficient online application capacity to serve user demand with acceptable service quality.
2. Faulty business capacity management maintains inadequate customer care and supporting service capacity to provide acceptable customer care for popular (e.g., viral) applications with rapidly rising user demand…or faulty applications that cause customer care volumes to surge.

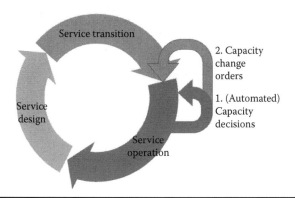

Figure 6.2   Automatic capacity management in the service life cycle.

6.1.2 Fast Start-Up and Slow Start-Up Capacity

As shown in Figure 6.3, online application capacity is actually increased in one of two ways:

1. Fast start-up by *reconfiguring a preexisting application instance,* such as increasing the number of online "worker" components supported by a single application instance's load balancer. As the application's management visibility, controllability, and service delivery infrastructure is already online, merely allocating, configuring, and deploying another application service capacity component should be relatively quick. Since fast start-up capacity fulfillment actions rely on preexisting application component instances for management visibility, controllability, and support functions, a fast start-up capacity growth action merely has to
   a. Allocate resource capacity to support the incremental of application service component capacity.
   b. Configure that component of application service capacity.
   c. Integrate that component of application service capacity with the preexisting application instance.
   d. Verify proper operation of newly allocated and configured application service component, so this is nominally fast start-up capacity compared to creating a new application instance.
   e. Order preexisting application to apply user workload to the new service component capacity.
      All of these actions can be completed fairly quickly so the additional application capacity starts up fast.

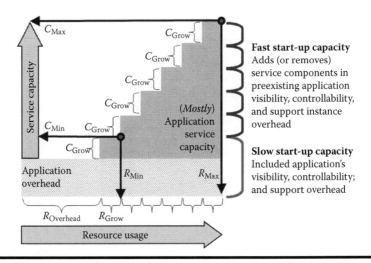

Figure 6.3   Fast and slow start-up application capacity.

2. Slow start-up by *creating a new application instance.* Creating a new application instance involves allocating and configuring the management visibility, controllability, and support framework, as well as allocating and bringing up application service components to serve user demand. Allocating, initializing, and verifying the visibility, controllability, and support overhead mechanisms must be completed before application service component capacity can be finalized, verified, and brought into service. If bringing a new application instance into service involves loading a large database or creating a complex configuration, then it might take tens of minutes or longer to complete allocation, initialization, configuration, and validation actions before the application is ready for service. Thus, introducing new application capacity via a new application instance is inherently slower than growing application capacity of a preexisting application instance.

In addition, fast start-up actions that add application service (rather than overhead) components are inherently more resource efficient because "all" of the incremental virtual resource capacity serves user demand. In contrast, slow start-up actions are primarily about bringing application instance overhead frameworks online so that application service components can be quickly added (and removed). There is often an architectural trade-off: while a richer management visibility, controllability, and support application instance framework consumes more resources and start-up time than a minimal framework, it can enable the fast start-up actions to be faster and more resource efficient because they can leverage preexisting management visibility, controllability, and support mechanisms rather than having to allocate their own resources and start-up time.

Likewise, application capacity can be reduced by releasing and deallocating some application service components to reduce the application instance's online capacity (nominally fast degrowth), or the entire application instance can be retired, released, and completely removed from service (nominally slow degrowth).

Fundamentally, the CSC's service capacity management must intelligently balance slow start-up capacity actions and fast start-up capacity actions to assure that sufficient application capacity is available online in the right geographies to serve user demand with acceptable service quality.

6.2 Simplified Capacity Management Model

Figure 6.4 visualizes application capacity management as two interlocked processes:

- **Capacity decision processes**—Compare current, historic, and forecast application demand to currently online application capacity, as well as considering alarm, performance, fault, and other information to the policies and criteria in the organization's capacity plan, to decide the following:
  - If a capacity change order should be dispatched, and if so,
  - Exactly what capacity change order should be issued.
  Capacity management decision risks are considered in Section 6.2.2.

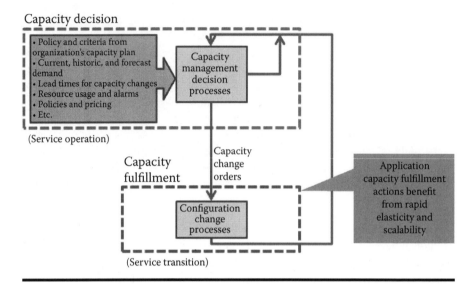

Capacity decision

(Service operation)

Capacity fulfillment

Capacity change orders

(Service transition)

Figure 6.4 Simplified application capacity management.

■ **Capacity fulfillment processes**—Execute the specific capacity change orders requested by capacity decision processes or human operations staff to manipulate both the target application instance(s) and the underlying CSP resources to fulfill the requested configuration change(s) to online application capacity. Automatically executed capacity fulfillment actions are analogous to traditional change management actions, defined as "judicious use of means to effect a change, or a proposed change, to a product or service" (ISO/IEC/IEEE, 2010-12-15). Capacity fulfillment risks are considered in Section 6.2.1.

6.2.1 Capacity Fulfillment (Change) Uncertainties (Risks)

The change management actions requested by automated capacity decision processes or human operations staff are fundamentally vulnerable to uncertainties/risks at two levels:

1. **CSP-attributable risks**—Changing online application capacity requires some change of the virtual resources and/or functional component as-a-service allocated to the CSC, as well as proper execution of some change management action by the management and orchestration CSP. *Quality Measurement of Automated Lifecycle Management Actions* (QuEST Forum, 2015-08) defines the following primary quality measurements, which usefully characterize the CSP fulfillment risks that the CSC must manage:

   a. **On-time service delivery (OTS)**—The on-time service delivery of CSPs can be measured as one measures the on-time delivery performance of a pizzeria. The service provider offers a promise time (e.g., "30 minutes or less" for a popular US-based pizza delivery chain), and customers evaluate delivery performance against that promise time. The target for on-time service delivery will generally be less than 100% (e.g., 90% on-time delivery target), and there may be some remedy if delivery exceeds the promise time (e.g., "pizza delivered in 30 minutes or less, or your pizza is free"). Note that capacity change fulfillment performance may vary across time and space, such as worse on-time service delivery performance during peak usage periods.

b. **Service quality (SQ)**—This essentially captures right-first-time performance for a requested change management action. For example, if the CSP delivers a purportedly operational virtual resource instance in response to the CSC's request, and the CSC finds the resource to be inoperable (aka dead on arrival or DOA), then that event is captured as a service quality impairment against the CSP. Occasionally, resource allocation requests will fail, just like occasionally, network packets are dropped and transactions occasionally fail.

2. **CSC-attributable risks**—Some aspects of a change management action are likely to be coordinated and executed by the CSC, such as draining user traffic away from a target component before deallocating it or testing new application service capacity before bringing it into service. Faulty execution of these actions can impact user service quality.

6.2.2 Capacity Decision Uncertainties (Risks)

As explained in Sections 4.5, "Data, Information, Knowledge and Wisdom," and 4.6, "Quality Model for Cloud-Based Applications," management and orchestration systems process concrete data elements to execute capacity decision processes that automatically generate appropriate capacity change requests. While product quality issues (Section 4.3) with the management and orchestration systems or data quality issues (Section 4.4) with the management information can cause capacity decision errors, the wisdom, knowledge, and high-level information that is embodied in the CSC's capacity management plan should broadly mitigate capacity management risks. In particular, the CSC's capacity management strategy and plan should balance the CSC's desire to carry minimal online application capacity to minimize their opex against the consequences of unacceptable user service quality due to one of the following risks:

■ **Faulty demand forecast**—inaccurate demand forecast risk (Table 20.4)—Future demand is inherently uncertain. In general, the farther into the future, the greater the uncertainty. For example, demand 1 minute from now is likely to be very similar to current demand; but demand 1, 2, or 3 hours from now can be quite different from now, and demand days, weeks, or months from now can be very, very different from demand now.

■ **Failure of application service component or capacity**—VM premature release (failure) risk (Table 14.2), (semi?) permanent loss of cloud service risk (Table 25.1)—An application component in production service can fail, thereby taking some application capacity out of service.

■ **Degraded resource delivery**—VM scheduling latency risk (Table 14.4), packet loss risk (Table 15.1), network-delivered throughput risk (Table 15.4)—Resource service quality delivered by CSPs can vary across time due to risks related to cloud characteristics of multitenancy (Section 1.4.3) and resource pooling (Section 1.4.6). The result is that a particular application configuration may no longer be delivering sufficient resource throughput to serve the same user workload with acceptable quality, and thus, some configuration change actions may be necessary to maintain user service quality with adequate online application reserve capacity.

■ **Stale management visibility**—Stale vision risk (Table 19.3)—Performance management data used by capacity decision processes (e.g., resource utilization data) are inherently stale because the data are collected over some measurement window (e.g., 15 minutes, 5 minutes, 1 minute, 15 seconds) and then made available to the capacity decision process. Thus, the capacity decision process might not become aware of some capacity-impacting condition until after the performance measurement window closes and the data propagates through various intermediate systems.

■ **Tardy capacity fulfillment action**—Requested capacity change action can be delivered late (i.e., beyond the CSP's promise time). Thus, reserve capacity must cover longer lead time intervals, longer than the service provider's promise time.

■ **Explicitly failed capacity fulfillment action**—VNF life cycle management (execution) risks (Table 23.2)—Requested capacity change action can fail outright with some error return code. Thus, the capacity decision process must reevaluate the original capacity decision and request another capacity change action.

■ **Implicit (silent) failure of capacity fulfillment action**—VM dead on arrival (DOA) risk (Table 14.1)—The CSP purports to have successfully executed the requested capacity change action, but subsequent testing or usage reveals that the capacity change action was not actually correct. In this case, the capacity decision process must both address the failed service capacity and request an appropriate mitigating capacity change action.

6.3 Understanding Application Demand and Demand Management

Applications generally experience cyclical patterns of demand over days, weeks, and seasons with random variations over milliseconds, seconds, and minutes. The following list is from longest time frame to shortest time frame:

- **Life cycle demand pattern** (e.g., years or months)—Demand for a particular application will follow a life cycle with small initial demand, some level of typical demand across the application's popular period, followed by declining demand, and eventually, the application is removed from service.
- **Seasonality**—Usage patterns for most application services exhibit some seasonality, such as increased consumer e-commerce activity leading up to year-end holidays.
- **Weekly**—Usage for most applications demonstrates some weekly patterns of demand. For example, demand on a Tuesday or Thursday is often materially different from demand on a Saturday or Sunday.
- **Daily**—Humans have daily patterns of activity: nominally 8 hours of sleep, 8 hours of work, and the remaining 8 hours accommodating leisure, dining, and other activities. Applications consumed directly or indirectly by human users often have demand patterns that are correlated with daily human activities; some applications are primarily consumed when users are working, relaxing, commuting, or whatever. Figure 6.5 visualizes (15-minute) workload for a sample communications application on a typical Thursday.

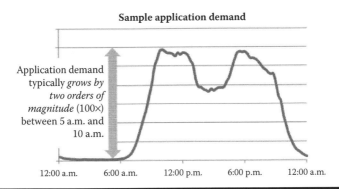

Figure 6.5   Sample daily demand pattern for a human-oriented application.

- **Random variations**—Superimposed on daily, weekly, seasonal, and life cycle patterns of demand are minute-by-minute, second-by-second, and millisecond-by-millisecond random variations. For example, the peak demand window in Figure 6.5 was 10:00 a.m. thru 10:15 a.m.; however, user demand was not uniform every minute, second, and millisecond across that 15-minute period. The busiest minute, busiest second, and busiest millisecond in that measurement window undoubtedly exceeded that 15-minute average value.

Figure 6.6 visualizes common application demand management strategies, as well as rapid elasticity and scalability, that are used to address cyclical and random variations in user demand.

- **Queues and buffers**—Applications rely on message buffers and work queues to smooth random variations in workloads across microseconds and milliseconds.
- **Load balancers**—Applications that rely on load balancers or application distribution controllers can use those components to balance workloads across pools of components or application instances.
- **Overload controls**—When queues, buffers, and load balancers can't mitigate user service impact of inadequate online capacity, applications often engage overload or congestion controls to minimize user service impact of an overload episode.
- **Workload placement**—Operational policies, supported by client configurations and other mechanisms, can place (i.e., distribute) user workloads across a suite of online application instances to broadly align user demand with online application capacity.

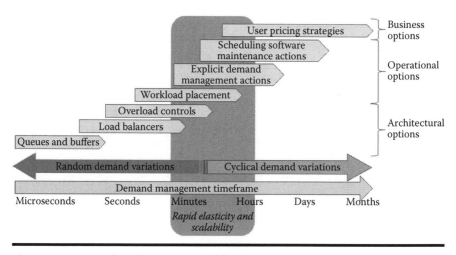

Figure 6.6 Typical application demand management strategies.

- **Rapid elasticity and scalability**—Rapid elasticity and scalability often takes between several minutes (for nominally fast start-up capacity) and several hours (for nominally slow start-up capacity) to bring additional application capacity online. This topic is considered throughout this chapter.
- **Explicit demand management actions**—In some cases, application service providers may opt to take explicit demand management actions to shape workload, such as deferring some lower-priority or nonurgent work to lower-usage periods.
- **Scheduling maintenance actions**—Maintenance actions for CSCs, CSPs, or others in the cloud service delivery chain can potentially impact available online capacity, so plans are often made to minimize the risk of user service impact due to those maintenance actions. For example, a CSC might move their production capacity out of a cloud data center while a major retrofit is underway or defer software updates during capacity emergency periods.
- **User pricing strategies**—Pricing strategies for application service can materially shape patterns of user demand. Readers may remember telephony pricing in the 20th century when long distance pricing was highest from 8 a.m. to 5 p.m. weekdays, with a significant discount from 5 p.m. to 11 p.m. (evenings), and calling was cheapest of all after 11 p.m. and on weekends. The discounts were large enough to push some demand from peak daytime periods to evening and night/weekend periods, thereby enabling telephone companies to both reduce demand peaks and increase usage in off-peak periods. Time of day, day of week, spot market, discounts, and other advanced pricing strategies can shape (e.g., smooth) service demand across time.

6.4 Understanding Online Application Capacity

Application demand from users is served by the supply of online application capacity. When the supply of online application capacity equals or exceeds user demand, then all users can be served with acceptable service quality; when demand exceeds the supply of online application capacity, then at least some users will experience unacceptable service quality or outright service rejection (e.g., through actions of overload or congestion control mechanisms). As shown in Figure 6.7, online application capacity can be factored into three broad bands:

1. **Working** (or productive) **capacity**—The portion of online capacity that actually serves user demand is said to be productive, or working, capacity. Random variations in demand (explained in Section 6.3, "Understanding Application Demand and Demand Management") mean that the instantaneous productive capacity varies from minute to minute, second to second, and millisecond to millisecond. However, the level of productive capacity is determined by what is necessary to serve offered workload with acceptable

Figure 6.7 Online application capacity.

demand in the measurement period of interest (e.g., a 5-minute performance measurement window). By analogy, four tires provide sufficient productive or working capacity for an automobile to drive properly.

2. **Reserve capacity**—Beyond the level of productive capacity required to serve current user demand with acceptable service quality, prudent CSCs will hold reserve application capacity online to mitigate the risk of user service impact due to the following:

a. **Inevitable failures**—Occasionally, some hardware, software, or human failure will impact some online application component, thereby rendering some portion of application capacity unavailable or unfit for service. It is prudent to maintain sufficient online reserve capacity (sometimes called *redundant* capacity) to instantaneously mitigate user service impact due to such capacity-impacting failure events.

b. **Lead time demand**—Just like ordering a pizza, fulfilling any capacity change fulfillment action takes a finite period of time. Sufficient reserve application capacity should be held online to serve rising demand through the entire application capacity change lead time period.

c. **Nonforecast demand events**—There is always uncertainty in forecasts of future demand, so sufficient reserve application capacity should be held online to mitigate some level of nonforecast demand surge. For example, the Loma Prieta (California) earthquake that occurred during a live broadcast of 1989 World Series baseball game triggered a nonforecast demand surge in communications services as viewers tried to contact friends and loved ones in the San Francisco area. The nature of the application service, customer expectations, and other factors will influence the level of reserve capacity appropriate to mitigate nonforecast demand events.

By analogy, one spare tire in the trunk of an automobile provides sufficient reserve capacity to mitigate the risk of a flat tire for most motorists.

3. **Excess capacity**—Online application capacity beyond what is necessary to cover both current productive and reserve capacity needs is excessive and represents pure waste to be eliminated. By analogy, carrying a second spare tire in the trunk of an automobile is excessive and wasteful for most motorists. Usage-based pricing of virtual resources (enabled by measured service, Section 1.4.2) means that CSCs can reduce their operating expenses by releasing cloud resources when excess online application capacity is released.

The exact application configuration required to serve a particular workload can vary across time and space because of the following:

■ Actual performance of virtual compute, memory, storage, networking, and functional components offered as-a-service that serve the target application may vary. For example, volume throughput risk (Table 16.5) or network-delivered throughput risk (Table 15.4) may throttle the actual application service capacity available to serve users, and packet loss risk (Table 15.1) may cause additional application capacity to be consumed with retransmitted, retried, and perhaps repeated work.

■ Settings of configuration parameters alter how much overhead processing the application instance must perform that impacts the remaining capacity available to serve user traffic. For example, generating richer debug logs and performance data consumes application resource capacity that would otherwise be available to serve user workload.

Thus, nominal application configuration recommendations for particular user workloads should be treated as guidance, like government fuel economy ratings on automobiles, rather than rigid specifications.

6.5 Canonical Application Capacity Management Model

Figure 6.8 visualizes application management in the quality model style from Chapter 4, "Cloud Service Qualities."

■ A *capacity plan* coalesces wisdom, knowledge, and information driving capacity management. According to ISO/IEC 20000-1 (ISO/IEC, 2011-04-15),

The capacity plan shall include at least:
  a) current and forecast demand for services;
  b) expected impact of agreed requirements for availability, service continuity and service levels;

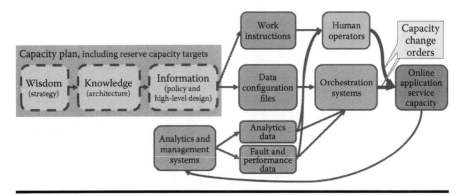

Figure 6.8   Canonical application capacity management model.

      c)   time-scales, thresholds and costs for upgrades to service capacity;

      ...

      f)   procedures to enable predictive analysis, or reference them…

Operationally, the capacity plan for a cloud-based application is likely to cover the following information:

- **Application instance policies**—How many application instances should be online at any time, and in what geographic regions?
- **Reserve capacity targets**—How much spare online application capacity above working capacity should be held to mitigate the capacity-related service quality risks?
- **Capacity decision input data**—What data are considered when making capacity management decisions?
- **Capacity change decision criteria**—What conditions (e.g., triggers) should prompt the capacity decision process to reevaluate capacity management decisions?
- **Capacity action selection and coordination policy**—When should fast start-up (aka horizontal) growth or degrowth of preexisting application instances be ordered versus when should slow start-up actions to create a new application instance or terminate a preexisting application instance be ordered?
- **Capacity placement policy criteria**—How should online application capacity growth and degrowth action requests be distributed across multiple (e.g., geographically distributed) CSP data centers?

■ *Data*, especially configuration files and descriptors, for a "reinterpretable representation of information in a formalized manner suitable for communication, interpretation, or processing," is a key element of the capacity plan. This data representation of the capacity plan serves as a primary input to automated orchestration systems as well as work instructions for human operators.

- *Orchestration systems* process configuration data, along with *analytics* and *fault and performance data* from analytics and management systems to make automatic capacity decisions and request *capacity change orders*, which configure the *online application service capacity* available to serve users.
- Occasionally, catastrophic or multipoint failures, unforecast demand surges, or other extraordinary events will overwhelm automated mechanisms executing capacity plans. *Work instructions* (e.g., methods of procedure) derived from the capacity plan will inform *human operators* when to override automated orchestration systems and advise what corrective actions to take to return the application to normal operation. Note that human override of overriding automated systems is likely to cover two rather different operational scenarios:

  1. **Faulty fulfillment actions**—Some capacity fulfillment actions hang, fail, or otherwise are not completed acceptably fast, so a human operator intervenes to manually configure sufficient online application to serve demand. Human operators may then troubleshoot the original capacity fulfillment problem.

  2. **Situations beyond the designed scope of automated mechanisms**— The goal of delivering new services and value faster will drive CSCs to bring services to market when life cycle automations are good enough to cover the vast majority of operational scenarios, but CSCs are unlikely to delay release until automations cover all possible scenarios. Often, there will still be a human operator somewhere, and as soon as he/she becomes aware of an emergency situation that increases risks to user service quality, like an incident that could or has impacted a cloud data center hosting application capacity or an extraordinary surge in user demand (e.g., media, entertainment, or disaster event), then he/she is likely to manually order capacity change actions to minimize the risk (or duration) of surging user demand outstripping online application capacity.

Figure 6.9 highlights the primary quality vulnerabilities of the canonical application capacity management model of Figure 6.8.

- **Product errors** (Section 4.3)—Orchestration, analytics, management, and other systems in the service management workflow and service delivery path are vulnerable to product quality problems that produce incorrect output from correct inputs.
- **Data errors** (Section 4.4)—Data used as input to orchestration and other systems, as well as formal work instructions used by human operators, can include data quality impairments (Section 4.4. Correct processing of faulty (input) data generally produces faulty results.

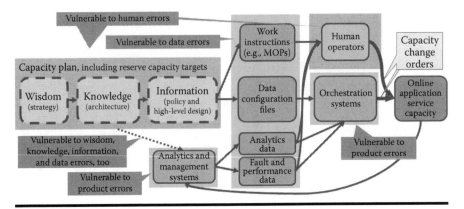

Figure 6.9 Quality risks for the canonical application capacity management model.

- **Human errors**—Human operators are expected to promptly and diligently follow work instructions and documented procedures, but they occasionally make mistakes (aka procedural errors) that produce faulty results.
- **Wisdom/knowledge/information quality** (Section 4.5)—The wisdom, knowledge, and information captured in the capacity plan can implicitly or explicitly include risks, limitation, or flaws. For example, the capacity planning wisdom, knowledge, and modeling information that underpins a CSC organization's capacity plan might recommend targeting 20% reserve capacity based on a set of assumptions. Correctly adhering to the recommended 20% reserve capacity target may fail to assure sufficient online application capacity if any of assumptions are violated, or if there is an error in the wisdom, knowledge, modeling, or other information embodied in the capacity plan. Flaws in the wisdom, knowledge, information, or data in the capacity plan often arise from one or more of the following: Visibility risks (Chapter 19), service policy risks (Chapter 20), human error risk (Table 22.4); life cycle management (execution) risks (Chapter 23); or unknown-unknown risks (Chapter 26).

6.6 Lean Application Capacity Management Strategy

Figure 6.10 visualizes the high-level methodology for achieving lean application capacity to minimize a CSC's expenses related to online application capacity:

- **Working capacity** serves offered workload. This is productive capacity.
- **Reserve capacity** mitigates user service impact of nonforecast demand surges, covers lead time demand, and supports high-availability mechanisms. Reserve

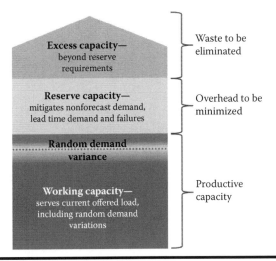

Figure 6.10 Lean application capacity management.

capacity is an overhead to be intelligently minimized. This is considered in Section 6.6.1, "Reduce Reserve Application Capacity Targets."

■ **Excess capacity** beyond reserve requirements is pure waste to be eliminated. This is considered in Section 6.6.2, "Eliminate Excess (Wasted) Application Capacity."

Continual service improvement (Chapter 9) drives out excess capacity via approaches like perfect capacity management (Section 6.8).

6.6.1 *Reduce Reserve Application Capacity Targets*

As explained in Section 6.4, reserve capacity is held to mitigate the risk of user service quality impact due to the following:

1. Inevitable failures
2. Lead time demand
3. Nonforecast demand events

Holding the risk of user service quality impact constant, one can minimize the level of reserve capacity required by methodically addressing each of these factors individually:

■ Reducing reserves required to mitigate inevitable failures (Section 6.6.1.1).
■ Reducing reserves required to mitigate lead time demand (Section 6.6.1.2).
■ Reducing reserves required to mitigate nonforecast demand events (Section 6.6.1.3).

6.6.1.1 Reducing Reserves Required to Mitigate Inevitable Failures

Highly available services are engineered to have no single point of failure (SPOF). This means that sufficient redundant capacity is held online (e.g., active) or nearline (e.g., standby) so that user service can be recovered following a failure without producing unacceptable service impact or outage for users. For example, a modern commercial jet aircraft is engineered to take off, maneuver, and land with only one of its two engines operating; thus, the jet engine is not an SPOF. Technically, that configuration is called $1 + 1$ ($N + K$) because one engine (N) is sufficient to serve the thrust (workload) required to take off, maneuver, and land the aircraft, and an additional engine (K) provides protection (redundancy). As Figure 6.11 illustrates, the percentage of online reserve capacity consumed by "+1" (or $K = 1$) redundancy decreases as the number N of working elements increases. Considering the aircraft example again, one recognizes that a twin-engine aircraft must be engineered with nominally 200% of required thrust to fulfill the no SPOF requirement (i.e., one reserve engine represents 50% of total nominal thrust), while a four-engine aircraft can be engineered with nominally 133% of required thrust (i.e., one reserve engine represents only 25% of total nominal thrust). Thus, having each element serve a smaller portion (nominally 1/Nth of workload) means that the percentage of reserve capacity required for a fixed "+K" level of redundancy decreases. Note that all-active arrangements of pooled workers (rather than standby components protecting active workers) are lower risk because undetected, or silent, failures are less likely to remain undetected on components actively serving user workloads than on nominally standby components that are largely idle.

While high-availability mechanisms mitigate the risk of nominally "single-point" failures, occasionally, there are catastrophic or multipoint failures that overwhelm a single application instance's high-availability mechanisms. For example, a data center fire might trigger an emergency power-off (EPO) action that de-energizes

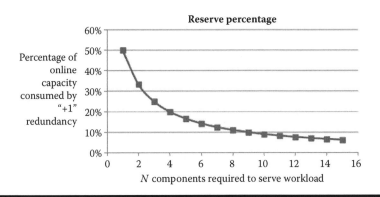

Figure 6.11   Reserve capacity consumed with N + 1 redundancy.

multiple racks or rows of equipment, or a natural disaster like an earthquake could render an entire data center unavailable. Service impact from catastrophic or multipoint failures is generally mitigated by disaster recovery plans, which recover user service into geographically distant data centers to minimize the risk of a single catastrophic event (e.g., earthquake) impacting recovery capacity. The primary figure of merit for disaster recovery planning is the recovery time objective (RTO). RTO is the time between a disaster declaration (or automatic activation of disaster recovery protocols) and the time until user service is recovered. Critical services may be engineered with sufficient geographically distributed online redundant capacity to achieve an RTO of seconds or minutes. Services with more generous RTOs (e.g., hours or days) might plan to allocate disaster recovery capacity on the fly following a catastrophic event rather than carrying online georedundant reserve capacity. Cloud computing in general, and virtual resources in particular, can make georedundant disaster recovery arrangements less costly than with traditional deployment options.

In addition to hard failures, which render one or more components totally unavailable for service, subcritical failure conditions can cause resource throughput or performance to be curtailed, which reduces the actual application capacity available to serve users. For example, the following risks can diminish the actual capacity available to service user workload for a specific application configuration:

- Network-delivered throughput risk (Table 15.4)
- Packet loss risk (Table 15.1)
- Volume throughput risk (Table 16.5)

Higher-quality infrastructure service reduces the need to hold reserve capacity online to mitigate episodes of curtailed throughput of nominally working capacity.

6.6.1.2 Reducing Reserves Required to Mitigate Lead Time Demand

As explained in Section 6.4, cloud-based application capacity can often grow via fast start-up capacity actions (e.g., adding service components to preexisting application instances) or via slow start-up capacity actions (i.e., creating a new application instance). Reserves held against lead time demand must cover rising demand in the actual capacity growth lead time period. The longer the actual lead time period, the greater the risk that demand may increase, and thus, the greater the reserve must be. Actual capacity growth lead times will vary, but those variations can usefully be factored into four categories:

1. **Typical or promise time for capacity change actions**—The majority of syntactically and semantically correct configuration change actions should be completed successfully within a reasonable (nominally "typical") time. *Quality Measurement of Automated Lifecycle Management Actions* (QuEST Forum,

2015-08) measures this with traditional service delivery models of a promise time committed by the service provider against which one determines if the delivery was within the promise time (i.e., on time) or the delivery exceeded the promise time (i.e., late). The objective and quantitative quality measurement is thus the percentage of on-time deliveries. Just as it is infeasible to engineer a real system for perfect (i.e., 100.00000%) service availability, it is impractical to engineer for 100% on-time delivery against a reasonable promise time. Practically, some on-time delivery percentage (perhaps 85% to 95%) of capacity change requests will complete within the service provider's promise time or typical completion time.

2. **Tardy capacity change actions**—Inevitably, some portion of capacity change requests will fail to be completed within the promise time. CSCs must serve their users with acceptable service quality even when their CSPs occasionally fail to meet their promise times for capacity change actions.

3. **Unsuccessful capacity change actions**—Not all requested capacity change actions will be successful, or right-first-time. Occasionally, semantically and syntactically correct capacity change actions will fail to be completed successfully. Unsuccessful automated life cycle management actions, including capacity change actions, can be measured via the service quality (SQ) metric of the QuEST Forum (2015-08). Capacity plans and decision processes will often request different capacity change actions (e.g., growing capacity of a different application instance or growing in a different way) to mitigate capacity change actions that fail outright.

4. **DOA (silent failure) capacity change actions**—On rare occasions, automated life cycle management actions will silently malfunction so that the virtual machine, service component, or other resource is not fit for purpose. Attempts to use the resource—either before or after production traffic is applied—will eventually reveal that the component is inoperable. For example, virtual network configuration or connectivity might be incorrect, or the wrong application image may have been loaded into the virtual machine. Inoperable resources must be methodically removed from service and released, and replacement capacity ordered, all of which prolongs the time to actually bring requested capacity into service.

Actual lead times are materially different for each of these four categories, and service provider qualities will influence distribution of actual lead times. Capacity plans and decision processes should hold sufficient online reserve capacity to serve offered workload in the actual lead time intervals between when a capacity change is requested and when requested application capacity is online and available to serve user workload. As a practical matter, capacity plans might engineer lead time demand reserves to cover perhaps two to four times the service provider's promised time for each capacity change action. Lead time demand reserves might be smaller for service providers with excellent on-time delivery performance, right-first-time service quality, and low DOA rates.

6.6.1.3 Reducing Reserves Required to Mitigate Nonforecast Demand Events

The future is inherently uncertain, and there is always a risk that unforeseen events will create a surge in demand that outstrips online application capacity. Thus, some online application capacity can be held in reserve to mitigate the risk of nonforecast demand surges. Shortening capacity fulfillment lead times can shorten the forecasting horizon, which reduces the risk of forecasting errors. Better analytics tools and algorithms applying more high-quality data can reduce the risk of forecasts being wrong. Review, and revision when necessary, of demand forecasts by human experts may further reduce the risk of forecasting error.

6.6.2 Eliminate Excess (Wasted) Application Capacity

As illustrated in Figure 6.12, excess online application represents pure waste to the CSC that should be eliminated to reduce the CSC's usage of virtual infrastructure resources, which should reduce operating expense for the CSC. Eliminating online application capacity that is above reserve capacity requirements requires several actions:

1. Decide that current online application capacity sufficiently exceeds reserve requirements that the cost savings benefit is deemed to outweigh the direct costs and user service quality risks associated with deallocating the excess online application capacity. If the CSP does not lower the CSC's usage charges for releasing a unit of previously allocated (but now excess) capacity, then there is no reward to the CSC to offset the risk and operational complexity of reducing online capacity. As there are costs and risks associated with

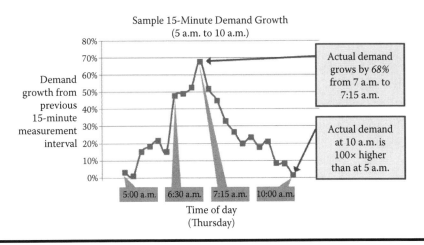

Figure 6.12 Sample morning demand ramp.

growing application capacity in the future, the CSC must also balance the risks and rewards of shrinking online capacity now and expanding capacity in the future rather than simply holding excess capacity. Considering the example of Figure 6.7, application complexity and CSP pricing may not make it worthwhile for a CSC to shrink online application capacity in the middle of the day when many user take lunch, but a dramatic day/night pattern of demand makes reducing capacity late at night and regrowing capacity early each morning a practical strategy to boost operational efficiency.

2. Select exactly which unit of application capacity is most appropriate to release.
3. Drain or migrate user workload being served by the selected unit of application capacity.
4. Decide when it is acceptably safe to take the selected component or application instance offline.
5. Terminate the selected component or application instance.
6. Formally release virtual compute, memory, storage, networking, and functional component services that supported the component or application instance that was terminated.

The following characteristics enable CSCs to prudently attack excess online capacity:

1. Supporting rapid and reliable mechanisms for workload drainage/migration away from targeted components or application instances.
2. Rapidly and reliably terminating targeted components or application instances.
3. Favorable billing treatment of resource release actions. For example, there should be no resource termination or release charges, and usage charging should cease the instant the CSC requests release rather than rounding usage up to the next hour, day, etc.

6.7 Managing Capacity Emergencies

Occasionally, events will unfold that automated systems are unable to manage successfully, resulting in a capacity emergency during which user demand outstrips instantaneously available online application capacity. These capacity emergencies are likely to be caused by one or more the following risks:

- Insufficient spare capacity (target) risk (Table 20.1)—Holding minimal spare or reserve capacity online increases the risk that a failure or demand surge will trigger a capacity emergency.
- Inaccurate demand forecast risk (Table 20.4)—Profound forecasting errors, like failing to predict unusual demand patterns related to major sporting or entertainment events, can produce capacity emergencies.

- Faulty scaling decision criteria risk (Table 20.3)—Faulty scaling decision criteria can cause demand growth to outpace automated capacity growth, which can ultimately produce a capacity emergency.
- Visibility risks (Chapter 19)—Not knowing the true level of user demand and current state of all service components.
- CSP catastrophe risks (Chapter 25)—CSP catastrophes can overwhelm normal capacity reserves and high-availability mechanisms.
- Network outage risk (Table 15.5)—Network outages, including within a cloud data center, can render significant portions of application service capacity inoperable or unreachable; partitioned application service capacity or data can complicate service recovery.
- Volume outage risk (Table 16.4)—Storage outages can prevent application software from properly processing user requests, thus rendering service effectively unavailable.

Aggressive management of capacity emergencies by human operators is useful in these situations. Human operators should be provided with both clear instructions on when to override automated capacity management systems and initiate emergency capacity growth actions. For example, if operations staff see an event of national or regional significance unfold on CNN in real time, those operators should have the ability and authority to initiate appropriate emergency capacity growth actions to grow application capacity ahead of surging demand rather than relying on automated systems to try and follow the demand surge.

6.8 Perfect Capacity Management

Figure 6.12 illustrates the percentage demand growth per 15 minute-interval for the morning demand ramp of the sample application demand shown in Figure 6.7. Note that from 6:15 a.m. thru 8:15 a.m., user demand increases by approximately 50% every 15 minutes, and demand continues to increase rapidly thru midmorning. Attempting to scale online application capacity by simple *reacting* to 15-minute performance management data or threshold-crossing alarms is risky if capacity fulfillment actions take several minutes (or longer) to complete and occasionally fail.

The alternative to making capacity decisions by simply reacting to performance management data and threshold-crossing alarms is predictive capacity decisions. Most applications have fundamentally cyclical patterns of demand; for instance, demand is often much greater at 10 a.m. than it is at 5 a.m. for our sample application in Figure 6.7 and for myriad other applications that serve human users. Predictive analytics can forecast short-term demand, and that forecast can be used to drive near-real-time capacity change orders. If upper control limits are exceeded, then additional (perhaps emergency) capacity growth actions can be triggered; if lower control limits are exceeded, then online capacity can be retired (or pending capacity growth actions can be cancelled). Predictive capacity management decisions can be continuously improved by methodically comparing actual capacity plans to *perfect* capacity plans.

PJM Interconnection, a large North American electric power provider, developed *perfect dispatch* to minimize operating expenses of their electricity generation facilities while assuring reliable power delivery to customers. PJM defines perfect dispatch (PJM Interconnection, 2014) as the least-cost electric power production operating plan assuring $N + 1$ protection of generating capacity and full knowledge of (nominally future) conditions in the analysis period. In essence, perfect dispatch is the theoretically optimal operational plan for generating electric power to serve a day's actual demand while maintaining +1 spare generating capacity as a hedge against brownouts/blackouts. By comparing a prior day's actual electricity generation plan with the day's *perfect dispatch* plan, which delivered exactly enough power to serve actual demand plus the level of spare capacity stipulated by the organization's operational policies, operators can identify imperfections to focus their continuous improvement activities onto to squeeze waste and inefficiency out of electric power production.

The notion of perfect dispatch can be applied to application capacity management to construct nominally "perfect capacity" plans that are *technically perfect* and *economically perfect* capacity plans to serve a particular day's actual demand. By comparing the day's actual online capacity, economically perfect capacity, technically perfect capacity, and actual demand, one can see opportunities for application capacity management optimization to reduce waste.

Figure 6.13 overlays perfect application capacity concepts onto the sample daily application demand pattern of Figure 6.7.

- **Actual demand**—The lowest line on Figure 6.13 represents the actual service demand from application users for a particular day.
- **Technically perfect capacity**—The dashed line immediately above actual demand on Figure 6.13 represents the smallest online application capacity

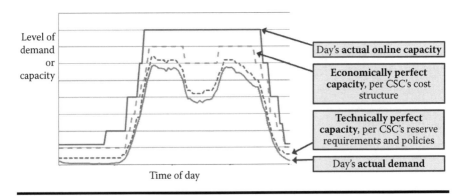

Figure 6.13 Perfect application capacity.

that is technically feasible that complies will the CSC's reserve requirements and other operational policies assuming that the CSC had perfect foresight of actual user demand. Technically perfect capacity would have the minimum technically feasible online capacity to serve actual demand while continuously fulfilling the CSC's reserve capacity requirement (e.g., +1 online redundancy) so that no single failure would reduce online application capacity below what is needed to serve all user workload with acceptable service quality. For example, if the CSC has configured an application instance to serve 100 active users per service component and there were 403 active users in a measurement period, then technically perfect capacity would have 6 service components: 5 service components are required to serve 403 users with acceptable service quality, and CSC policy requires 1 spare service component.

■ **Economically perfect capacity**—The dashed line above technically perfect capacity on Figure 6.13 represents the economically optimum online application capacity plan that minimizes the CSC's operating expenses and complies with the CSC's reserve capacity policy. The economically perfect capacity plan is driven by the CSP's usage-based pricing model, such as resource allocation and termination charges, as well as resource holding costs. If the expected cost savings of a capacity change action (e.g., reducing online application capacity in the late morning when users take lunch breaks and rebuilding online application capacity in early afternoon when they return) does not outweigh the direct costs of the capacity change actions, then the action is not justified, or economically perfect.

■ **Actual online capacity**—The solid line at the top of Figure 6.13 reflects the application capacity that was actually online in the target day.

The perfect capacity lines of Figure 6.13 enable one to visualize (shown in Figure 6.14) three concrete areas for a CSC to improve their operational efficiencies.

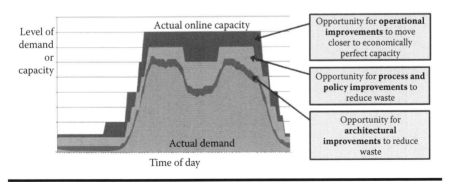

Figure 6.14 Improvement opportunities in the context of perfect application capacity.

■ Opportunities for **operational improvements**—The gap between actual online capacity and economically perfect capacity should be the CSC's primary focus of efficiency improvement because that gap represents pure waste: application capacity held beyond what is economically optimum based on current cost structures. For example, more frequent capacity change actions can enable actual online application capacity to track closer to economically perfect capacity.

■ Opportunities for **process and policy improvements**—The gap between economically perfect capacity and technically perfect capacity is primarily driven by two factors:
  – **(Risk-based) reserve requirement**—Mitigates nonforecast demand, lead time demand, and failures, so improving demand forecasting, shortening capacity fulfillment lead times, and minimizing the frequency and footprint of failures should enable reserve requirements to be reduced.
  – **Cost structure**—Usage-based pricing of CSP resources, application software, and CSC costs may not make it cost effective to drive capacity all the way to the architecturally perfect online application capacity level.

■ Opportunities for **architectural improvements**—The gap between technically perfect capacity and actual demands represent potential improvements/enhancements. Note that the overhead and other costs associated with fulfilling architecturally perfect capacity may not be cost effective for either the CSC or the CSP.

If CSCs can materially reduce their usage-based charges for cloud resources by releasing resources when application demand declines (e.g., overnight) and if capacity change actions both have a low transaction cost and are reliable, then sophisticated CSCs will strive for perfect capacity management. Continuous improvement actions focused on both driving actual online capacity closer to economically perfect capacity and driving economically perfect capacity closer to actual demand can minimize a CSC's operating expenses.

Chapter 7

Testing Cloud-Based Application Services

The most authoritative reference on software testing offers the following*:

> The primary goals of testing are to:
>
> - *provide information about the quality of the test item and any residual risk* in relation to how much the test item has been tested; to
> - find defects in the test item prior to its release for use; and to
> - *mitigate the risks to the stakeholders of poor product quality.*

Section 7.1, "Testing, Uncertainty, and Cloud-Based Applications," considers both knowledge-based uncertainty (Section 7.1.1) and stochastic uncertainty (Section 7.1.2) of cloud-based applications. Section 7.2, "Testing, Verification, and Validation," reviews standard testing concepts and terminology. Figure 7.1 is a simplified version of a figure from ISO/IEC/IEEE 29119-1, *Software Testing Concepts and Definitions*, which visualizes how standard test processes and other elements

---

* From clause 5.1, "Introduction to Software Testing," of ISO/IEC/IEEE 29119-1:2013, *Software Testing Concepts and Definitions* (ISO/IEC/IEEE, 2013-09-01).

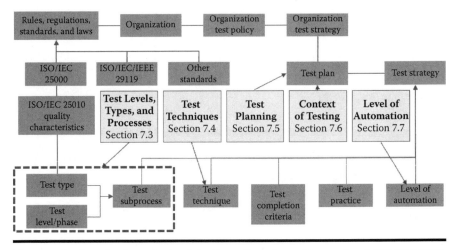

Figure 7.1 Standard context of testing. (Based on Figure 1 of ISO/IEC/IEEE, *29119-1—Software Testing—Part 1: Concepts and Definitions*, Geneva, Switzerland: ISO/IEC/IEEE, 2013-09-01.)

relate. How several of those test elements evolve as applications evolve to cloud deployment is considered separately:

- Test levels, types, and processes (Section 7.3)
- Test techniques (Section 7.4)
- Test planning (Section 7.5)
- Context of testing (Section 7.6)
- Level of automation (Section 7.7)

The following cloud-centric test techniques are considered:

- **Scalability testing** (Section 7.8)—Verifies that rapid elasticity and scalability (Section 1.4.5) of the application service works properly.
- **Risk control testing** (Section 7.9)—Verifies that the application's risk controls and treatments work properly.
- **Sensitivity (or dose–response) testing** (Section 7.10)—Quality impairments related to virtualized compute, memory, storage, or networking service contribute to the stochastic uncertainties (Section 7.1.2) facing cloud-based applications. Sensitivity testing characterizes how application service quality is impacted by variations in infrastructure service quality, which enables improvements to make application service more robust to infrastructure quality variations.
- **Automated acceptance testing for service transitions** (Section 7.11)— Automated acceptance testing is a component of faster service transitions.

Section 7.12 summarizes risk-based testing of cloud-based applications.

7.1 Testing, Uncertainty, and Cloud-Based Applications

The ISO/IEC/IEEE 29119 suite of software and system engineering standards* is the most authoritative reference on software testing. *Testing* is defined by ISO/IEC/IEEE 29119-1 (ISO/IEC/IEEE, 2013-09-01) as a "set of activities conducted to facilitate discovery and/or evaluation of properties of one or more test items."[†] Broadly speaking, "facilitate discovery" means reducing uncertainties; as explained in Chapter 3, "Risk and Risk Management," risk management focuses on reducing uncertainties. As explained in Section 3.1, it is useful to factor uncertainty into the following:

- Knowledge-based uncertainty (Section 7.1.1)
- Stochastic uncertainty (Section 7.1.2)

Figure 7.2 visualizes how uncertainties apply to cloud service customers (CSCs) in the context of user service quality risk.

7.1.1 Knowledge-Based Uncertainty

Knowledge-based (or epistemic) uncertainty is variability due to inadequate knowledge. There are inevitably some unknown residual defects in applications, data artifacts, operational policies, and procedures when they are first released. Software reliability growth theory (Musa, 1999) posits that there is a finite number of software defects in a piece of software executing a fixed operational profile. Figure 7.3 gives a sample software reliability growth model with cumulative testing effort on the *x*-axis and number of defects discovered on the *y*-axis. When testing begins, it is relatively easy to discover defects, but as those defects are corrected and testing continues, it requires more and more effort to detect and localize the remaining residual defects. Testing seeks to discover these residual defects (i.e., gain knowledge of their existence) so they can be corrected (especially treatments: replace or remove the risk source [Section 3.3.1] or change the risk likelihood [Section 3.3.2]) or otherwise mitigated.

As shown in Figure 7.3, the test effort—and thus cost—to find the next residual defect increases dramatically as one gets closer to finding the "last" residual defect in a software product when operated in a particular context of use. As it is seldom commercially feasible to test a software product until the last residual defect is uncovered,

---

* The ISO/IEC/IEEE 29119 family of software and systems engineering standards includes the following:
  - ISO/IEC/IEEE 29119-1:2013, *Software Testing—Part 1: Concepts and Definitions*
  - ISO/IEC/IEEE 29119-2:2013, *Software Testing—Part 2: Test Processes*
  - ISO/IEC/IEEE 29119-3:2013, *Software Testing—Part 3: Test Documentation*
  - ISO/IEC/IEEE 29119-4:2015, *Software Testing—Part 4: Test Techniques*
† IT Infrastructure Library (ITIL®) offers a similar definition of *test* as "an activity that verifies that a configuration item, IT service, process etc. meets its specification or agreed requirements" (Axelos Limited, 2011).

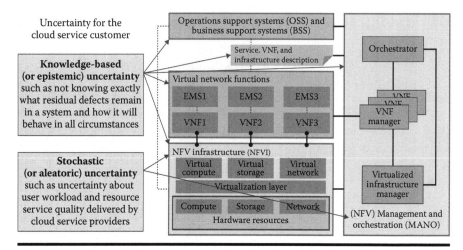

Figure 7.2   Cloud service customer uncertainties. EMS, element management system; NFV, network functions virtualization; VNF, virtualized network function.

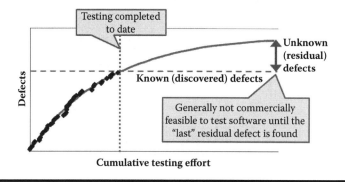

Figure 7.3   Sample software reliability growth model.

organizations make a risk-based decision that balances the upside benefit of releasing imperfect software into production sooner to deliver new services and value faster against the likelihood that a residual defect will produce unacceptable quality impact to some stakeholder. Note that while residual defects are routinely detected and reported after software is released to production, the costs for debugging, correcting, and deploying corrective patches for a defect are significantly higher for defects discovered in production operation than for defects discovered during normal testing.

7.1.2 Stochastic Uncertainty

Stochastic (or aleatoric) uncertainty is variability due to the nature of phenomena. Random demand variations, cache performance, fine-grained (e.g., microsecond- or millisecond-level) resource scheduling, queuing, and other inherently variable characteristics of an application's operational environment produce some level of inherent stochastic uncertainty in application service quality delivered to users. Chaotic systems exhibit stochastic uncertainty. Figure 7.4 visualizes the stochastic uncertainty in transaction latency exhibited by an application executing on virtualized resources. As the workload applied to the virtualized application instance increases from 60% of nominal capacity to 85% of nominal capacity to full-rated (nominal 100%) capacity, the slowest 1 in 1,000,000 transactions gets materially slower as scheduling, queuing, and other delays inevitably accumulate for a tiny fraction of transactions.

Both the fundamental and practical nature of cloud infrastructure increases stochastic uncertainties regarding quality of virtualized infrastructure resource services delivered to cloud-based applications, especially the following:

- **Multitenant sharing of physical infrastructure**—The key cloud characteristics of resource pooling (Section 1.4.6) and multitenancy (Section 1.4.3) mean that cloud infrastructure service providers must address inevitable resource contention problems when multiple application software component instances desire the same resource at exactly the same instant. Practically, the infrastructure will serialize nominally simultaneous resource access requests so they can be served by finite physical infrastructure. For example, when a real-time clock event fires (e.g., a 1-millisecond timer interrupt) or when network packets arrive to be processed, the infrastructure selects which application software component instance executes immediately and which application software component instance(s) is made to wait. As shown in Figure 7.4, as utilization of resources increases, the rate of contention events increases, and thus, the frequency for which some application instance is made to wait grows.
- **Application workload placement variability**—Cloud infrastructure service providers manage the key characteristics of on-demand self-service (Section 1.4.4) and rapid elasticity and scalability (Section 1.4.5) across

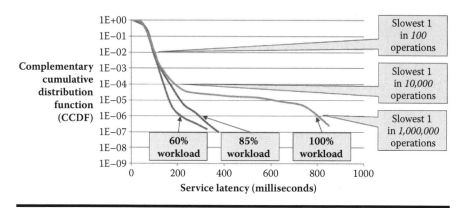

Figure 7.4 Sample stochastic uncertainty in service latency of a virtualized application.

pooled, shared resources by intelligently placing application component instances to optimize the infrastructure service provider's operational efficiency. Over time and across cloud data centers, the actual workloads that are competing for resources with a particular CSC's application software instance will vary. For example, a particular CSC's application component instance may be sharing compute, memory, storage, and networking resources with a web server one day, with a security application another day, and with a social networking application later in the week. Undoubtedly, different neighboring applications will place different resource demands on the underlying physical resource, which changes the nature and profile of multitenant resource contention events, which impact user service quality (per previous bullet item).

■ **Physical resource variability**—Virtualized compute, memory, storage, and networking are ultimately implemented via physical equipment. Cloud infrastructure service providers will purchase and deploy the physical infrastructure that best serves their business needs for cost, performance, power consumption, and overall operational efficiencies, and rely on software technologies, especially virtualization, to mask any operational and performance differences of equipment between equipment versions and infrastructure suppliers. Inevitably, somewhat different infrastructure equipment will be deployed and operated by each cloud infrastructure service provider across time and space, such as by deploying newer, better-performing processors as they become available. Application software component instances executed on those different physical infrastructure elements may exhibit small—or not so small—differences in performance.

■ **Access and wide area networking** between the cloud data center and the user's device can exhibit stochastic packet loss, latency, and jitter, which impacts user service qualities.

Stochastic variability often manifests as chronic service quality impairments.

7.2 Testing, Verification, and Validation

Two foundational concepts in this area of art* are as follows:

■ **Verification** is defined by ISO/IEC 25000 (ISO/IEC, 2005-08-01) as "confirmation, through the provision of objective evidence, that specified requirements have been fulfilled." For example, a functional requirement can be verified via a test case executed on a test bed.

---

* ITIL offers similar definitions (Axelos Limited, 2011):
  • **Verification**—An activity that ensures that a new or changed IT service, process, plan or other deliverable is complete, accurate, reliable and matches its design specification.
  • **Validation**—An activity that ensures a new or changed IT service, process, plan or other deliverable meets the needs of the business. Validation ensures that business requirements are met even though these may have changed since the original design.

■ **Validation** is defined by ISO/IEC 25000 (ISO/IEC, 2005-08-01) as "confirmation, through the provision of objective evidence, that the requirements for a specific intended use or application have been fulfilled." For example, a use case can be validated on a production environment before the target service component or system serves general user traffic.

Figure 7.5 visualizes the relationship between verification, validation, and testing.

As shown in Figure 7.6, testing is a core part of five of the ISO/IEC/IEEE 15288 standard system life cycle processes:

1. **Implementation process** (Section 5.2.7)—ISO/IEC/IEEE 15288:2015 clause 6.4.7.3.b includes the following:
   "Throughout the Implementation process the Verification process is used to objectively confirm the system element's conformance to requirements and the product's quality characteristics. The Validation process is used to objectively confirm the element is ready to be used in its intended operational environment according to stakeholder requirements" (ISO/IEC/IEEE, 2015-05-15).

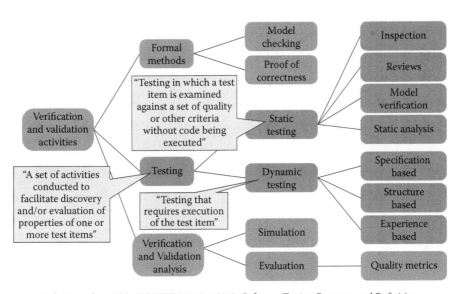

Definitions from ISO/IEC/IEEE 29119-1:2013, *Software Testing Concepts and Definitions*

Figure 7.5 Hierarchy of verification and validation activities. (From Figure A.1 of ISO/IEC/IEEE, *29119-1—Software Testing—Part 1: Concepts and Definitions*, Geneva, Switzerland: ISO/IEC/IEEE, 2013-09-01.)

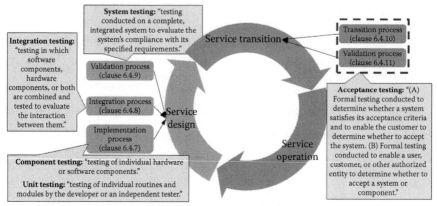

Definitions from ISO/IEC/IEEE 25765:2010, *Systems and Software Engineering Vocabulary*

Figure 7.6   Testing in the application service life cycle.

Standard testing activities in the implementation phase are as follows:

  a. **Component testing**—"testing of individual hardware or software components" (ISO/IEC/IEEE, 2010-12-15).

  b. **Unit testing**—"testing of individual routines and modules by the developer or an independent tester" (ISO/IEC/IEEE, 2010-12-15).

2. **Integration process** (Section 5.2.8)—Standard testing activities in the integration process are as follows:

  a. **Integration testing**—"testing in which software components, hardware components, or both are combined and tested to evaluate the interaction between them" (ISO/IEC/IEEE, 2010-12-15).

3. **Verification process** (Section 5.2.9)—Standard testing activities in the verification process include the following:

  a. **System testing**—"testing conducted on a complete, integrated system to evaluate the system's compliance with its specified requirements" (ISO/IEC/IEEE, 2010-12-15).

4. **Transition process** (Section 5.2.10)—ISO/IEC/IEEE 15288 includes the following activities in part "b) Perform the transition" of the standard transition process:

  "4 *Demonstrate* proper installation of the system

  7 *Demonstrate* the installed system is capable of delivering its required functions

  8 *Demonstrate* the functions provided by the system are sustainable by the enabling systems"

Primary testing activities in the transition phase are for *acceptance testing*: "(A) Formal testing conducted to determine whether a system satisfies its acceptance criteria and to enable the customer to determine whether to accept the system. (B) Formal testing conducted to enable a user, customer, or other authorized entity to determine whether to accept a system or component" (ISO/IEC/IEEE, 2010-12-15). Passing acceptance tests often means that some responsibility, accountability, and legal liability shifts from one organization that developed the produce or service to the organization that will operate it. Note that some support for automated acceptance testing of service transitions is expected to support automated life cycle management actions (aka service transitions), especially acceptance testing of scaling actions.

5. **Validation process** (Section 5.2.11)—Acceptance testing (defined previously) is a key activity of the validation process.

Figure 7.7 maps the verification and validation activities of Figure 7.5 to relevant application service life cycle processes of Figure 5.3:

- Implementation process (Section 5.2.7)—Static testing techniques like inspections, reviews and, static analysis are routine during implementation activities. Some dynamic testing is often completed as part of unit testing.
- Integration process (Section 5.2.8)—Dynamic testing, especially specification-based testing, is a key part of integration testing. Some static testing techniques may also be applied.
- Verification process (Section 5.2.9)—Extensive dynamic testing is the foundation of system verification. Static testing and formal methods may be applied, especially to system-level data artifacts like configuration files and methods of procedure.
- Transition process (Section 5.2.10).
- Validation process (Section 5.2.11)—Dynamic testing is the heart of acceptance testing.

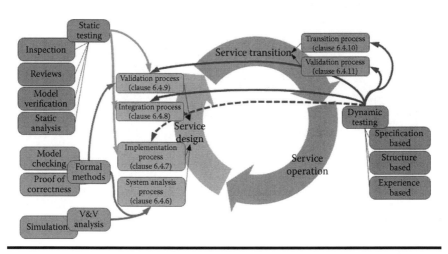

Figure 7.7 Verification and validation activities by application service life cycle processes.

Formal methods and simulation (e.g., Monte Carlo techniques) are often used by the system analysis process (Section 5.2.6).

The cloud encourages continuous integration/delivery models in which new software releases are brought into production to initially serve a small portion of user traffic. If that initial traffic is served with acceptable quality, then it can serve an increasing portion of the workload until the previous release is drained of all traffic and retired from service. Effectively, this canary testing model shifts some testing out of the service design phase into the service transition phase, and perhaps even into the service operation phase, such as with Netflix's Simian Army.

7.3 Test Levels, Types, and Processes

Figure 7.8 expands the test type, test level/phase, and test subprocess boxes of Figure 7.1 as a simplified version of ISO/IEC/IEEE 29119-1 Figure 2, "The relationship between the generic test sub-process, test levels and test types."

Test type is defined as a "group of testing activities that are focused on specific quality characteristics…EXAMPLE Security testing, functional testing, usability testing, and performance testing" (ISO/IEC/IEEE, 2013-09-01). Table 7.1 shows how standard product quality characteristics and subcharacteristics map naturally to many standard test types. Testing activities often focus on assessing the characteristics and subcharacteristics of these quality models. For example, Table 7.1

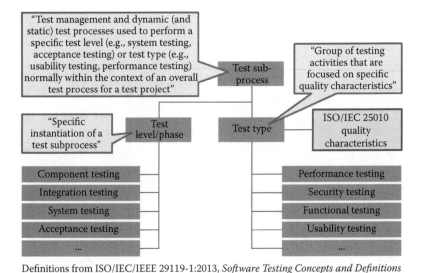

Definitions from ISO/IEC/IEEE 29119-1:2013, *Software Testing Concepts and Definitions*

Figure 7.8 Test level, type, and process.

Table 7.1   ISO/IEC 25010 Product Qualities and Test Types

ISO/IEC 25010 Product Quality Characteristics and Subcharacteristics	*ISO/IEC/IEEE 29119-1 Test Types*
Functional suitability	Functional testing
Functional completeness	
Functional correctness	
Functional appropriateness	
Performance efficiency	*Performance testing*—type of testing conducted to evaluate the degree to which a test item accomplishes its designated functions within given constraints of time and other resources. *Load testing*—type of performance efficiency testing conducted to evaluate the behavior of a test item under anticipated conditions of varying load, usually between anticipated conditions of low, typical, and peak usage.
Time behavior	
Resource utilization	
Capacity	
Compatibility	*Compatibility testing*—type of testing that measures the degree to which a test item can function satisfactorily alongside other independent products in a shared environment (coexistence) and, where necessary, exchanges information with other systems or components (interoperability).
Coexistence	
Interoperability	
Usability	Functional, user, and general usability testing *Procedure testing*—type of functional suitability testing conducted to evaluate whether procedural instructions for interacting with a test item or using its outputs meet user requirements and support the purpose of their use.
Appropriateness recognizability	
Learnability	
Operability	
User error protection	
User interface aesthetics	

(*Continued*)

Table 7.1 (Continued)   ISO/IEC 25010 Product Qualities and Test Types

ISO/IEC 25010 Product Quality Characteristics and Subcharacteristics	*ISO/IEC/IEEE 29119-1 Test Types*
Accessibility	*Accessibility testing*—type of usability testing used to measure the degree to which a test item can be operated by users with the widest possible range of characteristics and capabilities.
Reliability	*Reliability testing*—type of testing conducted to evaluate the ability of a test item to perform its required functions, including evaluating the frequency with which failures occur, when it is used under stated conditions for a specified period of time.
Maturity	*Stress testing*—type of performance efficiency testing conducted to evaluate a test item's behavior under conditions of loading above anticipated or specified capacity requirements, or of resource availability below minimum specified requirements.
Availability	
Fault tolerance	*Endurance testing*—type of performance efficiency testing conducted to evaluate whether a test item can sustain a required load continuously for a specified period of time.
Recoverability	*Backup and recovery testing*—type of reliability testing that measures the degree to which system state can be restored from backup within specified parameters of time, cost, completeness, and accuracy in the event of failure.
Security	*Security testing*—type of testing conducted to evaluate the degree to which a test item and associated data and information are protected so that unauthorized persons or systems cannot use, read, or modify them, and authorized persons or systems are not denied access to them.
Confidentiality	
Integrity	
Nonrepudiation	
Accountability	
Authenticity	

(Continued)

Table 7.1 (Continued)   ISO/IEC 25010 Product Qualities and Test Types

ISO/IEC 25010 Product Quality Characteristics and Subcharacteristics	*ISO/IEC/IEEE 29119-1 Test Types*
Maintainability	*Maintainability testing*—test type conducted to evaluate the degree of effectiveness and efficiency with which a test item may be modified.
Modularity	
Reusability	
Analyzability	
Modifiability	
Testability	
Portability	*Portability testing*—type of testing conducted to evaluate the ease with which a test item can be transferred from one hardware or software environment to another, including the level of modification needed for it to be executed in various types of environment.
Adaptability	
Replaceability	
Installability	*Installability testing*—type of portability testing conducted to evaluate whether a test item or set of test items can be installed as required in all specified environments.

shows how common test types align with ISO/IEC 25010 product quality characteristics and subcharacteristics.

Several additional types of testing are relevant for cloud-based applications (Table 7.2):

- Scalability testing (Section 7.8)
- Risk control testing (Section 7.9)
- Sensitivity (or dose–response) Testing (Section 7.10)
- Automated acceptance testing for service transitions (Section 7.11)

7.4 Test Techniques

The standard defines *test (design) techniques* as "activities, concepts, processes, and patterns used to construct a test model that is used to identify test conditions for a test item, derive corresponding test coverage items, and subsequently derive or

Table 7.2   Test Types for Section III, "Cloud Service Quality Risk Inventory," Items

Cloud Service Quality Risk Inventory Item	Reference	Primary Test Type
Virtualized Network Function (VNF) Product Risks	**Chapter 13**	
Faulty VNF configuration specification risk	Table 13.1	Installability testing Maintainability testing Scalability testing (Section 7.8)
Residual defect in VNF life cycle management script risk	Table 13.2	
Residual product defect risk	Table 13.3	System testing Scalability testing (Section 7.8)
Virtual Machine (VM) Risks	**Chapter 14**	
VM dead-on-arrival (DOA) risk	Table 14.1	Risk control testing (Section 7.9) Sensitivity (or dose–response) testing (Section 7.10)
VM premature release (failure) risk	Table 14.2	
VM stall risk	Table 14.3	
VM scheduling latency risk	Table 14.4	
VM clock error risk	Table 14.5	
VM placement policy violation risk	Table 14.6	
Virtual Networking Risks	**Chapter 15**	
Packet loss risk	Table 15.1	Risk control testing (Section 7.9) Sensitivity (or dose–response) testing (Section 7.10)
Packet delay risk	Table 15.2	
Packet jitter (delay variation) risk	Table 15.3	
Network delivered throughput risk	Table 15.4	
Network outage risk	Table 15.5	
Virtual network diversity compliance violation risk	Table 15.6	

(Continued)

Table 7.2 (Continued) Test Types for Section III, "Cloud Service Quality Risk Inventory," Items

Cloud Service Quality Risk Inventory Item	Reference	Primary Test Type
Virtual Storage Risks	**Chapter 16**	
Storage access reliability risk	Table 16.1	Risk control testing (Section 7.9) Sensitivity (or dose–response) testing (Section 7.10)
Storage access latency risk	Table 16.2	
Volume capacity risk	Table 16.3	
Volume outage risk	Table 16.4	
Volume throughput risk	Table 16.5	
Virtualized Application Latency Risks	**Chapter 17**	
Tail application latency risk	Table 17.1	Scalability testing (Section 7.8) risk control tresting (Section 7.9) Sensitivity (or dose–response) testing (Section 7.10)
Typical application latency risk	Table 17.2	
Service Integration Risks	**Chapter 18**	
Wrong element used risk	Table 18.1	System testing Installability testing Scalability testing (Section 7.8) Maintainability testing
System/service integration defect	Table 18.2	
Element operational conditions violated	Table 18.3	Sensitivity (or dose–response) testing (Section 7.10)
Faulty service delivery architecture risk	Table 18.4	Scalability testing (Section 7.8) risk control testing (Section 7.9)
Faulty service control architecture risk	Table 18.5	
Faulty service workflow risk	Table 18.6	System testing Installability testing Scalability testing (Section 7.8) Maintainability testing

(*Continued*)

Table 7.2 (Continued)   Test Types for Section III, "Cloud Service Quality Risk Inventory," Items

Cloud Service Quality Risk Inventory Item	Reference	Primary Test Type
Visibility Risks	**Chapter 19**	
Obstructed vision risk	Table 19.1	Analysis
Blurred vision risk	Table 19.2	
Stale vision risk	Table 19.3	
Mirage risk	Table 19.4	
Service Policy Risks	**Chapter 20**	
Insufficient spare capacity (target) risk	Table 20.1	Analysis
Faulty resource placement policy risk	Table 20.2	Sensitivity (or dose–response) testing (Section 7.10)
Faulty scaling decision criteria risk	Table 20.3	Analysis Sensitivity (or dose–response) testing (Section 7.10)
Inaccurate demand forecast risk	Table 20.4	Analysis Sensitivity (or dose–response) testing (Section 7.10)
Accountability Risks	**Chapter 21**	
Incomplete accountability risk	Table 21.1	Analysis
Conflicting accountability risk	Table 21.2	
Ambiguous demarcation risk	Table 21.3	
Ambiguous service-level objective risk	Table 21.4	
Human and Organizational Risks	**Chapter 22**	
Organization and incentive design risk	Table 22.2	Analysis
Human process risk	Table 22.3	
Human error risk	Table 22.4	

(*Continued*)

Table 7.2 (Continued)   Test Types for Section III, "Cloud Service Quality Risk Inventory," Items

Cloud Service Quality Risk Inventory Item	Reference	Primary Test Type
Life Cycle Management (Execution) Risks	**Chapter 23**	
VNF life cycle management (execution) risks	Table 23.2	System testing Installability testing
Network service life cycle management (execution) risks	Table 23.3	Maintainability testing Scalability testing (Section 7.8) risk control testing (Section 7.9)
Forwarding graph service life cycle management (execution) risks	Table 23.4	Sensitivity (or dose–response) testing (Section 7.10)
Virtual link service life cycle management (execution) risks	Table 23.5	
Functional-Component-as-a-Service Quality Risks	**Chapter 24**	
Functional-component as-a-service outage downtime risk	Table 24.2	Scalability testing (Section 7.8) risk control testing (Section 7.9)
Functional-component as-a-service reliability risk	Table 24.3	Sensitivity (or dose–response) testing (Section 7.10)
Functional-component as-a-service latency risk	Table 24.4	
Cloud Service Provider Catastrophe Risks	**Chapter 25**	
(Semi?) permanent loss of cloud service risk	Table 25.1	Disaster recovery testing
(Semi?) permanent loss of CSC data risk	Table 25.2	

(*Continued*)

Table 7.2 (Continued)   Test Types for Section III, "Cloud Service Quality Risk Inventory," Items

Cloud Service Quality Risk Inventory Item	Reference	Primary Test Type
Unknown-Unknown Risks	**Chapter 26**	
Fundamental business/ operations disruption risk	Table 26.1	Analysis Fuzz testing
Emerging technology risk	Table 26.2	
Flawed standards risk	Table 26.4	
Faulty infrastructure capex reduction risk	Table 26.5	
Faulty cloud service provider (CSP) opex reduction risk	Table 26.6	

select test cases" (ISO/IEC/IEEE, 2013-09-01). The standard factors test design techniques into three categories, visualized in Figure 7.9.

■ **Specification-based testing**—Defined as "testing in which the principal test basis is the external inputs and outputs of the test item, commonly based on a specification, rather than its implementation in source code or executable software. Synonyms for specification-based testing include black-box testing and closed box testing" (ISO/IEC/IEEE, 2013-09-01).

■ **Structure-based testing**—Defined as "dynamic testing in which the tests are derived from an examination of the structure of the test item.... Synonyms for structure-based testing are structural testing, glass-box testing, and white box testing" (ISO/IEC/IEEE, 2013-09-01).

■ **Experience-based testing**—Described by ISO/IEC/IEEE 29119-1 (ISO/IEC/IEEE, 2013-09-01) as testing based on the knowledge and experience of testing and operating similar systems and previous releases of the target system.

Scalability testing (Section 7.8), risk control testing (Section 7.9), sensitivity (or dose–response) testing (Section 7.10), and automated acceptance testing for service transitions (Section 7.11) are likely to primarily rely on structure-based

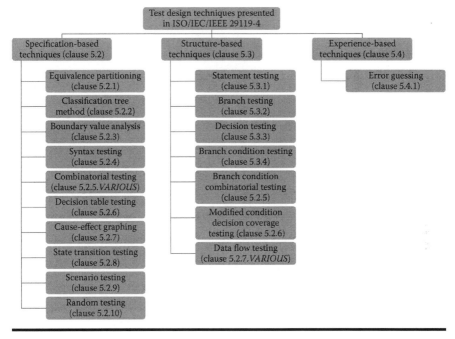

Figure 7.9   High-level test techniques presented in ISO/IEC/IEEE 29119-4:2015.

and experience-based testing techniques. Cloud computing has also enabled chaos testing, like the Simian Army, which is an advanced fault insertion testing model.

7.5 Test Planning

Figure 7.10 visualizes the standard test planning process from ISO/IEC/IEEE 29119-2, *Test Processes* (ISO/IEC/IEEE, 2013-09-01). Deploying an application service on the cloud rather than traditionally materially changes the test context; relevant changes to the *understand context* (designated activity *TP1* by ISO/IEC/IEEE 29119-2) activity are considered in Section 7.6, "Context of Testing."

In addition to general project risks, the new and evolved risks to user service quality raised when deploying an aptplication service onto the cloud should be considered when planning application testing. In particular, user service quality risks identified when executing the organization's risk management process should be considered in test planning.

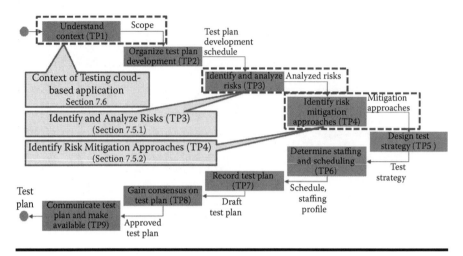

Figure 7.10 Test planning process. (From Figure 6 of ISO/IEC/IEEE, *29119-1— Software Testing—Part 1: Concepts and Definitions*, Geneva, Switzerland: ISO/IEC/IEEE, 2013-09-01.)

7.5.1 Identify and Analyze Risks (TP3)

Section IV, "Cloud Service Quality Risk Assessment and Management," in general, and Chapter 28, "Risk Assessment Process," in particular, produce risk identification and risk analysis artifacts that are useful in test planning. In particular, test planning should consider the following items:

- **Risk condition**—Identifies the nature of a service quality hazard.
- **Risk cause**—Gives the proximal and/or ultimate causes of the service quality risk. Test cases would likely trigger, coerce, or emulate the proximal risk cause.
- **Risk controls**—Enumerates the risk controls that are or will be deployed to treat the risk. Test cases can verify the effectiveness of those controls.
- **Risk owner**—The risk owner has primary accountability for reducing the risk likelihood by completing root cause analysis and deploying appropriate corrective actions. Test cases can verify that sufficient data are produced by the target application and supporting systems to do the following:
  - **Drive rapid fault localization** so appropriate (i.e., right-first-time) recovery actions can be quickly initiated.
  - **Defensibly indict the true risk owner**, thereby minimizing time spent finger-pointing and establishing accountability.
  - **Enable (offline) true root cause analysis by the risk owner** so that corrective actions can be taken to reduce the risk likelihood.

- **Risk type likelihood**—Chronic events (as well as less frequent acute events) that are not seamlessly, automatically, and successfully controlled will both impact users' quality of experience and drive up operating expenses for the CSC.
- **User impact of successfully controlled risk event**—Testing can assure that the actual user impact of successfully controlled risk events is no worse than the engineered objectives. Testing can also drive improvements to minimize the user service impact to exceed those objectives.
- **Risk control effectiveness**—Every unsuccessful risk control action may require intervention of a human operator to localize the trouble, restore service, and return the application to normal working order. This manual intervention both prolongs the duration of user service impact and drives up operating expenses for the CSC. Testing can boost the effectiveness of risk control mechanisms.
- **User impact of unsuccessfully controlled risk event**—Testing can characterize the likely user service impact of risk events that defeat primary risk controls and are ultimately addressed by others controls, procedures, and policies.

7.5.2 Identify Risk Mitigation Approaches (TP4)

Testing is not a *treatment* for user service quality risks in that it doesn't replace or remove the risk source (Section 3.3.1), change the risk consequences (Section 3.3.3), change the risk likelihood (Section 3.3.2), etc. Instead, testing *facilitates discovery* of the knowledge-based (epistemic) uncertainty regarding residual defects and of stochastic (aleatoric) uncertainty regarding performance and behavior in real-world operation. That knowledge then drives either of the following:

- **Corrections** to software, configuration, scripts, procedures, etc., to replace or remove the risk source (Section 3.3.1), change the risk consequences (Section 3.3.3), or change the risk likelihood (Section 3.3.2).
- **Decisions** by the CSC organization to share the risk with external party (Section 3.3.4), retain the risk (Section 3.3.5), reject accountability (Section 3.3.6), or avoid the risk (Section 3.3.7).

Organizations employ *risk-based testing*, defined as "testing in which the management, selection, prioritisation, and use of testing activities and resources are consciously based on corresponding types and levels of analyzed risk" (ISO/IEC/IEEE, 2013-09-01). The CSC organization's risk appetite in general, and test policy and strategy in particular, drives the nature and extent of application testing to remove uncertainties regarding user service quality.

7.6 Context of Testing

According to ISO/IEC/IEEE 29119-2, the first step in test planning is to *understand context* (TP1). The general context of use of cloud-based applications materially differs from the context of use of traditionally deployed applications in several ways:

- Vastly more service transitions (Section 7.6.1)
- Less consistent resource service quality (Section 7.6.2)
- Shorter service life cycles (Section 7.6.3)

Application-specific context of use should also consider the following:

- ISO/IEC 25010 quality in use characteristics (Section 7.6.4)
- ISO/IEC 25010 product quality characteristics (Section 7.6.5)

7.6.1 Vastly More Service Transitions

The key cloud computing characteristic of rapid elasticity and scalability (Section 1.4.5) coupled with pay-as-you-go resource pricing based on measured service (Section 1.4.2) assures that application capacity-scaling actions (i.e., service transitions) are likely to be vastly more common than service transitions of traditionally deployed applications. As discussed in Chapter 6, closely tracking online application capacity with actual user demand can lead to many discrete scaling actions per day: growing capacity ahead of rising demand (e.g., in the morning when humans wake) and shrinking capacity to follow declining demand (e.g., in the evening when humans go to sleep). Actual scaling actions executed are likely to be a mix of "fast" start-up actions (e.g., adding resources to preexisting application instances) and "slow" start-up actions (e.g., creating new application instances), and corresponding degrowth actions when demand wanes.

Given that scaling actions are vastly more frequent than other transitions (e.g., onboarding, release management), CSCs are likely to invest more to

- Identify residual defects in scaling code so it can be corrected to reduce frequency of failed scaling actions…and the associated expenses of mitigating failed scaling actions.
- Reduce time and effort required to execute acceptance tests to validate successful execution of scaling actions so scaled capacity can be brought into service as fast as possible with the lowest cost.
- Improve the coverage/reliability of acceptance testing for scaling actions, thereby reducing the frequency of dead-on-arrival application capacity change actions escaping acceptance testing to deliver unacceptable service quality to users.

Specifically, high-quality CSCs and their integrators and suppliers are likely to expect fast and reliable automated acceptance testing for service transitions (Section 7.11) that can be executed before user traffic is applied to the scaled application service capacity.

7.6.2 Less Consistent Resource Service Quality

The key cloud characteristics of resource pooling (Section 1.4.6) and multitenancy (Section 1.4.3) mean that cloud-based applications may experience greater stochastic uncertainty in resource service quality than traditionally deployed applications hosted on dedicated hardware. Thus, CSCs are likely to invest to assure that user service quality is unlikely to be unacceptably impacted by stochastic variations in cloud service provider quality. In particular, high-quality CSCs, their integrators, and suppliers are likely to properly design their software and execute sensitiivty (or dose-response) testing (Section 7.10).

7.6.3 Shorter Service Life Cycles

CSCs desire to accelerate the pace of service innovation, which means that the application service life cycle will iterate more often for cloud-based services than for traditionally deployed services. Practically, this means more frequent onboarding, release management, and disposal activities compared to traditional application deployments.

7.6.4 ISO/IEC 25010, Quality-in-Use Characteristics

Quality in use was introduced in Section 4.2.3 and detailed in Table 4.3. Table 7.3 considers the implications for each quality-in-use characteristic and subcharacteristic:

1. Changes for cloud application service deployment compared to traditional application deployment.
2. Implications to testing cloud-based application service deployment.

7.6.5 ISO/IEC 25010, Product Quality Characteristics

ISO/IEC 25010 product qualities were introduced in Section 4.3 and detailed in Table 4.2. Table 7.4 considers the implications for each product quality characteristic and subcharacteristic:

1. Changes for cloud application service deployment compared to traditional application deployment.
2. Implications to testing cloud-based application service deployment.

Table 7.3 Quality-in-Use Context Changes for Cloud Application Service Deployment

Quality-in-Use Characteristics and Subcharacteristics	Changes for Cloud Application Service Deployment Compared to Traditional Deployment	Cloud Testing Implications
Effectiveness	Agile methods (Section 11.2) enable more rapid, incremental improvements in effectiveness than traditional development models.	Test cases must be agile to track with evolving application functionality.
Efficiency	The closer application operation comes to "perfect capacity," the lower the CSC's costs can be. Rapid (i.e., short capacity change lead time) and reliable (i.e., right-first-time) capacity change actions enable greater efficiency. Smaller units of capacity change enable online capacity to track closer to actual demand.	Application scaling must be thoroughly tested.
Satisfaction	Ability for individual users to personalize their experience via self-service mechanisms boosts customer satisfaction.	Self-service provisioning/ configuration by end users must be thoroughly tested.
Usefulness	Not materially different between cloud and traditional deployment.	
Trust	Not materially different between cloud and traditional deployment.	
Pleasure	Not materially different between cloud and traditional deployment.	
Comfort	Not materially different between cloud and traditional deployment.	
Freedom from Risk		
Economic risk mitigation	Not materially different between cloud and traditional deployment.	
Health and safety risk mitigation	Not materially different between cloud and traditional deployment.	

(Continued)

Table 7.3 (Continued)   Quality-in-Use Context Changes for Cloud Application Service Deployment

Quality-in-Use Characteristics and Subcharacteristics	Changes for Cloud Application Service Deployment Compared to Traditional Deployment	Cloud Testing Implications
Environmental risk mitigation	Cloud deployment can be more environmentally responsible (greener) because of the following: • Lower carbon footprint due to elastic, lean operation of online application capacity • Minimal "wasted" hardware because resource pooling and multitenancy enable CSP to maximize resource utilization	Environmentally conscious users may require some certification of environmental risk mitigation by CSC, their CSPs, and other suppliers.
Context Coverage		
Context completeness	Agile development techniques with rapid service innovation encourage cloud-based applications to evolve more complete coverage of target and adjacent market contexts.	Agile test cases must assure context coverage is adequately tested.
Flexibility	Openness of cloud service components and offerings should reduce supplier lock-in compared to traditional architectures.	Testing with multiple component configurations verifies flexibility.

7.7 Level of Automation

ISO/IEC/IEEE 29119-1 offers the following test automation examples (ISO/IEC/IEEE, 2013-09-01):

- Test case management;
- Test monitoring and control;
- Test data generation;
- Test case generation;
- Test case execution;
- Test environment implementation and maintenance; and
- Session-based testing.

Table 7.4 Product Quality Testing Considerations for Cloud Application Service Deployment

Product Quality Characteristics and Subcharacteristics	Changes for Cloud Application Service Deployment Compared to Traditional Deployment	Cloud Testing Implications
Functional Suitability		
Functional completeness	Requirements and implementation must cover cloud-centric application features.	Testing must cover cloud-centric features.
Functional correctness		
Functional appropriateness	Cloud-centric applications must adopt an appropriate cloud-native architecture to efficiently scale capacity to serve offered load.	Testing should verify cloud-native behaviors, like rapid elastic capacity scaling.
Performance Efficiency		
Time behavior	Cloud-based applications vulnerable to latency-based risks, especially the following: • Virtualized application latency risks (Chapter 17) • VM stall risk (Table 14.3) • VM scheduling latency risk (Table 14.4) • Packet delay risk (Table 15.2) • Packet jitter (delay variation) risk (Table 15.3) • Storage access latency risk (Table 16.2) • Functional-component-as-a-service latency risk (Table 24.4) Testing should verify that risk of unacceptable user service time behavior is tolerable.	
Resource utilization	Testing should capture resource usage as a function of workload to characterize resource utilization, especially the following: • Resource utilization with minimal workload (i.e., idle) • Resource utilization at maximum workload • Resource utilization at several workload levels between 0% and 100% capacity • Typical ratio between an increment of increased application workload capacity and the corresponding increase in resource consumption	

(Continued)

Table 7.4 (Continued)   Product Quality Testing Considerations for Cloud Application Service Deployment

Product Quality Characteristics and Subcharacteristics	*Changes for Cloud Application Service Deployment Compared to Traditional Deployment*	*Cloud Testing Implications*
Capacity	All real system instances have some practical capacity limits, such as the configured size of internal tables. Hard capacity limits for a single VNF instance should be explicitly specified.	Stable service operation to the hard capacity limit should be verified, along with proper operation of overload control mechanism when that limit is exceeded. Reliability and latency of elastic capacity change actions should be verified.
Compatibility		
Coexistence	Key cloud characteristics of resource pooling (Section 1.4.6) and multitenancy (Section 1.4.3) mean that applications must peacefully coexist with myriad other applications sharing the same cloud services.	Testing should verify that application can peacefully coexist on shared infrastructure with other application instances.
Interoperability	Not materially different between cloud and traditional deployment.	
Usability		
Appropriateness recognizability	On-demand self-service (Section 1.4.4) materially increases the usability scope of an application service.	Testing must verify that all on-demand self-service characteristics of an application are appropriate and usable.
Learnability		
Operability		
User error protection		
User interface aesthetics		
Accessibility		

(Continued)

Table 7.4 (Continued)   Product Quality Testing Considerations for Cloud Application Service Deployment

Product Quality Characteristics and Subcharacteristics	Changes for Cloud Application Service Deployment Compared to Traditional Deployment	Cloud Testing Implications
Reliability		
Maturity	Not materially different between cloud and traditional deployment.	
Availability	Cloud-based automated life cycle management supports automatic failure detection and recovery actions, often called self-healing.	• Fault insertion or adversarial testing must verify availability/ recoverability.
Recoverability		• Risk control testing (Section 7.9) verifies that risks are acceptably controlled.
Fault tolerance		• Sensitivity (or dose-response testing (Section 7.10) characterizes the limits of tolerability.
Security		
Confidentiality	Security is not considered in this book.	
Integrity		
Nonrepudiation		
Accountability		
Authenticity		
Maintainability		
Modularity	Cloud-based applications will be refactored to enable rapid elasticity and scalability (Section 1.4.5).	Scalability testing (Section 7.8).

(Continued)

Table 7.4 (Continued) Product Quality Testing Considerations for Cloud Application Service Deployment

Product Quality Characteristics and Subcharacteristics	Changes for Cloud Application Service Deployment Compared to Traditional Deployment	Cloud Testing Implications
Reusability	Cloud-based application services are likely to (re)use functional components offered as-a-service by cloud service providers or from other parties in the cloud ecosystem rather than building bespoke service components.	
Analyzability	Decoupling application software from underlying hardware, life cycle automation mechanisms, and functional components increases need to capture and analyze data to rapidly detect and robustly localize the cause of service quality impairments.	Fault insertion or adversarial testing, risk control testing (Section 7.9), and sensitivity (or dose-response) testing (Section 7.10) are opportunities to validate application analyzability. Consider if inserted impairment can be correctly deduced from the management visibility data produced by the application.
Modifiability	Cloud-based applications support rapid elasticity and scalability (Section 1.4.5) to enable perfect capacity management (Sections 6.8 and 32.4.2).	Scalability testing (Section 7.8) verifies ability to reconfigure application capacity online.
Testability	Improved testability enables CSC to deliver new services and value faster and to verify rapid elasticity and scalability (Section 1.4.5) configuration changes.	Applications should support automated acceptance testing for service transitions (Section 7.11).

(Continued)

Table 7.4 (Continued)   Product Quality Testing Considerations for Cloud Application Service Deployment

Product Quality Characteristics and Subcharacteristics	Changes for Cloud Application Service Deployment Compared to Traditional Deployment	Cloud Testing Implications
Portability		
Adaptability	Applications must support virtual resources, life cycle management mechanisms, and functional components offered by cloud service providers.	Automated regression and acceptance testing streamlines validation on different target environments.
Installability	Cloud-based applications are engineered for automated installation so instances can be deployed rapidly to serve growing/ shifting patterns user demand.	Automated installation mechanisms must be tested.
Replaceability	Applications should use standardized and open interfaces when possible to limit supplier lock-in and facilitate replaceability.	Cloud lowers barriers to replacing service components, so cloud service customers may take replaceability testing more seriously.

Additional levels of automation are possible for testing of cloud-based applications:

■ **Automated testing in service transition and service operation phases** (Section 7.11)—Cloud orchestration systems that automate life cycle management actions can be configured to automate test setup, execution, test analysis, and results (go/no-go) evaluation.

■ **Elastic test-bed capacity**—rapid elasticity and scalability (Section 1.4.5) and on-demand self-service (Section 1.4.4) mean that nominally unlimited test-bed capacity can be created on demand to overlap execution of many test cases to significantly reduce the time required to execute all test cases.

Usage-based (aka pay-as-you-go) licensing of specialty test tools can be an attractive alternative to purchasing testing software that is used rarely.

- **Advanced static analysis tools**—The cloud introduces standard interfaces at several key points in both the automated service life cycle management value chain and in the user service delivery value chain, such as for the management information elements passed by the CSC to the management and orchestration service provider to support automated life cycle management actions. Standardization of these interfaces encourages players in the ecosystem to develop advanced static analysis tools to efficiently detect defects and risks.
- **Automated fault insertion testing**—Like Netflix Chaos Monkey (https://github.com/Netflix/SimianArmy).

7.8 Scalability Testing

Testing is appropriate to verify that cloud-based applications and services properly support the key cloud characteristic of rapid elasticity and scalability (Section 1.4.5). Scalability testing should verify that online service capacity reliably increases and decreases with no user service impact or throughput bottlenecks across the supported capacity range of the target component. In addition, resource consumption should not accumulate (aka leak) as the number of growth and shrink cycles increases. Scalability testing should also verify that capacity change lead times and reliability are consistently within expectation. Scalability testing should also verify extreme growth scenarios in which the target application grows from small configuration to maximum capacity as fast as possible to mitigate capacity emergency scenarios.

Scalability testing should also verify service federation, especially the following:

- **Increasing service capacity by creating another application instance**—For both technical reasons (e.g., finite table sizes) and practical reasons (e.g., limiting the maximum footprint of failure), CSCs will sometimes wish to increase online service capacity by creating another application instance. Testing should verify that user workload can gracefully be migrated to a newly created (or other preexisting) application instance to enable arbitrarily large scalability.
- **Decreasing service capacity via consolidation and application instance shutdown**—Service demand inevitably decreases for cyclical and life cycle reasons. Applications should gracefully enable user workloads to be consolidated onto a smaller number of application service instances so that CSCs can efficiently manage decreasing demand as efficiently as they manage increasing demand.

7.9 Risk Control Testing

Risk control testing addresses the risks discussed in Section III, "Cloud Service Quality Risk Inventory," and Section 7.5.1. Risk control testing explicitly activates or emulates risk conditions in the target application to verify the following:

1. Risk event is rapidly detected.
2. Risk event is accurately identified and correctly localized.
3. Proper risk control is activated.
4. Risk control works successfully.
5. User service impact is no greater than the control's design objective.

Practically, risk control testing is an advanced form of negative, fault insertion, or adversarial testing that is focused on assuring that risk controls function properly.

7.10 Sensitivity (or Dose–Response) Testing

Application service quality delivered to end users is materially impacted by service quality of the compute, memory, storage, and networking resources that serve the target application instance. For example, additional latency in the service-critical path introduced by virtual machine (VM) stall risk (Table 14.3), VM scheduling latency risk (Table 14.4), or packet delay risk (Table 15.2) directly increases the transaction service latency experienced by end users of impacted transactions. Sensitivity (dose–response) testing characterizes the application service quality impact of stochastic variations in resource service throughput, performance, or quality.

Sensitivity testing of applications is analogous to dose–response or toxicity testing of chemicals. Dose–response or toxicity assessment is covered in Annex 8 of ISO/IEC 31010 (ISO/IEC, 2009-11). Figure 7.11 gives a sample dose–response curve: the *y*-axis captures the response observed in test subjects as a function of the chemical dose on the *x*-axis. Key insights from a dose–response (toxicity) analysis are as follows:

■ **No-observable-effect level (NOEL)**—The "dose" level at which a response is reliably presented. Operationally, this means that changes in the observed response rise above ordinary random variation in system behavior; responses below this threshold are unimportant.
■ **No-observable-*adverse*-effect level (NOAEL)**—The "dose" level that produces the minimally acceptable service quality (or maximum acceptable *adverse* effect). By definition, adverse effects are undesirable and unacceptable, so one avoids doses that exceed the NOAEL.

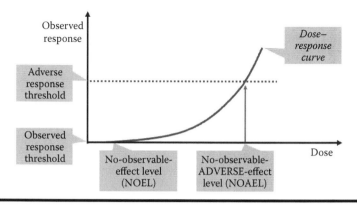

Figure 7.11 Sample dose–response analysis.

While cloud-based applications are not hazardous substances that can produce adverse health consequences to plants, animals, or humans after they are exposed to sufficiently large doses, the underlying dose–response methodology is useful for characterizing the user service quality impact of some stochastic risk to virtual network, VM, and virtual storage service quality. Figure 7.12 shows a hypothetical dose–response chart of unacceptable application transactions per million as a function of virtual network packet loss for packet loss rates of 10^{-7}, 10^{-6}, 10^{-5}, 10^{-4}, and 10^{-3}. As no unacceptable transactions were observed with 10^{-6} packet loss but some unacceptable transactions were observed with 10^{-5}, the NOEL is somewhere between 10^{-5} and 10^{-6} packet loss. Packet loss of 10^{-4} produced a rate of unacceptable transactions below the adverse response threshold of 10 unacceptable (aka defective) transactions per million, and 10^{-3} produced unacceptable transactions significantly above the 10 defective packets per million (DPM) adverse response

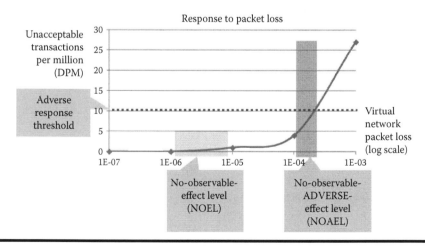

Figure 7.12 Hypothetical dose–response analysis of packet loss.

threshold; thus, the NOAEL is between 10^{-4} and 10^{-3} packet loss. CSCs will generally target resource service-level objectives (SLOs) to be near the NOEL. One expects that when resource quality approaches or exceeds the NOAEL, application service quality is likely to be degraded for some users.

Inevitably, different application components have different resource sensitivities. For example, packet loss on a transmission control protocol (TCP) link carrying performance management data may have no observable affect on user service quality, while lost or late real-time transport protocol (RTP) packets in a real-time voice or video stream may force the client device to engage lost packet compensation mechanisms, which can impact their user's quality of experience. Thus, testers must carefully consider the following:

1. Whether tested impairments are broad (e.g., all Internet Protocol [IP] packets flowing to/from the target application) or narrow (e.g., RTP packets carried to or from the target application).
2. How user service quality impact will be objectively and quantitatively measured.

7.11 Automated Acceptance Testing for Service Transitions

As shown in Figure 7.13, acceptance testing applies to service transitions at two points in the application service life cycle:

- **General, preproduction acceptance testing** verifies that a service is fit for use, including that rapid elasticity and scalability functionality is operable.
- **Specific, production acceptance testing** verifies that a particular configuration change (e.g., scaling up capacity of an online application) was completed

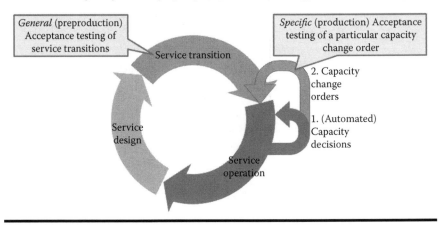

Figure 7.13 Types of automated acceptance tests for service transitions.

successfully and that user traffic can be safely applied to the transitioned service or component. Traditionally, after configured capacity of a physical system is increased by adding one or more hard disk drives, compute blades, etc., some acceptance tests are run before deeming the configuration change acceptable; if these test results are not acceptable, then the configuration change might be rolled back, or diagnosed and corrected. Traditionally, specific production acceptance tests were manually executed as part of a physical configuration change maintenance action; sometimes, extended acceptance testing was used, such as soaking or burning in new hardware elements over a weekend with test traffic before accepting the capacity for production service. The contextual change of vastly more service transitions (Section 7.6.1) means that an automated validation process (Section 5.2.11) is essential to reduce the opex associated with each service transition action, as well as to shorten cycle times to accelerate the pace of service innovation. Automating acceptance testing after a service transition action prior to applying user traffic to the reconfigured application service capacity and/or component(s) is essential to assure that user service quality is not impacted by inevitable service transition failures.

Clause 8.4.2 of ISO/IEC/IEEE 29119-2 considers test design and implementation processes, and this provides a useful framework for methodically considering automated acceptance testing of cloud-based applications (Figure 7.14).

- **Identify feature sets (TD1)**—Automated acceptance tests must assure that the transitioned component(s) deliver acceptable service quality, as well as operable management visibility and controllability.
- **Derive test conditions (TD2)**—Automated acceptance tests should not impact user service quality.

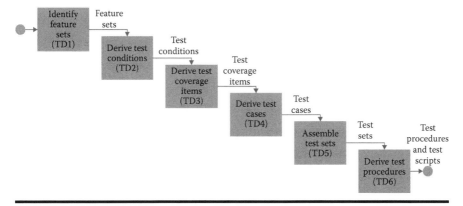

Figure 7.14   Simplified ISO/IEC/IEEE 29119-2 test design process.

- **Derive test coverage items (TD3)**—Testing should cover the service component being transitioned, as well as that component's interworking with components adjacent in the service delivery, service support, and management visibility/controllability chains. Automated acceptance testing of growth actions should verify correct operation before production user traffic is applied. Automated acceptance testing of degrowth/shrink actions should verify that resources have been properly released and that the CSC is no longer being charged for those resources to assure that the CSC enjoys the cost savings benefit of reducing online service capacity.
- **Derive test cases (TD4)**—Note that test cases used for specific, production acceptance testing should not impact production traffic; general, preproduction acceptance testing is executed on a preproduction instance, so live user traffic is not affected.
- **Assemble test sets (TD5)**—Assembling suites of tests is a normal test design activity.
- **Derive test procedures (TD6)**—These details are specific to the target application component and specific service transition action.

7.12 Summary

Risk-based test planning should leverage the service quality risk assessment (Chapter 28) to identify the risk conditions, causes, and controls that warrant testing. The organization's risk appetite, test policy, and test strategy drives the nature and extent of the CSC's test plans. Testing can remove uncertainty surrounding application operational characteristics, behavior, and quality, especially the following:

- **Knowledge-based (epistemic) uncertainties**, such as residual defects.
- **Stochastic (aleatoric) uncertainties**, such as how behavior is impacted by variations in the operational environment.

Knowledge derived from testing then drives the following:

- **Corrections** to software, configuration, scripts, procedures, etc., to replace or remove the risk source (Section 3.3.1), change the risk consequences (Section 3.3.3), or change the risk likelihood (Section 3.3.2).
- **Decisions** by the CSC organization to share the risk with an external party (Section 3.3.4), retain the risk (Section 3.3.5), reject accountability (Section 3.3.6), or avoid the risk (Section 3.3.7).

Several new or improved application test techniques become important for cloud-based applications:

■ **Scalability testing** verifies that cloud-centric rapid elasticity and scalability features enable an online application's capacity to be rapidly and reliably increased and decreased to serve changing demands.

■ **Sensitivity or dose–response testing of impaired cloud resources** characterizes the application service quality impact of degraded or curtailed service delivered by cloud service providers to the target application. Results of this sensitivity or dose–response testing are used to establish SLOs for resource service quality delivered by cloud service providers to the target application.

■ Cloud orchestration mechanisms enable **automated validation testing of service transitions** (e.g., elastic application capacity changes) to shorten application capacity change fulfillment intervals, as well as reducing the cost of those capacity changes and reducing the probability of failure due to human (aka procedural) error.

■ Advanced **static analysis, model verification, and simulation tools** are likely to be available from the cloud ecosystem to enable efficient and effective verification of application architecture, design, implementation, and configuration data earlier, which both reduces costs and shortens the service design phase.

On-demand self-service (Section 1.4.4) and rapid elasticity and scalability (Section 1.4.5) enable automation of test-bed allocation, configuration, and teardown/release to increase test agility. Connecting test-bed automation with aggressive test automation improves test efficiency and effectiveness. More frequently run automated tests should simplify debugging and defect identification because less will have changed since the previous successful test execution, which further improves efficiency and controls the risk of defects escaping into production to produce unacceptable user service quality.

Chapter 8

Service Design, Transition, and Operations Processes

As explained in Section 1.5, information technology (IT) service management is the set of "capabilities and processes to direct and control the service provider's activities and resources for the design, transition, delivery and improvement of services to fulfill the service requirements" (ISO/IEC, 2011-04-15). The IT Infrastructure Library (ITIL®) methodically considers the IT service management life cycle in five volumes:

- *ITIL Service Strategy* (Cannon, 2011-07-29)
- *ITIL Service Design* (Hunnebeck, 2011-07-29)
- *ITIL Service Transition* (Rance, 2011-07-29)
- *ITIL Service Operation* (Steinberg, 2011-07-29)
- *ITIL Continual Service Improvement* (Lloyd, 2011-07-29)

Service design, service transition, and service operation are the fundamental cycle of IT service management.

This chapter explicitly considers changes to service design, transition, and operations processes that cloud service customers (CSCs) are likely to make to reduce their operating expenses and increase service agility, and the user service quality risks associated with those changes. The chapter is organized as follows:

- Changes driven by key characteristics of cloud computing (Section 8.1)
- Service design considerations (Section 8.2)
- Service transition considerations (Section 8.3)
- Service operation considerations (Section 8.4)
- Summary (Section 8.5)

Note that although process activities are placed into one life cycle phase (e.g., service design, service transition, service operation) for pedagogical reasons, tasks associated with each process activity often span multiple life cycle phases.

8.1 Changes Driven by Key Characteristics of Cloud Computing

The defining characteristics of cloud computing enumerated in Section 1.4 drive fundamental changes to CSCs' service design, transition, and operation practices. Consider likely changes associated with several of the key characteristics:

- **Rapid elasticity and scalability** (Section 1.4.5)—Chapter 6 considered how rapid elasticity and scalability are likely to impact CSCs' capacity management activities. Lean application capacity management coupled with usage-based pricing enabled by measured service (Section 1.4.2) means that CSCs who use just-in-time online resource capacity can reduce their operating expenses by scaling online application capacity up and down so that they don't hold—and thus pay for—excessive online capacity. Lean capacity management of applications, just like lean manufacturing, can materially reduce waste and costs, but poorly executed lean capacity management (or poorly designed policies) will impact users when insufficient application capacity is online to serve instantaneous user demand with acceptable service quality.
- **On-demand self-service** (Section 1.4.4) is a key enabler of increased operational efficiency and reduced operating expenses by CSCs. On-demand self-service operates at two levels:
  - **End user self-service**—On-demand self-service enables end users to tailor services to their needs and tastes. This implies the following:
    - **A higher degree of service configuration/personalization for each end user**—Note that this can increase service complexity for the CSC.
    - **Increased self-care by end users**—Increased use of self-care by end users both reduces the CSC's opex and enhances scalability because it is faster to scale up the capacity of self-care systems than it is to hire and train customer care agents.

- **CSC self-service**—Automated life cycle management services offered by cloud service providers enable CSCs to fulfill service change requests much faster and more efficiently than traditional life cycle management actions that relied on manual execution by human staff. Faulty policies or plans for automatic execution of life cycle management actions raise a material risk to user service quality. While the initial risk of residual defects in automated life cycle scripts may be higher than in traditional methods of procedure because automated systems often require far more detailed instructions, the risk of faulty execution is generally lower for automated systems. So as residual defects in life cycle management actions are detected and corrected through testing and production use, the reliability of those actions should materially improve.

■ **Measured service** (Section 1.4.2)—Metered delivery of cloud services does not directly impact user service quality, but it does impact the CSC's costs. Pay-as-you-go charging for cloud resources and functional components offered as-a-service provides visibility to where the organization's costs lie, and CSCs can use those details to better manage and align their costs with their business. CSC organizations are likely to audit resource and functional-component-as-a-service charges assessed by their cloud service provider, or engage the services of a cloud auditor,* to assure that they are not being overcharged. After all, spurious resource and functional-component-as-a-service charges from cloud service providers directly increase a CSC's costs.

■ **Multitenancy** (Section 1.4.3)—Cloud service providers rely on multitenancy and resource sharing of their physical infrastructure to increase utilization of their capital investment in equipment, facilities, and data centers, and maximize their value to the enterprise. CSCs must monitor that the resource service quality delivered by their cloud service providers is not compromised by reckless efforts to maximize resource utilization, so the CSC can take appropriate actions to assure that application service quality delivered to the CSC's users is not adversely impacted by cloud infrastructure or functional-component-as-a-service quality issues.

8.2 Service Design Considerations

ITIL defines service design to include "the design of the services, governing practices, processes and policies required to realize the service provider's strategy and

---

* *Cloud auditor* is a standard role in the cloud ecosystem, which is defined by ISO/IEC 17788:2014 as a "cloud service partner with the responsibility to conduct an audit of the provision and use of cloud services."

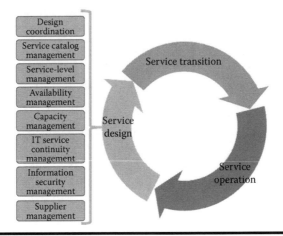

Figure 8.1 Service design phase processes.

to facilitate the introduction of services into supported environment" (Axelos Limited, 2011). The service design phase integrates application software with cloud infrastructure and functional components offered as-a-service into a service offering that can be successfully transitioned into production and be operated by the CSC organization. As shown in Figure 8.1, the primary processes of the service design phase are as follows:

- Design coordination (Section 8.2.1)
- Service catalog management (Section 8.2.2)
- Service-level management (Section 8.2.3)
- Availability management (Section 8.2.4)
- Capacity management (Section 8.2.5)
- IT service continuity management (Section 8.2.6)
- Information security management (Section 8.2.7)
- Supplier management (Section 8.2.8)

8.2.1 Design Coordination

ITIL design coordination "ensures the consistent and effective design of new or changed IT services, service management information systems, architectures, technology, processes, information and metrics" (Axelos Limited, 2011). Design coordination includes the following subprocesses:

- Design coordination support
- Service design planning
- Service design coordination and monitoring

- Technical and organizational service design
- Service design review and request for change (RFC) submission

This activity largely coordinates the application service life cycle tasks of Chapter 5, so refer to Chapter 5 for details on risks related to reducing opex and shortening cycle time while delivering acceptable quality to service users.

Rapid elasticity and scalability (Section 1.4.5) and on-demand self-service (Section 1.4.4) enable more agile development and deployment processes, which reduces the level of design coordination required. For example, as organizations can quickly implement, test, deploy, and try small service changes, and then pivot based on user feedback, less formal, up-front design coordination is necessary.

8.2.2 Service Catalog Management

ITIL service catalog management is "the process responsible for providing and maintaining the service catalogue and for ensuring that it is available to those who are authorized to access it" (Axelos Limited, 2011). As CSCs accelerate the pace of service innovation, the rate of additions, changes, and deletions to the organization's service catalog is likely to increase. Depending on the organization's business and service strategy, the rate of service catalog changes for cloud-based offerings could be significantly greater than for traditionally deployed services. While CSCs are likely to revamp the service catalog management processes to support rapid service innovation such as giving agile service teams more responsibility for maintaining their service catalog entries, those process changes not tied directly to cloud deployment and are unlikely to directly impact user service quality. Successful enhancements to an organization's service catalog management systems and processes should support the overarching business objectives of improving efficiency and enabling acceleration in the pace of service innovation.

8.2.3 Service-Level Management

ITIL service-level management is "the process responsible for negotiating achievable service level agreements and ensuring that these are met" (Axelos Limited, 2011). Broadly speaking, service-level management is a primary focus of this work: assuring that service reliability, latency, availability, and quality delivered to users meet the CSC's expectations. As shown in Figure 8.2, CSCs have several primary external service boundaries to manage:

1. As **provider of customer-facing application service** to end users. Service-level management of customer-facing service is fundamentally the same for cloud-based application services as for traditionally deployed application services.

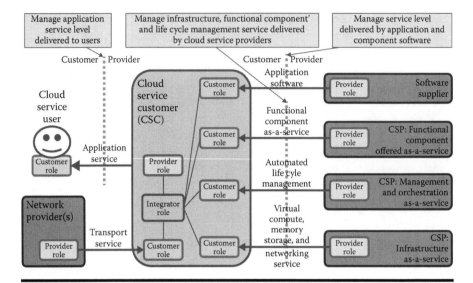

Figure 8.2 Service management in the accountability framework. CSP, cloud service provider.

2. As **consumer of resource-facing services** offered by cloud service providers. The service levels of virtualized compute, memory, storage, and networking service, as well as functional components offered and automated life cycle management, materially impact the customer-facing application service offered by the CSC. The remainder of this section considers how CSCs manage the resource service levels.

3. As **consumer of application and component software** offered by software suppliers. This service-level management activity assures that application and component software deliver service quality that meets the CSC's expectations.

Service-level management includes the following subprocesses:

■ **Identification of service requirements**—CSCs should construct service-level specifications (SLSs, Section 4.1.4, "Service-Level Objectives, Specifications, and Agreements") for the application software and components that comprise their service as well as the virtual resources and functional components offered as-a-service that the target application relies upon. Service-level targets and specifications should cover cloud service provider risks identified during risk assessment (Section IV, "Cloud Service Quality Risk Assessment and Management"), especially the following:

  – Virtual machine risks (Chapter 14)
  – Virtual networking risks (Chapter 15)

- Virtual storage risks (Chapter 16)
- Life cycle management (execution) risks (Chapter 23)
- Functional-component-as-a-service quality risks (Chapter 24)

Service-level thresholds should be set based on engineering judgment and validated via sensitivity (or dose-response) testing (Section 7.10).

■ **Design and maintenance of the service-level management framework—** "Trust but verify" is a prudent strategy; thus, CSCs should trust their suppliers and cloud service providers to meet the agreed-upon SLS but deploy monitoring mechanisms to objectively and quantitatively measure delivered service level to verify actual conformance to the agreed-upon SLS. Practical considerations make it infeasible for the CSC to monitor all relevant cloud service qualities for all virtual resource, functional-component-as-a-service, and automated life cycle management services consumed, so the CSC must balance visibility risks (Chapter 19) against broader business considerations of affordability (i.e., reduced opex) and time to market (i.e., accelerated pace of service innovation) to engineer and deploy a service-level framework that matches the organization's risk appetite.

■ **Agreements sign-off and service activation—**Rapid elasticity and scalability (Section 1.4.5) coupled with on-demand self-service (Section 1.4.4) means that cloud service provider service-level agreements (SLAs) or operations-level agreements (OLAs) should be agreed on in advance to maximize the pace of service innovation and agility.

■ **Service-level monitoring and reporting—**Cloud service provider quality measurements should be regularly compared to agreed-upon service levels. Root cause analysis should be executed and appropriate corrective actions deployed to drive continuous service improvement. Recurring or chronic underperformance may require more substantial remedies.

8.2.4 Availability Management

ITIL availability management "defines, analyses, plans, measures and improves all aspects of the availability of IT services, and ensures that all IT infrastructures, processes, tools, roles etc. are appropriate for the agreed service level targets for availability" (Axelos Limited, 2011). Availability management includes three subprocesses:

■ **Design services for availability—**This activity assures that the service architecture has no single point of failure (e.g., avoid faulty service delivery architecture risk, Table 18.4) and has an appropriate mechanisms to automatically detect and recover service following inevitable failure events. Note that instead of attempting to restore or repair a failing application instance, rapid elasticity and scalability (Section 1.4.5) coupled with on-demand self-service (Section 1.4.4) means that human or automatic mechanisms can simply start a new application instance to serve user demand and terminate the faulty application instance.

▪ **Availability testing**—Assures that automatic failure detection and recovery mechanisms operate rapidly and reliably. Risk control testing (Section 7.9) and techniques like negative or adversarial testing via tools like the Simian Army support this activity.

▪ **Availability monitoring and reporting**—The CSC should assure that there are sufficient service probes and monitoring mechanisms deployed, along with fault, alarm, performance, and configuration reporting, such that the true service state of the application is known so troubleshooting and corrective actions are promptly initiated. Rich tools and mechanisms offered by cloud service providers can provide robust monitoring and reporting, and this can be correlated with data from application components and other sources to give deeper insight into the true state of application service. In addition, sufficient data should be retained to enable effective root cause analysis of inevitable service quality impairment episodes and accurate reporting of application service quality performance.

8.2.5 Capacity Management

CSC capacity management was covered in Chapter 6 "Lean Application Capacity Management." As shown in Figure 8.3, lean application capacity management is executed in the service operation phase to drive service transition actions. However, appropriate activities in the service design phase are essential to enable the reduced opex and service agility potential of rapid elasticity and scalability.

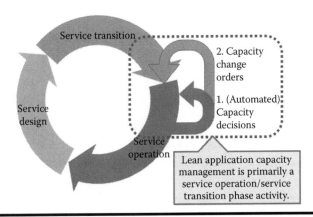

Figure 8.3 Application capacity management in the service management life cycle.

8.2.6 IT Service Continuity Management

IT service continuity management (ITSCM) "ensures that the IT service provider can always provide minimum agreed service levels, by reducing the risk to an acceptable level and planning for the recovery of IT services. IT service continuity management supports business continuity management" (Axelos Limited, 2011). Two fundamental disaster scenarios that challenge IT service continuity are as follows:

- **Data center disaster**—Some natural or man-made event (e.g., tornado, fire, act of war) renders some or all application capacity hosted in a physical data center unavailable.
- **Network segmentation**—Some natural or man-made event (e.g., force majeure, terrorism) renders some application instances hosted in one or more physical data centers unreachable.

The industry uses recovery time objective (RTO) and recovery point objective (RPO) to quantitatively characterize disaster recovery (aka service continuity) performance:

- **Recovery time objective** (RTO)—The time it takes to recover service to an alternate application instance, typically located in a geographically distant data center so that no single event can impact both data centers. Disaster recovery actions are often initiated by an enterprise manager formally activating a disaster recovery plan, but critical applications that demand rapid recovery often rely on automatic mechanisms to initiate georedundant recovery following disasters. Typically, RTO specifies how many minutes, hours, or days it should take to recover service for most or all impacted service users.
- **Recovery point objective** (RPO)—Changes to application data that occur after the last successful data backup or replication event will be lost on disaster recovery. RPO specifies how many seconds, minutes, or hours of data changes can be lost when recovering from a disaster.

CSCs are vulnerable to cloud service provider catastrophe risks (Chapter 25) as well as the continuity-related enterprise risk items of Section 3.1.2. ITSCM includes the following subprocesses:

- **Design for continuity**—Architecting, designing, developing, and testing disaster recovery and business continuity mechanisms that meet the organization's RTO and RPO. Geographically distributed redundancy (aka georedundancy) is often used for disaster recovery of critical services that require a short RTO. Rapid elasticity and scalability (Section 1.4.5) enables disaster recovery models that were not practical for traditionally deployed applications, including disaster-recovery-as-a-service offerings.

- **ITSCM support**—Assuring roles and responsibilities for addressing disasters is essential to assure that disaster recovery objectives will be met.
- **ITSCM training and testing**—Periodic disaster drills and related ITSCM training and testing are essential to assure that disaster recovery objectives will be met.
- **ITSCM review**—Periodic review of service continuity risks, expectations, and plans enables the CSC to track evolving risks.

Note that the cloud makes it more attractive to maintain an online application instance in several geographically distributed data centers, and it is often faster and cheaper to elastically grow online application capacity of nonimpacted service instances to mitigate a disaster than to start up a new (cold) service instance.

8.2.7 Information Security Management

ITIL information security management "supports business security and has a wider scope than that of the IT service provider, and includes handling of paper, building access, phone calls etc. for the entire organization" (Axelos Limited, 2011). Per Section 2.5, security topics are outside of this work's perimeter of consideration. However, the cloud enables significant automation of information security management processes.

8.2.8 Supplier Management

ITIL supplier management is "the process responsible for obtaining value for money from suppliers, ensuring that all contracts and agreements with suppliers support the needs of the business, and that all suppliers meet their contractual commitments" (Axelos Limited, 2011). Supplier management includes the following:

- Providing the supplier management framework
- Evaluation of new suppliers and contracts
- Establishing new suppliers and contracts
- Processing of standard orders
- Supplier and contract review
- Contract renewal or termination

Usage-based pricing is a practical way for organizations to tie their software costs more closely to their revenue, and rapid elasticity and scalability (Section 1.4.5) and on-demand self service (Section 1.4.4) make usage-based pricing more practical than with traditional deployments. Supplier management with usage-based pricing is more complicated than traditional arrangements, so CSC organizations may need to enhance their supplier management systems, policies, and processes.

8.3 Service Transition Considerations

ITIL service transition "ensures that new, modified or retired services meet the expectations of the business" (Axelos Limited, 2011). On-demand self-service (Section 1.4.4) coupled with rapid elasticity and scalability (Section 1.4.5) of cloud resources enables CSCs to aggressively automate service transition activities to dramatically shorten cycle times, reduce costs, and reduce vulnerability to human errors. Note that lean application capacity management (Chapter 6) and increased application service agility are likely to dramatically increase the rate of service configuration change (i.e., transition) actions. Traditionally, organizations would carefully plan service transitions to minimize the absolute number of service transitions like software updates or capacity growth actions to minimize the risk of service-impacting incidents. With cloud computing, service transitions like software upgrades and capacity growth/degrowth shift from being rare to routine, business-as-usual actions. A key service quality challenge is to assure that application service transitions can be executed reliably enough so that even with dramatically higher rates of service transition actions, the CSC's expectations for service reliability, latency, availability, and quality can be achieved.

As shown in Figure 8.4, the primary processes of the service transition phase are as follows:

- Transition planning and support (Section 8.3.1)
- Change management (Section 8.3.2)
- Change evaluation (Section 8.3.3)
- Service asset and configuration management (Section 8.3.4)
- Release and deployment management (Section 8.3.5)
- Service validation and testing (Section 8.3.6)
- Knowledge management (Section 8.3.7)

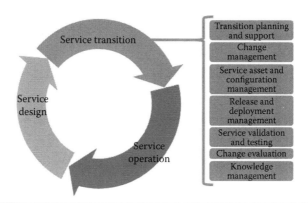

Figure 8.4   Service transition phase processes.

8.3.1 Transition Planning and Support (Project Management)

ITIL transition planning and support is "the process responsible for planning all service transition processes and coordinating the resources that they require" (Axelos Limited, 2011). This is primarily an overarching project management function covering the following:

- Project initiation
- Project planning and coordination
- Project control
- Project reporting and communication

While the specific activities associated with service transition of cloud-based applications are different from those of traditionally deployed applications, project management of those activities need not be fundamentally different.

8.3.2 Change Management

ITIL change management is "the process responsible for controlling the lifecycle of all changes, enabling beneficial changes to be made with minimum disruption to IT services" (Axelos Limited, 2011). Note that major configuration changes are considered via the change evaluation (Section 8.3.3) process. Change management includes the following subprocesses:

- Change management support
- Assessment of change proposals
- RFC logging and review
- Assessment and implementation of emergency changes
- Change assessment by the change manager
- Change assessment by the change advisory board (CAB)
- Change scheduling and build authorization
- Change deployment authorization
- Minor change deployment
- Postimplementation review and change closure

Lean application capacity management and self-healing, and automated life cycle management in general, strive to automatically initiate, execute, and complete configuration change actions without direct human involvement. As a result, the overall number of configuration changes executed against a cloud-based application service are likely to be much, much higher than for a traditionally deployed application service. This vast increase in the number of changes to be assessed, managed, and executed will likely prompt CSCs to overhaul their change management processes. To reduce their costs, CSCs will reengineer their processes so that humans are *on* the change management loop for routine actions rather than *in* the change management loop. This presents CSCs with several strategic questions:

1. What changes will they permit orchestration and automated life cycle management systems to autonomously assess, plan, authorize, and execute without explicit human approval?
2. What criteria will orchestration and automated life cycle management systems use to make go/no-go authorization decisions before autonomously executing a change action?
3. What criteria will human operators use to determine when autonomously initiated change management actions should be aborted, canceled, or otherwise overridden by manual actions?
4. Should the cadence of changes requiring explicit human approval be aligned or coordinated with execution of fully automated configuration change actions?

An organization's answers to these questions may evolve over time. Orchestration and automated life cycle management actions are unlikely to fully automate all change actions, so CSCs will require hybrid change management processes where all or some of the change planning, assessment, and authorization is performed by humans and all or some of the scheduling and execution is performed by orchestration and automated life cycle management systems.

8.3.3 Change Evaluation

ITIL change evaluation is "the process responsible for formal assessment of a new or changed IT service to ensure that risks have been managed and to help determine whether to authorize the change" (Axelos Limited, 2011). Change evaluation includes the following subprocesses:

- Change evaluation prior to planning
- Change evaluation prior to build
- Change evaluation prior to deployment
- Change evaluation after deployment

Agile methods, especially continuous delivery, shrink the magnitude of change from one delivery to the next, which reduces the overall risk for any particular change. However, major changes will require human assessment, planning, and authorization. As on-demand self-service (Section 1.4.4) and rapid elasticity and scalability (Section 1.4.5) materially shorten the execution intervals and costs associated with both routine and major infrastructure-related changes, CSCs may rework their change evaluation processes for major changes as well.

8.3.4 Service Asset and Configuration Management

ITIL service asset and configuration management is "the process responsible for ensuring that the assets required to deliver services are properly controlled, and that accurate and reliable information about those assets is available when and where it is needed" (Axelos Limited, 2011). The cloud fundamentally changes the service asset and configuration management problem for CSCs because they no longer have direct control, visibility, responsibility, or accountability for the physical compute, memory, storage, and networking assets or the functional components offered as-a-service that are resources for their customer-facing application services; instead, the infrastructure service provider controls configuration management of physical resources and other infrastructure aspects that are invisible to the CSC. Moreover, on-demand self service (Section 1.4.4) coupled with rapid-elasticity and scalability (Section 1.4.5) may prompt cloud service providers to unobtrusively reconfigure their virtual resources and functional components offered as-a-service on the fly to boost the cloud service provider's operational efficiency, such as migrating an application's virtual machine instance from one physical server to another. Thus, service asset and configuration management systems, policies, and processes for CSCs are likely to be materially different from traditional solutions.

8.3.5 Release and Deployment Management

ITIL release and deployment management is the "process responsible for planning, scheduling and controlling the build, test and deployment of releases, and for delivering new functionality required by the business while protecting the integrity of existing services" (Axelos Limited, 2011). Release and deployment management includes the following subprocesses:

- Release management support
- Release planning
- Release build
- Release deployment
- Early life support
- Release closure

Cloud orchestration and automated life cycle management automates the release deployment process, and on-demand self-service (Section 1.4.4) coupled with rapid elasticity and scalability (Section 1.4.5) encourage far more frequent release deployment actions, which accelerates the pace of service innovation. Profoundly increasing the rate of release deployment actions for cloud-based applications will prompt organizations to streamline and rework their release management planning, building, supporting, and closure processes to maximize the pace of service innovation at the lowest cost.

8.3.6 Service Validation and Testing

ITIL service validation and testing is "the process responsible for validation and testing of a new or changed IT service. Service validation and testing ensures that the IT service matches its design specification and will meet the needs of the business" (Axelos Limited, 2011). This topic was covered in Chapter 7, "Testing Cloud-Based Application Services"; automated acceptance testing for service transitions (Section 7.11) will materially change this process for cloud-based applications.

8.3.7 Knowledge Management

ITIL defines knowledge management as the "process responsible for sharing perspectives, ideas, experience and information, and for ensuring that these are available in the right place and at the right time" (Axelos Limited, 2011). Increased automatic data collection coupled with powerful analytics increases the information, knowledge, and wisdom available across the service design, transition, operations, and continual service improvement processes, so knowledge management processes are likely to be revised for the cloud. Chapter 9, "Continual Service Improvement," considers this topic further.

8.4 Service Operation Considerations

ITIL service operation "coordinates and carries out the activities and processes required to deliver and manage services at agreed levels to business users and customers" (Axelos Limited, 2011). As shown in Figure 8.5, the primary processes of the traditional service operation phase are as follows:

- Event management (Section 8.4.1)
- Incident management (Section 8.4.2)
- Problem management (Section 8.4.3)

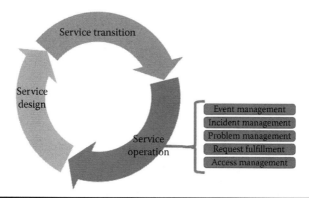

Figure 8.5   Traditional service operation phase processes.

- Request fulfillment (Section 8.4.4)
- Access management (Section 8.4.5)

8.4.1 Event Management

ITIL defines event as "a change of state that has significance for the management of an IT service or other configuration item" (Axelos Limited, 2011). Event management is the process for managing events throughout their life cycle and includes the following subprocesses:

- Maintenance of event-monitoring mechanisms and rules
- Event filtering and first-level correlation
- Second-level correlation and response selection
- Event review and closure

Automated life cycle management mechanisms, especially automated self-healing, should minimize the number of events requiring operator involvement. For example, if a virtualized compute, memory, storage, or networking resource fails, then cloud orchestration mechanisms can "self-heal" the impacted application instance by automatically allocating, configuring, and introducing to service new virtual component(s) and releasing the failed resources.

8.4.2 Incident Management

As shown in Figure 8.6, the meaning of incident in the context of ITIL is essentially the same as in ISO/IEC/IEEE 25765:2010 (Section 4.1.2).

Incident management is the process for managing the life cycle of an incident (rather than resolving the underlying problem, which is considered in Section 8.4.3, "Problem Management"), including the following subprocesses:

- Incident management support
- Incident logging and categorization
- Immediate incident resolution by first-level support
- Incident resolution by second-level support
- Handling of major incidents
- Incident monitoring and escalation
- Incident closure and evaluation
- Proactive user information
- Incident management and reporting

The on-demand self-service (Section 1.4.4) characteristic of cloud computing drives organizations to deploy powerful self-care systems, which automate many incident management tasks, and automated life cycle management and self-healing mechanisms will automate others. Fundamental changes to the underlying problem

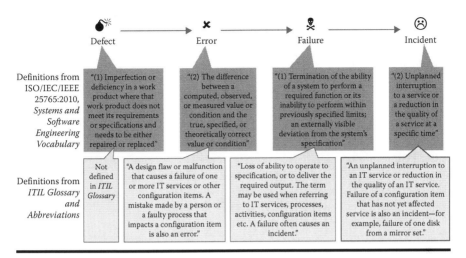

Figure 8.6   Incident for both ITIL and ISO/IEC/IEEE.

management (Section 8.4.3) process will likely drive more profound changes to the incident management processes implemented by CSCs.

8.4.3 *Problem Management*

The ITIL definition of problem is "a cause of one or more incidents" (Axelos Limited, 2011). The ISO/IEC/IEEE definition is essentially the same.* Problem management is the process of managing problems to service restoration. Root cause analysis and deployment of corrective actions is considered in Chapter 9, "Continual Service Improvement."

Section III, "Cloud Service Quality Risk Inventory," catalogs the primary proximal and ultimate causes of service quality problems that confront cloud-based applications above and beyond the risks confronting traditionally deployed applications. Fault localization and root cause analysis of cloud-based applications is inherently more complicated than problem management of traditionally deployed applications because the decoupled, decomposed, dynamic, and multivendor environment makes it more challenging to detect, localize, recover, and ultimately correct defects than with a traditional one-throat-to-choke accountability model (Section 12.2, "Differences between VNF and PNF Deployments"). To treat these risks, both

---

* The primary ISO/IEC/IEEE 25765:2010 (ISO/IEC/IEEE, 2010-12-15) definitions of *problem* are as follows:
  (1) difficulty, uncertainty, or otherwise realized and undesirable event, set of events, condition, or situation that requires investigation and corrective action
  (2) difficulty or uncertainty experienced by one or more persons, resulting from an unsatisfactory encounter with a system in use

cloud service providers and CSCs are likely to gather more alarm, fault, performance, and configuration data than with traditional deployments to enable rapid, reliable, and automated fault detection and localization. Automated life cycle management, especially self-healing mechanisms, should enable some fraction of problems of cloud-based application to be automatically detected and resolved without operator intervention. As automated self-healing mechanisms mature, the portion of problems that can be automatically detected and resolved will grow. However, true root cause analysis of the underlying failure is necessary to drive corrective actions to eliminate the fundamental problem. Virtualization platforms often support mechanisms to capture a full snapshot of the failed component, which can subsequently be examined off-line to improve the efficiency and effectiveness of root cause analysis.

ITIL problem management subprocesses can be factored into two groups:

■ **Substantially impacted**—Rich alarm, fault, performance, and configuration data are likely to be collected by both CSCs and cloud service providers to automate detection, localization, and repair of as many problems as possible. The automated systems, policies, and operational procedures used by CSCs and cloud service providers to support these problem management subprocesses are likely to be materially different from traditional deployment models. The following subprocesses are likely to be substantially impacted:
  – Proactive problem identification—The cloud introduces a range of new problem causes; Section III, "Cloud Service Quality Risk Inventory," for details.
  – Problem categorization and prioritization—May be automated by self-healing mechanisms.
  – Problem diagnosis and resolution—rapid elasticity and scalability (Section 1.4.5) often enables replacement service components to be quickly instantiated to restore service, and root cause of the failure can be analyzed off-line. Note that virtualization enables new ways to capture failure data for off-line analysis (e.g., taking a snapshot image of a failed component and associated configuration data).
■ **Minimally impacted**—These subprocesses are likely to be largely the same for traditional and cloud-based applications:
  – Problem error and control
  – Problem closure and evaluation
  – Major problem review
  – Problem management reporting

8.4.4 Request Fulfillment

ITIL defines service request as "a formal request from a user for something to be provided—for example, a request for information or advice; to reset a password; or to install a workstation for a new user" (Axelos Limited, 2011). The process responsible for managing service requests is called request fulfillment. The on-demand self-service (Section 1.4.4) characteristic of cloud computing drives organizations to deploy powerful self-care systems, which automate the key processes of request fulfillment:

- Request fulfillment support
- Request logging and categorization
- Request model execution
- Request monitoring and escalation
- Request closure and evaluation

Effective self-care systems can improve end users' quality of experience by enabling them to better tailor their service experience to their needs while reducing the workload on the CSC's human customer support staff.

8.4.5 Access Management

ITIL access management is "the process responsible for allowing users to make use of IT services, data or other assets" (Axelos Limited, 2011). Per Section 2.5, security topics, including access management, are outside of this work's perimeter of consideration.

8.5 Summary

As shown in Figure 8.7, the cloud enables organizations to automate many IT service management activities, which reduces CSC staffing levels, thereby reducing the organization's operating expenses.

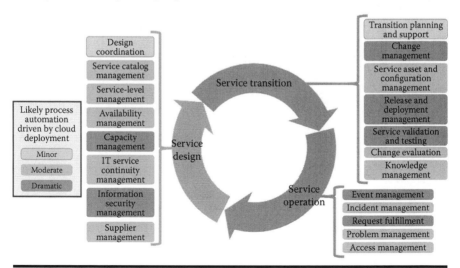

Figure 8.7 Likely cloud-enabled automation of IT service management processes.

Chapter 9

Continual Service Improvement

The Information Technology Infrastructure Library (ITIL®) defines continual service improvement as follows:

> Continual service improvement ensures that services are aligned with changing business needs by identifying and implementing improvements to IT services that support business processes. The performance of the IT service provider is continually measured and improvements are made to processes, IT services and IT infrastructure in order to increase efficiency, effectiveness and cost effectiveness. (Axelos Limited, 2011)

This chapter considers how continual service improvement is applied to minimize the risk that the application service reliability, latency, quality, and availability delivered to cloud service users will be compromised by a cloud service customer's (CSC's) efforts to deliver new services and value faster and improve operational efficiency. Continual service improvement is considered in the following sections:

- The plan–do–check–act cycle (Section 9.1)
- The seven-step improvement model and the data–information–knowledge–wisdom model (Section 9.2)
- Aligning PDCA cycles (Section 9.3)

9.1 Plan–Do–Check–Act Cycle

ISO 9001:2015, *Quality Management System Requirements*, clause 0.3.2 "Plan–Do–Check–Act Cycle," offers the most authoritative reference on the plan–do–check–act (or PDCA) cycle (Figure 9.1):

- **Plan**—"establish the objectives of the system and its processes, and the resources needed to deliver the results in accordance with customers' requirements and the organization's policies, and identify and address risks and opportunities" (ISO, 2015-09-15)
- **Do**—"implement what was planned" (ISO, 2015-09-15)
- **Check**—"monitor and (where applicable) measure processes and the resulting products and services against policies, objectives, requirements and planned activities, and report the results" (ISO, 2015-09-15)
- **Act**—"take actions to improve performance, as necessary" (ISO, 2015-09-15)

Continual service improvement seeks to identify and deploy specific refinements to an organization's policies, processes, and practices that produce reproducible, sustainable improvements to the organization's performance. Figure 9.2 visualizes PDCA cycles across time. Standard policies, processes, and practices establish a baseline context for execution of PDCA. Ideally, each PDCA cycle drives improvement actions, which are incorporated into the plans for the next iteration, thereby enabling incrementally better performance over time. Periodically, the improved policies, processes, and practices are consolidated into a revised standard baseline context for the future, thereby making the improvements sustainable across time.

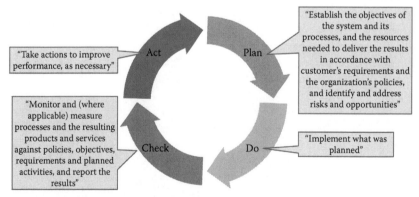

Definitions from ISO 9001:2015, *Quality Management System Requirements*

Figure 9.1 Standard plan–do–check–act cycle.

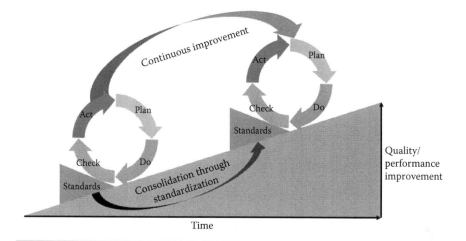

Figure 9.2 Continuous improvement and plan–do–check–act cycles.

PDCA improvement cycles are fundamental to the following:

- **ISO 9000 quality management**—Section 9.1.1, "PDCA in ISO 9000 Quality Management"
- **ISO 31000 risk management**—Section 9.1.2, "PDCA in ISO 31000 Risk Management"
- **ISO 20000 information technology (IT) service management**—Section 9.1.3, "PDCA in ISO 20000 IT Service Management"
- **ITIL continual service improvement**—Section 9.2, "The Seven Step Improvement Model and the Data–Information–Knowledge–Wisdom Model"

9.1.1 PDCA in ISO 9000 Quality Management

ISO 9001 states, "the PDCA cycle enables an organization to ensure that its processes are adequately resourced and managed, and that opportunities for improvement are determined and acted on" (ISO, 2015-09-15). Figure 9.3 illustrates how ISO 9001:2015 quality management system requirements clauses map onto the PDCA cycle.

9.1.2 PDCA in ISO 31000 Risk Management

Risk assessment (Section IV, "Cloud Service Quality Risk Assessment and Management") operates within a risk management framework. Figure 9.4 illustrates how the ISO 31000 risk management process maps onto the PDCA cycle.

- **Plan**—ISO 31000 clause 4.3 considers design of framework for managing risk.
- **Do**—ISO 31000 clause 4.4, "Implementing Risk Management," is both a framework for managing risk and the risk management process itself.

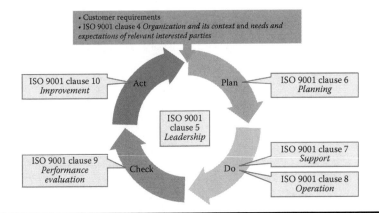

Figure 9.3 Plan–do–check–act cycle from ISO 9001. (Based on Figure 2 of ISO, *9001—Quality Management Systems—Requirements,* Geneva, Switzerland: International Organization for Standardization, 2015-09-15.)

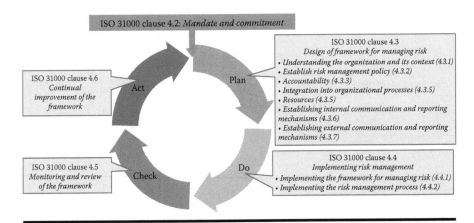

Figure 9.4 ISO 31000 risk management framework. (From Figure 2 of ISO, *31000—Risk Management Principles and Guidelines,* Geneva, Switzerland: International Organization for Standardization, 2009-11-15.)

- Check—ISO 31000 clause 4.5 considers monitoring and review of the framework.
- Act—ISO 31000 clause 4.6 considers continual improvement of the framework.

9.1.3 PDCA in ISO 20000 IT Service Management

The introduction of ISO/IEC 20000-1:2011 describes how an IT service management systems (SMS) maps onto the PDCA cycle (Figure 9.5). Figure 9.6 illustrates how clauses from ISO/IEC 20000-1:2011 align with the PDCA cycle.

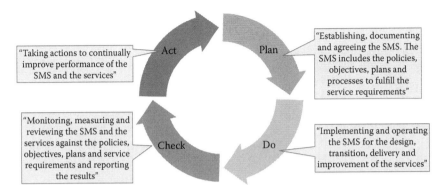

Text from ISO/IEC 20000-1:2011, *Management System Requirements*

Figure 9.5   PDCA Principles in ISO 20000 IT service management. SMS, service management system.

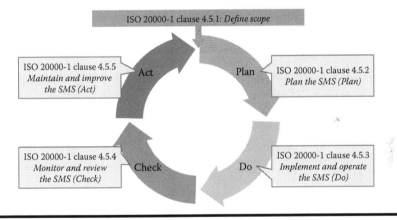

Figure 9.6   PDCA requirements in ISO 20000. SMS, service management system.

9.2 Seven-Step Improvement Model and the Data–Information–Knowledge–Wisdom Model

ITIL continual service improvement relies on a seven-step improvement model. Figure 9.7 overlays seven-step improvement onto the general PDCA model of Figure 9.1:

- **Identify vision, goals, and strategy for improvement**—A critical starting point for any improvement program is agreeing on the vision and goals of the target end state (e.g., accelerated pace of service innovation and reduced opex without unacceptable user service quality) and a strategy (e.g., use Agile and

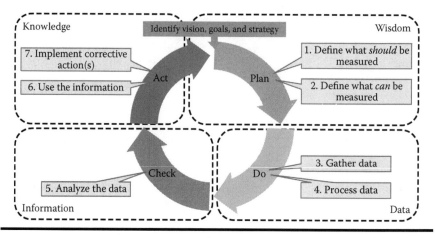

Figure 9.7 Seven-step improvement model.

DevOps methods, deploy on cloud, automate life cycle management activities, reengineer IT service management practices).

1. **Define what should be measured**—The vision, goals, and strategy for improvement frame what should be measured, such as reduction in operating expenses and acceleration in the pace of service innovation.
2. **Define what can be measured**—Unfortunately, it is often infeasible to directly measure performance against vision and goals. Thus, one must carefully consider exactly what objective and quantitative measurements can practically and reliably be made.
3. **Gather data**—Having defined key measurements, one collects primary data required for those measurements (e.g., time-stamped event records).
4. **Process data**—Collected data (e.g., time-stamped event records) is processed into measurements (e.g., transaction latencies), which can be further processed into derived information (e.g., 99th-percentile latency, etc.).
5. **Analyze the data**—Measurement and processed data can be analyzed to spot trends and patterns. Deeper analysis can identify proximal and distal (ultimate) root causes and other contributory factors.
6. **Use the information**—Analysis drives recommendations for corrective actions, which are presented to decision makers.
7. **Implement corrective action(s)**—Corrective actions approved by decision makers are implemented. Plans for the next PDCA iteration will measure and check the efficacy of those corrective actions to determine if further improvements are appropriate.

Figure 9.7 also overlays the data–information–knowledge–wisdom (DIKW) model that was introduced discussed in Section 4.5:

- **Data (do)**—Gathering data (step 3) and processing data (step 4) are clearly data-oriented activities.
- **Information (check)**—Analyzing the data (step 5) produces information, like who, what, when, and where about actual performance.
- **Knowledge (act)**—Using the information to propose corrective actions that can be offered to decision makers (i.e., step 6 using the information) gets at *how* system performance may have differed from expectations and suggests corrective actions, which are addressed in step 7 (implement corrective actions).
- **Wisdom (plan)**—Understanding what one should measure in support of the organization's vision, goals, and strategy (step 1) and deciding what the organization actually can measure (step 2) requires wisdom.

Figure 9.8 lays the seven steps alongside the DIKW pyramid, with implementation hints on the right-hand side of the visualization.

- **Automated data collection**—Cloud infrastructure, management, orchestration, service components, and applications are likely to automatically collect reams of service performance data to support operations, management, orchestration, and analytics needs, as well as to enable usage-based pricing.

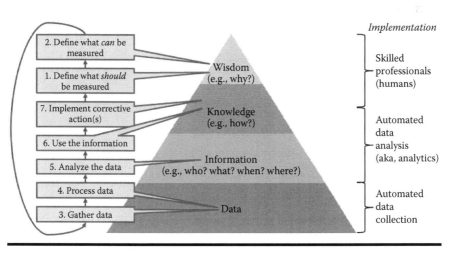

Figure 9.8   Seven-step PDCA and DIKW.

Falling costs of storage make it increasingly feasible to capture "all" data that might be useful for off-line and root cause analysis.

■ **Automated data analysis**—Advanced management, orchestration, and analytics systems are likely to perform a wide range of sophisticated data analysis activities like event correlation, trend spotting, and performance characterization. Automated data analysis tools typically operate at three levels:

1. **Descriptive**, which characterize actual operation, such as of a specific product or service instance
2. **Predictive**, which suggest relationships, such as fault correlations
3. **Prescriptive**, which serve as recommendations engines, such as perfecting elastic capacity management decisions

■ **Skilled (human) professionals**—Results of automated data analysis are input for skilled (human) professionals, who ultimately propose perfective and corrective actions, and leaders, who make decisions for each recommended action. More complete data sets combined with more powerful analytics tools enable deeper off-line root cause analyses, which produce better and more compelling recommendations. The skilled human professionals who consume the automated data analysis can thus be more productive because they are freed from having to gather, process, and analyze raw data.

9.3 Aligning PDCA Cycles

Rather than independent and uncoordinated IT service management, risk management, and quality management, PDCA cycles, big data, and analytics techniques enable CSCs to align and integrate their continuous improvement activities. Focusing simultaneously on minimizing non-value-adding activities to minimize opex and cycle time while holding user service quality to acceptable levels enables better allocation of scarce resources for improvements to the actions with the highest benefit to the organization. Operationally, CSCs should explicitly include continual service improvement in their normal service design, transition, operations, and management activities. In particular, CSCs should do the following:

1. Identify key performance characteristics to improve, which **should be measured**, such as the following:
   a. **Opex reduction relative to baseline**—Ideally one measures all of the non-value-adding (aka, waste) activities recognized through lean computing activities, discussed in Chapter 10, "Improving Operational Efficiency of Cloud-Based Applications."
   b. **Acceleration in pace of service innovation relative to baseline**—Ideally, one measures the time to complete each activity in the application service life cycle activities of Chapter 5, "Application Service Life Cycle."

c. **Delivered user service quality relative to baseline**—Ideally, one objectively and quantitatively measures all of the characteristics applicable to the target service from Section 27.5, "Establish Service Quality Objectives."

2. Select or define objective and quantitative measurements likely to impact key performance characteristics that **can be measured.**

3. Automatically **gather data.**

4. **Process data** into easier-to-use information products.

5. **Analyze the data** to compare actual performance to targets and control limits.

6. **Use the analyzed information** to formulate corrective actions to improve performance of key characteristics. A primary use case for analyzed data is to validate and calibrate assumptions about risks, such as the probability of a risk event occurring, the probability of an event occurrence being successfully controlled, and the likely impact of both successfully and unsuccessfully controlled risk events. This information feeds into *risk analysis* activities (Section 28.3) and can impact the results of *risk evaluation* activities (Section 28.4).

7. **Implement the corrective actions** selected by CSC decision makers.

Chapter 10

Improving Operational Efficiency of Cloud-Based Applications

A standard goal of the cloud* is as follows:

> From the [cloud service] customers' perspective, *cloud computing offers the users value by enabling a switch from a low efficiency and asset utilization business model to a high efficiency one.*

This chapter considers the topic of improving operational efficiency of cloud-based applications via the following sections:

- What is efficiency? (Section 10.1)
- Efficiency, capacity, and utilization (Section 10.2)
- Direct inputs to application service (Section 10.3)
- Vision to improve CSC's operational efficiency (Section 10.4)
- Lean computing for cloud service customers (Section 10.5)
- Recognizing waste in the cloud (Section 10.6)
- Respect and operational efficiency (Section 10.7)
- Continuous improvement of operational efficiency (Section 10.8)

---

* From clause 6.2 of ISO/IEC 17788, *Cloud Computing Overview and Vocabulary* (ISO/IEC, 2014-10-15).

10.1 What Is Efficiency?

The Information Technology Infrastructure Library (ITIL®) defines *efficiency* as

> a measure of whether the right amount of resource has been used to deliver a process, service or activity. An efficient process achieves its objectives with the minimum amount of time, money, people or other resources. (Axelos Limited, 2011)

Figure 10.1 offers a canonical model of an information technology (IT) service component like a virtualized network function (VNF). The VNF—technically an ITIL *configuration item**—consumes infrastructure resources as input (i.e., compute, memory, networking, and storage) and delivers some IT service as output.

Figure 10.2 visualizes efficiency of a target service component as the quantity of customer-facing service output produced divided by the quantity of resource-facing service input consumed. Reducing the quantity of resource-facing service input consumed to produce a fixed output by a service component (or producing more output with the same resource input) improves its efficiency.

Figure 10.3 applies the component efficiency model of Figure 10.2 to the canonical architecture of Figure 1.1 to show that application service efficiency is the ratio of application output delivered to cloud service users divided by the resource inputs consumed. To minimize operating expense, cloud service customers (CSCs) want to engage the smallest and lowest-cost fleet of resources to serve their users with acceptable service quality. This chapter assumes that user service quality expectations are held constant, so reducing resources to the point that service quality requirements are violated is unacceptable.

10.2 Efficiency, Capacity, and Utilization

Efficiency is different from capacity. ITIL defines *capacity* as follows:

> The *maximum throughput* that a configuration item or IT service can deliver.... capacity may be the size or volume—for example, a disk drive.

---

* *Configuration item* is defined by ITIL as follows:

> Any component or other service asset that needs to be managed in order to deliver an IT service. Information about each configuration item is recorded in a configuration record within the configuration management system and is maintained throughout its lifecycle by service asset and configuration management. Configuration items are under the control of change management. They typically include IT services, hardware, software, buildings, people and formal documentation such as process documentation and service level agreements. (Axelos Limited, 2011)

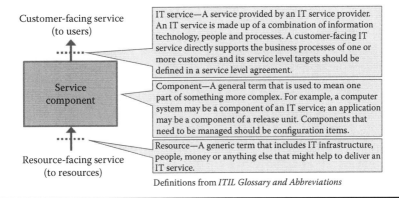

Figure 10.1   Canonical service component model.

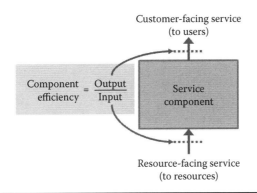

Figure 10.2   Component efficiency as a ratio.

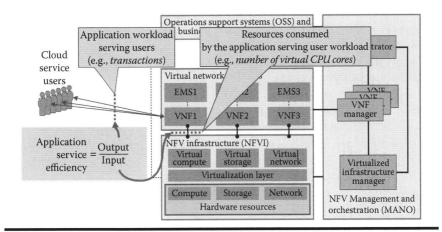

Figure 10.3   Simplified operational efficiency of cloud-based applications. EMS, element management system; NFV, network functions virtualization.

In the context of capacity ratings, maximum throughput is generally understood to mean maximum *steady-state* throughput that can be served with acceptable service quality, especially acceptable reliability and performance.

Rapid elasticity and scalability enables one to reconfigure the maximum throughput (i.e., capacity) that a VNF can deliver rapidly to respond to user demand and business needs. However, at any instant in time, a particular VNF has a deterministic resource configuration, which establishes the maximum throughput (i.e., capacity) that the VNF can deliver.

ISO/IEC/IEEE 24765 defines *utilization* as "a ratio representing the amount of time a system or component is busy divided by the time it is available." The relationship of capacity and utilization is best understood via two practical scenarios:

- If *utilization* of a VNF's current online *capacity* is too *high*, then orchestration mechanisms will leverage rapid elasticity to allocate and add additional resources to change the VNF's configuration and increase its maximum throughput/*capacity*.
- If *utilization* of a VNF's current online *capacity* is too *low*, then orchestration mechanisms will reconfigure the VNF to a smaller configuration with a smaller maximum throughput/*capacity* and return the excess resources to the cloud service provider.

10.3 Direct Inputs to Application Service

The focus of this chapter is to minimize a CSC's direct resource inputs to deliver application service to cloud users in their service operation and service transition phases, thereby maximizing the CSC's application service efficiency. The diligence and decisions taken in the service design phase establish the cost models and performance characteristics that drive the feasible and likely operational efficiencies of the service transition and operation phases, such as the nature, extent, and quality of automation mechanisms.

As explained in Chapter 5, "Application Service Life Cycle," and Section 8.2, "Service Design Considerations," the service design phase covers needs assessment, requirements, architecture, design, implementation, integration, and verification of the application itself, as well as creation of the governing practices, processes, and policies required to realize the service provider's strategy and to facilitate the introduction of services into the CSC's supported environment. As those service design activities are not a direct cost of service production, the efficiencies of service design are not considered in this chapter. Excluding the service design phase and the costs of selling, a CSC's service production costs are visualized in Figure 10.4:

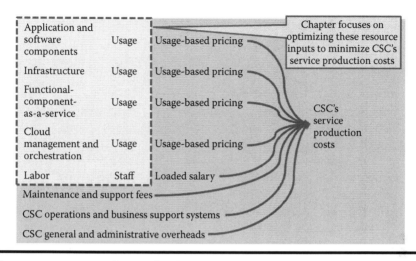

Figure 10.4   CSC service production costs.

- **Application software and service components** charges paid to software suppliers.
- **Compute, memory, storage, and networking resources** charges paid to infrastructure cloud service providers. Note that the usage-based price charged by the infrastructure cloud service provider covers the power and space consumed by the physical equipment that serves the compute, memory, storage, and networking resources to the CSC's application service component instances.
- **Functional components offered as-a-service** usage charges paid to cloud functional-component-as-a-service providers.
- **Management and orchestration** service charges paid to cloud management and orchestration service provider(s).
- **Labor** of CSC's operations, administration, maintenance, provisioning, and other staff and managers.
- Service of CSC's **operations and business support systems** to CSC's IT organization.
- **Maintenance and support fees** to suppliers.
- **General and administrative overhead.**

Maximizing the utilization efficiency of application and software components, infrastructure, management, orchestration, functional components offered as-a-service, and staff is the focus of this chapter. Minimizing the pricing of those resources is a separate topic beyond the scope of this work.

10.4 Vision to Improve CSC Operational Efficiency

As shown in Figure 10.5, CSCs improve their efficiency of operating cloud-based applications via four intertwined threads:

1. **Increasing automation** so CSC staffing for operations, administration, customer care, provisioning, and management can be reduced. Practically, humans are moved from being *in the loop* executing operations, administration, support and provisioning actions to being *on the loop* monitoring and optimizing those autonomous operations, and rapidly intervening if the automations fail to function properly.

2. **Rapidly elastic application and resource configurations** so online capacity and resource consumption can closely match actual user demand. Practically, this means growing online application capacity and resource consumption during busy periods, and shrinking online application capacity and resource consumption when application usage is low.

3. **Maximizing resource efficiency of serving a particular application workload.** Practically, this means selecting and configuring service components and architectures that require less resource input to serve user demand with acceptable service quality.

4. **Improving quality.** Every software defect that is activated, random failure event that occurs, or life cycle management action that fails causes automated systems and/or human operators to detect the trouble, localize the problem, and take appropriate corrective actions, all of which consume resources that would have been expended if the failure had not occurred. As shown in

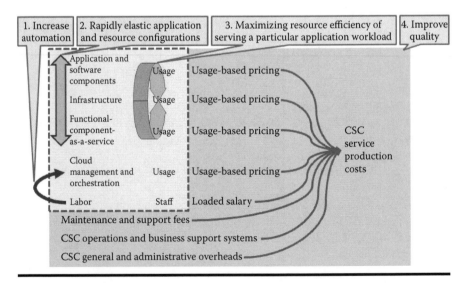

Figure 10.5   Primary strategies to improve CSC operational efficiency.

Figure 10.6, life cycle management actions that are not completed with quality (i.e., *not* right-first-time) require additional time and effort—and perhaps user service impact—to detect, localize, rework, restore service, and resolve. Note that the cost of reworking an automated life cycle management action that is not right-first-time is often higher than the cost of a successful manual execution. Thus, maximizing the portion of automatic, as well as manual, life cycle management actions that complete right-first-time improves operational efficiency by eliminating expensive manual rework.

Figure 10.7 visually compares elasticity and resource efficiency.

■ **Rapid elasticity** enables the online service capacity offered by the CSC to be rapidly changed to whatever level the CSC desires. As explained in Chapter 6, "Lean Application Capacity Management," the CSC will carry online capacity to serve cyclical demand plus random demand variations,

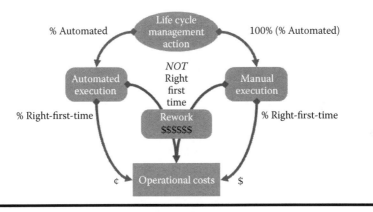

Figure 10.6   Automation, quality, and operational efficiency.

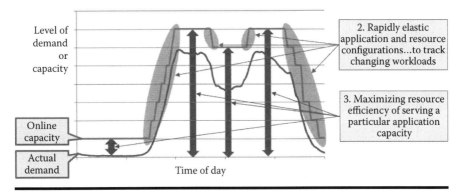

Figure 10.7   Capacity-related operational efficiencies.

as well as a small increment of reserve capacity to mitigate the risk of infrastructure or component failure, as well as of unforecast surges in demand and other problems. Key qualities for rapid elasticity include the following:

- **Capacity fulfillment lead time**—How long does it take for a requested capacity change action to complete?
- **Capacity fulfillment reliability**—What portion of capacity fulfillment actions are completed right-first-time?
- **Granularity of capacity change actions**—Governs how close online application capacity can come to the CSC's target. For example, if the CSC wants to deploy 1737 units of online capacity and online capacity is currently 1500 units, then can they grow by 237 units of capacity, or only by 240 units, or 250 units, or 500 units?
- **Cost of capacity change action**—Both cloud service providers and CSCs must expend resources to execute a requested capacity change action, such as allocating or releasing one or more infrastructure resources, manipulating both infrastructure and application component configurations, and validating that the capacity change is executed successfully before user traffic is applied to the altered application capacity. Regardless of whether those configuration change expenses are monetized (e.g., as a fee for each capacity change action) or not, ultimately, some organization must cover those costs.

▪ **Resource efficiency** is logically the ratio of application service output to resource inputs, like serving X users with Y virtual machine instances. Particular application configurations, like automobiles, have optimal levels of service output. For instance, a sedan might comfortably seat four passengers, while a full-size sport-utility vehicle might comfortably seat seven. Transporting fewer passengers—or serving less user workload—than the engineered capacity reduces efficiency. Fortunately, application service components generally offer more configuration flexibility than automobiles. Note that unlike with automotive fuel efficiency (e.g., 21 miles per gallon for city driving), cloud resources are typically quantized (e.g., as virtual machine instances) rather than being fluid (e.g., gallons of fuel); thus, resource efficiency is somewhat messier to objectively and quantitatively measure. Nevertheless, relative resource efficiency is more straightforward: requiring less resource input to serve a given workload with acceptable service quality is better than requiring more resource input.

Thus, sophisticated CSCs will strive for perfect capacity management with maximum resource efficiency to optimize or boost overall efficiency.

10.5 Lean Computing for Cloud Service Customers

Lean thinking methodically squeezes inefficiencies out of processes to deliver higher quality faster and with less waste. *Lean Computing for the Cloud* (Bauer, 2016) applies lean manufacturing and just-in-time principles to cloud computing to improve efficiency across the entire cloud service delivery chain. This section applies lean thinking to simultaneously derisk a CSC's application service innovation and reduce their operating expenses without compromising the service reliability, latency, quality, and availability delivered to their end users. Figure 10.8 shows the lean house visualization for CSCs. The goal of lean computing is to *sustainably achieve the shortest lead time, best quality and value, and highest customer delight at the lowest cost.* The twin pillars of lean computing are respecting partners across the cloud service delivery chain to eliminate waste and non-value-adding effort (Section 10.7) and continuous improvement to squeeze out waste and non-value-adding activities (Section 10.8). Recognizing waste and non-value-adding activities (Section 10.6) enables continuous improvement of lean performance. Key lean principles can be usefully applied to CSC operations, especially shifting from a push-oriented (aka supply- or capacity-driven) operation to a demand-driven operation, leveling the workload to improve utilization, and improving quality to reduce rework.

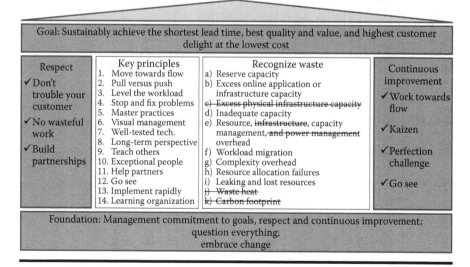

Figure 10.8 Lean "house" for cloud service customers. (From Bauer, *Lean Computing for the Cloud,* Piscataway, NJ: Wiley-IEEE Press, 2016.)

10.6 Recognizing Waste in the Cloud

Any time, resources, or effort expended beyond the bare minimum required to fulfill the customers' expectations is nominally waste; any waste that can be squeezed out of the service delivery chain should ultimately reduce lead time, service delivery latency, and/or costs for at least one organization in the value chain. Squeezing wasted time out of the value chain directly supports the lean goal to "sustainably achieve the shortest lead time," and eliminating wasted resources directly supports "highest customer delight at the lowest cost."

Before one can engineer wasted time, resource, or effort expenditures out of the value chain, one must first recognize those non-value-adding items. Bauer (2016) offered the following categories of waste in the context of cloud computing to consider:

- Reserve (or spare) capacity (Section 10.6.1)
- Excess online application capacity (Section 10.6.2)
- Excess online infrastructure capacity (Section 10.6.3)
- Excess physical infrastructure capacity (Section 10.6.4)
- Inadequate (online) application capacity (Section 10.6.5)
- Infrastructure overhead (Section 10.6.6)
- Capacity management overhead (Section 10.6.7)
- Resource overhead (Section 10.6.8)
- Power management overhead (Section 10.6.9)
- Workload migration (Section 10.6.10)
- Complexity overhead (Section 10.6.11)
- Resource allocation (and configuration) failure (Section 10.6.12)
- Leaking and lost resources (Section 10.6.13)
- Waste heat (Section 10.6.14)
- Carbon footprint (Section 10.6.15)

While some of these items are pure waste (e.g., *leaking and lost resources* [Section 10.6.13]), which organizations should strive to completely eliminate, many of these items are more nuanced that must be carefully balanced. An organization's risk appetite drives the balance of operational costs, complexities, and user service quality risks of extremely aggressive online application capacity management against the likely cost savings that is right for the organization. For example, online application *reserve (or spare) capacity* (Section 10.6.1) explicitly treats the risk of *inadequate (online) application* capacity (Section 10.6.5), so reducing the "waste" of *reserve (or spare)* capacity increases the risk of *inadequate (online) application* capacity. Risk appetite drives the optimal level of reserve capacity is for a particular organization that cost *reserve (or spare) capacity* against the business risk of *inadequate (online) application* capacity.

10.6.1 Reserve (or Spare) Capacity

As explained in Chapter 6, "Lean Application Capacity Management," reserve capacity is application capacity held online to minimize the user service quality impact of the following:

- Application service component failures, including those due to infrastructure failures
- Nonforecast application demand
- Lead time demand
- Episodes when cloud resource instances deliver less-than-rated throughput, such as due to demand from other infrastructure users

While some level of reserve application capacity is prudent, CSCs should carefully consider the level of reserve capacity that balances the organization's appetites for both operational efficiencies and cost savings (which argue for less reserve capacity) and desire to assure acceptable service quality despite inevitable unforeseen failures and events (which argues for more reserve capacity).

10.6.2 Excess Online Application Capacity

Application capacity beyond the application service provider's reserve requirement is deemed excess and thus is pure waste to be eliminated. Overengineering application performance is also a waste of capacity. Investments in application architecture, features, or resources that provide imperceptible or gratuitous improvements in users' quality of experience are likely to be wasteful.

10.6.3 Excess Online Infrastructure Capacity

Excess online infrastructure capacity is waste to the cloud infrastructure service provider, not the CSC.

10.6.4 Excess Physical Infrastructure Capacity

Excess physical infrastructure capacity is waste to the cloud infrastructure service provider, not the CSC.

10.6.5 Inadequate (Online) Application Capacity

Inadequate online application capacity disappoints customers and squanders end user (i.e., the CSCs' customers') goodwill. An inadequate online capacity event occurs when instantaneous user demand outstrips instantaneously available online application capacity. Inadequate online application capacity accrues costs (aka waste) to the CSC organization via the following:

- Loss of end-user goodwill due to unacceptable service quality during capacity emergency incidents
- Effort for emergency capacity management actions
- Effort for root cause analysis and corrective actions for capacity emergency events
- Penalty payments for service-level agreement (SLA) violations during the capacity emergency
- Negative publicity

Waste attributed to inadequate capacity explicitly covers the following:

- Loss of end-user and partner goodwill due to the capacity emergency
- Effort for emergency capacity management actions taken by parties in the value stream
- Effort for root cause analysis and corrective actions for capacity emergency events

CSCs must carefully balance the risk of carrying excess online application capacity (Section 10.6.2) and excess reserve (or spare) capacity (Section 10.6.1) against the risk of inadequate (online) application capacity (Section 10.6.5) to optimize their business results.

10.6.6 Infrastructure Overhead

Cloud infrastructure overhead is waste to the cloud infrastructure service provider, not the CSC.

10.6.7 Capacity Management Overhead

Application capacity management consumes resources for the following:

- Application demand forecasting
- Application capacity decision and planning
- Application demand/response measurement and modeling
- Simulation to support capacity decision and planning
- Application capacity fulfillment actions
- Infrastructure capacity decision and planning
- Infrastructure capacity fulfillment actions
- Testing infrastructure resources before they are delivered to applications
- Detecting faulty (e.g., dead-on-arrival [DOA]) infrastructure resources
- Testing new application capacity before it is brought into service

- Mitigating capacity fulfillment failures
- Infrastructure resources consumed bringing application capacity online
- Infrastructure resources consumed after decision to release online application capacity

Depending on the roles and responsibilities for application capacity life cycle management, the split of resource consumption and other overhead costs paid directly by the CSC versus indirectly through charges by their cloud service provider will vary. However, regardless of how the overhead is charged back to the CSC, some organization in the cloud service delivery chain is covering each of these costs.

Application capacity decision, planning, and fulfillment actions are essentially overhead because they do not serve application end users. These overhead activities have three primary costs:

1. Compute, memory, storage, and networking resources consumed to execute these overhead functions, which increases usage-based charges to the cloud infrastructure service provider
2. Time consumed executing these functions, which increases application capacity lead time
3. Human staff supervising both automatic and manual capacity management actions

CSCs must carefully balance their investment in complex capacity management overhead against waste from both excess online application capacity (Section 10.6.2) and inadequate (online) application capacity (Section 10.6.5).

10.6.8 Resource Overhead

Infrastructure service providers are likely to support a very small number of virtual resource types to reduce their complexity and maximize their operational efficiency. Any application inefficiency or wasted resources because the resources offered by the infrastructure service provider are not configured optimally for the application are covered in this category, such as the following:

- Resource instances that offer more compute, memory, storage, or networking throughput than the application component can productively consume. For instance, if an application requires only a medium-size capacity resource, but the cloud service provider offers only small and large sizes, then the CSC accepts the large size knowing that a portion of the resource capacity is beyond what they will ever need.
- Resource instances that have the wrong ratio of resource capacities and thereby limit application performance/throughput.

- Wasted physical capacity because the physical equipment is not optimal for the job. Hardware designed specifically to solve a particular task, like floating-point mathematical operations, can be more efficient than general-purpose hardware at that particular function but is often less efficient at other common functions. For example, a computationally intensive application might perform more efficiently on a graphics processor rather than on a general-purpose processor. The excess resources consumed when running a particular job on suboptimal hardware compared to resource consumption on some "optimal" hardware is considered overhead for the target infrastructure. Any software application running on general rather than bespoke hardware will likely be unable to fully and continuously utilize all hardware capacity, but careful planning can minimize overall waste by simultaneously reducing resource overhead, complexity, and other factors.

Note that resource overhead must be balanced against other costs, especially complexity overhead (Section 10.6.11). As Section 31.1, "Containerization as an Analog for Cloud Computing," will discuss, the shipping industry achieved massive improvements in operational efficiency by standardizing on a handful of sizes for intermodal shipping containers, in part by minimizing the complexity of supporting a larger variety of container sizes.

10.6.9 Power Management Overhead

Power management overhead is waste to the cloud infrastructure service provider, not the CSC.

10.6.10 Workload Migration

Moving an active resource instance (e.g., virtual machine) from one physical hardware element to another, or a user session from one application or component instance to another, wastes infrastructure resources (e.g., network bandwidth to move volatile data) and risks impacting user service quality.

Migrations of CSC resource instances are typically requested for one of the following reasons:

1. **Increase cloud service provider's operational efficiency** either so that more CSCs can be served with existing online resource capacity or to permit some capacity to be removed from service for maintenance actions or be powered off to reduce the cloud service provider's costs. Better initial placement of CSC resources might have eliminated the need for subsequent migration.
2. **Mitigate some infrastructure service quality problem**, such as relieving congestion of an overextended physical resource. Better initial CSC workload placement and better CSP operational policies might have eliminated

the infrastructure service quality problems that prompted a workload migration action.

3. **Decommission data center infrastructure equipment.** Compute, memory, storage, and networking hardware eventually wears out or fails for well-known physical reasons. Infrastructure service providers will decommission infrastructure equipment as it reaches the end of its useful service life, and they gracefully drain workload from that equipment before shutting it down. Note that infrastructure service providers may treat hardware elements as consumable items (think lightbulbs), which are discarded when they fail, rather than as repairable items, so when the quota of maximum allowable hardware failures is exceeded, then a rack, pod, or container of equipment may be decommissioned.

Workload migration actions attempt to mitigate some deeper problem, so one should minimize both the waste associated with each workload migration event as well as the underlying root cause that drives the complexity and bother of ordering a workload migration action.

10.6.11 Complexity Overhead

Generally speaking, simple is fast, and simple is reliable; complexity increases the number of "moving parts" that could break or fail, and thus which must be monitored, managed, and maintained. Excess complexity in cloud computing includes the following:

- Multiple supported service configuration options
- Too many supported technology and product options
- Too many supported virtual resource configuration options
- Too many different software versions
- Too many different software tools and processes
- Complex self-service provisioning and other tools
- Overly complex training required

10.6.12 Resource Allocation (and Configuration) Failure

Attempts to allocate resources to fulfill an application's capacity management change request occasionally fail, such as due to the following:

- Insufficient infrastructure resources online
- Outright infrastructure failure
- Incomplete resource fulfillment, such as not all requested resources being successfully delivered
- Undetected infrastructure failure causes allocated resource to be DOA
- Resource allocation being unacceptably slow

Every failed resource allocation or configuration action forces the CSC, or systems working on the CSC's behalf, to waste effort on the following:

1. Detecting the resource-related failure event
2. Cleaning up the resource-related failure event
3. Planning an alternate configuration change to address the original need that prompted the requested resource-related configuration change request
4. Executing—and hence accruing additional completion latency and complexity—of the alternate configuration change action

10.6.13 Leaking and Lost Resources

Rapid elasticity and scalability (Section 1.4.5) coupled with on-demand self-service (Section 1.4.4) will increase the frequency of capacity configuration change events. Inevitably, some resource release and configuration actions will be improperly requested and/or fail to complete properly. Resources that the CSC did not successfully release, and thus that they continue to pay for, represent pure waste to the CSC.

10.6.14 Waste Heat

Waste heat is waste to the cloud infrastructure service provider, not the CSC.

10.6.15 Carbon Footprint

Carbon footprint is waste to the cloud infrastructure service provider, not the CSC. However, the customers of a CSC's service offering may be concerned with the carbon footprint of products and services they consume, so those customers may expect CSCs to minimize the carbon footprint of their cloud service delivery chain.

10.7 Respect and Operational Efficiency

Figure 10.9 illustrates the key respect boundaries for CSC organizations to consider:

1. CSC to their cloud service users—Users expect application service to be available on demand with acceptable service quality at a fair price.
2. CSC to their infrastructure, management, and orchestration cloud service providers—CSCs expect to pay a fair price for cloud infrastructure, management, and orchestration service that is delivered right-first-time within promised times, and with infrastructure service quality that continuously achieves all service-level specifications.

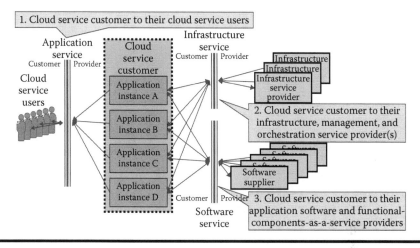

Figure 10.9 Key respect boundaries.

3. CSC to their software suppliers and functional-component-as-a-service—
CSCs expect to pay a fair price for the value delivered by application components and functional-component-as-a-service offerings.

Both parties across each of these respective boundaries should work to establish
a partnership with their counterparty so they can productively collaborate across
the value chain to sustainably achieve the shortest lead time, best quality and value,
and highest customer delight at the lowest cost. Lean is based on win–win partnership rather than gaming practical and operational aspects of the service delivery
chain to optimize one organization's performance, such as by pushing waste and/or
inefficiency up or down the value chain. Partners focus on eliminating waste and
inefficiencies rather than finding and exploiting gaps in their counterparty's pricing
or operational policies.

Providers should explicitly try to avoid troubling their customers with annoy-
ances like the following:

■ **Having to do wasteful work**—Entirely eliminate wasteful, low-value work
rather than pushing it up or down the value chain. For example, pushing
tedious tasks from the organization providing a service onto the consumers of
the service disrespects the consumers by burdening them with additional work.
■ **Receiving faulty products and services**—Broken products and low-quality
services disrupt a customer's operations and cause them to waste time and
effort to localize the faulty product or service, correct any of their work that
was compromised by the faulty product or service, and repair, replace, or
work around the faulty product or service.

- **Having to wait**—Customers never like to wait. While customers expect instant illumination when they flip on a light switch, they will generally tolerate slightly longer delays for on-demand self-service (Section 1.4.4) and rapid elasticity and scalability (Section 1.4.5) for cloud-based applications and resources. Customers increasingly find anything less than instant gratification annoying, and suppliers who deliver value faster to customers gain competitive advantage.
- **Having unrealistic expectations**—While suppliers do not control their customers' expectations, honest and timely communications can minimize the risk of expectations mismatch.
- **Being overloaded with superfluous or extraneous data**—Burying useful information under mountains of redundant or low-value data wastes precious time and attention of customers, staff, and suppliers.
- **Failing to share relevant information on a timely basis**—Working without all relevant information increases the risk of making poor decisions and avoidable errors, and nobody likes to be forced into that situation. Timely disclosure of all relevant information, such as known problem lists and best estimates of delivery schedules, demonstrates respect for customers.

A critical enabler of respect is to ensure that accountabilities and responsibilities are properly aligned because it is undesirable to hold organizations and individuals accountable for factors beyond their reasonable control. Likewise, costs and prices should be properly aligned so that all parties in the value chain are properly incentivized to reduce wasteful work rather than simply shifting it up or down the value chain.

10.8 Continuous Improvement of Operational Efficiency

As explained in Chapter 9, continual service improvement is an essential part of quality, risk, and service management; continuous improvement is also a pillar of lean computing. Section 10.8.1 reviews the four elements of the continuous improvement pillar. Section 10.8.2, "Plan–Do–Check–Act Alignment," considers how lean continuous improvement can be integrated with the IT service, quality, and risk management plan–do–check–act (PDCA) cycles to maximize the efficiency of continuous service improvement activities. Section 10.8.3, "Measure and Analyze Waste," considers what a CSC organization should measure to gather objective and quantitative data about potentially non-value-adding activities.

10.8.1 Continuous Improvement Pillar

The four elements of the lean continuous improvement pillar are as follows:

- **Work toward flow.** Traditional IT capacity management and release management processes were often executed quarterly, or perhaps even less frequently. As discussed in Chapter 6, "Lean Application Capacity Management," cloud computing (especially rapid elasticity and scalability [Section 1.4.5]) enables application capacity management to be demand driven with smaller and more frequent capacity change actions for online capacity to track closer to service demand. To thrive in a vastly more dynamic cloud environment, CSC organizations shift from a batch- and maintenance-window-oriented operating model to a flow model of nearly continuous, just-in-time configuration changes.
- **Kaizen,** meaning continuous improvement for its own sake, such as methodically reducing the CSC's technical debt. Eliminating waste, shortening cycle time, and improving the quality of experience for service users are useful goals even if the benefit cannot be rigorously quantified in monetary terms. While the cost saving, cycle time reduction, or service quality benefit of finding and fixing any single residual defect is hard to quantify, the organization's costs, cycle times, and customer satisfaction are adversely impacted by the residual defects that do escape to the field, so eliminating defects reduces both the risk of poor future performance and the costs associated with troubleshooting and repair.
- **Perfection challenge**. An organization's stretch goal should be perfection rather than merely being good enough. Perfect capacity management in Section 6.8 is an excellent example of the perfection challenge for application capacity management.
- **Go see.** An important aspect of lean manufacturing is to visit the shop floor to go see, ask why, and show respect to enable continuous improvement. While cloud-based application service is not produced on a shop floor that can usefully be visited and physically observed, there are reams of service measurement and other data that are produced, and the staff supporting operations, administration, maintenance, and provisioning, as well as end users, can be observed directly or indirectly via service measurements. Careful analysis of both direct and indirect observation data is a key enabler of continuous improvement. "Eating your own dog food" (aka dogfooding) and DevOps (see Section 11.3, "DevOps Thinking about Service Strategy") are common go-see strategies for ICT.

10.8.2 Plan–Do–Check–Act Alignment

Chapter 9, "Continual Service Improvement," explained that PDCA cycles were at the heart of IT service, quality, and risk management. To minimize non-value-adding activity, lean continual improvement efforts to reduce operating expense and shorten schedule intervals should appropriately align the organization's PDCA infrastructure and processes.

Figure 10.10 visualizes how lean continuous improvement fits into the standard PDCA framework:

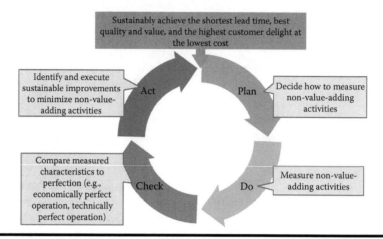

Figure 10.10   PDCA principles in lean computing for the cloud.

- **Plan**—recognize waste (see Section 10.6, "Recognizing Waste in the Cloud," and Section 10.8.3, "Measure and Analyze Waste") and develop appropriate objective and quantitative measurements of non-value-adding activities.
- **Do**—measure waste and non-value-adding activities
- **Check**—compare measured waste to theoretically perfect operation, such as perfect capacity management (Section 6.8)
- **Act**—execute improvements and repeat

10.8.3 Measure and Analyze Waste

Cloud and big data make it practical to collect large amounts of usage, performance, fault, alarm, configuration, and quality data, which can be analyzed offline to identify and quantify non-value-adding activities. Organizations should leverage these technologies to explicitly measure and analyze the following levels of waste:

- Reserve (or spare) capacity (Section 10.6.1)—Analyze actual data to determine if the organization's reserve capacity target is too high, too low, or just right for their risk appetite.
- Excess online application capacity (Section 10.6.2)—Perfect capacity management (Section 6.8) is a best practice for identifying excess online application capacity.
- Inadequate (online) application capacity (Section 10.6.5)—user service quality data should capture episodes of inadequate online capacity.
- Capacity management overhead (Section 10.6.7)—Audits can determine the resources devoted to capacity management overhead activities.

- Resource overhead (Section 10.6.8)—patterns of actual resource utilization can give insight into resource overheads.
- Workload migration (Section 10.6.10)—Event and other logs should indicate every workload migration event, so the frequency, service impact, and costs associated with workload migration can be characterized.
- Complexity overhead (Section 10.6.11)—Broader analysis of processes and patterns of resource consumption can identify complexities that might be simplified to reduce waste.
- Resource allocation (and configuration) failure (Section 10.6.12)—All resource allocation and configuration failure events are pure waste to be analyzed and corrected to drive continuous improvement.
- Leaking and lost resources (Section 10.6.13)—Audits of usage-based charges against configuration and capacity fulfillment changes can identify leaking and lost resource waste.

Note that collecting and storing performance, fault, alarm, configuration, and quality data itself consumes resources, so organizations should balance the costs of gathering and storing data against the likely waste reductions enabled via appropriate analysis of the data.

10.9 Holistic Operational Efficiency Improvements

The cloud enables operational efficiencies at two other levels:

- **End to end**—Beyond merely automating life cycle management of application service components, other elements in the value chain can also benefit from cloud. For example, service assurance probes can potentially leverage the benefit of the cloud just as service delivery components can; rather than having to physically install service probes near end users, one can use software-based service probes running on cloud infrastructure located in the appropriate geography. Lowering the cost of service monitoring enables the CSC to reduce their costs or do more service monitoring, or both.
- **Working smarter**—All of the performance, usage, fault, alarm, configuration, and other data gathered and analyzed for cloud-based applications give CSCs a deeper understanding of the true operating characteristics of their service. Sophisticated organizations will leverage these data to gain deeper insights into the true causes of wasted resources and wasted time in their operations so they can make better decisions about investments to improve operational efficiency. Making better decisions about where to focus scarce resources is the essence of working smarter.

Chapter 11

Service Strategy

The Information Technology Infrastructure Library (ITIL®) service strategy "defines the perspective, position, plans and patterns that a service provider needs to execute to meet an organization's business outcomes" (Axelos Limited, 2011). A successfully executed cloud service strategy enables the organization to deliver new service and value faster with improved efficiency and acceptable user service quality. When sufficient time and cost are squeezed out of the application design, transition, and operation life cycle, organizations can shift their business strategy to exploit more business opportunities, such as focusing service offerings on smaller and smaller market segments.

This chapter is organized as follows:

- Traditional service strategy (Section 11.1)
- Agile thinking about service strategy (Section 11.2)
- DevOps thinking about service strategy (Section 11.3)
- Transparency and cost alignment (Section 11.4)
- Quality expectations across time (Section 11.5)
- Risk thinking about service strategy (Section 11.6)
- Technology refresh considerations (Section 11.7)

11.1 Traditional Service Strategy

ITIL service strategy includes the following main processes:

- Strategy management for information technology (IT) services (Section 11.1.1)
- Service portfolio management (Section 11.1.2)
- Financial management for IT services (Section 11.1.3)

■ Demand management (Section 11.1.4)
■ Business relationship management (Section 11.1.5)

11.1.1 Strategy Management for IT Services

Strategy management frames "an organization's perspective, position, plans and patterns with regard to its services and the management of those services" (Axelos Limited, 2011). Strategy management includes three subprocesses:

■ **Strategic service assessment**—Essentially a market assessment. This activity is fundamentally the same regardless of whether the organization will deploy their application on the cloud or traditionally. However, as organizations are able to deliver new services and value faster with improved efficiency, they can consider smaller markets with smaller investments (due to improved efficiency), so they may refine and focus their service offerings to better serve the needs of those particular markets.
■ **Service strategy definition**—Essentially how the organization will address the assessed market. Reducing the organization's operating expenses (i.e., cost structure) and accelerating the pace of service innovation should enable the organization to address opportunities that traditionally were unprofitable or otherwise inaccessible, and somewhat different strategies may be appropriate for those new or smaller segments.
■ **Service strategy execution**—Lay out plans to execute against their strategy, including how the organization will achieve their expected opex reductions and accelerate the pace of service innovation with acceptable risk. This is likely to be impacted by Agile thinking about service strategy (Section 11.2), DevOps thinking about service strategy (Section 11.3) and risk thinking about service strategy (Section 11.6).

11.1.2 Service Portfolio Management

Service portfolio management "ensures that the service provider has the right mix of services to meet required business outcomes at an appropriate level of investment" (Axelos Limited, 2011). Service portfolio management includes three subprocesses:

■ **Define and analyze new or changed services**—Analyze additions or changes to the organization's portfolio of service offerings. An accelerated pace of service innovation coupled with reduced operating expenses (especially for unsuccessful/failed service offerings) enables the organization to define and try far more service offerings than were traditionally possible.
■ **Approve new or changed services**—Drive decisions for proposed additions or changes to the organization's portfolio of service offerings. Materially lower

up-front costs reduce the risk of unsuccessful services offerings, so organizations can streamline and accelerate "go" decisions to design and try new or changed services.

■ **Service portfolio review**—Periodically review the organization's portfolio of offered services and adjust as appropriate. Accelerated pace of service innovation with improved efficiency reduces the business risks to try and deploy services, which may lead to more services entering the organization's portfolio; thus, service portfolio review processes may need to be streamlined.

11.1.3 Financial Management for IT Services

Financial management concerns budgeting, accounting, and charging related to the organization's service offerings. Financial management is beyond the scope of this work.

11.1.4 Demand Management

Demand management is "responsible for understanding, anticipating and influencing customer demand for services" (Axelos Limited, 2011); ITIL defines no associated subprocesses. Rapid elasticity means that cloud service customers (CSCs) can focus primarily on demand generation and rely on Lean application capacity management (Chapter 6) to assure that sufficient application capacity is online to serve users with acceptable service quality.

11.1.5 Business Relationship Management

Business relationship management concerns maintaining the positive relationship with an organization's customers, specifically, managing a CSC's relationship with their application service users. Integrating the lean principle of respect (see Section 10.7) into business relationships with partners across the service value chain supports the lean goal to sustainably achieve the shortest lead time, best quality and value, and highest customer delight at the lowest cost.

11.2 Agile Thinking about Service Strategy

The popular Agile development model is well suited to the goal of increasing the pace of service innovation to deliver new services and value faster. Fortunately, the key characteristics of cloud computing, especially rapid elasticity and scalability (Section 1.4.5) and on-demand self-service (Section 1.4.4) efficiently enable key principles of Agile. Figure 11.1 highlights two Agile principles that map directly onto service management life cycle topics that were explicitly considered in Section II, "Analyzing the Cloud Service Customer's Problem."

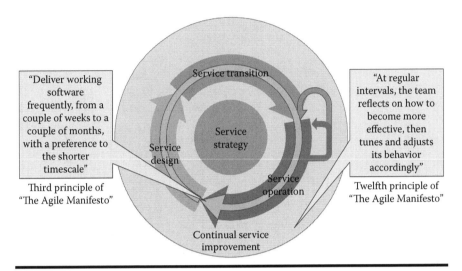

Figure 11.1   Selected Agile principles in the service management life cycle.

- Third Agile principle—"Deliver working software frequently, from a couple of weeks to a couple of months, with a preference to the shorter timescale" (Beck, Beedle, and others)—Agile teams accelerate the application service life cycle (Chapter 5) to transition new releases into service between every few weeks and every few months.
- Twelfth Agile principle—"At regular intervals, the team reflects on how to become more effective, then tunes and adjusts its behavior accordingly" (Beck, Beedle, and others)—This principle is well aligned with continual service improvement (Chapter 9) and continuous improvement of operational efficiency (Section 10.8).

Figure 11.2 visualizes how four Agile principles map directly onto the lean computing "house" discussed in Chapter 10.

- First Agile principle—"Our highest priority is to satisfy the customer through early and continuous delivery of valuable software" (Beck, Beedle, and others)—The first Agile principle is well aligned with the lean computing goal to sustainably achieve the shortest lead time, best quality and value, and highest customer delight at the lowest cost.
- Eighth Agile principle—"Agile processes promote sustainable development. The sponsors, developers, and users should be able to maintain a constant pace indefinitely" (Beck, Beedle, and others)—Respect for customers, employees, and partners drives a lean thinking to sustainable solutions.

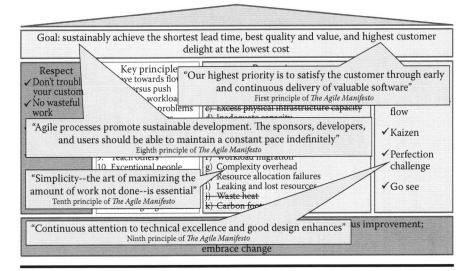

Figure 11.2   Selected Agile principles in the lean house for cloud service customers.

- Ninth Agile principle—"Continuous attention to technical excellence and good design enhances agility." (Beck, Beedle, and others)—This is the perfection challenge of the continuous improvement pillar.
- Tenth Agile principle—"Simplicity—the art of maximizing the amount of work not done—is essential" (Beck, Beedle, and others)—Eliminating complexity overhead and non-value-adding activities is a fundamental tenet of lean thinking.

The remaining principles from the *Agile Manifesto* (Beck, Beedle, and others) are consistent with earlier discussions in Section II, "Analyzing the Cloud Service Customer's Problem," or are beyond the scope of this work.

- Second Agile principle—"Welcome changing requirements, even late in development. Agile processes harness change for the customer's competitive advantage."
- Fourth Agile principle—"Business people and developers must work together daily throughout the project."
- Fifth Agile principle—"Build projects around motivated individuals. Give them the environment and support they need, and trust them to get the job done."
- Sixth Agile principle—"The most efficient and effective method of conveying information to and within a development team is face-to-face conversation."
- Seventh Agile principle—"Working software is the primary measure of progress."
- Eleventh Agile principle—"The best architectures, requirements, and designs emerge from self-organizing teams."

11.3 DevOps Thinking about Service Strategy

As the industry lacks a standard definition of DevOps, we'll use Wikipedia's definition:

> DevOps (a clipped compound of development and operations) is a culture, movement or practice that emphasizes the collaboration and communication of both software developers and other information-technology (IT) professionals while automating the process of software delivery and infrastructure changes. It aims at establishing a culture and environment where building, testing, and releasing software can happen rapidly, frequently, and more reliably.*

Figure 11.3 visualizes the key DevOps linkage between the application development life cycle and the service operations life cycle: tested software produced by the development life cycle is transitioned directly into service operations, and feedback from service operation flows directly into planning and coding of the next software release. This feedback, plan and code, build, test, update and release, service transition, and service operation cycle accelerates so that new software releases are delivered in weeks, days, or even hours—nominally *continuous* delivery—rather than taking months. Making smaller and more frequent software changes, which are then (*continuously*) integrated and tested makes it easier to localize defects, which can then be corrected quickly to improve development efficiency.

Deploying incrementally improved service to users (nominally) continuously enables organizations to rapidly tweak the features and functionality of their application to better serve their target market, or quickly abandon an application that is found to be less popular than expected. Rapid elasticity and scalability (Section 1.4.5) along with a rich ecosystem of off-the-shelf service components and automated life cycle management make DevOps easier to deploy for cloud-based applications than for traditionally deployed applications.

11.4 Transparency and Cost Alignment

Usage-based pricing of cloud resources coupled with on-demand self-service (Section 1.4.4) and rapid elasticity and scalability (Section 1.4.5) gives CSCs clarity over where their resource costs are incurred, so they can make better business decisions to improve operational performance. In particular, organizations can better align resource costs for service design, transition, and operation with specific

---

* Retrieved from https://en.wikipedia.org/wiki/DevOps, 07/21/16.

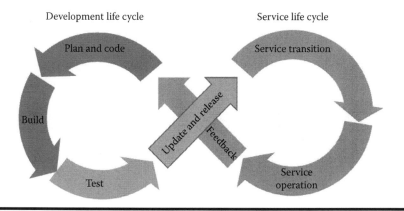

Figure 11.3   Simplified DevOps visualization.

service offerings. Deeper understanding and alignment of costs for specific service offerings enable business leaders to make more informed investment decisions to maximize likely returns to the business.

11.5 Quality Expectations across Time

Sophisticated organizations will explicitly decide if their objectives for service quality should vary across time and space. Figure 11.4 illustrates two common models for service quality targets. The *x*-axis gives the number of service users, which will vary across time. The *y*-axis gives the organization's service quality target, such

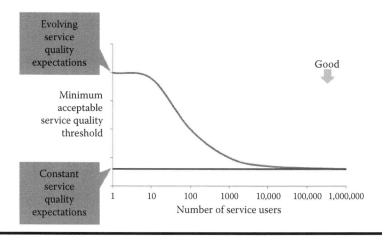

Figure 11.4   Constant and evolving quality expectations.

as the maximum acceptable rate of defective service operations or the maximum acceptable response time. Two basic models are illustrated.

- *Evolving* service quality expectations—In a rapid-innovation and fail-fast model, organizations are more concerned with trying a service with target users so they can evolve, tweak, and refine their service into a successful offering. Organizations are often more interested in getting a roughly right version to early adopters than they are in perfecting the quality of what might be an unsuccessful service offering. As the service offering evolves toward success and the number of service users grows, the organization raises their quality expectations to assure acceptance by a broader range of users.
- *Constant* service quality expectations—Organizations with strong brands often set a constant service quality expectation to support the brand's reputation for quality to assure that even the very first service user enjoys the same quality with the new service that they do with the organization's other, more mature service offerings.

If and how service quality expectations vary across time and space is an important strategic question for a CSC organization to address.

11.6 Risk Thinking about Service Strategy

While Section IV, "Cloud Service Quality Risk Assessment and Management," considers risk management in depth, appropriately integrating risk-based thinking into the organization's service strategy assures that decision makers have sufficient information to maximize the likelihood that the target cloud-based application will deliver the business benefits that the organization expects without unacceptable service quality for users. Thus, risk management should be fundamentally tied to an organization's service strategy. Strategic risk-based thinking is considered in the following sections:

- ISO 9001 risk-based thinking (Section 11.6.1)
- Risk IT thinking (Section 11.6.2)
- Gut check on risk appetite (Section 11.6.3)

11.6.1 ISO 9001 Risk-Based Thinking

The 2015 version of the world's preeminent quality document, ISO 9001, *Quality Management System Requirements*, added the following to clause 0.1, "General":

> Risk-based thinking enables an organization to determine the factors that could cause its processes and its quality management system to deviate from the planned results, to put in place preventive controls to

minimize negative effects and to make maximum use of opportunities as they arise. (ISO, 2015-09-15)

Clause 0.3.3, "Risk-Based Thinking," includes the following:

To conform to the requirements of this International Standard, an organization needs to plan and implement actions to address risks and opportunities. Addressing both risks and opportunities establishes a basis for increasing the effectiveness of the quality management system, achieving improved results and preventing negative effects.

Appropriately linking CSC service strategy with the organization's quality management processes can streamline plan–do–check–act continual improvement efforts and drive timely preventive actions to preclude defects from escaping the service design phase into the service transition and service operation phases, where they can drive up the organization's costs and adversely impact user service quality.

11.6.2 Risk IT Thinking

ISACA's Risk IT (ISACA, 2009) offers six principles for considering IT-related risks:

- **Connect to business objectives**—Enterprises invest in cloud-based applications in pursuit of business benefits like reduced operating expenses and accelerated pace of service innovation. The organization's service strategy should be clearly linked to the organization's desired business outcome.
- **Align management of IT-related business risk with overall enterprise risk management risk**—Cloud-related risks (e.g., Section III, "Cloud Service Quality Risk Inventory") should be considered alongside other business opportunities and hazards (aka risks). Methodical consideration of risks and all treatment options enables better decisions. For example, making risk treatment decisions to avoid the risk (Section 3.3.7) by delaying a potential service offering until, say, a technology matures is best considered in the larger context of enterprise risk management. Note that shifting to a usage-based, pay-as-you-go model for compute, memory, storage, networking, and other cloud-based resources improves a CSC's alignment of costs with revenue, which reduces uncertainty regarding capital investment decisions.
- **Balance the costs and benefits of managing IT-related risks**—Risks facing the organization should be prioritized and treated based on the organization's risk appetite and risk tolerances to optimally manage the risks facing the organization.
- **Promote fair and open communication about IT-related risks**—Open, honest, transparent, and timely discussions of risks, likelihoods, consequences, and treatment options enables business leaders to make better decisions.

- **Establish the right tone from the top and enforce personal accountability for operating within acceptable and well-defined tolerance levels**—Clear decisions about risk appetites, risk tolerance, and risk treatment decisions enable efficient and effective actions. Clear assignment of accountabilities for risk ownership, treatment, monitoring, and management assures better outcomes.
- **Risk management is a continuous process and part of daily activities**— Risks arise, evolve, and change over time, such as when new products and services are offered by suppliers and competitors, or as more information is gathered about risks, or for myriad other reasons. Thus, organizations should regularly reassess the landscape of risks and opportunities facing the CSC and take appropriate actions to assure that the organization's level of risk remains tolerable.

These risk-thinking principles should be considered when a CSC organization constructs their service strategy.

11.6.3 Gut Check on Risk Appetite

Organizations, services, customers, and market contexts vary widely, so different organizations inevitably have different risk appetites. Figure 11.5 visualizes key risk appetites for a hypothetical service offering as a function of the number of service users. The relative magnitudes of these three appetites may drive organizations to make different decisions about appropriate risk treatments and controls. Consider the implications of each hypothetical appetite curve:

- Appetite for **rapid service innovation**—Rapid service innovation, especially fast time to market, is critical for success of application service offerings, so those CSC organizations will have a high appetite for rapid service innovation

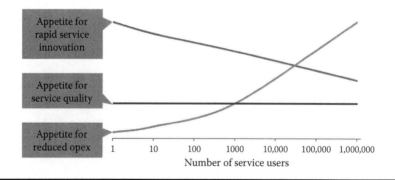

Figure 11.5 Hypothetical risk appetites by service popularity.

and short time to market. The organization aggressively innovates to get their first users, and their appetite for rapid service innovation declines relative to other appetites as their user base grows.

■ Appetite for **reduced opex**—Successful businesses always consider their costs, but when a service is rapidly innovating for a small to modest user population (e.g., in a trial or limited deployment), reducing opex is far less important than continuing to innovate to grow the business (or deciding to abandon the service). Ultimately, organizations often treat a successful service offering as a cash cow by focusing more on reducing operating expenses for the service (e.g., by reducing investment in new features and functionality) to maximize bottom-line returns to the business.

■ Appetite for **service quality**—To manage reputational risks, organizations offering branded services may insist that user service quality expectations are the same regardless of whether there is a single user or a million users (as shown in Figure 11.5). In other cases, organizations may operate (possibly unbranded) services on a limited, free, trial, or pilot basis with lower service quality expectations, and then increase service quality expectations for their branded, generally available offerings to larger numbers of users. Note that mass market adopters often have less tolerance for poor service quality than early adopters, who might be poorly served by current market offerings and thus are willing to tolerate worse service quality to enjoy a service better suited to their particular needs.

Readers should consider how their own organization's appetites for rapid service innovation, reduced opex, and service quality change (or not) across time, across services and markets, and across other dimensions. Appropriately characterizing and linking the organization's risk appetites to the service strategy enables better focus, communication, and decision making.

11.7 Technology Refresh Considerations

Many organizations have legacy applications that are periodically refreshed and rehosted onto new technology platforms when the previous platform reaches end of life, perhaps every 3 to 7 years. When organizations refresh their current traditionally deployed applications, many will decide to deploy their updated application onto the cloud. As Section II, "Analyzing the Cloud Service Customer's Problem," has discussed in general, and this chapter has considered in particular, refreshing an organization's processes along with the underlying compute, memory, storage, and networking technology is essential to achieving the full potential to deliver new services and value faster with improved operational efficiency.

CLOUD SERVICE QUALITY RISK INVENTORY

III

User service quality of cloud-based applications is vulnerable to the 14 risk vectors shown in Figure III.1 and the risk types summarized in Table III.1. Chapter 12, "Factoring Cloud Service Quality Risks," derives the 14 risk vectors of Figure III.1, and subsequent chapters consider each risk vector and the associated risk types.

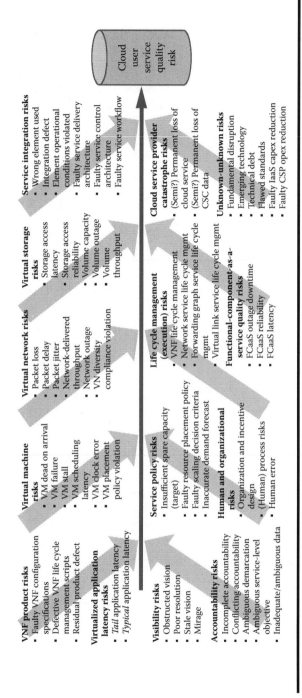

VNF product risks
- Faulty VNF configuration specifications
- Defective VNF life cycle management scripts
- Residual product defect

Virtualized application latency risks
- *Tail* application latency
- *Typical* application latency

Virtual machine risks
- VM dead on arrival
- VM failure
- VM stall
- VM scheduling latency
- VM clock error
- VM placement policy violation

Virtual network risks
- Packet loss
- Packet delay
- Packet jitter
- Network-delivered throughput
- Network outage
- VN diversity compliance violation

Virtual storage risks
- Storage access latency
- Storage access reliability
- Volume capacity
- Volume outage
- Volume throughput

Service integration risks
- Wrong element used
- Integration defect
- Element operational conditions violated
- Faulty service delivery architecture
- Faulty service control architecture
- Faulty service workflow

Visibility risks
- Obstructed vision
- Poor resolution
- Stale vision
- Mirage

Accountability risks
- Incomplete accountability
- Conflicting accountability
- Ambiguous demarcation
- Ambiguous service-level objective
- Inadequate/ambiguous data

Service policy risks
- Insufficient spare capacity (target)
- Faulty resource placement policy
- Faulty scaling decision criteria
- Inaccurate demand forecast

Human and organizational risks
- Organization and incentive design
- (Human) process risks
- Human error

Life cycle management (execution) risks
- VNF life cycle management
- Network service life cycle mgmt
- Forwarding graph service life cycle mgmt
- Virtual link service life cycle mgmt

Functional-component-as-a-service quality risks
- FCaaS outage downtime
- FCaaS reliability
- FCaaS latency

Cloud service provider catastrophe risks
- (Semi?) Permanent loss of cloud service
- (Semi?) Permanent loss of CSC data

Unknown–unknown risks
- Fundamental disruption
- Emerging technology
- Technical debt
- Flawed standards
- Faulty IaaS capex reduction
- Faulty CSP opex reduction

Cloud user service quality risk

Figure III.1 User service quality risks confronting cloud service customers. CSC, cloud service customer; CSP, cloud service provider; FCaaS, functional-component-as-a-service; IaaS, infrastructure-as-a-service; VM, virtual machine; VN, virtual network; VNF, virtualized network function.

Table III.1   Inventory of Cloud User Service Risks

Item	Reference	Page
Virtualized Network Function (VNF) Product Risks	**Chapter 13**	**249**
Faulty VNF configuration specification risk	Table 13.1	251
Residual defect in VNF life cycle management script risk	Table 13.2	252
Residual product defect risk	Table 13.3	252
Virtual Machine (VM) Risks	**Chapter 14**	**257**
VM dead-on-arrival (DOA) risk	Table 14.1	259
VM premature release (failure) risk	Table 14.2	260
VM stall risk	Table 14.3	261
VM scheduling latency risk	Table 14.4	262
VM clock error risk	Table 14.5	263
VM placement policy violation risk	Table 14.6	264
Virtual Networking (VN) Risks	**Chapter 15**	**269**
Packet loss risk	Table 15.1	271
Packet delay risk	Table 15.2	271
Packet jitter (delay variation) risk	Table 15.3	272
Network-delivered throughput risk	Table 15.4	272
Network outage risk	Table 15.5	273
VN diversity compliance violation risk	Table 15.6	273
Virtual Storage Risks	**Chapter 16**	**277**
Storage access reliability risk	Table 16.1	279
Storage access latency risk	Table 16.2	279
Volume capacity risk	Table 16.3	280
Volume outage risk	Table 16.4	280
Volume throughput risk	Table 16.5	281

(Continued)

Table III.1 (Continued)   Inventory of Cloud User Service Risks

Item	Reference	Page
Virtualized Application Latency Risks	**Chapter 17**	**283**
Tail application latency risk	Table 17.1	284
Typical application latency risk	Table 17.2	285
Service Integration Risks	**Chapter 18**	**289**
Wrong-element-used risk	Table 18.1	292
System/service integration defect	Table 18.2	292
Element operational conditions violated	Table 18.3	293
Faulty service delivery architecture risk	Table 18.4	293
Faulty service control architecture risk	Table 18.5	294
Faulty service workflow risk	Table 18.6	294
Visibility Risks	**Chapter 19**	**295**
Obstructed vision risk	Table 19.1	297
Blurred vision risk	Table 19.2	298
Stale vision risk	Table 19.3	299
Mirage risk	Table 19.4	300
Service Policy Risks	**Chapter 20**	**303**
Insufficient spare capacity (target) risk	Table 20.1	306
Faulty resource placement policy risk	Table 20.2	307
Faulty scaling decision criteria risk	Table 20.3	307
Inaccurate demand forecast risk	Table 20.4	308
Accountability Risks	**Chapter 21**	**309**
Incomplete accountability risk	Table 21.1	310
Conflicting accountability risk	Table 21.2	311
Ambiguous demarcation risk	Table 21.3	312
Ambiguous service-level objective risk	Table 21.4	313
Inadequate/ambiguous data risk	Table 21.5	313

(Continued)

Table III.1 (Continued)   Inventory of Cloud User Service Risks

Item	Reference	Page
Human and Organizational Risks	**Chapter 22**	**317**
Organization and incentive design risk	Table 22.2	320
Human process risk	Table 22.3	321
Human error risk	Table 22.4	321
Life Cycle Management (Execution) Risks	**Chapter 23**	**325**
VNF life cycle management (execution) risks	Table 23.2	330
Network service life cycle management (execution) risks	Table 23.3	331
Forwarding graph service life cycle management (execution) risks	Table 23.4	332
Virtual link service life cycle management (execution) risks	Table 23.5	333
Functional-Component-as-a-Service Quality Risks	**Chapter 24**	**335**
Functional-component-as-a-service outage downtime risk	Table 24.2	336
Functional-component-as-a-service reliability risk	Table 24.3	336
Functional-component-as-a-service latency risk	Table 24.4	338
Cloud Service Provider (CSP) Catastrophe Risks	**Chapter 25**	**339**
(Semi?) permanent loss of cloud service risk	Table 25.1	340
(Semi?) permanent loss of cloud service customer (CSC) data risk	Table 25.2	340
Unknown-Unknown Risks	**Chapter 26**	**343**
Fundamental business/operations disruption risk	Table 26.1	345
Emerging technology risk	Table 26.2	346
Technical debt risk	Table 26.3	346
Flawed standards risk	Table 26.4	347
Faulty infrastructure capex reduction risk	Table 26.5	347
Faulty CSP opex reduction risk	Table 26.6	348

Chapter 12

Factoring Cloud Service Quality Risks

Cloud user service quality risks potentially impact service reliability, latency, availability, or overall quality delivered to cloud service users. Section 12.2, "Differences between Virtualized Network Function and Physical Network Function Deployments," Section 12.3, "European Telecommunications Standards Institute Network Functions Virtualization Quality Accountability Framework," and Section 12.4, "Rumsfeld Risks," derive the 14 risk vectors shown in Figure III.1 that are considered in the subsequent chapters of Section III, "Cloud Service Quality Risk Inventory." Before considering how to factor risk vectors, we shall consider how to characterize risks (Section 12.1).

12.1 Risk Capture

Figure 12.1 shows the basic risk capture model used in this work: some *risk cause* is activated to produce a *risk condition*, which produces *service consequences*, which results in *service quality impact*.

It is useful to factor risk causes into the following:

- **Proximal** risk causes are the immediate cause of a risk event.
- **Distal** factors are the deeper and ultimate causes of a risk event, sometimes called root causes.

Figure 12.2 visualizes a sample linkage between a risk event and proximal and distal causes for the risk of degraded audio quality of a voice-over-internet protocol (IP)

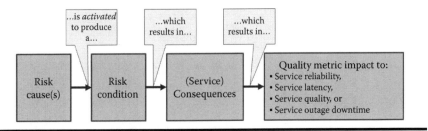

Figure 12.1 Risk identification model.

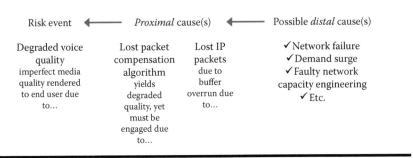

Figure 12.2 Sample proximal and distal causes.

service. The lost packet compensation algorithm on the user's device can produce degraded quality when it tries to conceal episodes of packet loss. Episodes of packet loss can be caused because buffers in some intermediate system are full, so packets are discarded. Buffers in an intermediate system might be driven to overflow because of a network link or intermediate system failure, because of a surge in network demand, because of faulty network capacity engineering, or for other reasons.

Figure 12.3 visualizes the linkage between key risk concepts used by this analysis:

- **Risk vectors**—Section 12.3, "European Telecommunications Standards Institute Network Functions Virtualization Quality Accountability Framework," and Section 12.4, "Rumsfeld Risks," factor user service quality risk into 14 vectors, which are covered in Chapters 13 thru 26.
- **Risk types**—Each risk vector contains two or more specific risk types, which are methodically analyzed.
- **Risk causes**—Each risk type has likely proximal (immediate) and distal (deeper, ultimate) causes.
- **Risk controls**—Risk controls are deployed to minimize the likelihood of a risk event occurring.
- **Risk consequences**—When a risk event occurs, its effects can cascade into consequences such as unacceptable user service quality.

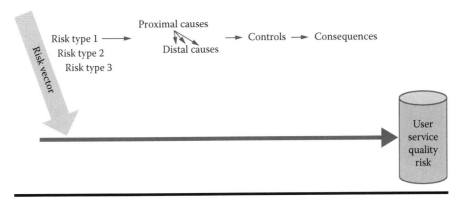

Figure 12.3   Key risk concepts.

Risks will be captured with the following information:

1. Risk **name**—typically based on the root cause of the risk
2. Primary risk **cause(s)**—describes the root (i.e., distal or ultimate) causes of the risk
3. Risk **condition**—describes the impaired condition produced when the risk cause is activated
4. Risk **consequence**—how the risk condition is likely to impact user-facing application service
5. Risk **impact**—identifies how user service reliability, service latency, service quality, and/or service outage downtime is likely to be impacted

Identified risks are summarized in tabular form in Table 12.1.

Table 12.1   Risk Summary Statement

Attribute	Value
Risk **name**	Typically the name of the document section detailing the risk
Risk **cause(s)**	Describes the fundamental root cause(s) of the risk
Risk **condition**	Explains the technical mechanism(s) of the fundamental root cause(s)
Risk (service) **consequence**	Explains how the uncontrolled risk condition is likely to impact user-facing application service
Risk **impact**	Describes how user service reliability, latency, quality, or downtime is likely to be impacted

12.2 Differences between Virtualized Network Function and Physical Network Function Deployments

There are seven fundamental differences between virtualized network function (VNF) and physical network function (PNF) deployments, each of which raises several risks:

1. **Software is decoupled from hardware**—raises the following risks:
   a. Service integration risks (Chapter 18)
   b. Visibility risks (Chapter 19)
   c. Accountability risks (Chapter 21)
   d. Service policy risks (Chapter 20)
2. **Shared compute, memory, storage, and networking infrastructure**—raises the following risks:
   a. Virtual machine risks (Chapter 14)
   b. Virtual networking risks (Chapter 15)
   c. Virtual storage risks (Chapter 16)
   d. Virtualized application latency risks (Chapter 17)
3. **Automated resource and application life cycle management**—raises the following risks:
   a. Service integration risks (Chapter 18)
   b. Visibility risks (Chapter 19)
   c. Accountability risks (Chapter 21)
   d. Service policy risks (Chapter 20)
   e. Life cycle management (execution) risks (Chapter 23)
4. **Automated network service life cycle management**—raises the following risks:
   a. Service integration risks (Chapter 18)
   b. Visibility risks (Chapter 19)
   c. Accountability risks (Chapter 21)
   d. Service policy risks (Chapter 20)
   e. Life cycle management (execution) risks (Chapter 23)
5. **Dynamic operations**—raises the following risks:
   a. Visibility risks (Chapter 19)
   b. Service policy risks (Chapter 20)
6. **Increasingly complex multivendor environment**—raises the following risks:
   a. Service integration risks (Chapter 18)
   b. Visibility risks (Chapter 19)
   c. Accountability risks (Chapter 21)
   d. Service policy risks (Chapter 20)

7. **"Virtualized" demark or reference points**—raises the following risks:
   a. Visibility risks (Chapter 19)
   b. Accountability risks (Chapter 21)

12.3 European Telecommunications Standards Institute Network Functions Virtualization Quality Accountability Framework Risks

Figure 12.4 calls out the highest-level role-based service quality risks per the European Telecommunications Standards Institute (ETSI) network functions virtualization (NFV) quality accountability framework (QAF). Let us consider each party's risk factors (from left to right).

■ **Cloud service user risks**—Associated with end users and their devices, including the following:
   – User/human error
   – Device failure or configuration error
   – Battery exhaustion

   As these risks are not materially different for VNF-based services than they are for PNF-based services, they are not considered in this analysis.

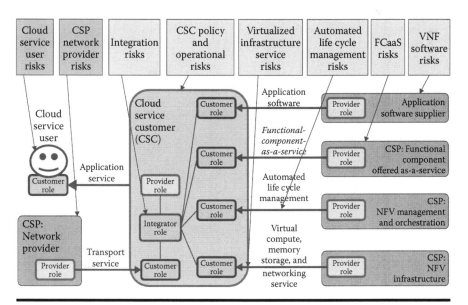

Figure 12.4   Risk attributability model of NFV quality accountability framework.

- **Cloud service provider (CSP) network provider risks**—Associated with access and wide area transport service providers, including the following:
  - Wireless coverage holes and quality impairments
  - Wireline and/or wireless access network quality impairments
  - Handoff risks when a user's network service transitions between technologies (e.g., LTE to/from Wi-Fi) or between network edge devices (e.g., base stations, access points)
  - Network outages
  - Network congestion
  - Software-defined networking (SDN)—wide area SDN risks not considered in this work

  When all application service components and included functional-component-as-a-service instances are located in a single cloud data center, the network service provider risks for cloud-based application deployment are similar to the risks for traditional application deployment. When application service components and/or included functional-component-as-a-service instances are distributed across multiple cloud data centers that communicate via network provider services, then the additional network-related service quality risks must be considered. Instead of considering inter–data center networking risks separately from intra–data center networking, the virtual networking risks (Chapter 15) category will cover relevant inter–data center risks; after all, inter–data center networking risks appear fundamentally the same to application service components as intra–data center networking impairments.
- **Integration risks**—Integrating VNF software onto cloud infrastructure, management, and orchestration platforms with other platform components and transport services to enable high-quality user services raises several primary risk factors:
  - Service integration risks (Chapter 18)
  - Visibility risks (Chapter 19)
  - Service policy risks (Chapter 20)
  - Virtualized application latency risks (Chapter 17)
- **Cloud service customer (CSC) policy and operational risks**—Operating a cloud-based network service raises several primary risk factors:
  - Accountability risks (Chapter 21)
  - Service policy risks (Chapter 20)
  - Human and organizational risks (Chapter 22)
  - CSP catastrophe risks (Chapter 25)
- **Virtualized infrastructure cloud service risks**—Operating of cloud infrastructure as-a-service carries several primary risk factors:
  - Virtual machine risks (Chapter 14)
  - Virtual networking risks (Chapter 15)
  - Virtual storage risks (Chapter 16)
  - CSP catastrophe risks (Chapter 25)

- **Automated life cycle management risks**—Cloud relies on automated life cycle management actions to dynamically respond to changing patterns of user demand, failures, and other routine events. While automation of life cycle management actions reduces the per-configuration-change risk of human/procedural error, the frequency of configuration change events is likely to be vastly higher than with traditional application deployments. Primary risk factors that might compromise this goal include the following:
  - Service integration risks (Chapter 18)
  - Visibility risks (Chapter 19)
  - Service policy risks (Chapter 20)
  - Life cycle management (execution) risks (Chapter 23)
- **Functional component offered as-a-service risks**—Service quality delivered to CSC users may rely on one or more functional components offered as-a-service like database-as-a-service or load-balancing-as-a-service. The primary risks are considered in the following:
  - Functional-component-as-a-service quality risks (Chapter 24)
- **VNF software risks**—Application service quality delivered by a VNF instance to a CSC provider in the context of an application service carries several primary risk factors:
  - VNF product risks (Chapter 13)

12.4 Rumsfeld Risks

On February 2, 2002, Donald Rumsfeld made his famous risk management statement:

> As we know, there are known knowns, there are things we know we know.
>
> We also know there are known unknowns. That is to say we know there are some things we do not know.
>
> But there are also unknown unknowns, the ones we don't know we don't know.*

Unknown-Unknown Risks are considered in Chapter 26.

---

* Retrieved from http://www.rsdsolutions.com/donald-rumsfeld-risk-guru, 11/18/15.

Chapter 13

Virtualized Network Function Product Risks

ISO/IEC/IEEE 29119-1 defines *product risk* as the "risk that a product may be defective in some specific aspect of its function, quality or structure" (ISO/IEC/IEEE, 2013-09-01). As shown in Figure 13.1, the product risks to user service quality facing virtualized network functions (VNFs) fall into three broad categories:

- Faulty VNF configuration specification risk (Table 13.1)
- Residual defect in VNF life cycle management script risk (Table 13.2)
- Residual product defect risk (Table 13.3)

VNF product risks are considered in the following sections:

- Captured risks (Section 13.1)
- Baseline risk context (Section 13.2)
- Risk causes (Section 13.3)
- Risk controls (Section 13.4)
- Risk treatments (Section 13.5)

13.1 Captured Risks

Network element outages and problems have traditionally been factored into three buckets:

- **Hardware**—Traditional hardware risks are replaced by virtual machine risks (Chapter 14), virtual networking risks (Chapter 15), and virtual storage risks (Chapter 16) in the cloud.

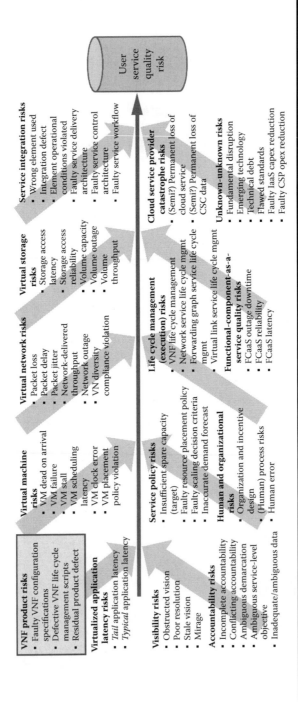

Figure 13.1 Context of VNF product risks. CSP, cloud service provider; FCaaS, functional-component-as-a-service; IaaS, infrastructure-as-a-service; VM, virtual machine; VN, virtual network.

Table 13.1   Faulty VNF Configuration Specification Risk

Attribute	*Value*
Risk **name**	Faulty VNF configuration specification risk.
Risk **root cause**	Operational envelope and/or parameters for target element are incompletely or incorrectly documented in machine- or human-readable configuration specifications.
Risk **condition**	Human integrator, automated management, and orchestration systems and/or operations staff unknowingly drives target element outside of its engineered operational envelope.
Risk (service) **consequence**	Working outside of its engineered operational envelope, the target element may fail to serve traffic with acceptable service quality. For example, • Workload beyond the target element's engineered envelope may be rejected via congestion controls. • Workload with protocol settings outside of the target element's configured envelope may be rejected as unsupported. Note that the risk of the target element crashing when driven outside of its operational envelope is deemed a residual product defect risk (Table 13.3).
Risk **impact**	Primary risk impacts: • Service quality and service reliability impact when some legitimate, syntactically and semantically correct workload may be rejected. • Service latency impact when requests are delayed due to increased queuing etc. • Service availability if fault detection, localization, and automatic service recovery mechanisms fail to operate properly.

■ **Software**—Product software risks remain, and they are captured as residual product defect risk (Table 13.3).
■ **Procedural**—Procedural risks are profoundly transformed with network functions virtualization (NFV) because of automated life cycle management. To enable automated life cycle management, VNF suppliers deliver scripts and configuration information, which introduce faulty VNF configuration specification risk (Table 13.1) and residual defect in VNF life cycle management script risk (Table 13.2). Those scripts are integrated with the cloud

Table 13.2 Residual Defect in VNF Life Cycle Management Script Risk

Attribute	Value
Risk **name**	Residual defect in VNF life cycle management script risk.
Risk **root cause**	Residual defect in design, structure, syntax, semantics, or other aspect of VNF's life cycle management script escapes from the supplier's development and testing processes.
Risk **condition**	Residual defect is activated to become an error, which causes the requested VNF life cycle management action to not complete perfectly within the expected time.
Risk (service) **consequence**	Resulting condition of the VNF impacts user service.
Risk **impact**	Primary risk impacts: • Service reliability—Impacted operations fail. • Service outage—Primary functionality of target element is impacted, or service capacity of target element is lost. Secondary risk impacts: • Service latency—Impacted operations are delayed (e.g., due to expiration of timeout). • Service quality—Impacted operations are completed with diminished functionality.

Table 13.3 Residual Product Defect Risk

Attribute	Value
Risk **name**	Residual product defect risk.
Risk **root cause**	Residual defect in supplier's product design, software, documentation, or other artifacts escapes from the supplier's development and testing processes.
Risk **condition**	Residual defect is activated in production service to become an error.
Risk (service) **consequence**	Error condition escalates into some user-impacting service failure.
Risk **impact**	Primary risk impacts: • Service reliability—Impacted operations fail. • Service outage—Primary functionality of target element is impacted, or service capacity of target element is lost.

infrastructure, management, and orchestration (considered as service integration risks in Chapter 18) and are vulnerable to life cycle management (execution) risks (Chapter 23).

13.2 Baseline Risk Context

VNF suppliers deliver

1. VNF software
2. VNF life cycle management scripts
3. VNF configuration specifications
4. Human-readable VNF documentation, procedures, and training
5. Technical support services

VNF software is expected to properly install with cloud infrastructure, management, and orchestration that fully conform to the VNF's configuration specifications. The VNF instance should then fulfill functional and quality expectations.

Product/supplier-attributable failures to properly install and function on supported cloud platforms will be captured as problem reports filed by (or on behalf of) the cloud service customer (CSC) against the supplier. Those risk events will primarily be measured via

■ Number of problem reports, such as TL 9000 NPR1, NPR2, and NPR3
■ Product-attributable service outage downtime, such as TL 9000 SO4 and SO3

13.3 Risk Causes

The likely causes of faulty VNF configuration specification risk events include

1. Engineered limit of some cloud resource characteristic not correctly specified
2. Engineered limit of some cloud resource characteristic not adequately verified
3. Implicit limit on some previously unrecognized or improperly understood operational characteristic of cloud resource
4. Syntactical or semantic error in specification of configuration information for virtualized resources

The likely causes of residual defect in VNF life cycle management script risk events include

1. Residual defect in VNF life cycle management script
2. Implicit (unstated) precondition for successful execution of VNF life cycle management script

3. Insufficient testing/verification of cloud resource instances before use, thus resulting in an inoperable VNF component or instance
4. Insufficient (automated or stipulated) testing prior to detect dead-on-arrival (DOA)/inoperable VNF component or instance before deeming VNF life cycle management action successful

The likely causes of residual product defect risk for VNFs are fundamentally the same as the risks for physical network function (PNFs). In addition, changes in the VNF's operational environment may expose previously inaccessible or otherwise untested residual defects, especially configuration-related defects.

13.4 Risk Controls

VNF suppliers control all VNF product risks by deploying robust quality management systems including thorough review and validation of all work products, along with root cause analysis and corrective actions of defects that escape. VNF suppliers control faulty VNF configuration specification risk and residual defect in VNF life cycle management script risk by

- Fully documenting VNF configuration specifications via appropriate industry standard mechanisms, syntaxes, and semantics so they can be verified via formal methods
- Testing all VNF life cycle management actions on several cloud infrastructure, management, and orchestration platforms under realistic usage scenarios
- Generating detailed alarms and fault logs for configuration and life cycle management anomalies and errors detected at runtime
- Assuring that VNF configurations can be safely rolled back to a known-good state if anomalies or errors are detected while executing a VNF life cycle management action

Cloud service providers who operate cloud infrastructure, management, and orchestration control these risks by

- Generating detailed alarms and fault logs for configuration and life cycle management anomalies and errors detected at runtime

13.5 Risk Treatments

Potential risk treatment options (see Section 3.3) for VNF product risks are as follows:

- **Replace or remove the risk source**—CSCs may have the option of entirely replacing a risky VNF from one supplier with a VNF from another supplier. Exercising this option may be simple in the early stages of service design but becomes increasingly expensive as the application moves from service design thru transition to deployment and operation.

- **Change the risk likelihood**—Assuring that the CSC's operational environment and the VNF supplier's (and service integrator's) test beds closely match reduces the risk of configuration defects escaping to production. Engineering the network service to minimize the likelihood of the VNF being pushed outside of this verified operational configuration reduces the risk of exposing residual configuration defects. Assuring that the infrastructure-as-a-service and management and orchestration service providers strictly guarantee and enforce platform compatibility as they evolve and upgrade their platforms minimizes the risk of underlying configuration details changing beneath the VNF and thus exposing residual defects.

- **Change the risk consequences**—Maintaining sufficient spare online VNF capacity so that user service can be rapidly recovered if a VNF-related failure event occurs can minimize user service consequences. Engineer VNF and network services so that no faulty VNF or life cycle management action can initiate a failure cascade; for example, VNF instances should be fully decoupled so that failures cannot propagate from one VNF instance to another.

- **Share the risk with an external party**—One can share faulty VNF configuration specification risk, residual defect in VNF life cycle management script risk, and residual product defect risk with the VNF supplier via remedies attached service-level agreements. Service integrators may also share accountability for discovering and resolving faulty VNF configuration specification risk and residual defect in VNF life cycle management script risk associated with the CSC's operational scenario.

- **Retain the risk**—The default assumption is that the CSC assures that their VNF instances, and their overall network services, continuously operate within the VNF's engineered parameters.

- **Reject accountability**—It is generally infeasible for CSC to escape overall accountability to their customers for failures related to products engineered into their application without negatively impacting customer goodwill.

- **Avoid the risk**—Specific VNF-related risks of can be avoided either by using a software-as-a-service offering or by deploying a PNF instead of using a VNF.

Chapter 14

Virtual Machine Risks

This chapter considers following virtual machine risks that can produce unacceptable user service quality for applications hosted on impacted virtual machine instances (see Figure 14.1):

- VM dead on arrival (DOA) risk (Table 14.1)
- VM premature release (failure) risk (Table 14.2)
- VM stall risk (Table 14.3)
- VM scheduling latency risk (Table 14.4)
- VM clock error risk (Table 14.5)
- VM placement policy violation risk (Table 14.6)

14.1 Context

Figure 14.2 visualizes virtual compute risks in the canonical cloud accountability context of Figure 1.3: application software executes from virtual compute and memory resources offered by a cloud infrastructure service provider, and impairments to those virtual machine instances directly impact execution of hosted application software.

Figure 14.3 visualizes virtual infrastructure as a service product in the context of the NFV architecture. Cloud service customers are service consumers of virtual compute, memory, storage, and networking services to host their VNFs. Infrastructure CSPs are service providers of virtual compute, memory, storage, and networking services, and the NFV architecture defines the Vn-Nf reference point as the demark between a consumer and a provider for infrastructure services.

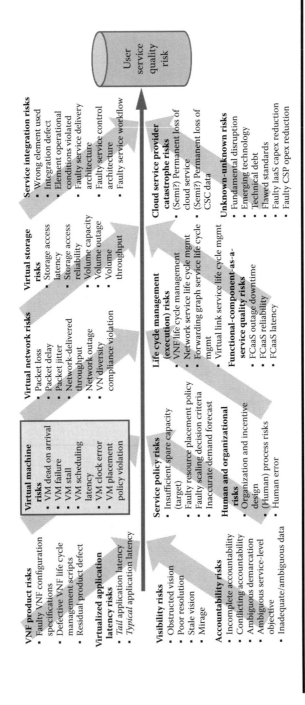

Figure 14.1 Virtual machine risks in cloud risk fishbone. CSP, cloud service provider; FCaaS, functional-component-as-a-service; IaaS, infrastructure-as-a-service; VM, virtual machine; VN, virtual network.

Table 14.1 VM Dead on Arrival (DOA) Risk

Attribute	Value
Risk **name**	VM dead on arrival (DOA) risk.
Primary risk cause(s)	Purportedly operational virtual machine instance is delivered to the CSC that is actually partially or totally inoperable. A proximal cause may be a nonresponsive VM.
Risk **condition**	The VM fails to provide the expected service for the VNFC instance applied to it.
Risk **consequence**	VNFC instance hosted by the DOA VM is partially or totally inoperable and thus unable to properly serve offered load with acceptable quality.
Risk **impact**	• If VM DOA is promptly detected, then lead time for requested fulfillment action will be longer than as the impacted VNF must be driven to a known state, DOA VM must be properly released, and the impacted configuration change action re-executed. As the DOA VM was probably ordered as part of a scaling operation, the additional capacity will be delayed, which increases the risk that rising application demand will outstrip online application capacity. • If partially or totally inoperable VNFC/VM instance is not detected before the instance enters production, then some user service impact may be required to trigger detection of the DOA VM instance.

ETSI NFV Service Quality Metrics (ETSI, 2014-12) includes several useful virtual machine service quality metrics. Figure 14.4 visualizes virtual machine quality metrics from (ETSI, 2014-12) across the virtual machine's life cycle.

- **VM Dead-On-Arrival** (DOA) (covered by VM dead on arrival [DOA] risk [Table 14.1]) as shown in Figure 14.4, this metric captures purportedly correct virtual machine instances provided by the cloud service provider that are found to be inoperable.
- **VM Premature Release Ratio** (covered by VM premature release [failure] risk [Table 14.2]), as shown in Figure 14.4, captures virtual machine instances that fail or are terminated for reasons other than CSC request.

Table 14.2   VM Premature Release (Failure) Risk

Attribute	Value
Risk **name**	VM premature release (failure) risk.
Primary risk cause(s)	An operational VM instance hosting some VNF software component instance fails.
Risk **condition**	VM unexpectedly (from cloud service customer's perspective) stops providing service.
Risk **consequence**	Active, in-flight, or pending operations associated with the impacted VNFC(s) are lost unless they can be retried or recovered by high availability mechanisms or self-healing actions.
Risk **impact**	Primary impacts: • Service reliability due to lost transaction(s) • Service functionality due to loss of volatile state data • Secondary impacts: • Service outage downtime if failure is not promptly recovered within the system requirements • Service latency and service quality for retried/ recovered operations

- **VM Stall** (covered by VM stall risk [Table 14.3]) captures cases where an unacceptable virtual resource throughput is delivered to the CSC's application software for a brief period. As shown in Figure 14.5, VM stall events that persist beyond the maximum acceptable stall time are deemed premature release events and thus are likely to activate application high availability mechanisms to failover service to other components.
- **VM Scheduling Latency** (covered by VM scheduling latency risk [Table 14.4]) captures cases where the infrastructure fails to execute the CSC's software to service real-time timer and network events interrupts promptly. For example, Figure 14.6 gives a sample complementary cumulative distribution function of an actual performance for 1 millisecond timer interrupts for an application hosted on virtualized infrastructure. In this case, the slowest 1 millisecond timer tick is late by 5 milliseconds or more, and that delay may cascade into service latency jitter experienced by service users.
- **VM Clock Error** (covered by VM clock error risk [Table 14.5]) captures errors in the real-time clock value reported by a virtual machine instance. Practically, this is the difference between true real (i.e., UTC) time and the

Table 14.3   VM Stall Risk

Attribute	Value
Risk **name**	VM stall risk.
Primary risk cause(s)	Infrastructure pauses execution of a runnable VM instance, such as due to live migration or resource contention/sharing.
Risk **condition**	Runnable VNFC software hosted on the impacted VM instance VM does not execute for a period of time.
Risk **consequence**	Response latency for pending and in-flight work increases and new requests are queued. When the stall condition clears pending and in-flight work continues, and the backlog of queued work is processed. The longer the stall event is, the greater the risk that pending, in-flight, and new requests will be noticeably slower, timeout and be retried, or even abandoned by users. Long VM stall events are likely to appear to the VNF or other systems as component failures and prompt an automatic high availability recovery action (e.g., failover away from the stalled VM component). Failover and recovery may cause some or all of the pending, in-flight, and new requests to be lost.
Risk **impact**	Primary impact is to service latency, service quality, and service reliability. Service availability is impacted if the failure is not promptly recovered within the system requirements.

clock time reported by the virtual infrastructure. These clock errors often cascade into faulty timestamps, which can complicate event correlation, usage records, and so on.

In addition to these core virtual machine execution metrics (above), ETSI (2014-12) offers several orchestration-related virtual machine metrics that are useful (see Figure 14.7):

■ **VM Provisioning Latency** (covered by VNF life cycle management [execution] risks [Table 23.2]) captures the interval between request and response for VM allocation.

Table 14.4   VM Scheduling Latency Risk

Attribute	Value
Risk **name**	VM scheduling latency risk.
Primary risk cause(s)	Infrastructure (e.g., hypervisor) fails to promptly schedule application software to run in response to timer or input/output interrupts.
Risk **condition**	Timer (e.g., every 1 millisecond) event expires or network traffic is received, but instead of instantly running VNFC software to address that event in real time (i.e., preempting other VNFs sharing physical resources), the infrastructure/hypervisor waits and thereby adds latency into real-time service delivery.
Risk **consequence**	As shown in Figure 14.6, latency between the actual time when a timer event should have expired or an input/output event occurred and when the appropriate VNFC software module is executed can add excess latency into the critical path of user service delivery as well as impact timing accuracy for some periodic events such as media streaming.
Risk **impact**	Primary impact is to service latency and service quality.

- **VM Provisioning Failures** (covered by VNF life cycle management [execution] risks [Table 23.2]) captures the portion of syntactically and semantically correct VM allocation requests that were properly fulfilled within the maximum acceptable time.
- **VM Dead on Arrival** (covered by VM dead on arrival [DOA] risk [Table 14.1]).
- **VM Placement Policy Compliance** (covered by VM placement policy violation risk [Table 14.6]) captures how strictly the cloud service provider adheres to the cloud service customer's resource placement (e.g., anti-affinity) rules across space and time.
- **Failed VM Release Ratio**—While failing to properly process resource release actions does not impact the user service quality risk, it can cause the CSC to be overcharged for resources.

Table 14.5   VM Clock Error Risk

Attribute	Value
Risk **name**	VM clock error risk.
Primary risk cause(s)	Real-time clock value provided by virtual machine instance differs from actual (i.e., UTC) time, perhaps by milliseconds or more.
Risk **condition**	Clock synchronization errors between different VNFCs in the same VNF, or between VNFs. For example, a simultaneous event recorded by different VNFCs may show different timestamps, then making actual sequence (or simultaneity) of events difficult to determine after the fact.
Risk **consequence**	• Faulty update timestamps on files can cause mayhem. • Faulty timestamps on messages and events can violate order assumptions, create temporal errors on billing events, and confound trouble localization and root cause analysis efforts by confusing the chain of causality. • Services requiring synchronization with remote devices or other components may be unable to properly sync and result in failure or loss of functionality.
Risk **impact**	Prolonged service impact duration due to difficulty with trouble localization and root cause analysis due to misleading times.

14.2 Captured Risks

Virtual machine risks based on the NFV Software Quality Metrics are captured as

- VM dead on arrival (DOA) risk (Table 14.1)
- VM premature release (failure) risk (Table 14.2)
- VM stall risk (Table 14.3)
- VM scheduling latency risk (Table 14.4)
- VM clock error risk (Table 14.5)
- VM placement policy violation risk (Table 14.6)

Table 14.6   VM Placement Policy Violation Risk

Attribute	Value
Risk **name**	VM placement policy violation risk.
Primary risk cause(s)	Cloud service provider fails to fully enforce placement policy rules across the entire life cycle of applicable VM instances.
Risk **condition**	In violation of the CSC's anti-affinity rules, both primary and protecting VNFC instances are placed into the same infrastructure failure group so that failure of that infrastructure element risks violating single point of failure assumptions of the CSC's high availability architecture.
Risk **consequence**	Some infrastructure failure simultaneously impacts both primary and protecting components, which overwhelms an application's high availability architecture. Note that policy violations, which place virtual machines into different jurisdictions, could break legal constraints, such as data privacy laws.
Risk **impact**	Primary service impact: • Service outage downtime Secondary service impact: • Service latency, reliability, and quality degrade as remaining VNFCs struggle to recover impacted user service. • Reduced service capacity resulting in activation of overload controls and associated shedding of load.

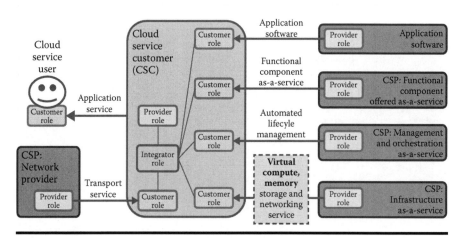

Figure 14.2   Virtual machine risks in accountability context.

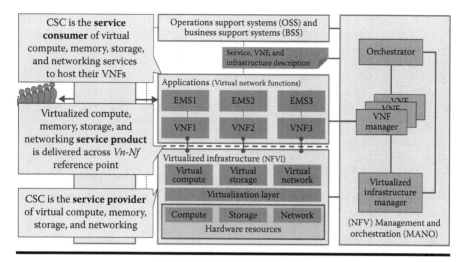

Figure 14.3 **Infrastructure as a service product in the NFV architecture.**

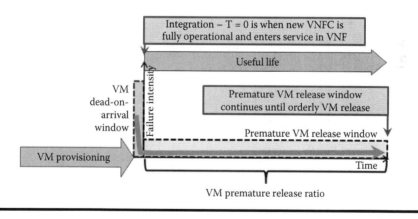

Figure 14.4 **Virtual Machine Failure Metrics across VM life cycle. (From Figure 4 of ETSI,** *INF 010 NFV Service Quality Metrics.* **Sophia Antipolis, France: European Telecommunications Standard Institute, 2014-12.)**

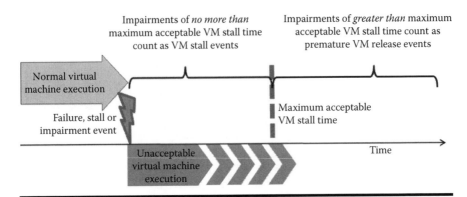

Figure 14.5 Virtual machine stall and premature release. (From Figure 6 of ETSI, *INF 010 NFV Service Quality Metrics*. Sophia Antipolis, France: European Telecommunications Standard Institute, 2014-12.)

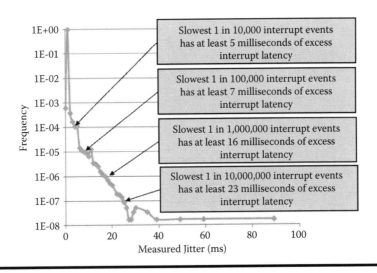

Figure 14.6 Sample 1 millisecond timer interrupt scheduling latency.

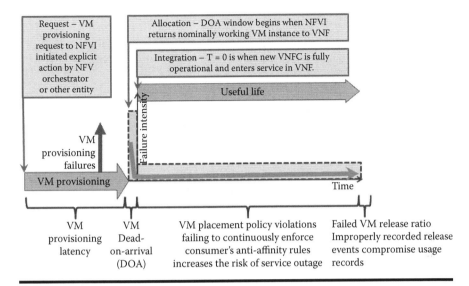

Figure 14.7   VM orchestration metrics. (From Figure 10 of ETSI, *INF 010 NFV Service Quality Metrics*. Sophia Antipolis, France: European Telecommunications Standard Institute, 2014-12.)

Chapter 15

Virtual Networking Risks

Cloud-based applications rely on virtual network services for communication between distributed application software components (VNFCs), functional components offered as a service and supporting systems, along with wide area and access networking to communicate with end users' devices. As shown in Figure 15.1, user service quality is vulnerable to the following virtual networking risks:

- Packet loss risk (Table 15.1)
- Packet delay risk (Table 15.2)
- Packet jitter (delay variation) risk (Table 15.3)
- Network delivered throughput risk (Table 15.4)
- Network outage risk (Table 15.5)
- VN diversity compliance violation risk (Table 15.6)

15.1 Context

As shown in Figure 15.2, virtual networking service is delivered by infrastructure cloud service providers to enable communications between the cloud service customers application, functional components, other systems, and transport services.

Figure 15.3 illustrates standard (ETSI, 2014-12) service quality metrics for virtual networking service delivered by infrastructure service providers to cloud service customers across the Vn-Nf reference point.

- **Packet Loss Ratio** (covered by packet loss risk [Table 15.1]) is the rate of packets that are either never delivered to the destination or delivered to the destination. As shown in Figure 15.4, if an episode of packet loss persists

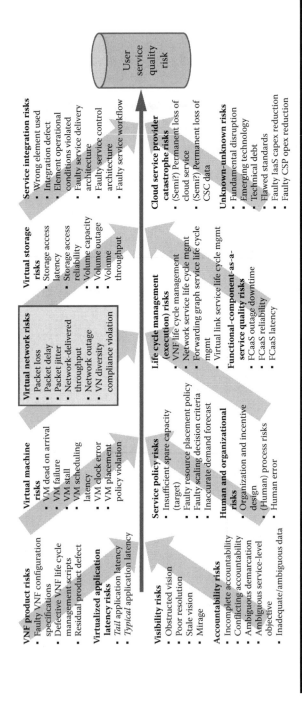

VNF product risks
- Faulty VNF configuration specifications
- Defective VNF life cycle management scripts
- Residual product defect

Virtualized application latency risks
- *Tail* application latency
- *Typical* application latency

Virtual machine risks
- VM dead on arrival
- VM failure
- VM stall
- VM scheduling latency
- VM clock error
- VM placement policy violation

Virtual network risks
- Packet loss
- Packet delay
- Packet jitter
- Network-delivered throughput
- Network outage
- VN diversity compliance violation

Virtual storage risks
- Storage access latency
- Storage access reliability
- Volume capacity
- Volume outage
- Volume throughput

Service integration risks
- Wrong element used
- Integration defect
- Element operational conditions violated
- Faulty service delivery architecture
- Faulty service control architecture
- Faulty service workflow

Visibility risks
- Obstructed vision
- Poor resolution
- Stale vision
- Mirage

Accountability risks
- Incomplete accountability
- Conflicting accountability
- Ambiguous demarcation
- Ambiguous service-level objective
- Inadequate/ambiguous data

Service policy risks
- Insufficient spare capacity (target)
- Faulty resource placement policy
- Faulty scaling decision criteria
- Inaccurate demand forecast

Human and organizational risks
- Organization and incentive design
- (Human) process risks
- Human error

Life cycle management (execution) risks
- VNF life cycle management
- Network service life cycle mgmt
- Forwarding graph service life cycle mgmt
- Virtual link service life cycle mgmt

Functional-component-as-a-service quality risks
- FCaaS outage downtime
- FCaaS reliability
- FCaaS latency

Cloud service provider catastrophe risks
- (Semi?) Permanent loss of cloud service
- (Semi?) Permanent loss of CSC data

Unknown-unknown risks
- Fundamental disruption
- Emerging technology
- Technical debt
- Flawed standards
- Faulty IaaS capex reduction
- Faulty CSP opex reduction

User service quality risk

Figure 15.1 Virtual network risks in cloud user service risk fishbone. CSP, cloud service; FCaaS, functional-component-as-a-service; IaaS, infrastructure-as-a-service; VM, virtual machine; VN, virtual network.

Table 15.1   Packet Loss Risk

Attribute	Value
Risk **name**	Packet loss risk.
Risk **root cause**	Some IP packets between VNFC instances (intra-VNF traffic) or between VNFC instances and other PNFs, VNFs, or functional components offered as a service (inter-VNF traffic) are lost due to congestion, buffer overflow, transient failure event, etc.
Risk **condition**	Application packets that are lost must be detected and retransmitted, recovered, concealed, or presented as a failure to the service user.
Risk **consequence**	Packet loss detection as well as retry/retransmission or other recovery mechanism adds latency to the user's response time; packet concealment mechanisms (e.g., for bearer traffic) impact the user's quality of experience.
Risk **impact**	Service latency and service quality of impacted operations are worse.

Table 15.2   Packet Delay Risk

Attribute	Value
Risk **name**	Packet delay risk.
Risk **root cause**	Physical and virtual networking infrastructure, equipment, and facilities produce networking latency for intra-VNF and/or inter-VNF communications. Suboptimal resource placement decisions, policies, failures, and other operational characteristics can increase that packet delay.
Risk **condition**	More elements and facilities in the networking path increase the risk of one-way packet delay.
Risk **consequence**	Virtual networking packet delay adds to overall service latency experienced by end users.
Risk **impact**	Typical service latency is higher (i.e., worse).

Table 15.3   Packet Jitter (Delay Variation) Risk

Attribute	Value
Risk **name**	Packet jitter (delay variation) risk.
Risk **root cause**	Physical or virtual network queuing, congestion, collisions, and other factors cause some packets to have significantly greater one-way transmission latency than typical packet delay.
Risk **condition**	Packets on some intra-VNF and/or inter-VNF communication links may experience extreme latency variation (jitter).
Risk **consequence**	Extreme latency variations may appear to end users as tail latency events.
Risk **impact**	Service latency is worse for impacted operations; extreme jitter events may cause impacted operations to be unacceptably slow, thereby impacting service reliability or service quality.

Table 15.4   Network Delivered Throughput Risk

Attribute	Value
Risk **name**	Network delivered throughput risk.
Risk **root cause**	Virtual network infrastructure fails to deliver rated network throughput for CSC's VNF and/or network service due to physical or virtual network impairment, congestion, etc.
Risk **condition**	Network traffic may be throttled (rate limited) or dropped.
Risk **consequence**	Throughput (e.g., service capacity) of CSC's application is limited and application's congestion/overload controls may activate. Components begin retransmitting dropped packets, which may further stress overloaded network links leading to more pervasive service impact.
Risk **impact**	Application service capacity may be limited. Service latency, quality, and reliability are likely to be impacted. Extreme events can cause elements to activate congestion controls, which deliberately reject user traffic.

Table 15.5   Network Outage Risk

Attribute	Value
Risk **name**	Network outage risk.
Risk **root cause**	Some intra-VNF or inter-VNF virtual network links are inoperable or unavailable.
Risk **condition**	At least some intra-VNF and/or inter-VNF virtual networking is unavailable, so timeouts and retries/retransmissions are unsuccessful. VNF's high availability mechanism is likely to activate.
Risk **consequence**	Impacted application or VNF has partial or total loss of functionality or capacity. Impacted application or VNFs may be simplex exposed.
Risk **impact**	Impacted application service or VNF experiences partial or total loss of functionality or capacity outage. Active user sessions and pending user requests may be lost.

Table 15.6   VN Diversity Compliance Violation Risk

Attribute	Value
Risk **name**	VN diversity compliance violation risk.
Risk **root cause**	Some intra-VNF or inter-VNF virtual network links fail to meet virtual network diversity requirements stipulated by CSC.
Risk **condition**	VNF or network service is at risk that some physical network equipment or facility (e.g., link) failure will overwhelm the application's high availability architecture.
Risk **consequence**	Physical or virtual network failure event produces an application service outage.
Risk **impact**	Impacted application service or VNF experiences a functionality or capacity loss outage. Active user sessions and pending user requests may be lost.

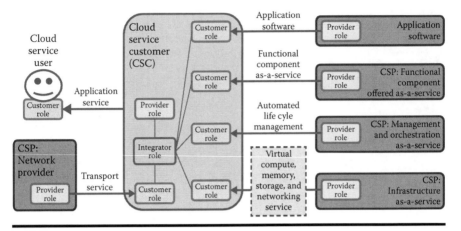

Figure 15.2 Virtual network risks in accountability context.

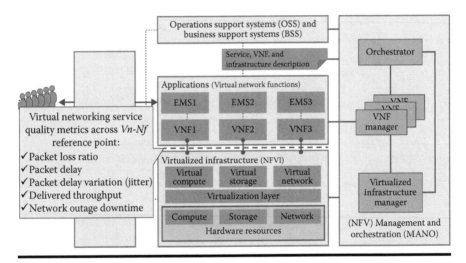

Figure 15.3 Virtual networking quality metrics in the reference architecture.

beyond the maximum acceptable network transient time, then the impairment is measured as network outage downtime rather than packet loss.

■ **Packet Delay** (covered by the packet delay risk [Table 15.2]) is the elapsed time between a packet being sent from one VNFC's guest OS instance to the time it is received by the destination VNFC's guest OS instance.

■ **Packet Delay Variation (jitter)** (covered by the packet jitter [delay variation] risk [Table 15.3]) is the variance in packet delay.

■ **Network Delivered Throughput** (covered in network delivered throughput risk [Table 15.4]).

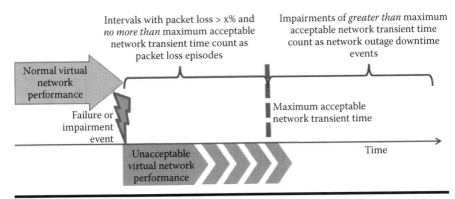

Figure 15.4 Virtual network packet loss and outage downtime metrics. (From Figure 8 of ETSI, *INF 010 NFV Service Quality Metrics*. Sophia Antipolis, France: European Telecommunications Standard Institute, 2014-12.)

■ **Network Outage Downtime** (covered by network outage risk [Table 15.5])— As shown in Figure 15.4, network outage downtime characterizes virtual network impairments that persist for longer than the maximum acceptable network transient time.

Figure 15.5 offers a simple example of how virtual network risks confronting cloud service customers is related to how application service components are placed onto physical infrastructure equipment. Imagine a sample distributed cloud-based application with two frontend components FE1 (hosted in location 1) and FE2 (hosted in location 2), and one backend component BE1 (hosted in location 1). While virtual networking assures that both the FE1:BE1 and FE2:BE1 virtual links

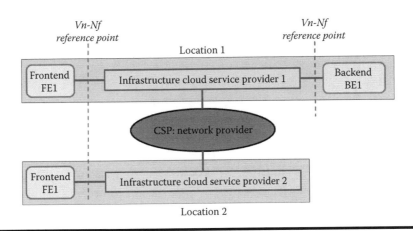

Figure 15.5 Application component distribution example.

appear functionally identical to the CSC's application, the FE2:BE1 virtual link carries materially higher packet loss risk (Table 15.1), packet delay risk (Table 15.2), packet jitter (delay variation) risk (Table 15.3), and network outage risk (Table 15.5) because additional networking equipment and facilities are included in the critical service delivery path for traffic that flows between location 2 and location 1 than for traffic that remains within a single data center. Thus, the CSC and CSP resource placement policies can impact the virtual networking risks facing a cloud-based application service.

15.2 Captured Risks

Virtual networking risks are captured as

- Packet loss risk (Table 15.1)
- Packet delay risk (Table 15.2)
- Packet jitter (delay variation) risk (Table 15.3)
- Network delivered throughput risk (Table 15.4)
- Network outage risk (Table 15.5)
- VN diversity compliance violation risk (Table 15.6)

Chapter 16

Virtual Storage Risks

Application services rely on persistent storage to host user data, configuration information, and other application information elements. Cloud-based applications typically rely on virtual storage services of cloud service providers to host their persistent data. As shown in Figure 16.1, virtual storage presents the following user service quality risks:

- Storage access reliability risk (Table 16.1)
- Storage access latency (Table 16.2)
- Volume capacity risk (Table 16.3)
- Volume outage risk (Table 16.4)
- Volume throughput risk (Table 16.5)

As shown in Figure 16.2, virtual storage service is delivered by infrastructure cloud service providers to host user data, configuration information, and other application information elements.

Storage risks are usefully factored into those affecting an entire storage volume versus risks that manifest against individual files or records. Risks related to individual storage/file operations:

- Storage access reliability risk (Table 16.1)
- Storage access latency (Table 16.2)

Risks related to entire storage volumes:

- Volume capacity risk (Table 16.3)
- Volume outage risk (Table 16.4)
- Volume throughput risk (Table 16.5)

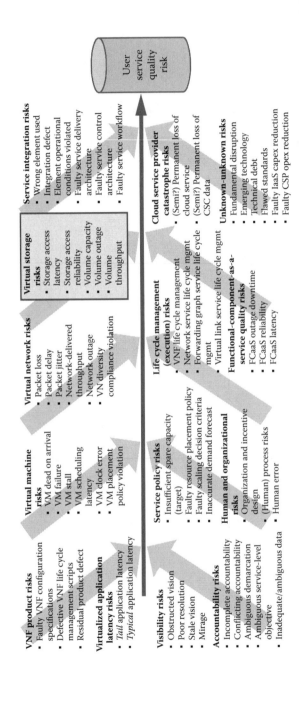

VNF product risks
- Faulty VNF configuration specifications
- Defective VNF life cycle management scripts
- Residual product defect

Virtualized application latency risks
- *Tail* application latency
- *Typical* application latency

Virtual machine risks
- VM dead on arrival
- VM failure
- VM stall
- VM scheduling latency
- VM clock error
- VM placement policy violation

Virtual network risks
- Packet loss
- Packet delay
- Packet jitter
- Network-delivered throughput
- Network outage
- VN diversity compliance violation

Virtual storage risks
- Storage access latency
- Storage access reliability
- Volume capacity
- Volume outage
- Volume throughput

Service integration risks
- Wrong element used
- Integration defect
- Element operational conditions violated
- Faulty service delivery architecture
- Faulty service control architecture
- Faulty service workflow

Visibility risks
- Obstructed vision
- Poor resolution
- Stale vision
- Mirage

Accountability risks
- Incomplete accountability
- Conflicting accountability
- Ambiguous demarcation
- Ambiguous service-level objective
- Inadequate/ambiguous data

Service policy risks
- Insufficient spare capacity (target)
- Faulty resource placement policy
- Faulty scaling decision criteria
- Inaccurate demand forecast

Human and organizational risks
- Organization and incentive design
- (Human) process risks
- Human error

Life cycle management (execution) risks
- VNF life cycle management
- Network service life cycle mgmt
- Forwarding graph service life cycle mgmt
- Virtual link service life cycle mgmt

Functional-component-as-a-service quality risks
- FCaaS outage downtime
- FCaaS reliability
- FCaaS latency

Cloud service provider catastrophe risks
- (Semi?) Permanent loss of cloud service
- (Semi?) Permanent loss of CSC data

Unknown-unknown risks
- Fundamental disruption
- Emerging technology
- Technical debt
- Flawed standards
- Faulty IaaS capex reduction
- Faulty CSP opex reduction

User service quality risk

Figure 16.1   Virtual storage risks. CSP, cloud service provider; FCaaS, functional-component-as-a-service; IaaS, infrastructure-as-a-service; VM, virtual machine; VN, virtual network.

Table 16.1   Storage Access Reliability Risk

Attribute	*Value*
Risk **name**	Storage access reliability risk.
Risk **root cause**	Failure in virtual storage system, configuration (e.g., file locking), congestion, operational status (e.g., maintenance action), etc., prevents CSC virtual storage requests from being successfully served.
Risk **condition**	Semantically and syntactically correct file access or manipulation request (i.e., open, close, read, write, lock, seek) fails to complete in the maximum acceptable time.
Risk (service) **consequence**	VNF cannot access, manipulate, or store some data object.
Risk **impact**	Service reliability and/or quality impacted because some functionality or information is unavailable.

Table 16.2   Storage Access Latency Risk

Attribute	*Value*
Risk **name**	Storage access latency risk.
Risk **root cause**	Resource contention, operational status (e.g., maintenance actions), configuration limitations, or other factors cause delays in accessing or manipulating stored information.
Risk **condition**	Storage access latency directly increases time to complete operations.
Risk (service) **consequence**	Impacted operations will be slower. User or application operations may fail if storage access latency exceeds timeout values for application software components.
Risk **impact**	Service latency, as excess storage latency usually adds to the latency experienced by the end user. Service reliability or quality if operation latency is unacceptable and user abandons their request or if the VNF is unable to deliver requested functionality with latency specified by SLA.

Table 16.3 Volume Capacity Risk

Attribute	Value
Risk **name**	Volume capacity risk.
Risk **root cause**	Infrastructure service provider is unable or unwilling to make sufficient storage capacity available to CSC to fulfill their request to create or write a file.
Risk **condition**	VNF's request to create a file or write data is denied.
Risk (service) **consequence**	VNF is unable to complete some operation (e.g., creating a new user profile, saving some user artifact, etc.).
Risk **impact**	Service reliability due to operation failure.

Table 16.4 Volume Outage Risk

Attribute	Value
Risk **name**	Volume outage risk.
Risk **root cause**	Virtual storage is unavailable due to planned or unplanned service outage.
Risk **condition**	All access requests to files held on the impacted volume fail.
Risk (service) **consequence**	VNF is unable to complete some operation (e.g., retrieving a user's profile, saving some user artifact).
Risk **impact**	Service reliability due to operation failure.

Table 16.5   Volume Throughput Risk

Attribute	Value
Risk **name**	Volume throughput risk.
Risk **root cause**	CSC demand, failure, maintenance action, operational policies or practices, and/or poor infrastructure design/configuration prevent the infrastructure service provider from delivering committed storage throughput to VNF.
Risk **condition**	Virtual storage infrastructure fails to deliver rated throughput, which may limit service performance or ability to meet committed SLA.
Risk (service) **consequence**	VNF throughput may be limited by storage throughput; VNF work queues may overflow so user requests are rejected or excessive latency is introduced.
Risk **impact**	Service latency from queuing due to storage throughput limitations. Service reliability due to request timeouts, queue filling, and workload shedding.

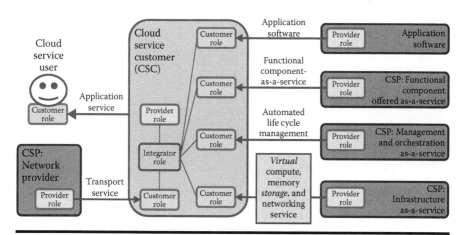

Figure 16.2   Virtual storage risks in accountability context.

Chapter 17

Virtualized Application Latency Risks

Virtualization technology imposes a modest latency overhead to support multi-tenancy (Section 1.4.3), resource pooling (Section 1.4.6), and other enablers of cloud computing. This overhead creates both tail application latency risk (Table 17.1) and typical application latency risk (Table 17.2). Figure 17.1 illustrates how these risks fit into cloud risk fishbone.

As shown in Figure 17.2, virtualization adds some processing overhead between application software and the physical hardware resources. This incremental overhead is normally very small, but resource contention from infrastructure software and other applications sharing the underlying resources, as well as other factors, often cause application latency to be somewhat greater than similar natively deployed applications. Some of the causes of virtualized application typical and tail latency risks are as follows:

- **Decomposed infrastructure architectures**—Decomposing persistent storage from compute and memory increases resource access and increases overheads compared to dedicated and composed architectures.
- **Resource placement**—Placement of an application's virtualized resources impacts latency to access that resource; placing the underlying physical resource on a different blade, chassis, row, or data center can materially change typical application service latency.
- **Resource contention**—Multitenancy configurations further exacerbate resource access due to resource contention between components.
- **Infrastructure technologies and sharing policies**—Cloud service provider's infrastructure architecture and operational policies and configurations

Table 17.1   Tail Application Latency Risk

Attribute	Value
Risk **name**	Tail application latency risk—extraordinary latency on the slowest few transactions (e.g., slowest 1 in 10,000).
Risk **root cause**	Virtualization technology in general, and resource sharing in the context of cloud in particular, occasionally delays scheduling resources to instantly serve a particular VNF's need (e.g., letting another application's processing run to completion or another workload be scheduled according to the infrastructure's resource scheduling policy). Any time the hypervisor or a virtualized compute, memory, networking, or storage resource is switched away from the target application's context, incremental application service latency may accrue: 1. When application software waits to be scheduled onto the resource 2. Due to context switching of resources back to serve the application Any time the infrastructure executes another workload (e.g., another VNF or some infrastructure, management, or orchestration "overhead" workload) when the target VNF is runnable adds latency to the target VNF's operation.
Risk **condition**	A small portion of VNF operations (e.g., slowest 1 in 50,000) can be materially slower than typical VNF operation latency, thus giving inconsistent service quality to users.
Risk (service) **consequence**	Impacted operations complete materially slower than non-impacted operations.
Risk **impact**	A portion of users will experience significantly worse service latency; extreme tail latency events will be abandoned by end users or timed out by requesting systems, resulting in service reliability impairments.

Table 17.2 Typical Application Latency Risk

Attribute	Value
Risk **name**	Typical application latency risk—additional latency on typical (e.g., slowest 1 in 10) operations.
Risk **root cause**	Specific configuration of virtualized resources introduces application latency overhead due to • Decomposed infrastructure architectures • Suboptimal resource placement • Infrastructure technologies • Suboptimal infrastructure sharing policies Well-engineered, well-operated virtualized infrastructure imposes a minimal latency penalty on hosted applications, but suboptimal engineering, operations, workload characteristics, and other factors can produce nonnegligible latency compared to traditional deployment architectures.
Risk **condition**	Every access of a virtualized resource imposes an incremental latency penalty compared to natively deployed application configuration.
Risk **consequence**	Virtualized resource access latency penalties aggregate to make typical application service latency materially greater than a natively deployed application configuration.
Risk **impact**	Application's typical service latency is somewhat worse than native configurations.

impact the physical performance and overhead that application's will typically experience.

- **Failure or deficiency in virtualized application configuration,** such as not enough virtual resources allocated to handle the capacity or performance requirements.
- **Monitoring and metrics** collecting/reporting software may add overhead even though it increases visibility and facilitates trouble shooting. Note that finer measurement granularity (e.g., reporting performance data every 15 seconds instead of every 15 minutes) can increase this overhead.

Many studies have demonstrated that applications deployed on virtualized infrastructure tend to experience greater execution latencies than the natively deployed applications on equivalent or identical physical hardware. One result using the Riak database (https://en.wikipedia.org/wiki/Riak) is shown in Figure 17.3: database transaction latencies are given for the same application software either running

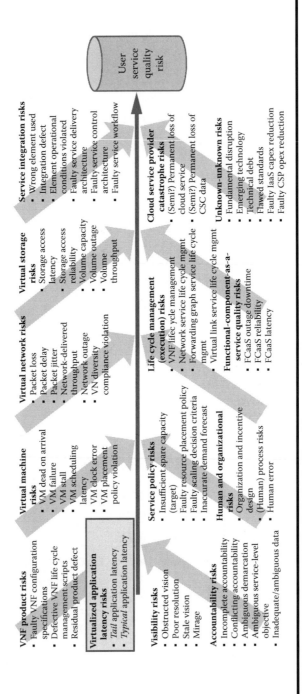

Figure 17.1 Virtualized application latency risks in cloud risk fishbone. CSP, cloud service provider; FCaaS, functional-component-as-a-service; IaaS, infrastructure-as-a-service; VM, virtual machine; VN, virtual network.

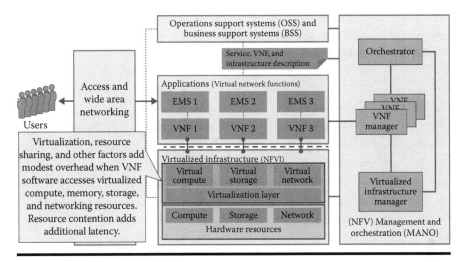

Figure 17.2 Virtualized application latency risks in accountability context.

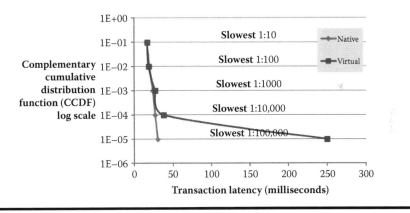

Figure 17.3 Application service latency on native and virtualized hardware.

natively (nonvirtualized) on "bare metal" or running in a KVM virtual machine instance on the same hardware. The native application running on bare metal gives statistically normal latency performance: the slowest 1 in 10 transactions takes 16.4 milliseconds, the slowest 1 in 100 transactions takes 19.4 milliseconds, the slowest 1 in 1,000 takes 23.6 milliseconds, and so on. The virtualized configuration roughly tracks latency of the bare-metal latency to the slowest 1 in 10,000, which takes 37.8 milliseconds, but the slowest 1 in 100,000 takes a whopping 249.6 milliseconds, which creates a significant latency tail. The practical implication is that at least a handful of transactions per 100,000 will experience vastly larger transaction latency than all other transactions.

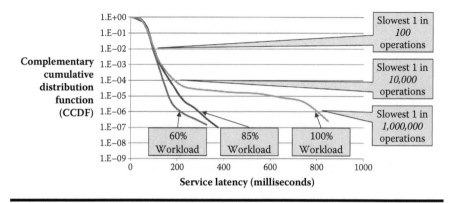

Figure 17.4 Sample application tail latency.

Section 7.1.2, "Stochastic Uncertainty," explained how increasing stochastic variations can manifest as increasing latency; Figure 17.4 shows increasing application tail latency.

Virtualized application latency risks are captured as

■ Tail application latency risk (Table 17.1)
■ Typical application latency risk (Table 17.2)

Chapter 18

Service Integration Risks

As shown in Figure 18.1, service integration creates and verifies a service implementation that combines VNF software with virtualized resources, functional components, management and orchestration, operations and support systems, and other elements to construct a valuable application service. As service integration is a large and complex task, cloud service customers often engage one or more service integration teams, so ownership of specific service integration risks is determined by the contractual arrangement that the cloud service customer makes with any organizations or suppliers that they contract with for integration services.

As shown in Figure 18.2, service integration carries several fundamental risks:

- Wrong element used risk (Table 18.1)
- System/service integration defect (Table 18.2)
- Element operational conditions violated (Table 18.3)
- Faulty service delivery architecture risk (Table 18.4)
- Faulty service control architecture risk (Table 18.5)
- Faulty service workflow risk (Table 18.6)

Note that service integration deliverables may include and/or impact Visibility Risks (Chapter 19) and Service Policy Risks (Chapter 20), but these risks are considered separately.

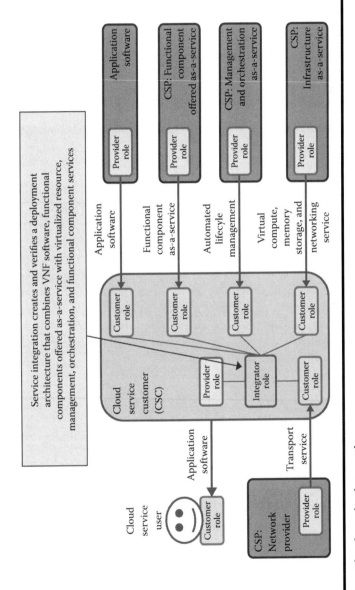

Figure 18.1   Cloud service integration.

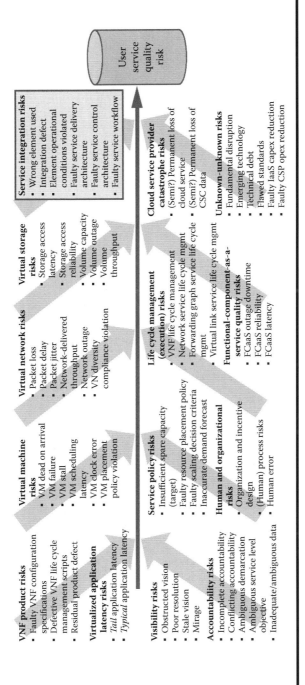

Figure 18.2 Service integration risks in cloud risk fishbone. CSP, cloud service provider; FCaaS, functional-component-as-a-service; IaaS, infrastructure-as-a-service; VM, virtual machine; VN, virtual network.

Table 18.1   Wrong Element Used Risk

Attribute	Value
Risk **name**	Wrong element used risk.
Risk **root cause**	VNF, functional component, management and orchestration offering, some other element is unable to meet fundamental requirements of the CSC's service offering. For example, if the mandatory bill of materials specifies the wrong VNF for the job.
Risk **condition**	Fully operational VNF or other service component does not deliver all features, functionality, or performance necessary for the application to service users with acceptable quality.
Risk (service) **consequence**	Service impact depends on the nature and magnitude of gap among features, functionality, or performance expected by the application service and what is delivered by the target element.
Risk **impact**	Service latency, reliability, quality, or outage downtime may be impacted.

Table 18.2   System/Service Integration Defect

Attribute	Value
Risk **name**	System/service integration defect.
Risk **root cause**	Proximal cause is typically a configuration or integration defect prevents one or more VNFs, functional components, or other elements from properly interworking to fulfill all service requirements.
Risk **condition**	Service components do not properly interwork to deliver acceptable user service quality.
Risk (service) **consequence**	Service impact depends on the nature of the integration defect.
Risk **impact**	Service latency, reliability, quality, or outage downtime may be impacted.

Table 18.3   Element Operational Conditions Violated

Attribute	Value
Risk **name**	Element operational conditions violated.
Risk **root cause**	Integration and service configuration fails to prevent one or more elements in the service chain from being driven outside of their operational profiles (e.g., offered workload exceeds component's maximum rated capacity). Note that incompletely or incorrectly specified element operational conditions are covered as faulty VNF configuration specification risk (Table 13.1).
Risk **condition**	Element rejects traffic or otherwise fails to properly serve some or all traffic.
Risk (service) **consequence**	Impact depends on the target element and how far outside of its operational envelope it is driven.
Risk **impact**	Service availability, latency, reliability, and/or quality may be impacted.

Table 18.4   Faulty Service Delivery Architecture Risk

Attribute	Value
Risk **name**	Faulty service delivery architecture risk.
Risk **root cause**	Elements are not arranged in a proper service architecture to fulfill service requirements. For example, service architecture includes a single point of failure or is unable to properly scale some aspect of service functionality or capacity.
Risk **condition**	Service architecture fails to fulfill all service requirements even when all VNFs, functional components, and elements are operating properly.
Risk (service) **consequence**	Service impact depends on the nature of the architectural error or deficiency.
Risk **impact**	Service latency, reliability, quality, or outage downtime may be impacted.

Table 18.5 Faulty Service Control Architecture Risk

Attribute	Value
Risk **name**	Faulty service control architecture risk.
Risk **root cause**	VNFs, functional components, and other service elements are not arranged to give CSC adequate management controllability. For example, restoring service following some failure or maintenance event requires a larger and/ or longer service impact than might have been feasible with a better architecture.
Risk **condition**	Crude and coarse management and control actions must be taken because more refined management and control mechanisms, policies, and procedures are not adequately supported.
Risk (service) **consequence**	Service impact depends on the nature of the service control deficiency.
Risk **impact**	Service latency, reliability, quality, or outage downtime (including impact of recovery actions) may be worse than what is technically feasible.

Table 18.6 Faulty Service Workflow Risk

Attribute	Value
Risk **name**	Faulty service workflow risk.
Risk **root cause**	Residual defect in an automated life cycle management script or method of procedure (MOP) for an application or service chain.
Risk **condition**	Executing faulty service workflow places service into an impaired or risky operational state.
Risk (service) **consequence**	Service impact depends on the nature of the impaired or risky operational state.
Risk **impact**	Service latency, reliability, quality, or outage downtime may be impacted.

Chapter 19

Visibility Risks

Visibility risks create uncertainty as to the true state of user demand, service components, or underlying resources. Without full, accurate, and timely visibility into the true operational status of all service components and facilities of an application service, it is difficult to detect, localize, and resolve of inevitable service quality impairments or adjust the application's configuration to improve operational efficiency. Incomplete, incorrect, or stale knowledge of the true state of a service can prompt incorrect actions or inactions (i.e., failing to act), both of which can impact user service quality. As shown in Figure 19.1, we factor these visibility risks as follows:

- Obstructed vision risk (Table 19.1)
- Blurred vision risk (Table 19.2)
- Stale vision risk (Table 19.3)
- Mirage risk (Table 19.4)

Uncertainty as to the true state of user demand, service components, or underlying resources arises for four fundamental reasons:

- **Obstruction** (obstructed vision risk [Table 19.1])—One doesn't have visibility to some particular point in the service delivery chain, so one has to guesstimate the true state of that point by interpolating or extrapolating (or guessing) state from other nearby—or not-so-nearby—measure points that one can see. All sorts of scary things can hide in dark corners…
- **Poor Resolution or Blurred Vision** (blurred vision risk [Table 19.2])—The data returned from a measurement point may be inaccurate or uncertain for a variety of reasons. For instance, statewide average employment, salary, education, or similar statistics for a state give little insight into characteristics of

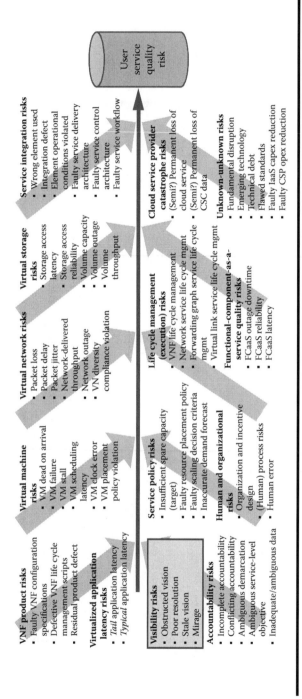

Figure 19.1 Visibility risks in cloud risk fishbone. CSP, cloud service provider; FCaaS, functional-component-as-a-service; IaaS, infrastructure-as-a-service; VM, virtual machine; VN, virtual network.

Table 19.1   Obstructed Vision Risk

Attribute	*Value*
Risk **name**	Obstructed vision risk.
Risk **root cause**	Likely root causes: • **Sensor or data collector** is not deployed close enough to target service demark or between components. For example, if data are gathered on the input to component A and the output of component C, but nothing on component B, which processes data between A and C, then it may be difficult to localize a service impairment to component A, B, or C. • **Statistical sampling**—Strategies that rely on statistical sampling "obstruct" visibility of components or service flows that are not sampled. For example, if a service provider proactively monitors only, say, 10% of the service workers in a load shared pool, then they have implicitly obstructed their visibility to the remaining 90% of the service worker instances. • **Organizational or trust boundary blocks visibility**—Cloud service customers may not be offered full and timely visibility to all (or any?) fault, alarm, performance, and configuration data for the resources serving their application that held by the cloud service provider.
Risk **condition**	Organization is unaware of service quality, performance, or fault status at a particular point in the service chain so no corrective actions are initiated, and/or localizing the true root cause of a service impairment takes longer because indirect fault localization methods must be applied.
Risk (service) **consequence**	1. Organization may be unaware of a failure, impairment, or risk. 2. Organization may not be able to rapidly localize a known failure, impairment, or risk to its true root cause.
Risk **impact**	The duration of service latency, reliability, and quality problems naturally extends when obstructed visibility means the organization is unaware of a problem and/or is unable to rapidly localize the cause of the problem so that appropriate corrective actions can be taken.

Table 19.2 Blurred Vision Risk

Attribute	Value
Risk **name**	Blurred vision risk.
Risk **root cause**	Likely root causes: • **Too many impairment or event types aggregated into a single measurement** to resolve true state. For example, aggregating all 4XX SIP errors into a single measurement obscures the true nature of server failures. • **Too many events aggregated into a single measurement** to resolve true state. For example, aggregating all measurements into 15-minute measurement buckets, rather than 1 minute buckets. • **Inaccurate or unreliable measurement process** so data do not reflect true state. For example, VM clock error causes the real-time read by a VNFC to be slightly different from true universal (UTC) time, resulting in slightly inaccurate timestamps. • **Measurement process alters target state**, like how enabling verbose recording of debug data can alter an application's timing characteristics.
Risk **condition**	Measurement, aggregation, and/or reporting mechanisms obscure the true state.
Risk (service) **consequence**	Homogenization, consolidating, averaging, or otherwise blurring of reported data make it hard to pinpoint the root cause of service impairment. If the problem cannot be sufficiently localized to enable a fine-grained corrective action (e.g., repairing or migrating a single VNFC), then a cruder and perhaps more impactful corrective action may be necessary (e.g., restarting an entire VNF instance rather than simply one component instance).
Risk **impact**	Coarser corrective actions that impact more users may be required if the problem is not localized sufficiently to rely on minimally impacting, fine-grained corrective actions.

a particular town or neighborhood within that state. Averaging performance across a pool of worker components or across a suite of virtual links can obscure individual elements that are severely impaired.

■ **Staleness** (stale vision risk [Table 19.3])—Data inevitably reach the service management systems or staff milliseconds, seconds, minutes, or longer after the measurement was taken. The true current state at the target measurement

Table 19.3 Stale Vision Risk

Attribute	Value
Risk **name**	Stale vision risk.
Risk **root cause**	Complex, inefficient, and/or slow data flows delay when automated systems and human staff receive data characterizing the state of service, components, resources, and workloads that can be used to drive corrective actions, optimizations, and general operations.
Risk **condition**	Likely root causes: • **Slow propagation** of fault, alarm, or configuration change events also yields faulty information on the true current state of the target application. • **Long measurement windows** (e.g., 15-minute performance management reporting windows) both blur data (by homogenizing 15 minutes of behavior into a single set of numbers) and guarantee that the data are somewhat stale (because it is the first time that the organization sees what happened at the beginning of the measurement window).
Risk (service) **consequence**	Stale data may delay activation of automatic self-healing and high availability mechanisms because they cannot activate until appropriate data reach them. Stale data may also compromise an organization's ability to localize and correct shorter duration transient events, like episodes of packet loss or VM scheduling latency, because by the time the data are available, the transient event has long since passed.
Risk **impact**	Less effective impairment detection, localization, and correction can prolong user service impact episodes.

point may be materially different by the time the data reach the service management system(s) or staff.

■ **Mirage** (mirage risk [Table 19.4])—Seeing something that is not actually true, often due to either a faulty conceptual model of the system or a faulty implementation of that model. For example, a "dreaming" element that reports it is successfully processing user traffic when it has actually failed (i.e., the element is "dreaming" that it is working properly when, in fact, it is "sleeping" and not processing traffic).

As an example, consider the physical visibility problem of the captain of the *RMS Titanic* after the ship struck an iceberg in the early hours of April 15, 1912.

Table 19.4 Mirage Risk

Attribute	Value
Risk **name**	Mirage risk.
Risk **root cause**	True state of a service component is not reported correctly.
Risk **condition**	A defect or failure prevents the true service state of a component from being correctly reported. Some organizations use the euphemism "dreaming" to describe the mirage situation in which a component has stopped functioning properly, but the control module is dreaming that everything is working properly, so it reports normal/green operational status to relevant management systems. Thus, element and network management systems and/or human operations staff must rely on secondary mechanisms and/or tedious troubleshooting to first recognize the faulty status report and then correct the true root cause of service impairment.
Risk (service) **consequence**	Mirage/dreaming incidents prolong duration of user service impact because fault localization, and perhaps even fault detection, is delayed.
Risk **impact**	Less effective impairment localization can prolong user service impact episodes.

To determine appropriate emergency actions, the captain needs to understand the true nature of the damage by addressing visibility risks:

- Unobstructed visibility—which watertight compartments are damaged?
- Unblurred visibility—how fast is each compartment taking on water?
- Fresh (not stale) visibility—how much water is in each compartment now?

Service integrators or CSCs should

1. Select VNFs that provide high visibility into their VNFCs, as well as the delivered service quality of their critical resources (e.g., virtualized compute, memory, storage, networking, and functional components used as-a-service)
2. Deploy service probes throughout the network service delivery path to independently assess true service performance, quality, and workload
3. Select infrastructure, management, orchestration, and functional component cloud service providers who offer fine-grained visibility into the service quality that they deliver to each of the CSCs, VNFs, and VNFCs

Accuracy and timeliness of fault, alarm, and other critical state data is routinely validated against ground-truth reality, such as comparing the timeliness and accuracy of the cloud service provider's alarming of an actual virtual machine error/failure event and when the application user service was impacted. Close monitoring and continuous improvement can reduce visibility risks over time.

Chapter 20

Service Policy Risks

As shown in Figure 20.1, wisdom, knowledge, and information drive service provider operational policies, which are captured in both the scripts that serve as inputs for automated systems and the work instructions that guide human operators. Leveraging insights of Section 4.6, "Quality Model for Cloud-Based Applications," we explicitly decouple the following risks:

- **Service policy risks**, which drive decisions and actions of automated systems and human operators; this topic is considered in this chapter.
- **Flawed translation of service policy into automation scripts** considered as faulty service workflow risk (Table 18.6).
- **Faulty execution of policy by automated systems** due to lifecycle management (execution) risks (Chapter 23), VM placement policy violation risk (Table 14.6), or VN diversity compliance violation risk (Table 15.6).
- **Flawed translation of service policy into human work instructions** considered as human process risk (Table 22.3).
- **Faulty execution of policy by human operators** considered as human error risk (Table 22.4).
- **Faulty input data** due to visibility risks (Chapter 19).

Figure 20.2 maps the following service policy risk items into the cloud risk fishbone:

- **Insufficient Spare Capacity (Target) Risk** (Table 20.1)—CSC organizations hold sufficient reserve or spare online application capacity to both cover capacity change lead times and mitigate the user service impact of failure events, demand forecasting errors, or other events that might otherwise push application demand above online capacity. Holding insufficient spare online application capacity increases the risk that some users will not receive

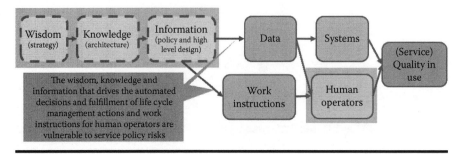

Figure 20.1 Service policy risks in the quality model for cloud-based applications.

acceptable user service quality. Figure 20.3 illustrates this risk in the context of the online application capacity model of Chapter 6, "Lean Application Capacity Management."

■ **Faulty Resource Placement Policy Risk** (Table 20.2)—Highly available architectures rely on primary and protecting components being placed in different failure groups so no single point of failure can produce a service outage. Policies that stipulate which components may not be placed into the same infrastructure failure group are called anti-affinity rules. CSCs must provide anti-affinity rules and other placement policy instructions to their cloud service providers, and (subject to CSP policies) cloud service providers must continuously enforce those placement rules. Faulty resource placement policy risk (Table 20.2) covers flawed anti-affinity and other placement rules being provided by the CSC; VM placement policy violation risk (Table 14.6) and VN diversity compliance violation risk (Table 15.6) cover flawed policy enforcement by the CSP.

■ **Faulty Scaling Decision Criteria Risk** (Table 20.3)—As explained in Chapter 6, "Lean Application Capacity Management," and shown in Figure 20.4, application capacity management is usefully decoupled into capacity decision processes and capacity fulfillment processes. Both automated and human capacity management decisions are made by comparing data on both the current and the forecast future state of the target application against some policy criteria. Faulty scaling decision criteria risk (Table 20.3) covers policy-related decision risks such as the following:

  – **Wrong data are considered**, for example, not considering all relevant alarm types and resource utilization metrics.

  – **Wrong decision criteria are used**, for example, using decision criteria thresholds that are too aggressive like waiting until resource utilization hits 95% before ordering a capacity growth action.

  – **Wrong policy response is requested**, for example, ordering only a small capacity growth action when the system is saturated in deep overload.

■ **Inaccurate Demand Forecast Risk** (Table 20.4)—Capacity planning decisions are based on forecasts of future demand. Profoundly wrong demand forecasts can cause capacity decision processes to produce faulty decisions.

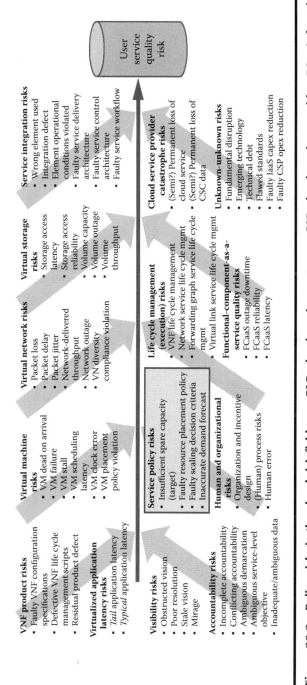

Figure 20.2 Policy risks in the cloud risk fishbone. CSC, cloud service customer; CSP, cloud service provider; FCaaS, functional-component-as-a-service; IaaS, infrastructure-as-a-service; VM, virtual machine; VN, virtual network; VNF, virtualized network function.

Table 20.1 Insufficient Spare Capacity (Target) Risk

Attribute	Value
Risk **name**	Insufficient spare capacity (target) risk.
Risk **root cause**	Target for spare online capacity is insufficient to serve offered load with acceptable service quality following failure event or some foreseen or unforeseen situation.
Risk **condition**	Automated systems and/or human staff correctly maintain the level of spare online capacity dictated by CSC policy, yet that level of reserve online capacity is insufficient to serve all user demand with acceptable service quality.
Risk (service) **consequence**	Some user workload is rejected via overload control mechanisms; other user service may experience increased service latency, reduced functionality, or other impairments.
Risk **impact**	Service reliability, latency, and/or quality.

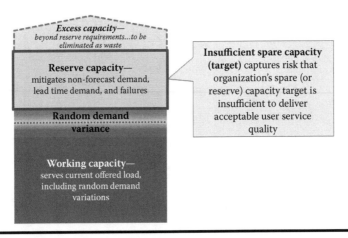

Figure 20.3 Insufficient spare capacity risk.

Table 20.2   Faulty Resource Placement Policy Risk

Attribute	Value
Risk **name**	Faulty resource placement policy risk.
Risk **root cause**	Policy for placing virtual machine, virtual networks, virtual storage, VNFs, or other service resources creates a single point of failure or otherwise risks service performance, throughput, or high availability operation.
Risk **condition**	• Primary and protecting application components are in the same infrastructure failure group, so high availability mechanisms do not work properly, or • Excess latency and packet loss introduced because components and/or resources are unnecessarily distributed.
Risk (service) **consequence**	Infrastructure failure simultaneously impacts both primary and protecting application components, thereby overwhelming the application's high availability architecture, or Excess packet latency, loss, and jitter accrue due to poor resource placement.
Risk **impact**	Service outage downtime, or perhaps only service quality, latency, and reliability impact.

Table 20.3   Faulty Scaling Decision Criteria Risk

Attribute	Value
Risk **name**	Faulty scaling decision criteria risk.
Risk **root cause**	Decision criteria for requesting application capacity growth or degrowth actions are faulty so insufficient capacity is online to cover offered workload.
Risk **condition**	• Growth is requested too late, including not allowing sufficient time to detect and mitigate failures when executing scaling actions (e.g., addressing dead-on-arrival VM instances). • Degrowth is requested too early. • Wrong growth or degrowth action is requested.
Risk (service) **consequence**	Insufficient application capacity is available to serve lead time demand.
Risk **impact**	Service latency, reliability, quality, or outage downtime impact.

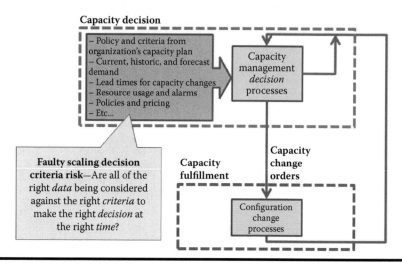

Figure 20.4 Faulty scaling decision criteria risk.

Table 20.4 Inaccurate Demand Forecast Risk

Attribute	Value
Risk **name**	Inaccurate demand forecast risk.
Risk **root cause**	Service demand forecast is materially wrong, such as failing to predict surging user demand.
Risk **condition**	Faulty user demand forecasts provided as input to application capacity decision processes and systems.
Risk (service) **consequence**	Insufficient application capacity is online to serve surging user demand, so overload controls may activate to shed some user demand.
Risk **impact**	Service latency, reliability, or quality impact.

Chapter 21

Accountability Risks

Project managers often use the following definitions of responsibility and accountability when constructing responsible–accountable–consulted–informed (RACI) charts:

- **Responsible—the doer**—"The 'doer' is the individual(s) who actually complete the task. The 'doer' is responsible for action/implementation. Responsibility can be shared. The degree of responsibility is determined by the individual with the 'A'" (Smith and Erwin).
- **Accountable—the buck stops here**—"The accountable person is the individual who is ultimately answerable for the activity or decision. This includes 'yes' or 'no' authority and veto power. Only one 'A' can be assigned to an action" (Smith and Erwin).

As multiple organizations are included in the value chain that delivers cloud-based application services to end users, it is crucial that the responsibilities and accountabilities of each party are back to back, meaning they are complete (no gaps) and interlocked (no overlaps). Clear and comprehensive accountabilities enable each party to focus tightly on their responsibilities; if an issue arises, then clear and comprehensive accountabilities should enable the root cause to be rapidly attributed to the appropriate party who can rapidly identify the true root cause.

Figure 21.1 highlights the four fundamental accountability risks onto the canonical service delivery model of Figure 4.4:

- Incomplete accountability risk (Table 21.1)
- Conflicting accountability risk (Table 21.2)

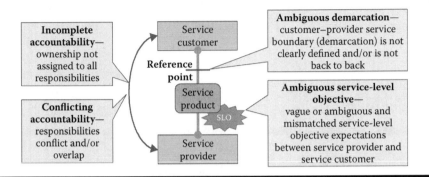

Figure 21.1 Accountability risks in the canonical service delivery model.

Table 21.1 Incomplete Accountability Risk

Attribute	Value
Risk **name**	Incomplete accountability risk.
Risk **root cause**	Responsibility and accountability for all functionality, operations, risks, and risk controls/treatments are not fully specified and agreed upon.
Risk **condition**	Incomplete, ill-defined, and non-agreed-upon accountability creates gaps that no party is responsible for, so no organization may be appropriately equipped to troubleshoot and correct problems that arise.
Risk **consequence**	1. Delays in isolating true root cause (because nobody owns it). 2. Delays in agreeing which party will debug and temporarily fix the problem (because nobody wants additional SLA liability). 3. Delays in deploying corrective actions because parties may not agree on exactly what corrective actions should be taken by which organizations, and perhaps who should pay for the work.
Risk **impact**	Risk events produce longer user service impact because of delays in isolating and fixing the problem.

Table 21.2 Conflicting Accountability Risk

Attribute	Value
Risk **name**	Conflicting accountability risk.
Risk **root cause**	Multiple parties believe they are accountable for the same functionality, responsibility, and/or risk, so multiple parties independently take actions that may collide and conflict. For example, multiple mechanisms or organizations try to simultaneously repair the same virtualized network function (VNF) component failure.
Risk **condition**	Two or more parties feel responsible for the same action(s) or accountable for the same risks.
Risk **consequence**	1. Failures because multiple parties simultaneously attempt conflicting actions. 2. Delayed fault localization and repair because different partys' actions conflict to create chaos and confusion. 3. Delays in deploying corrective action because party assigned accountability may not have architected their solution/service in a way that makes it straightforward to rapidly and effectively address the true root cause. 4. Wasted effort as multiple parties address the same issues.
Risk **impact**	More frequent impairment events that take longer to correct.

- Ambiguous demarcation risk (Table 21.3)
- Ambiguous service-level objective risk (Table 21.4)
- Inadequate/ambiguous data risk (Table 21.5)

Figure 21.2 illustrates accountability risks in the context of the cloud risk fishbone diagram.

Figure 21.3 highlights the primary accountability boundaries for cloud service customers on the canonical accountability model of Figure 1.3. In particular, cloud service customers should clarify the accountabilities that their software suppliers, integration suppliers, and cloud service providers of infrastructure, management, orchestration, and functional components offered as-a-service providers have toward them. Also, cloud service providers should clarify the accountabilities that they have toward both their cloud service users and the network providers that haul traffic to and from users.

Accountability risks are controlled via the following:

- Define clear responsibilities and accountability perimeters for organizations involved in service delivery, including for "all causes" and catastrophic/force majeure risks as well as for ordinary product/supplier-attributable impairments.

Table 21.3 Ambiguous Demarcation Risk

Attribute	Value
Risk **name**	Ambiguous demarcation risk.
Risk **root cause**	Demarcation between accountability parties is not clearly defined, so accountability for risk treatment and true root cause of service quality impairments cannot rapidly and reliably be agreed upon.
Risk **condition**	• Vague, ambiguous, impractical, or undefined accountability demarcation points create cracks that accountability for risk assessment, control, and treatment can fall into. • Risks may be ignored by all parties because they assume that their respective counterparties are addressing the risk, so no effective risk control may be deployed.
Risk **consequence**	1. Delays in agreeing on true root cause because no party believes they own the risk. 2. Delays in deploying corrective action because party ultimately assigned accountability may not have architected their solution/service in a way that makes it straightforward to rapidly and effectively address the true root cause. 3. Delays in detecting problems because no provider is monitoring them. In the worst case, it may result in initial failure reports originating from the end user.
Risk **impact**	More frequent impairment events that take longer to correct.

- ◾ Accountable parties have the resources, controls, processes, and structures to make it feasible and likely that they will fulfill their responsibilities.
- ◾ Identify key quality indicators (KQIs) for all critical inputs in the service delivery chain, establish quantitative service-level objectives for those KQIs, and monitor actual performance. If deployed KQIs do not cover relevant service quality characteristics, then evolve KQIs.

Table 21.4 Ambiguous Service-Level Objective Risk

Attribute	*Value*
Risk **name**	Ambiguous service-level objective risk.
Risk **root cause**	Sloppy or inadequate specification of service-level objectives means that the service provider's actual service quality target is materially different from the service customer's expectations.
Risk **condition**	Cloud service provider or VNF supplier delivers technically acceptable service quality, yet it is not adequate for the cloud service customer's application service.
Risk **consequence**	Poor user service quality.
Risk **impact**	Increased service latency, failed transactions, and/or degraded service quality.

Table 21.5 Inadequate/Ambiguous Data Risk

Attribute	*Value*
Risk **name**	Inadequate/ambiguous data risk.
Risk **root cause**	Fault and other data associated with a failure event are insufficient or otherwise inadequate to localize the problem and establish clear accountability.
Risk **condition**	Delays in agreeing which party is responsible for a service failure may delay troubleshooting and service restoration actions.
Risk **consequence**	Duration of service outage or impairment increases, while responsibility and accountability for troubleshooting and service restoration are debated.
Risk **impact**	More frequent impairment events that take longer to correct.

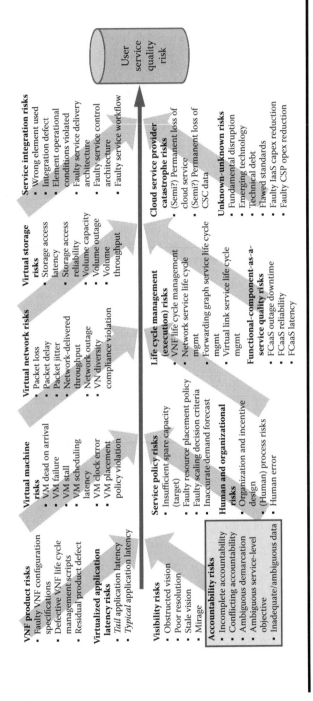

Figure 21.2 Accountability risks in the cloud risk fishbone. CSC, cloud service customer; CSP, cloud service provider; FCaaS, functional-component-as-a-service; IaaS, infrastructure-as-a-service; VM, virtual machine; VN, virtual network; VNF, virtualized network function.

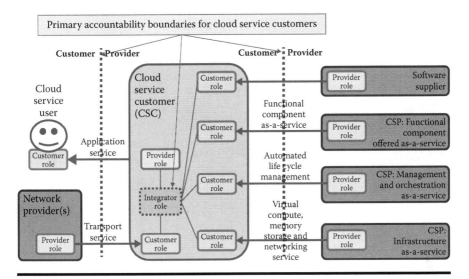

Figure 21.3 Primary accountability boundaries for cloud service customers.

Chapter 22

Human and Organizational Risks

Figure 22.1 offers a simplified view of organizations, processes, and humans:

- An **organization** is an administrative or business structure that is formed for a particular purpose, for example, a cloud service customer organization formed to offer some application service to end users, and a cloud service provider organization formed to offer infrastructure-, platform-, or software-as-a-service to cloud service customers. To effectively fulfill its purpose, an organization defines roles, responsibilities, measurements, and incentives.
- **Processes** and policies guide management and staff to better align their individual actions with the goals of the organization.
- **Human** managers and staff execute processes and follow policies to advance the purpose of the organization.

As shown in Figure 22.2, the quality model for cloud-based applications of Section 4.6 clarifies the practical distinction between process risks and human error risks.

- **Human process risk** (Table 22.3)—Work instructions and processes crystallize the organization's policies that guide day-to-day and emergency activities of managers and staff. For example, how are service outages managed? How are troubles localized? How is outage accountability assigned? How quickly are managers notified? How are suppliers' technical support organizations engaged? As a practical matter, these processes capture an organization's risk treatment decisions, like how much training staff must have to perform a job

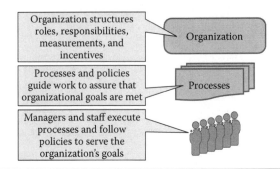

Figure 22.1 Humans, processes, and organizations.

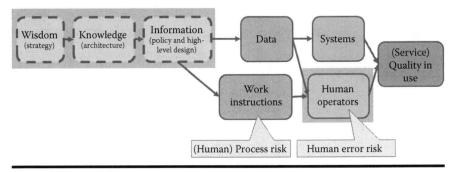

Figure 22.2 Human process and human error risks.

function, when to override automated mechanisms, and what actions to take in response to various service emergencies.

■ **Human error risk** (Table 22.4)—All humans occasionally make mistakes or errors such as due to fatigue, inattention, stress, or panic. Note that sabotage, vandalism, and other deliberate human acts are security risks (hence beyond the scope of this work) rather than quality risks (in scope for this work).

The industry has traditionally lumped both human process and error risks into the general notion of *procedural error,* which is defined as "an error that is the direct result of human intervention or error" (QuEST Forum, 2012-12-31). Table 22.1 highlights the distinction between human error risks and human process risks by factoring several examples and contributing factors of TL 9000 procedural errors.

In addition to human process and human error risks, there are higher-level organization and incentive design risks (Table 22.2). For example, faulty organizational design can decouple accountability for results (i.e., who is ultimately answerable) from responsibility and control of those results (i.e., who actually does the work), deploy misaligned incentives, and otherwise create a context that reduces the feasibility and likelihood of achieving the organization's objectives. Poorly

Table 22.1 Factoring TL 9000 Procedural Error (QuEST Forum, 2012-12-31) into Human Error and Process Risks, Human and Organizational Risks

Human Error Risk (Table 22.4)	Human Process Risk (Table 22.3)
Contributing factors [of procedural errors] can include but are not limited to the following:	
a. "Deviations from accepted practices or documentation"	
	b. "Inadequate training"
	c. "Unclear, incorrect, or out-of-date documentation"
	d. "Inadequate or unclear displays, messages, or signals"
	e. "Inadequate or unclear hardware labeling"
f. "Miscommunication"	
	g. "Nonstandard configurations"
	h. "Insufficient supervision or control"
i. "User characteristics such as mental attention, physical health, physical fatigue, mental health, and substance abuse"	
Examples of procedural error can include but are not limited to the following:	
a. "Removing the wrong fuse or circuit pack"	
b. "Not taking proper precautions to protect equipment, such as shorting out power, not wearing electrostatic discharge (ESD) strap, etc."	
c. "Unauthorized work"	
d. "Not following methods of procedures (MOPs)"	
e. "Not following the steps of the documentation"	

(*Continued*)

Table 22.1 (Continued)   Factoring TL 9000 Procedural Error (QuEST Forum, 2012-12-31) into Human Error and Process Risks, Human and Organizational Risks

Human Error Risk (Table 22.4)	Human Process Risk (Table 22.3)
f. "Using the wrong documentation"	
g. "Using incorrect or outdated documentation"	
	h. "Insufficient documentation"
	i. "Translation errors"
j. "User panic response to problems"	
k. "Entering incorrect commands"	
l. "Entering a command without understanding the impact"	

Table 22.2   Organization and Incentive Design Risk

Attribute	Value
Risk **name**	Organization and incentive design risk.
Risk **root cause**	Incentives, structure, and/or culture of an organization biases processes, policies, management, and staff to accept greater service quality risks or fails to incentivize reduction of risk.
Risk **condition**	Greater appetite for service quality risk than is consistent with organization's stated quality objectives, thereby creating greater risk of service-impacting failure events.
Risk **consequence**	Greater risk of service quality impairments occurring. Trouble localization and correction may also take longer, especially if those activities are not the highest-priority work in the organization.
Risk **impact**	More frequent service impairment events of somewhat longer duration.

Table 22.3 Human Process Risk

Attribute	Value
Risk **name**	Human process risk.
Risk **root cause**	Poorly documented or undocumented documented policies and procedures increase risks of poor outcomes and service-impacting failures.
Risk **condition**	Human procedural error can drive a system out of its normal and protected operating region, disable automatic alarms and control mechanisms, take wrong actions, or fail to promptly take right actions.
Risk **consequence**	Service-impacting failure event cascades from nominally correct execution of risky procedures, policies, or practices.
Risk **impact**	More frequent impairment events and/or longer duration of impact.

Table 22.4 Human Error Risk

Attribute	Value
Risk **name**	Human error risk.
Risk **root cause**	Human mistake or error, which might have been caused by inattention, fatigue, physical or mental health, substance abuse, etc.
Risk **condition**	Human procedural error can drive a system out of its normal and protected operating region, disable automatic alarms and control mechanisms, take wrong actions, or fail to promptly take right actions.
Risk **consequence**	The system is driven into a degraded or inoperable operating region, or prevented from returning to a normal operating region. User service quality is impacted when the system remains in the degraded or inoperable operating region.
Risk **impact**	More frequent impairment events and/or longer duration of impact.

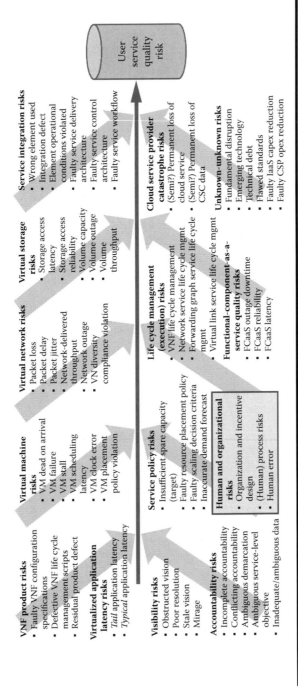

VNF product risks
- Faulty VNF configuration specifications
- Defective VNF life cycle management scripts
- Residual product defect

Virtualized application latency risks
- *Tail* application latency
- *Typical* application latency

Virtual machine risks
- VM dead on arrival
- VM failure
- VM stall
- VM scheduling latency
- VM clock error
- VM placement policy violation

Virtual network risks
- Packet loss
- Packet delay
- Packet jitter
- Network-delivered throughput
- Network outage
- VN diversity compliance violation

Virtual storage risks
- Storage access latency
- Storage access reliability
- Volume outage
- Volume throughput
- Volume capacity

Service integration risks
- Wrong element used
- Integration defect
- Element operational conditions violated
- Faulty service delivery architecture
- Faulty service control architecture
- Faulty service workflow

Visibility risks
- Obstructed vision
- Poor resolution
- Stale vision
- Mirage

Accountability risks
- Incomplete accountability
- Conflicting accountability
- Ambiguous demarcation
- Ambiguous service-level objective
- Inadequate/ambiguous data

Service policy risks
- Insufficient spare capacity (target)
- Faulty resource placement policy
- Faulty scaling decision criteria
- Inaccurate demand forecast

Human and organizational risks
- Organization and incentive design
- (Human) process risks
- Human error

Life cycle management (execution) risks
- VNF life cycle management
- Network service life cycle mgmt
- Forwarding graph service life cycle mgmt
- Virtual link service life cycle mgmt

Functional-component-as-a-service quality risks
- FCaaS outage downtime
- FCaaS reliability
- FCaaS latency

Cloud service provider catastrophe risks
- (Semi?) Permanent loss of cloud service
- (Semi?) Permanent loss of CSC data

Unknown-unknown risks
- Fundamental disruption
- Emerging technology
- Technical debt
- Flawed standards
- Faulty IaaS capex reduction
- Faulty CSP opex reduction

User service quality risk

Figure 22.3 Human and organizational risks in the cloud risk fishbone. CSC, cloud service customer; CSP, cloud service provider; FCaaS, functional-component-as-a-service; IaaS, infrastructure-as-a-service; VM, virtual machine; VN, virtual network; VNF, virtualized network function.

structured incentives can create a moral hazard that increases an organization's risk; for example, if bonus payments to management and staff are tied solely to maximizing opex savings with no consideration of the downside consequences of poor service quality, then sensible managers and staff will accept more service quality risk than is consistent with the organization's reputation for quality in pursuit of greater opex savings for the organization and greater bonus payments for themselves. Organizational culture may also discourage organizations from consider rare but high-impact black-swan risks (Taleb, 2010) or other hazards.

Figure 22.3 illustrates how human and organizational risks fit into the cloud risk fishbone.

Chapter 23

Life Cycle Management (Execution) Risks

Automation of virtualized network function (VNF) and application service life cycle management is fundamental both to delivering new services and value faster and to improving operational efficiency for cloud-based application services. While automated mechanisms can dramatically reduce the risk of human error risk (Table 22.4), the mechanisms that execute automated life cycle management actions are inevitably imperfect and will occasionally fail to perform flawlessly. Life cycle management (execution) risks cover the hazards that prevent syntactically and semantically correct life cycle management actions for cloud-based application services from being completed successfully.

As shown in Figure 23.1, life cycle management (execution) risks are easily understood in the context of the simplified application capacity management model of Chapter 6, "Lean Application Capacity Management."

- Automated capacity decisions are made by capacity management decision processes (vulnerable to life cycle management [execution] risks), which automatically compare data on the true state of the system (vulnerable to visibility risks, Chapter 19) to capacity change decision criteria (vulnerable to service policy risks, Chapter 20) and dispatch correct capacity change orders (vulnerable to faulty service workflow risk, Table 18.6) as appropriate.

- Automated capacity fulfillment mechanisms execute capacity change orders by executing configuration change processes (vulnerable to life cycle management [execution] risks) based on automation scripts (vulnerable to faulty service workflow risk, Table 18.6, and residual defect in VNF life cycle management script risk, Table 13.2), which rely both on knowledge of the true

Capacity decision

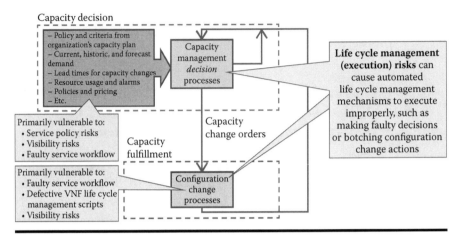

Figure 23.1 Life cycle management (execution) risks in the simplified application capacity management model.

system state (vulnerable to visibility risks, Chapter 19) and on proper execution of relevant components (vulnerable to virtual machine [VM] dead-on-arrival risk Table 14.1; faulty VNF configuration specification risk, Table 13.1; residual product defect risk, Table 13.3; etc.).

Industry has measured the quality of manually executed life cycle management actions for decades via industry standards like TL 9000 product category 7.1.1, *installation*, defined as "contracted or internal services to position, configure, remove, and/or adjust a hardware/software product within the network" such as "New equipment installation, Expansion installation, Upgrade installation, Equipment removal" (QuEST Forum, 2012-12-31). Industry has traditionally applied standard quality measurements like on-time delivery and right-first-time quality to life cycle management actions performed by humans. Suppliers routinely give a promise date for an installation to be completed, and customers assess the suppliers' on-time delivery performance against that promise date; right-first-time performance is self-explanatory. For traditional installations and other life cycle management actions, suppliers would offer a promise date (e.g., completed by next Friday). Automated life cycle management actions should execute much, much faster, so a promise *time* rather than promise *date* is more appropriate. Pizza delivery offers a useful analog for quality measurements of automated life cycle management actions: for instance, a pizza delivery company might promise to deliver the pizza in 30 minutes. Customers can easily evaluate on-time performance by comparing the time the pizza arrives against when they ordered it. Some suppliers even remedy late pizza deliveries with discounts up to and including not charging for food delivered late.

Quality Measurements of Automated Lifecycle Management Actions (QuEST Forum, 2015-08) aligned network functions virtualization (NFV) automated life cycle management actions (ETSI, 2014-12) with TL 9000 product categories so that traditional quality measurements like on-time service delivery and right-first-time service quality can usefully be applied. Table 23.1 shows how these automated life cycle management quality categories map into risk types. Figure 23.2 illustrates how these risk types fit into the cloud risk fishbone.

Applying the pizza delivery quality paradigm to automated life cycle management actions for cloud-based application services, one can measure the quality of those actions via the following standard TL 9000 quality measurements (QuEST Forum, 2012-12-31):

■ **On-time service delivery**—According to the *TL 9000 Measurements Handbook*,

> On-Time Delivery (OTD) measures timeliness of delivery of products to customers. ... The OTD measurement covers on-time delivery performance for any customer-initiated product order. (QuEST Forum, 2012-12-31)

> On-time service delivery measures the percentage of automated life cycle management actions completed within the service provider's *promise time*. For example, if a cloud service provider sets a promise time of 5 minutes for completing *VNF instantiate* actions, the on-time service delivery is the portion of automated life cycle management actions within the measurement period that are completed in 5 minutes or less. Cloud service providers and other suppliers can thus set reasonable *promise times* for fulfilling automated life cycle management actions (e.g., minutes) and realistic on-time service delivery targets (e.g., <100%). Both service providers and service customers can easily compare actual service delivery times to promise times to compute on-time service delivery performance.

■ **Service quality** (SQ)—According to the *TL 9000 Measurements Handbook*,

> Service Quality (SQ) measures performance of a service transaction to specified criteria. ... This measurement is used to provide quality measurement information for establishing the evaluation and continuous improvement of the service. The measurement is based on the number of defective service transactions and the total number of service transactions. (QuEST Forum, 2012-12-31)

> Inevitably, some automated life cycle management either will explicitly fail to be completed successfully or will promptly be found faulty. Service quality is used to measure right-first-time of automated life cycle management actions.

Table 23.1   Factoring Life Cycle Management Actions

Category Name and Definition (QuEST Forum, 2015-08)	Applicable NFV Management and Orchestration Operations (ETSI, 2014-12)	Life Cycle Management (Execution) Risks
Network element services—life cycle management services for network elements (aka virtualized network functions)	• Check VNF instantiation feasibility • Instantiate VNF • Update VNF software • Upgrade VNF software • Query VNF • Modify VNF • Terminate VNF • Scale VNF • Heal VNF	VNF life cycle management (execution) risks (Table 23.2)
Network service services—life cycle management for service delivery chains of physical and virtualized network functions	• Instantiate network service • Terminate network service • Update network service • Query network service • Scale network service	Network service life cycle management (execution) risks (Table 23.3)
Forwarding graph services—life cycle management for VNF forwarding graphs (VNFFGs)	• Create VNFFG • Delete VNFFG • Update VNFFG • Query VNFFG	Forwarding graph service life cycle management (execution) risks (Table 23.4)
Virtual link (VL) services—life cycle management for VLs	• Create VL • Delete VL • Update VL • Query VL	VL service life cycle management (execution) risks (Table 23.5)

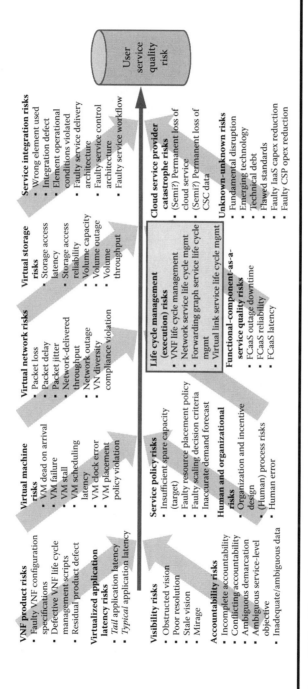

Figure 23.2 Life cycle management (execution) risks in cloud risk fishbone. CSC, cloud service customer; CSP, cloud service provider; FCaaS, functional-component-as-a-service; IaaS, infrastructure-as-a-service; VN, virtual network.

Table 23.2 VNF Life Cycle Management (Execution) Risks

Attribute	Value
Risk **name**	VNF life cycle management (execution) risks.
Risk **root cause**	Some chronic or acute problem with the cloud service provider (i.e., their hardware, software, operations, staff, or other factor) causes some syntactically and semantically correct VNF (aka network element) life cycle management action(s) to fail.
Risk **condition**	Some cloud service provider quality, integration, or other problem causes failure of one or more valid VNF life cycle management actions, such as the following: • Check VNF instantiation feasibility • Instantiate VNF • Update VNF software • Upgrade VNF software • Query VNF • Modify VNF • Terminate VNF • Scale VNF • Heal VNF
Risk (service) **consequence**	Cloud service customer's VNF service configuration not changed as requested; e.g., service capacity does not grow, failed components are not healed/repaired. Best-case scenario: cloud service customer's service configuration is unchanged…but service configuration could have been damaged (e.g., producing a support service–caused outage event).
Risk **impact**	Latency, reliability, availability, or general quality impairments to user service are possible, perhaps even partial or total loss of application service functionality or capacity.

■ **Support service–caused outages** (SSO)—According to the *TL 9000 Measurements Handbook*,

The SSO measurement provides insight into the impact of the organization's support service activities on the performance of the network. It is used to evaluate the downtime frequency delivered to the end user during product operation with a goal of reducing the frequency of these events, their associated cost, and their impact on customer satisfaction and revenue. (QuEST Forum, 2012-12-31)

Table 23.3 Network Service Life Cycle Management (Execution) Risks

Attribute	Value
Risk **name**	Network service life cycle management (execution) risks.
Risk **root cause**	Some chronic or acute problem with the cloud service provider (i.e., their hardware, software, operations, staff, or other factor) causes some syntactically and semantically correct (network) application service life cycle management action(s) to fail.
Risk **condition**	Some cloud service provider quality, integration, or other problem causes failure of one or more valid network application service life cycle management actions, such as the following: • Instantiate network service • Terminate network service • Update network service • Query network service • Scale network service For example, a request to scale a network service may fail to properly grow all VNFs and service components to assure that requested online application service capacity is available to serve offered load.
Risk (service) **consequence**	Cloud service customer's network service configuration not changed as requested, e.g., service capacity does not grow properly. Best-case scenario: cloud service customer's service configuration is unchanged…but service configuration could have been damaged (e.g., producing a support service–caused outage event).
Risk **impact**	Latency, reliability, availability or general quality impairments to user service are possible, perhaps even partial or total loss of application service functionality or capacity.

SSO measures toxic life cycle management actions that produce user service impact.

■ **Number of problem reports** (NPR)—According to the *TL 9000 Measurements Handbook.*

This measurement is used to evaluate the number of customer-originated problem reports related to the product and its associated processes during its General Availability (GA) and Retirement Phases. Problem reports may have a negative impact on the organization

Table 23.4 Forwarding Graph Service Life Cycle Management (Execution) Risks

Attribute	Value
Risk **name**	Forwarding graph service life cycle management (execution) risks.
Risk **root cause**	Some chronic or acute problem with the cloud service provider (i.e., their hardware, software, operations, staff, or other factor) causes some syntactically and semantically correct VNFFG (nominally software defined network [SDN] connectivity across a network application service) life cycle management action(s) to fail.
Risk **condition**	Some cloud service provider quality, integration, or other problem causes failure of one or more valid VNFFG service life cycle management actions, such as the following: • Create VNFFG • Delete VNFFG • Update VNFFG • Query VNFFG
Risk (service) **consequence**	Cloud service customer's VNFFG service configuration not changed as requested. Best-case scenario: cloud service customer's service configuration is unchanged…but service configuration could have been damaged (e.g., producing a support service–caused outage event).
Risk **impact**	Latency, reliability, availability, or general quality impairments to user service are possible, perhaps even partial or total loss of application service functionality or capacity.

(such as rework), on the customer (such as scheduling repeat site visits) and may jeopardize or affect the customer's business operations. Problem reports contribute to loss of end-user loyalty and customer satisfaction. (QuEST Forum, 2012-12-31)

NPR measures the number of problem reports filed by customers (e.g., cloud service customers) against their supplier (i.e., their cloud service provider who implements automated life cycle management services). For example, a support service–caused outage event or chronic service quality or

Table 23.5   Virtual Link Service Life Cycle Management (Execution) Risks

Attribute	Value
Risk **name**	VL service life cycle management (execution) risks.
Risk **root cause**	Some chronic or acute problem with the cloud service provider (i.e., their hardware, software, operations, staff, or other factor) causes some syntactically and semantically correct virtual networking link life cycle management action(s) to fail.
Risk **condition**	Some cloud service provider quality, integration, or other problem causes failure of one or more valid virtual network link service life cycle management actions, such as the following: • Create VL • Delete VL • Update VL • Query VL
Risk (service) **consequence**	Cloud service customer's VL service configuration is not changed as requested. Best-case scenario: cloud service customer's service configuration is unchanged…but service configuration could have been damaged (e.g., producing a support service–caused outage event).
Risk **impact**	Latency, reliability, availability, or general quality impairments to user service are possible, perhaps even partial or total loss of application service functionality or capacity.

on-time deliver problems may prompt cloud service customers to file problem reports against the applicable cloud service provider.

■ **Fix response time** (FRT) "measures the organization's overall responsiveness to customer-originated problem reports" (QuEST Forum, 2012-12-31).

■ **Overdue problem fix responsiveness** (OFR) "measures the responsiveness to customer-originated problem reports that are not fixed on time according to the counting rules for the Fix Response Time measurement" (QuEST Forum, 2012-12-31).

Life cycle management (execution) risks can impair the service quality, on-time service delivery, number of problem reports and outage performance of automated life cycle management actions.

Chapter 24

Functional-Component-as-a-Service Quality Risks

Application services offered by cloud service customers (CSCs) often rely on functional components offered as-a-service by cloud service providers (CSPs), like database-as-a-service and load-balancing-as-a-service. As these functional components often provide critical functionality in the service delivery path (e.g., load balancing), impairments of the service quality delivered by those components can adversely impact application service quality delivered to the CSC's end users.

NFV Service Quality Metrics (ETSI, 2014-12) considers service quality of technology components offered as-a-service as well as virtual machine, virtual networking, and orchestration metrics. Table 24.1 shows how technology-component-as-a-service (TcaaS) quality metrics defined by *NFV Service Quality Metrics* apply to functional-component-as-a-service (FCaaS) offerings that are used by CSCs. Figure 24.1 shows FCaaS quality risks in the context of the cloud risk fishbone.

CSPs offering functional components as-a-service to CSCs must manage risks that are similar to the user service quality risks that CSCs manage in the context of their end user–facing application service. As the FCaaS CSP is generally accountable for all causes of FCaaS service quality impairment, the CSC should select an FCaaS CSP who has both credible quality data demonstrating good service quality performance in the past and effective risk and quality management mechanisms in place to assure the feasibility and likelihood of delivering acceptable service quality in the future.

Table 24.1   Functional (Technology) Component Service Quality Metrics and Risk Types

Technology Component Service Quality Metric (from *ETSI, 2014-12*)	NFV Risk Type	Risk Capture Table
TcaaS service downtime	Functional-component-as-a-service outage downtime risk	Table 24.2
TcaaS service reliability	Functional-component-as-a-service reliability risk	Table 24.3
TcaaS service latency	Functional-component-as-a-service latency risk	Table 24.4

Table 24.2   Functional-Component-as-a-Service Outage Downtime Risk

Attribute	Value
Risk **name**	FCaaS outage downtime risk.
Risk **root cause**	Service-impacting outage (planned or unplanned) of cloud service FCaaS offering renders service unavailable to some or all of the CSC's application instances.
Risk **condition**	
Risk **consequence**	Partial or total functionality loss of the technology component prevents some or all of the CSC's application from delivering some functionality to end users.
Risk **impact**	Partial or total functionality loss of the target user service.

Table 24.3   Functional-Component-as-a-Service Reliability Risk

Attribute	Value
Risk **name**	FCaaS reliability risk.
Risk **root cause**	Some failure or impairment prevents the FCaaS from completing some or all of the requests from some or all of the CSC's application instances.
Risk **condition**	
Risk **consequence**	Failure of FCaaS requests issued by CSC application elements prevents the user service requests from being processed correctly within the maximum acceptable time.
Risk **impact**	Service reliability, and perhaps service quality, of impacted application transactions is impacted.

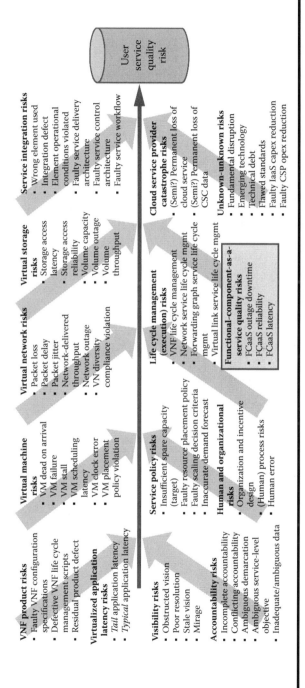

Figure 24.1 Functional-component-as-a-service quality in cloud risk fishbone. IaaS, infrastructure-as-a-service; VN, virtual network; VNF, virtualized network function.

Table 24.4   Functional-Component-as-a-Service Latency Risk

Attribute	Value
Risk **name**	FCaaS latency risk.
Risk **root cause**	Service latency of FCaaS requests is higher than expected, such as due to suboptimal resource placement (e.g., in a remote data center), service quality impairments of the virtualized infrastructure hosting the functional component offered as-a-service, etc.
Risk **condition**	Increased latency in the critical user service delivery path.
Risk **consequence**	Increased latency to serve application requests by CSC users.
Risk **impact**	Service latency is impacted; extreme latency impairments can manifest as service reliability problems.

Chapter 25

Cloud Service Provider Catastrophe Risks

Cloud service provider (CSP) organizations in general, and their physical data centers in particular, are vulnerable to catastrophic and force majeure risks, including the following:

- **Natural disasters** like flood, earthquake, tsunami, hurricane, volcano, etc.
- **Human-caused hazards** like terrorism, cyber attack, fire, product tampering, war, civil disorder and rioting, bankruptcy, etc.
- **Accidents and technology hazards** like civil infrastructure failures (loss of natural gas, water, sewerage, electricity), building collapse, hazardous material incidents, etc.

Business Continuity and Disaster Recovery Planning for IT Professionals (Snedaker, 2013) offers a comprehensive list of distal catastrophic risks confronting enterprises, including CSCs.

The fundamental risks presented to a cloud service customer (CSC) by a CSP catastrophe are as follows:

- **Prolonged or permanent loss of cloud service from impacted cloud data center**—(Semi?) permanent loss of cloud service risk (Table 25.1)—Some catastrophic event profoundly impacts a CSP's ability to deliver infrastructure, management, orchestration, and/or functional component from an impacted availability zone, data center, or region.
- **Prolonged or permanent loss of CSC data hosted in impacted cloud data center**—(Semi?) permanent loss of CSC data risk (Table 25.2)

Table 25.1 (Semi?) Permanent Loss of Cloud Service Risk

Attribute	Value
Risk **name**	(Semi?) permanent loss of cloud service risk.
Risk **root cause**	Natural disaster, human-caused hazard, accident hazard, or technology hazard causes delivery of infrastructure, management, orchestration, and/or functional component services from a cloud provider to unexpectedly cease.
Risk **condition**	CSC service is impacted until disaster recovery/business continuity plans are completed successfully to restore CSC services.
Risk (service) **consequence**	Partial or total functionality or capacity loss until CSC's disaster recovery actions can be completed.
Risk **impact**	User service impacted until disaster recovery actions can be completed, which is nominally the sum of the following: 1. The time for the CSC to declare a disaster and activate their disaster recovery plans. 2. The time to execute the CSC's disaster recovery/business continuity plan (nominally their recovery time objective [RTO]).

Table 25.2 (Semi?) Permanent Loss of CSC Data Risk

Attribute	Value
Risk **name**	(Semi?) permanent loss of CSC data risk.
Risk **root cause**	Catastrophic event causes data changes since last successful georedundant data replication or backup to be lost.
Risk **condition**	Changes to (volatile and nonvolatile) data that were not replicated or backed up to a nonimpacted location are permanently lost.
Risk (service) **consequence**	Service impact depends on the application and the nature of the data lost.
Risk **impact**	

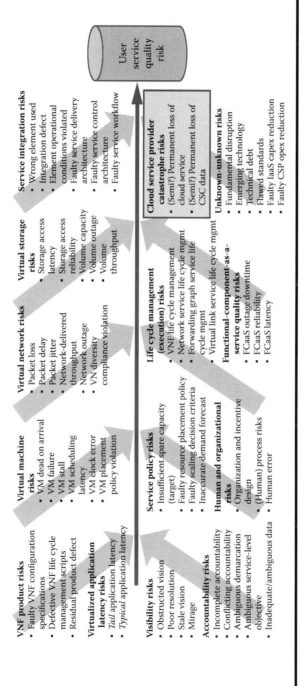

VNF product risks
- Faulty VNF configuration specifications
- Defective VNF life cycle management scripts
- Residual product defect

Virtualized application latency risks
- *Tail* application latency
- *Typical* application latency

Virtual machine risks
- VM dead on arrival
- VM failure
- VM stall
- VM scheduling latency
- VM clock error
- VM placement policy violation

Virtual network risks
- Packet loss
- Packet delay
- Packet jitter
- Network-delivered throughput
- Network outage
- VN diversity compliance violation

Virtual storage risks
- Storage access latency
- Storage access reliability
- Volume capacity
- Volume outage
- Volume throughput

Service integration risks
- Wrong element used
- Integration defect
- Element operational conditions violated
- Faulty service delivery architecture
- Faulty service control architecture
- Faulty service workflow

Visibility risks
- Obstructed vision
- Poor resolution
- Stale vision
- Mirage

Accountability risks
- Incomplete accountability
- Conflicting accountability
- Ambiguous demarcation
- Ambiguous service-level objective
- Inadequate/ambiguous data

Service policy risks
- Insufficient spare capacity (target)
- Faulty resource placement policy
- Faulty scaling decision criteria
- Inaccurate demand forecast

Human and organizational risks
- Organization and incentive design
- (Human) process risks
- Human error

Life cycle management (execution) risks
- VNF life cycle management
- Network service life cycle mgmt
- Forwarding graph service life cycle mgmt
- Virtual link service life cycle mgmt

Functional-component-as-a-service quality risks
- FCaaS outage downtime
- FCaaS reliability
- FCaaS latency

Cloud service provider catastrophe risks
- (Semi?) Permanent loss of cloud service
- (Semi?) Permanent loss of CSC data

Unknown-unknown risks
- Fundamental disruption
- Emerging technology
- Technical debt
- Flawed standards
- Faulty IaaS capex reduction
- Faulty CSP opex reduction

User service quality risk

Figure 25.1 Catastrophic cloud service provider risks. FCaaS, functional-component-as-a-service; IaaS, infrastructure-as-a-service; VM, virtual machine; VN, virtual network.

While some data center outages may be promptly repairable (e.g., severe equipment failures or emergency power-off situations), other outages are more persistent (e.g., structural collapse due to an earthquake). CSP catastrophe risks can cause an impacted CSP availability zone, data center, or perhaps even the entire organization to be incapable of serving CSC demand temporarily. Service continuity management (Section 8.2.6) disaster recovery plans should be designed to cope with data center failures that persist for indefinite periods, like repairing a data center after a major earthquake, flood, fire, etc. If the CSP has inadequate business continuity plans or for other reasons, then the CSP might be ruined or otherwise permanently unable to restore original service and/or data. Many CSCs will activate their disaster recovery plans promptly after their application is impacted by data center failure. User service can be gracefully returned to the impacted data center once it has been repaired and returned to full service.

As explained in Section 8.2.6, "IT Service Continuity Management," CSCs set target recovery time objectives (RTOs) and recovery point objectives (RPOs). Service integrators construct application architectures that meet those RTO and RPO requirements, and assure that virtualized network functions (VNFs) as well as infrastructure, management, orchestration, and functional component CSPs are selected and configured to support the CSC's RTO and RPO requirements. Periodic disaster drills assure that the CSC's disaster recovery and business continuity arrangements adequately mitigate both (semi?) permanent loss of cloud service risk (Table 25.1) and (semi?) permanent loss of CSC data risk (Table 25.2).

Figure 25.1 shows CSP catastrophe risks in the cloud risk fishbone.

Chapter 26

Unknown-Unknown Risks

As discussed in Section 12.4, "Rumsfeld Risks," there are always unknown-unknown risks: the things we don't know that we don't know. As risks must be identified before they can be controlled and treated, risk management for unknown-unknown risks must focus on identifying potential but not-yet-known risks. While unknown-unknowns are fundamentally unknowable, experts can speculate on the likely areas where these unknown-unknown risks will materialize. Best practices for exposing unknown-unknown risks are as follows:

1. Research activities to investigate potential market and operational disruptions and technical risks associated with emerging technologies
2. Vigilant monitoring of potentially disruptive competitors
3. Vigilant monitoring and analysis of quality and performance of our emerging technologies
4. Vigilant monitoring and analysis of industry reports of customers' and competitors' outages and service problems

As shown in Figure 26.1, the author's best guess of unknown-unknown risks that will confront cloud service customers (CSC) regarding the application service quality they deliver to their end users is as follows:

- **Fundamental business/operations disruption risk**—Table 26.1—Technologies like wireless communications and containerized shipping drove waves of creative destruction that reshaped telecommunications and manufacturing as well as logistics. Chapter 31, "Cloud and Creative Destruction," considers how cloud computing might drive a wave of Schumpeterian creative destruction through information technology (IT). Disruptive competitors enabled

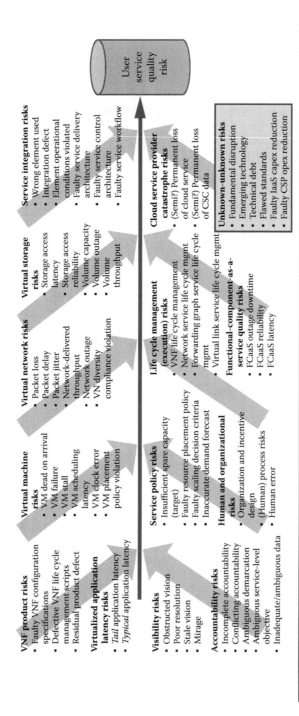

Figure 26.1 Unknown-unknown risk on the cloud risk fishbone. FCaaS, functional-component-as-a-service; IaaS, infrastructure-as-a-service; VM, virtual machine; VN, virtual network; VNF, virtualized network function.

Table 26.1 Fundamental Business/Operations Disruption Risk

Attribute	Value
Risk **name**	Fundamental business/operations disruption risk.
Risk **root cause**	Cloud computing and/or some related technology produces a fundamental disruption to information and communications technologies (ICT).
Risk **condition**	As discussed in Chapter 31, "Cloud and Creative Destruction," cloud computing triggers a wave of Schumpeterian creative destruction that disrupts IT, like how shipping containers completely upended the global transportation/logistics business or how wireless technology disrupted global telecommunications businesses. This change renders some fundamental business, market, operational, architectural, or other assumptions inoperable.
Risk (service) **consequence**	Disruptive competitors can alter customers' service expectations.
Risk **impact**	Hard to predict.

by new business models, operations, policies, and practices are an unknown-unknown risk.

- **Emerging technology risk**—Table 26.2—Virtualization, machine learning, software-defined networking, and a range of other technologies are rapidly evolving; some of those evolved technologies will materially impact the future direction and risks of cloud computing.
- **Technical debt risk**—Table 26.3—Deploying short-term fixes and work-arounds often helps to deliver new service and value faster but can overhang the business with technical debt. The risk of that technical debt can be hard to characterize.
- **Flawed standards risk**—Table 26.4—Official, emerging, or de facto standards may turn out to contain flaws, which create future risks, limitations, and opportunities.
- **Faulty infrastructure capex reduction risk**—Table 26.5—Cloud service providers (CSPs) who own and operate physical infrastructure may deploy some new infrastructure equipment in pursuit of cost improvements, which introduces new risks (e.g., compatibility problems) to CSCs' application user service quality.
- **Faulty CSP opex reduction risk**—Table 26.6—Some CSP attempts to improve their operational efficiency or performance by deploying some architectural, process, policy, or other change to their infrastructure, management and orchestration, or functional-component-as-a-service offering, which introduces new risks (e.g., compatibility problems) to application user service quality.

Table 26.2   Emerging Technology Risk

Attribute	Value
Risk **name**	Emerging technology risk.
Risk **root cause**	By definition, emerging technologies are immature, so limitations of the technology and best practices for deployment may not be fully understood.
Risk **condition**	Fundamental, yet poorly understood, technology limitations or optimal operational models leave key functionality, operational, or quality aspects of the service vulnerable in some way.
Risk (service) **consequence**	• Service quality, performance or functionality will be inferior to more mature technology instances and deployment models. • Disruptive competitors emerge.
Risk **impact**	Service quality, reliability, or latency is inferior to later-adopting competitors.

Table 26.3   Technical Debt Risk

Attribute	Value
Risk **name**	Technical debt risk.
Risk **root cause**	Technical debt is the gap between a short-term (aka quick-and-dirty) fix/work-around and a robust technical solution. Schedule pressure, limited resources, limited knowledge, or business considerations may prompt a project team to take the risk of running a technical debt by deploying quick-and-dirty fixes or designs rather than more robust and costly alternatives.
Risk **condition**	Quick-and-dirty fixes or work-arounds generally address an immediate failure or risk scenario, but often are not robust enough to fully address adjacent and related failure or risk scenarios. Thus, a failure event or scenario outside of the limited scope of the short-term fix/work-around may cascade into a user service–impacting failure.
Risk (service) **consequence**	Depends on both the nature of the short-term fix and the failure scenario.
Risk **impact**	

Table 26.4   Flawed Standards Risk

Attribute	Value
Risk **name**	Flawed standards risk.
Risk **root cause**	Emerging, new, or preexisting standard is suboptimal or flawed in the context of cloud computing or some cloud-based business model.
Risk **condition**	Standards compliance may compromise compatibility, functionality, performance, business model, or some other key aspect of the CSC's business.
Risk (service) **consequence**	Standards compliance exposes service providers to some previously unknown risk(s).
Risk **impact**	Hard to predict.

Table 26.5   Faulty Infrastructure Capex Reduction Risk

Attribute	Value
Risk **name**	Faulty infrastructure capex reduction risk.
Risk **root cause**	In pursuit of capital expense reductions, a CSP deploys equipment and/or architectures that create previously unknown service quality risks for applications hosted on target capex-optimized infrastructure.
Risk **condition**	Infrastructure incompatibility or technology limitations adversely impact application service quality, functionality, or performance.
Risk (service) **consequence**	Hard to predict.
Risk **impact**	

Table 26.6 Faulty CSP Opex Reduction Risk

Attribute	Value
Risk **name**	Faulty CSP opex reduction risk.
Risk **root cause**	In pursuit of opex reduction, infrastructure, management, orchestration, or functional component CSPs deploy policies, software, operational models, or architectures that raise previously unknown application service quality risks.
Risk **condition**	Virtual infrastructure, management, orchestration, or technology component service changes in some way that creates new application service quality risks for the CSC.
Risk (service) **consequence**	Hard to predict.
Risk **impact**	

CLOUD SERVICE QUALITY RISK ASSESSMENT AND MANAGEMENT

Chapter 3, "Risk and Risk Management," offered ISO 31000 as the world's preeminent risk management methodology. Section IV methodically applies ISO 31000 risk management to the cloud service customer's problem of reducing the likelihood that risks from Section III, "Cloud Service Quality Risk Inventory," yield unacceptable user service quality. At the highest level, the primary artifact of the cloud service customer's risk assessment process is often a spreadsheet, which is produced via the following steps:

1. User service quality risks for the target application are identified.
2. The likelihood and consequences of identified risk events are analyzed.
3. Risks are evaluated, rated, and ranked for treatment.
4. Recommendations for treatment for priority risks are made.
5. The cloud service customer decides which risk treatments to implement.
6. Selected risk treatments are implemented.
7. Performance is monitored and periodically reviewed to drive continuous improvement.

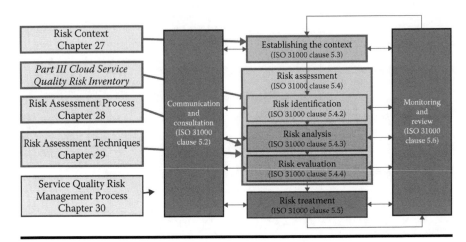

Figure IV.1 Organization of Part IV, "Cloud Service Quality Risk Assessment and Management."

Figure IV.1 visualizes how Section IV, "Cloud Service Quality Risk Assessment and Management," applies the ISO 31000 risk management processes to manage the service quality risk of cloud-based applications. This part is organized as follows:

■ **Risk Context** (Chapter 27)—Covers risk context, which frames the roles, responsibilities, decision criteria, and other important considerations that drive successful implementation of risk management.

■ **Risk Assessment Process** (Chapter 28)—Lays out the process for methodically assessing the user service quality risks challenging a cloud-based application service.

■ **Risk Assessment Techniques** (Chapter 29)—Considers the following categories of risk assessment techniques:
  – General risk identification and analysis techniques
  – Specialized risk identification and analysis techniques
  – Risk controls analysis techniques
  – Risk evaluation techniques
  – Additional techniques

■ **Service Quality Risk Management** (Chapter 30)—Connects the dots on risk assessment, treatment, monitoring, and continual service improvement. A sample outline of a risk assessment report is also offered.

Chapter 27

Risk Context

Figure 27.1 illustrates "establish the context" in the context of the ISO 31000 risk management process. The establish-the-context activity frames an organization's objectives and scope along with the internal and external parameters and criteria to be used by risk management activities.

Risk context has several components, which drive risk assessment activities, as shown in Figure 27.2.

- Internal context (Section 27.1) and external context (Section 27.2) guide risk ownership and influences risk criteria.
- Risk criteria (Section 27.3) guides risk rating and ranking of risks, and selection of risk treatments.
- Context of the risk management process (Section 27.4) guides both what treatment information is appropriate to enable a timely risk treatment decision, and who the cloud service customer (CSC) decision maker(s) are.
- Selected service quality objectives (Section 27.5).

27.1 Internal Context

ISO 31000 defines *internal context* as "internal environment in which the organization seeks to achieve its objectives" (ISO, 2009-11-15). ISO scopes the internal risk management context to cover the following (ISO, 2009-11-15):

- governance, organizational structure, roles and accountabilities;
- policies, objectives, and the strategies that are in place to achieve them;

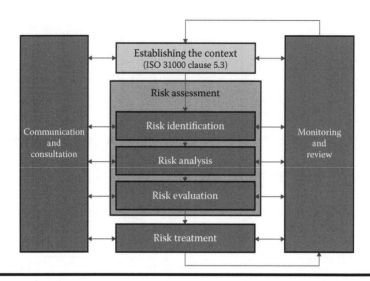

Figure 27.1   Establishing the context in risk management process.

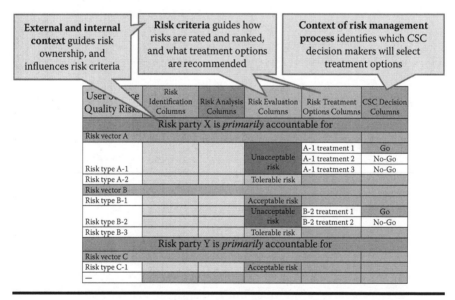

Figure 27.2   How risk context is used in a risk assessment table.

- capabilities, understood in terms of resources and knowledge (e.g., capital, time, people, processes, systems and technologies);
- the relationships with and perceptions and values of internal stakeholders;
- the organization's culture;

- information systems, information flows and decision-making processes (both formal and informal);
- standards, guidelines and models adopted by the organization; and
- form and extent of contractual relationships.

Table 27.1 maps the internal context examples from ISO 31000 to the applicable cloud service quality risk vector; Figure 27.3 illustrates the risk vectors often in the CSC's internal context.

Table 27.1   Internal Context Examples (ISO Guide 73)

"NOTE Internal context can include:" (ISO Guide 73)	Applicable Cloud Service Quality Risk Vector
"governance, organizational structure, roles and accountabilities"	Human and organizational risks (Chapter 22) Accountability Risks (Chapter 21)
"policies, objectives, and the strategies that are in place to achieve them"	Service policy risks (Chapter 20) Cloud service provider catastrophe Risks (Chapter 25) Unknown-Unknown Risks (Chapter 26)
"the capabilities, understood in terms of resources and knowledge (e.g., capital, time, people, processes, systems and technologies)"	Service policy risks (Chapter 20) Human and organizational risks (Chapter 22)
"information systems, information flows and decision making processes (both formal and informal)"	Service policy risks (Chapter 20) Human and organizational Risks (Chapter 22)
"relationships with, and perceptions and values of internal stakeholders"	Human and organizational risks (Chapter 22)
"the organization's culture"	Human and organizational risks (Chapter 22) Unknown-unknown risks (Chapter 26)
"standards, guidelines and models adopted by the organization"	Service policy risks (Chapter 20) Human and organizational risks (Chapter 22)
"form and extent of contractual relationships"	Accountability risks (Chapter 21)

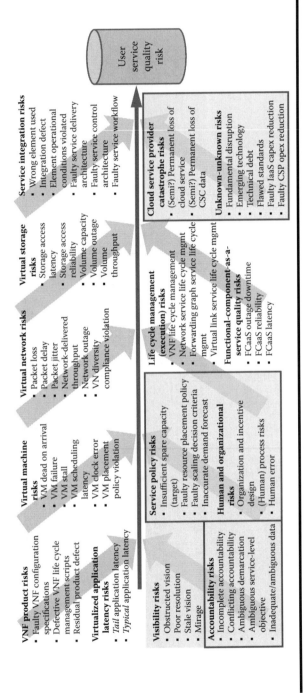

Figure 27.3   Cloud service quality risk vectors nominally in CSC's internal context. CSP, cloud service provider; FCaaS, functional-component-as-service; IaaS, infrastructure-as-a-service; VN, virtual network.

Figure 27.4 Risk culture. (From Figure 11 of ISACA, *The Risk IT Framework,* Rolling Meadows, IL: ISACA, http://www.isaca.org, 2009.)

The Risk IT framework (ISACA, 2009) (Figure 27.4) usefully factors an organization's risk culture along three dimensions:

- **Behavior toward taking risks**—On the spectrum from conservative, risk-averse to aggressive risk-taking cultures, where does the organization lie?
- **Behavior toward negative outcomes**—On the spectrum from a learning culture to a blaming culture, where does the organization lie?
- **Behavior toward policy compliance**—On the spectrum from compliance-oriented to noncompliance, where does the organization lie?

Specifics of each CSC's internal context will impact their risk criteria, quality objectives, analysis of risk, and selection of treatment options, as well as the ongoing monitoring and review that the CSC deploys to drive continuous improvement.

27.2 External Context

ISO 31000 defines external context as the "external environment in which the organization seeks to achieve its objectives" (ISO, 2009-11-15) and offers three samples of external context entities:

1. "Cultural, social, political, legal, regulatory, financial, technological, economic, natural and competitive environment, whether international, national, regional or local" (ISO, 2009-11-15)—considered in Section 27.2.1, "External Factors and Key Drivers."

2. "Key drivers and trends having impact on the objectives of the organization" (ISO, 2009-11-15)—considered in Section 27.2.1, "External Factors and Key Drivers."

3. "Relationships with, and perceptions and values of external stakeholders" (ISO, 2009-11-15)—considered in Section 27.2.2, "External Parties and Relationships."

27.2.1 External Factors and Key Drivers

Other factors in the external context that may impact cloud service quality risk management include the following:

- **Market**—Quality expectations of network services often vary widely based on market context, such as the following:
  - **Fixed versus mobile access**—Customers expect shorter postdial delay, fewer failed calls, and no dropped calls when using wireline telephony devices, but tolerate significantly worse quality via wireless devices.
  - **Enterprise versus consumer**—Enterprises often demand superior service quality to minimize the risk of degraded quality of interaction with their customers or suppliers or between their employees.
  - **Free versus pay**—Customers will often tolerate somewhat poorer quality for free service offerings.
  - **Regional variations**—Customers in different markets and geographies may have somewhat different service quality expectations.
- **Traditional service offerings**—The service quality of traditional (i.e., pre-cloud) offerings often serve as a baseline that end users will compare a cloud-based offering against. For example, traditional (precloud) wireline telephony services have short postdial delay times; will customers expect the postdial delay time of cloud-based telephony offerings to deliver the same postdial delay performance?
- **Disruptive service offerings**—Disruptive competitors may bring similar service offerings to market, possibly at dramatically lower price points (e.g., free to noncommercial end users). Service quality of those offerings may impact the market's overall service quality expectations.
- **Published (nominally independent) quality benchmarks**—Nominally independent organizations like J.D. Power, Consumers Union, and QuEST Forum publish quality reports on service offerings. The exact criteria used in those benchmarks often become specific focus areas for service providers, and achieving a favorable—ideally best-in-class—ranking in those surveys is often an objective of leading service provider organizations.
- **Regulatory reporting**—If applicable regulatory bodies mandate reporting of certain service outage or impairment events, then service providers often explicitly focus on minimizing the likelihood of any reportable events.

These external factors and key drivers impact user service quality expectations and can contribute to unknown-unknown risks (Chapter 26).

27.2.2 External Parties and Relationships

CSCs typically interact with the following external parties:

- **Cloud service users**, who are the end users of the CSC's application service
- Network **transport service providers**, who haul Internet Protocol (IP) packets between cloud service users' devices and the cloud service providers' points of presence
- Service **integrators**, who integrate applications with cloud infrastructure, management, orchestration, and technology components on behalf of the CSC
- One or more **cloud service provider** organizations, who offer cloud infrastructure, management, orchestration, and/or technology component services
- **Application software suppliers**

The Network Functions Virtualization Quality Accountability Framework (ETSI, 2016-01) describes the roles and responsibilities of each of these parties. All of these parties are part of the CSC's external context.

Section 12.3, "European Telecommunications Standards Institute Network Functions Virtualization Quality Accountability Framework Risks," roughly mapped service quality risk vectors to accountable parties. Note that virtualized application latency risks are more complicated. Typical application latency risks are driven by the selecting both virtualized network functions (VNFs) and cloud infrastructure that fulfill performance expectations (e.g., avoiding the wrong element used risk [Table 18.1]) and properly integrating VNFs with cloud infrastructure (i.e., avoiding system/service integration defect [Table 18.2]). Tail application latency risk is driven by virtual machine (VM) risks (e.g., VM scheduling latency risk [Table 14.4]), virtual network risks (e.g., packet loss risk [Table 15.1]), and virtual storage risks (e.g., storage access latency risk [Table 16.2]); however, residual product defect risk (Table 13.3) and other risks can also produce tail latency impairments.

27.3 Defining Risk Criteria

Risk criteria are defined follows:

> terms of reference against which the significance of a risk is evaluated…
> [and] should reflect the organization's values, objectives and resources.
> Some criteria can be imposed by, or derived from, legal and regulatory
> requirements and other requirements to which the organization sub-
> scribes. (ISO, 2009-11-15)

Risk criteria are thus the actionable guidance for how an organization's risk appetite should drive risk management decisions for a particular class of risk facing the organization. The standard ISO/IEC 31010 (ISO/IEC, 2009-11) stipulates six points that a risk criteria context should define.

1. The nature and types of consequences to be included and how they will be measured
2. The way in which probabilities are to be expressed
3. How a level of risk will be determined
4. The criteria by which it will be decided when a risk needs treatment
5. The criteria for deciding when a risk is acceptable and/or tolerable
6. Whether and how combinations of risks will be taken into account

Multiple risk criteria can be used for a single type of risk, and ideally, they will be precise and unambiguous. For example, the Dam Safety Office of the US Department of the Interior Bureau of Reclamation offers two quantitative risk criteria when evaluating safety of dams in the United States:

■ **Annualized failure probability** is defined as a "measure of risk Annualized Failure Probability, and uses a guideline of 1 in 10,000 per year for the accumulation of failure likelihoods from all potential failure modes that would result in life-threatening unintentional release of the reservoir. When the mean estimate is above this threshold level there is generally increasing justification to take action to reduce or better understand the risks. Below this threshold level there is generally decreasing justification to reduce or better understand the risks" (Dam Safety Office, 2011).
■ **Annualized life loss** risk criteria "…uses a guideline of 0.001 fatalities per year to address this measure of risk. When the mean estimate is above the guideline of 0.001 fatalities per year, there is generally increasing justification to take action to reduce or better understand the risks. There is generally decreasing justification to reduce or better understand the risks when they are below this guideline value" (Dam Safety Office, 2011).

CSC organizations not directly involved in critical and human life safety applications may not routinely work with quantified risk thresholds. If quantitative risk threshold criteria are not practical for a particular organization, then qualitative risk criteria may be more appropriate. While different industries and customers have rather different criticality factorizations and expectations, the US Federal Aviation Administration (FAA) gives clear, objective, and quantitative expectations, which can be generalized. The FAA's capability criticality ratings are as follows (FAA, 2008-01-08):

- **Routine**—"Loss of this capability would have a minor impact on the risk associated with providing safe and efficient local [National Airspace System] operations."
- **Essential**—"Loss of this capability would significantly raise the risk associated with providing safe and efficient local NAS operations."
- **Efficiency critical**—"Loss of this capability would raise to an unacceptable level the risk associated with providing safe and efficient local [National Airspace System] operations."
- **Safety critical**—"Loss would present an unacceptable safety hazard during transition to reduced capacity operation."

Qualitatively—and quantitatively, if possible—framing the criticality rating of a particular target application is often useful. After agreeing on these general risk appetite statements, they can be used to guide risk analysis, evaluation, and recommendation of treatment options.

27.4 Establishing the Context of the Risk Management Process

The CSC's risk management activities operate within the organization's process context, which includes the following:

- Business objectives, including schedule and resource constraints
- Enterprise decision-making processes
- Enterprise risk management processes
- Enterprise quality management systems
- Organizational relationships with internal parties
- Commercial relationships with external parties

This context will directly impact the following:

1. What CSC leader makes decisions about recommended risk treatments
2. What supporting data and analysis are required by that CSC leader to make a timely decision
3. How implementation of selected risks will be project-managed
4. Ongoing monitoring and review of target application

This context will also drive how risk management processes are integrated with the organization's overarching quality and enterprise management processes.

27.5 Establish Service Quality Objectives

Service quality risks must obviously be assessed against the application's service quality objectives. Section 27.5.1 begins by considering, what are quality objectives? One can establish service quality objectives via a three-step process:

1. Select quality objective metrics (Section 27.5.2)
2. Select service quality measurement point(s) (Section 27.5.3)
3. Set performance targets for each key quality objective (Section 27.5.4)

Ongoing monitoring and review, as well as continual service improvement (Chapter 9), should regularly evaluate if service quality objectives should be changed based on evolving market conditions, such as if a disruptive competitor enters the market, as business needs shift, or as a market matures and expectations evolve.

27.5.1 What Are Quality Objectives?

ISO 9001 (ISO, 2015-09-15) stipulates the following:
> The quality objectives shall:

> a. Be consistent with the quality policy;
> b. Be measurable;
> c. Take into account applicable requirements;
> d. Be relevant to conformity of products and services and to enhancement of customer satisfaction;
> e. Be monitored;
> f. Be communicated;
> g. Be updated as appropriate.

Section 4.1.4, "Service-Level Objectives, Specifications, and Agreements" explained that agreed-upon service-level objectives are typically captured in a service-level specification (Figure 27.5)

The European Telecommunications Standards Institute (ETSI, 2007-01) offers that service-level objectives should be as follows:

- Reachable with regard to the objectives
- Repeatable
- Assessable
- Understandable
- Meaningful

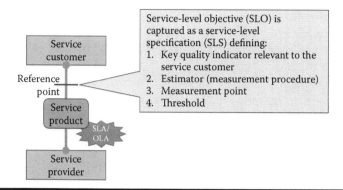

Figure 27.5 Service-level objectives. OLA, operations-level agreement; SLA, service-level agreement.

- Controllable with regard to the contract
- Affordable
- Mutually acceptable

Thus, a foundational element of any quality objective is the measurement definition; sloppy measurement definitions introduce uncertainty that will pervade and potentially compromise the entire quality and risk management processes.

27.5.2 Select Quality Objective Metrics

Ideally, user service quality objectives directly support the CSC organization's strategic goals, such as a strategic objective of achieving a particular Net Promoter Score or a specific ranking or target on an independent user quality measurement. For example, the JD Power Wireless Network Quality survey quantitatively assesses perceptions of end users' quality of experience:

> the semiannual study is based on 10 problem areas of the customer experience: dropped calls; calls not connected; audio issues; failed/late voicemails; lost calls; text transmission failures; late text message notifications; Web connection errors; slow downloads; and email connection errors. Network performance issues are measured as problems per 100 (PP100) network connections, with a lower score reflecting fewer problems and better overall performance.*

Thus, a CSC organization might select key quality indicators directly based on key characteristics from a quality-of-experience metric applicable to their target

---

* http://canada.jdpower.com/press-releases/2015-us-wireless-network-quality-performance
-study%E2%80%94volume-2, retrieved 11/16/15.

application. For example, if *calls not connected* was an applicable quality characteristic, then a service objective metric could be established for failed call attempts (i.e., *calls not connected*), which can be mapped into a concrete service reliability measurement (Section 4.2.1.1, "Service Reliability").

ISO/IEC 15939 (ISO/IEC, 2009-10-01) Annex D offers several criteria to evaluate a proposed measurement against, which can be useful when refining the measurement definition for a candidate quality objective:

- **Usefulness of the measurement** (Annex D.2)—Will the measurement drive useful decisions?
- **Confidence in the measurement definition** (Annex D.3)—Do you have confident understanding of all of the underlying data gathering, calculations, normalizations, and other details of producing the measurement?
- **Evidence of fitness for purpose** (Annex D.4)—Has effectiveness of the measurement been demonstrated?
- **Understandability of the measurement** (Annex D.5)—The measurement should be easy for CSC decision makers and staff to understand. Disturbance-oriented metrics where perfect performance is 0 are easier for most humans to understand than perfection-oriented metrics where perfect performance is 100%. For instance, most folks grasp the implication of 100 failures per million user requests compared to 10 failures per million user requests better than the difference between 99.99% and 99.999% service reliability.
- **Satisfactory measurement assumptions** (Annex D.6)—Are statistical sampling and other fundamental assumptions made by the measurement definition reasonable for the intended use?
- **Accuracy of measurement procedure** (Annex D.7)—How closely will the actual measurement procedure conform to the measurement definition? Will data be produced by measurement systems or by human observation? Will manipulation of those data deviate in any way from the formal measurement definition?
- **Repeatability of measurement method** (Annex D.8)—If the measurement is actually repeated under the same conditions with the same tools, staff, and so on, then will the same result be produced? Note that random measurement errors impact measurement repeatability.
- **Reproducibility of measurement method** (Annex D.9)—If the measurement is repeated under different conditions (e.g., different data-gathering tool, different staff), then will acceptable results be produced? Note that random measurement errors impact measurement reproducibility.

27.5.3 Select Service Quality Measurement Point(s)

One must identify the measurement point(s) for each service quality objective. Ideally, CSCs or end users will arrange back-to-back measurement points and service-level agreements/objectives to assure acceptable end-to-end service quality. For example, the primary measurement point for user service reliability might be at the application's front-end security/border element, where the cloud service provider first delivers user traffic to a CSC application element. As a practical matter, positioning measurement points at or near accountability boundaries or service demark points is helpful when establishing and managing service-level agreements.

27.5.4 Set Performance Targets for Each Key Quality Objective

Finally, one must set feasible and achievable quantitative performance objectives for each key user service quality indicator. Two performance objectives for each indicator are generally useful:

- **Target performance level** is the target for typical/normal operation, such as user service reliability of five defective transactions per million requests.
- **Worst acceptable performance level** beyond which corrective actions should be triggered, such as when user service reliability exceeds 10 defective transactions per million requests. Worst acceptable performance level is often used as the threshold in a service-level agreement. If that threshold is violated, then the service-level agreement might stipulate some remedy.

These performance targets should be appropriately aligned both with the organization's risk appetite (discussed in Section 27.3, "Defining Risk Criteria") and are appropriately aligned to support organizational objectives, such as financial liabilities for failing to meet end-user service-level agreements or reputational risks from high-visibility outages. Simplistically setting traditional quality targets may prove to be inappropriate for new and emerging technologies and service offerings. For instance, wireless telephony is successful despite having significantly longer postdial delays than wireline, and digital cable TV is successful despite having significantly slower channel change times than traditional analog cable TV. Nevertheless, organizations must start with some quality targets, so traditional targets are certainly a better starting point than no targets at all.

Note that quantitative performance objectives influence application deployment architecture and operational policies, as well as materially impacting risk. Fundamentally, performance objectives are positively correlated with risk: other things being equal, the higher the performance objectives, the greater the risk in achieving those objectives.

Chapter 28

Risk Assessment Process

This chapter applies ISO 31000 risk management processes to user service quality of cloud-based applications. As shown in Figure 28.1, this chapter is organized as follows:

- Purpose and context of risk assessment process (Section 28.1)
- Risk identification (Section 28.2)
- Risk analysis (Section 28.3)
- Risk evaluation (Section 28.4)
- Risk treatment (Section 28.5)

28.1 Purpose and Context of Risk Assessment Process

The primary output of a cloud user service quality risk assessment is a risk assessment table (Figure 28.2), which enables cloud service customer (CSC) leaders to decide which risk treatment options to pursue. Appropriate organizations are then assigned responsibility to implement each selected treatment option, and those organizations manage treatment implementation; implementation of treatment options is beyond the scope of the risk assessment activity.

Figure 28.3 visualizes how the ISO 31000 risk management activities discussed in this chapter support completion of a risk assessment table.

28.2 Risk Identification

The goal of the risk identification activity is to capture a complete set of the user service quality risks for the target service. The output of this activity is a partially

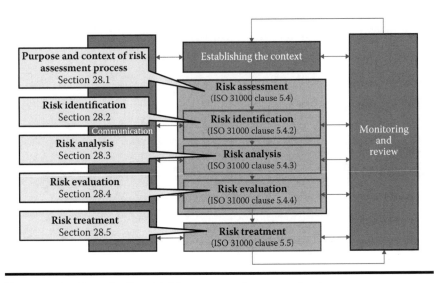

Figure 28.1 Organization of risk assessment process chapter.

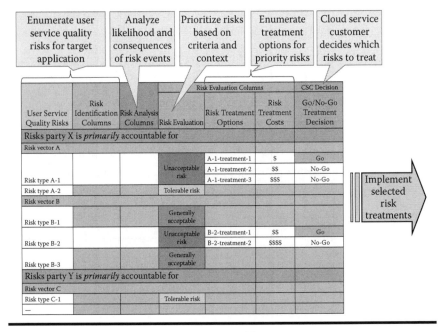

Figure 28.2 Overview of risk assessment table.

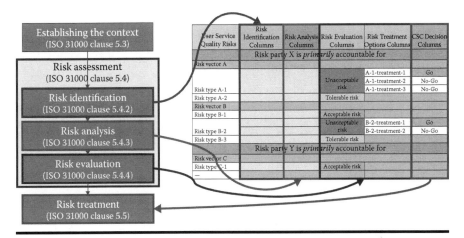

Figure 28.3   Process to risk assessment artifact linkages.

completed risk assessment table for the target service. The table includes the following:

1. A row for each risk type relevant to target service in the applicable risk context.
2. The following cells for each row are complete:
   a. **Named risk**—Use risk names from Section III, "Cloud Service Quality Risk Inventory," whenever possible.
   b. **Risk condition**—Summarizes the applicable risk condition for target service, such as which virtualized network function (VNF) or VNF component (VNFC) is at greatest risk.
   c. **Risk cause(s)**—Capture the high-likelihood risk causes for the target service and context.
   d. **Risk controls**—List relevant risk controls assumed to be included in the plan of record for the target service and context.
   e. **Risk owner**—From the external parties or relationships (Section 27.2.2) or the CSC's internal context (Section 27.1)
   f. **Service quality impact of unsuccessfully controlled risk event**—Tailor user service quality risks for target service.
3. Factor risk type rows by accountable party (i.e., the risk owner), and organize those risk type rows by risk vector per owner, for example, separate buckets for cloud service provider(s), service integrator, VNF suppliers, and risks retained by the CSC; within the cloud service provider block of risk vectors would be a portion given for virtual machine risks, virtual network risks, virtual storage risks, etc., with rows for each risk type listed by vector. For example, the ultimate cause of a virtual machine failure might be a faulty hardware component, but the CSC holds the infrastructure cloud service

provider accountable for all causes of virtual machine failure. The infrastructure cloud service provider must then manage the underlying risks of equipment, facilities, policies, and operations to assure that they can fulfill their service quality commitments to their CSCs.

Chapter 29, "Risk Assessment Techniques," especially Section 29.1, "General Risk Identification and Analysis Techniques," offers methods for risk identification that can be applied to populate fields in a risk assessment table.

28.3 Risk Analysis

According to ISO 31010,

> Risk analysis is about developing an understanding of the risk. It provides an input to risk assessment and to decisions about whether risks need to be treated and about the most appropriate treatment strategies and methods.
>
> Risk analysis consists of determining the consequences and their probabilities for identified risk events, taking into account the presence (or not) and the effectiveness of any existing controls. The consequences and their probabilities are then combined to determine a level of risk. (ISO/IEC, 2009-11)

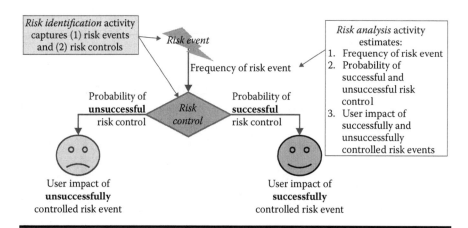

Figure 28.4 Risk identification versus risk analysis.

Figure 28.4 visualizes the key distinction between risk identification and risk analysis activities.

- **Risk identification** enumerates the relevant risk events and the risk controls that are included in the plan of record.
- **Risk analysis** estimates the frequency of risk events, the effectiveness of planned risk controls, and the likely user service impact of both successfully and unsuccessfully controlled risk events.

The estimated risk impact characteristics of Figure 28.4 enable deeper consideration and treatment of higher-priority risks.

Risk maps are often used to visualize and prioritize risks. The risk map in Figure 28.5 places magnitude of risk impact event (aka consequences) on the x-axis and probability of risk event on the y-axis. This style of risk map is routinely partitioned into four regions:

1. Low-probability, low-impact risks (nominally **low** risk)—These risks are generally accepted (aka retained) by the organization.
2. High-probability, low-impact risks (nominally **medium** risk)—These risks will generally be controlled by the organization.
3. Low-probability, high-impact risks (nominally **medium** risk)—These risks are often shared (e.g., insurance).
4. High-probability, high-impact risks (nominally **high** risk)—These risks are often the primary focus of risk treatment activities and will be aggressively treated and controlled.

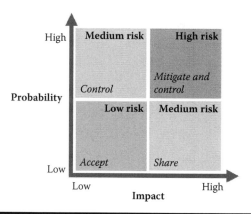

Figure 28.5   Canonical risk map.

The relative position on a risk map of a specific risk type in a particular context is determined by several factors:

1. Likelihood of risk event, such as how often underlying risk events occur. For example, how frequently is a particular VNFC instance to fail?
2. Adequacy and effectiveness of risk controls, such as how effectively the service impact of risk events can be controlled, especially the probability that a risk event will be successfully controlled. For example, how likely is it that the resiliency mechanisms protecting a particular VNFC instance will rapidly and reliably detect the VNFC failure and recover service to a protecting VNFC instance?
3. Ultimate service consequence, such as the following:
   a. User service impact of successfully controlled risk events. For example, what is the user service impact if a VNFC instance fails and service is successfully recovered to a protecting VNFC instance?
   b. User service impact of *un*successfully controlled risk events. For example, what is the user service impact if a VNFC instance fails but the failure is either not automatically detected or not successfully recovered via primary automated mechanisms?

The goal of this activity is to complete the risk analysis columns in the risk assessment table for the target service:

- **Risk type likelihood**—ideally, include a quantitative estimate of the frequency of risk events; as a fallback, a qualitative likelihood estimate can be given.
- **Risk control effectiveness**—probability that a risk incident will be successfully controlled.
- **User impact of successfully controlled risk event**, such as the nature and duration of user service impact.
- **User impact of unsuccessfully controlled risk events**, such as the nature and duration of user service impact.
- **Overall risk probability (*x*-axis) rating**, such as the *x*-axis on Figure 28.5, "Canonical risk map."
- **Overall risk impact (*y*-axis) rating**, such as the *y*-axis on Figure 28.5, "Canonical risk map."

Chapter 29, "Risk Assessment Techniques," reviews analysis methods for cloud user service quality risks, especially the following:

- General risk identification and analysis techniques (Section 29.1)—Primary techniques for risk identification and analysis of cloud service quality risk. Practitioners will use a handful of these techniques.

- Specialized risk identification and analysis techniques (Section 29.2)—Advanced techniques to consider a specific category of risk. Practitioners can use these techniques as needed.
- Risk controls analysis techniques (Section 29.3)—Techniques to identify and evaluate the effectiveness of risk controls. Practitioners will likely use a few of these techniques.

28.4 Risk Evaluation

Risk evaluation compares the results of risk analysis (Section 28.3) to the organization's risk criteria Section 27.3 to rate and ranks the risks, and recommend treatment options as appropriate. Risk evaluation begins with rating the risks previously identified and analyzed. Unacceptable/high/red, tolerable/medium/amber, and generally acceptable/low/green is the minimal practical set of risk ratings, but more demanding applications and more sophisticated organizations will use richer risk classifications. Organizations should tailor risk ratings for the target application, paying particular attention to user service quality consequences that the CSC has little appetite for. Organizations can start with the following baseline risk ratings:

- **Unacceptable** (aka high-priority) **risks**—color-coded red—hazards that carry a material risk of
  - "Severity 0" service outage that becomes a news event, impacts the enterprise's stock price, and/or triggers regulatory reporting/scrutiny
  - Reputational damage
- **Tolerable** (aka medium-priority) **risks**—color-coded amber—material risk of moderate to large numbers of users being occasionally impacted due to service quality impairments.
- **Generally acceptable** (aka low-priority) **risks**—color-coded green—acceptable or ordinary risks of doing business, including impact to a small to moderate numbers of users

Sophisticated organizations often add a fourth category for **opportunity** (color-coded blue) for risks that are *super*acceptable, meaning that the organization can take additional risk in pursuit of business value without exceeding generally acceptable levels of risk. Applying the automotive example of Section 6.4, carrying two spare tires in an automobile is an opportunity (blue risk) to improve efficiency by removing the second spare tire; carrying one spare tire in an automobile is generally acceptable (green risk); carrying no spare tire in an automobile may be tolerable (amber).

The primary additions to the risk assessment table via the risk evaluation to ultimately enable CSC leaders to make effective risk treatment decisions are as follows:

- **Risk rating**—Rates all identified and analyzed risks according to the agreed-upon risk rating scale.
- **Risk ranking**—Ranks risks requiring treatment in priority order.
- **Risk treatment options**—Recommend specific treatment options for high-priority risks. Section 3.3 detailed the fundamental risk treatment options one can consider:
  - Replace or remove the risk source (Section 3.3.1)
  - Change the risk likelihood (Section 3.3.2)
  - Change the risk consequences (Section 3.3.3)
  - Share the risk with external party (Section 3.3.4)
  - Retain the risk (Section 3.3.5)
  - Reject accountability (Section 3.3.6)
  - Avoid the risk (Section 3.3.7)
- **Risk treatment costs**—Estimates costs of each treatment option using CSC organization's cost accounting.

Risk IT (ISACA, 2009) suggests evaluating five parameters when evaluating and recommending a risk treatment:

- **Cost of treatment** to reduce risk to tolerable levels. Each risk treatment option carries a cost, which can be estimated.
- **Importance of risk**, indicated by position on the risk map.
- **Capability to implement risk treatment**—Organizations may not have the maturity or capability to successfully plan, implement, deploy, and operate some advanced risk treatments, so simpler risk treatments may be more appropriate choices. Ideally, the recommended risk treatment is routine and simple (as in, "keep it simple, stupid") for the organization to execute because exotic and unique treatments introduce additional risks.
- **Effectiveness of risk treatment**—How likely the treatment is to reduce the frequency and impact of the particular risk.
- **Efficiency of risk treatment**—The benefits of the risk treatment compared to the costs of the treatment.

Section 29.4, "Risk Evaluation Techniques," of Chapter 29, "Risk Assessment Techniques," reviews methods for practitioners to apply when evaluating service quality risks.

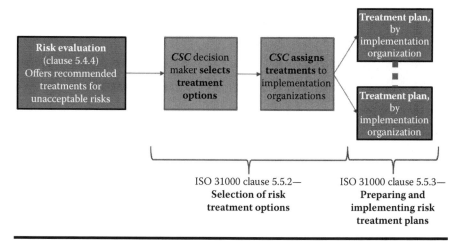

Figure 28.6 Recommended risk treatment process.

28.5 Risk Treatment

The risk assessment artifact is the primary input to the risk treatment activity. As shown in Figure 28.6, ISO 31000 breaks risk treatment into two steps:

1. Selection of risk treatment options—ISO 31000 clause 5.5.2
2. Preparing and implementing risk treatment plans—ISO 31000 clause 5.5.3

In the risk treatment phase, CSC decision makers then select treatment options to deploy and assign organizations to implement those treatment options. Implementation organizations then follow their respective processes to deploy selected treatments.

Chapter 29

Risk Assessment Techniques

This chapter reviews the risk assessment techniques given in ISO/IEC 31010 (ISO/IEC, 2009-11) and other standards to support risk identification, analysis, and evaluation of cloud user service quality risks facing cloud service customers (CSCs). These techniques are organized into the following categories:

- General risk identification and analysis techniques (Section 29.1)—Primary techniques for identification and analysis of cloud service quality risk. Practitioners are likely to use a handful of these techniques.
- Specialized risk identification and analysis techniques (Section 29.2)—Advanced techniques to consider for particular categories of risk. Practitioners will apply these techniques as needed.
- Risk control analysis techniques (Section 29.3)—Techniques to identify and evaluate the effectiveness of risk controls. Practitioners are likely to use several of these techniques.
- Risk evaluation techniques (Section 29.4)—Techniques to evaluate the level of risk. Practitioners will likely use one or more of these techniques.
- Additional techniques (Section 29.5)—Additional risk assessment techniques that are not broadly applicable to cloud user service quality risk assessment. Few practitioners will apply these techniques.

29.1 General Risk Identification and Analysis Techniques

The following techniques are generally useful for identification and analysis of user service quality risks of cloud-based applications:

- Influence diagrams (Section 29.1.1)
- Cause-and-effect analysis (Section 29.1.2)
- Failure mode effect analysis (Section 29.1.3)
- Structured interview and brainstorming (Section 29.1.4)
- SWIFT—structured "what-if" technique (Section 29.1.5)
- Fault tree analysis (Section 29.1.6)

As many of these techniques can yield similar results, practitioners should select the appropriate set of techniques and degree of diligence to execute based on the target service, availability of subject matter experts, and other considerations.

29.1.1 Influence Diagrams

Influence diagrams visualize the relationship between events and outcomes. Constructing influence diagrams for each of the service quality objectives of the target application can be useful. Figure 29.1 illustrates the risk types from Section III, "Cloud Service Quality Risk Inventory," that are most influential on user service reliability (i.e., producing failed user requests) for a sample application.

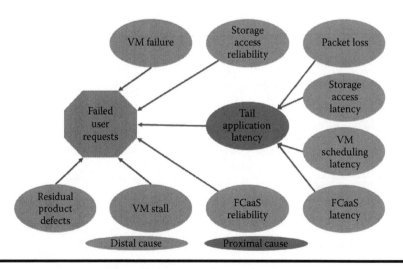

Figure 29.1 Sample influence diagram. FCaaS, functional-component-as-a-service.

29.1.2 Cause-and-Effect Analysis

Cause-and-effect analysis produces a fishbone or Ishikawa diagram and is covered in Annex B.17 of ISO/IEC 31010 (ISO/IEC, 2009-11). The cloud risk fishbone Figure III.1 derived in Section III, "Cloud Service Quality Risk Inventory," is the output of a cause-and-effect visualization of generic user service quality risks of cloud-based applications. Figure 29.2 illustrates how the canonical user service quality cause-and-effect fishbone can be tailored to a specific user service quality objective (user service reliability in this case) for a target application.

29.1.3 Failure Mode Effect Analysis

Failure mode effect analysis (FMEA) is covered in Annex B.13 of ISO/IEC 31010 (ISO/IEC, 2009-11) and Annex A.2 of CEI/IEC 300-3-9 (IEC, 1995). FMEA considers the system impact of failures of various system elements, such as the user impact of component failures for elements comprising a cloud-based application service. Table 29.1 shows a sample FMEA table.

- Each service component appears on a separate row (e.g., *Component 1, Component 2, Component 3*)
- Each of the user service quality objectives appears in a separate column (e.g., *Service Quality A, Service Quality B, Service Quality C*)
- Each cell in the table characterizes the impact to the relevant user service quality objective when the relevant service component fails. Likely options:
  - **No impact**—Component failure has no impact on this user service quality objective.
  - Impact to **some** service users, such as "Active user sessions served by this component lost."
  - Impact to **all** service users, such as "Function X unavailable to all users…" or "New user sessions (logins) unavailable…"

  Ideally, duration of service impact is also given, such as "Function X unavailable to all users for 15 seconds during failover."

If FMEA doesn't provide sufficient rigor (e.g., in a human safety–critical context), then hazard and operability analysis [HAZOP; covered in Annex B.6 of ISO/IEC 31010 (ISO/IEC, 2009-11) and Annex A.1 of CEI/IEC 300-3-9 (IEC, 1995)] can be used.

29.1.4 Structured Interview and Brainstorming

Structured interviews and brainstorming are considered in Annex B.2 and B.1 of ISO/IEC 31010 (ISO/IEC, 2009-11). The methodologies of these two techniques differ somewhat, but they both enable teams of experts to identify and roughly

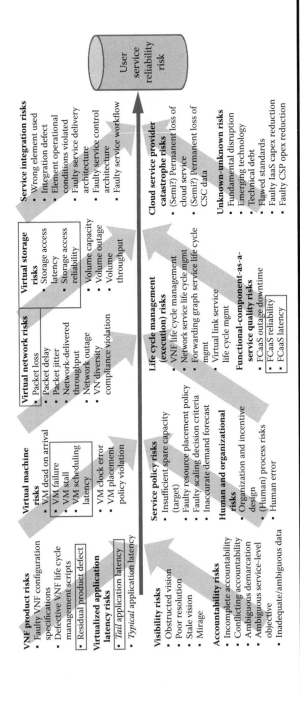

Figure 29.2 Sample cause-and-effect analysis for user service reliability risk. CSC, cloud service customer; FCaaS, functional-component-as-a-service ; IaaS, infrastructure-as-a-service; VN, virtual network.

Table 29.1 Sample FMEA Table

Service Component	Impact of Component Failure		
	Service Quality A	*Service Quality B*	*Service Quality C*
Component 1	Active user sessions served by component are lost	No impact	No impact
Component 2	No impact	Function X unavailable to all users for 15 seconds during failover	No impact
Component 3	No impact	No impact	New user sessions (logins) unavailable for 5 seconds during failover
...			

assess high-level risks to user service quality. Execution details will be tailored by the practitioner to the particular context and available subject matter experts. Likely discussion prompts for subject matter experts include the following:

1. What service quality risks keep you up at night?
2. Considering each Section III, "Cloud Service Quality Risk Inventory," risk vector individually, **what risk type(s) in each vector are you most concerned will impact service quality?**
3. Which of the risk vectors do you think will have the most impact on service quality?
4. Are there any other service quality risks not on the risk fishbone that worry you?

29.1.5 SWIFT—Structured "What-If" Technique

Structured "what-if" technique (aka SWIFT) is detailed in Annex B.9 of ISO/IEC 31010 (ISO/IEC, 2009-11). This team-based technique explicitly considers various what-if prompts to enable a comprehensive review of risks and controls. The risk fishbone from Section III, "Cloud Service Quality Risk Inventory," is useful as input when constructing what-if scenarios to consider, such as "what if a virtual machine instance is dead on arrival?"

Preliminary hazard analysis (PHA, considered in ISO/IEC 31010 Annex B.5 and Annex A.5 of CEI/IEC 300-3-9 [IEC, 1995]) is a more rigorous technique that can be deployed when necessary.

29.1.6 Fault Tree Analysis

Faults that impact target service qualities can be analyzed by constructing trees of fault events that can produce a particular service-impacting failure condition. Figure 29.3 visualizes how fault tree analysis relates to the risk capture model used in Section III, "Cloud Service Quality Risk Inventory."

The fault tree analysis methodology is given in Annex B.14 of ISO/IEC 31010 (ISO/IEC, 2009-11) and Annex A.3 of CEI/IEC 300-3-9 (IEC, 1995). At the highest level, fault tree analysis of user service risks has the following steps:

1. Identify the top-level failure events that produce the most severe service impacts to the most important service quality objectives (Section 27.5, "Establish Service Quality Objectives"), such as chronically excessive tail application latency.
2. Starting with the top failure event, capture the immediate (proximal) cause of each event in the tree until further levels of causality. For example, chronically excessive tail application latency can arise from any of the following (logical *or*):
   - **Virtual compute impairments** such as virtual machine (VM) stall risk (Table 14.3) events and VM scheduling latency risk (Table 14.4) episodes, perhaps in combination with other factors, can produce excessive service latency for impacted requests.

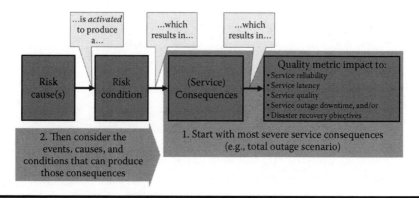

Figure 29.3   Fault tree analysis in the context of risk capture model.

- Virtual networking impairments such as packet loss risk (Table 15.1) episodes with timeout and retransmission or network delivered throughput risk (Table 15.4) episodes that cause requests to queue can produce excessive service latency for impacted requests.
- Virtual storage impairments such as excessive storage access latency risk (Table 16.2) and volume throughput risk (Table 16.5) events that cause requests to queue can produce excessive service latency for impacted requests.
- Functional component impairments, such as excessive functional-component as-a-service latency risk (Table 24.4) episodes, can add service latency to impacted requests.
- Faulty virtualized network function (VNF) configuration specification risk (Table 13.1) events can produce poorly configured VNFs that cause some requests to queue and thereby accrue excessive service latency.
- Element operational conditions violated (Table 18.3)—Driving service components out of their operational envelope can cause some requests to queue or otherwise accrue excessive service latency.
3. Consider the logical conditions (e.g., condition x *and* condition y) that are necessary to activate the higher-level failure condition, such as which VNF components (VNFCs) are vulnerable to VM stall risk (Table 14.3) events that can produce excessive application tail latency.
4. As shown in Figure 29.4, all of these conditions can be arranged into a logical tree of fault conditions. One can often estimate the probability of each failure scenario. Reducing the probability of failure scenarios and removing entire branches of the fault tree can reduce risk.

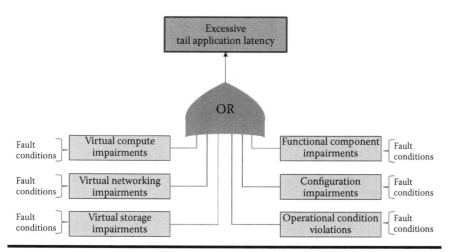

Figure 29.4 Sample (top-level) fault tree analysis.

29.2 Specialized Risk Identification and Analysis Techniques

Some categories of user service quality risk are best considered with specialized techniques.

- **Scenario analysis** is considered in Annex B.10 of ISO/IEC 31010 (ISO/IEC, 2009-11). Scenario analysis describes how the future might unfold, typically as best case, worst case, and expected case. Scenario analysis is useful when considering visibility risks, accountability risks, service policy risks, human and organizational risks, cloud service provider catastrophe risks, and unknown-unknown risks (Figure 29.5).
- **Business impact analysis** is covered in Annex B.11 of ISO/IEC 31010 (ISO/IEC, 2009-11). As shown in Figure 29.6, business impact analysis can be used to better characterize critical cloud service provider requirements, drive requirements for disaster recovery time objective (RTO) and recovery point objective (RPO), and consider risk treatments for cloud service provider catastrophe risks.
- **Reliability-centered maintenance** (RCM) is covered in Annex B.22 of ISO/IEC 31010 (ISO/IEC, 2009-11). According to ISO/IEC 31010 (ISO/IEC, 2009-11), "Reliability centred maintenance (RCM) is a method to identify the policies that should be implemented to manage failures so as to efficiently and effectively achieve the required safety, availability and economy of operation for all types of equipment." RCM can be applied to maintenance and operations activities for cloud-based applications.
- **Human reliability assessment** (HRA) is considered in Annex B.20 of ISO/IEC 31010 (ISO/IEC, 2009-11) and Annex A.6 of CEI/IEC 300-3-9 (IEC, 1995). HRA considers the impact of humans on system performance. As shown in Figure 29.7, HRA can be useful when considering human and organizational risks, as well as how human operators address visibility, accountability, and other risks when events are not correctly addressed by automated management and orchestration mechanisms.

29.3 Risk Control Analysis Techniques

Identifying applicable risk controls and estimating their effectiveness is an important aspect of risk assessment. Practitioners often select one or more of the following techniques for risk assessment:

- Layers-of-protection analysis (LOPA; Section 29.3.1)
- Hazard analysis and critical control points (HACCP; Section 29.3.2)
- Event tree analysis (ETA; Section 29.3.3)
- Bow-tie analysis (Section 29.3.4)

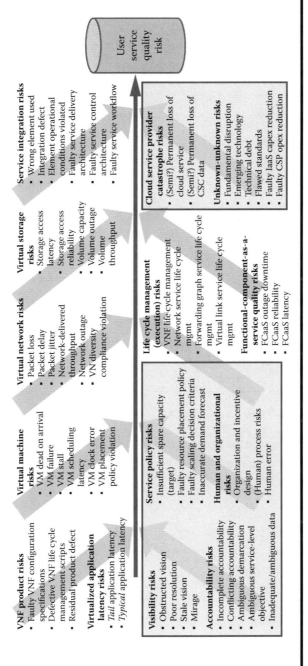

Figure 29.5 Applicability of scenario analysis technique.

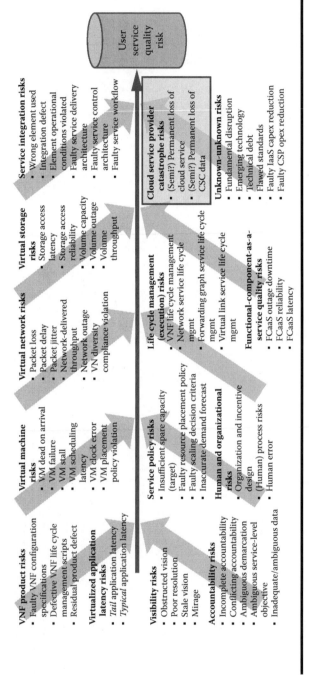

Figure 29.6 Applicability of business impact analysis technique.

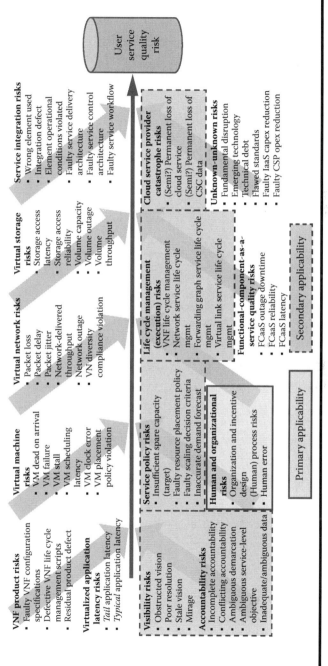

Figure 29.7 **Applicability of human reliability assessment technique.**

29.3.1 Layers-of-Protection Analysis

Layers-of-protection analysis (LOPA) is covered in Annex B.18 of ISO/IEC 31010 (ISO/IEC, 2009-11). LOPA considers the independent protection layers (IPLs) between a particular cause of harm and an adverse consequence. Figure 29.8 gives a hypothetical LOPA visualization for a chemical processing plant. Four layers of prevention are engineered into the hypothetical chemical process:

1. The process is designed with a valve to manipulate processing.
2. Automatic process control mechanisms control the value.
3. Alarms alert human operators to intervene when control limits are exceeded.
4. Safety mechanism automatically engages when limits are further exceeded.

Four layers of mitigation are provided:

1. Active protection mechanisms engage when conditions further deteriorate.
2. Passive protection mechanisms physically contain a problem.
3. Plant emergency response is activated when physical containment is breached.
4. Community emergency response is initiated when necessary.

While cloud-based applications do not require the same protection rigor as a chemical processing plant, the notion of layered protection is useful when analyzing risk controls. Figure 29.9 visualizes the nominal layers of control protecting the user service quality of a cloud-based application:

■ **Robust service design**—Robust service design, supported by rigorous architecture and supplier selection diligence, is the foundation of user service quality risk control. For example, well-designed service components effectively

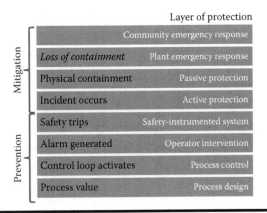

Figure 29.8 Sample chemical processing plant layers-of-protection analysis.

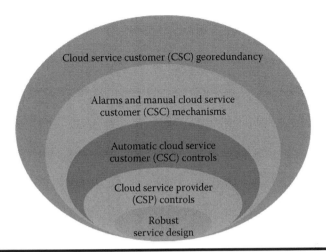

Figure 29.9   Canonical application of layers-of-protection analysis.

contain errors, and well-designed application software methodically detects and appropriately treats failures returned by service components to minimize the risk of failure cascades.

■ **Cloud service provider controls**—Infrastructure and functional component cloud service providers deploy service monitors and control mechanisms to assure that acceptable service quality is continuously delivered to their CSCs.

■ **Automatic CSC controls**—Orchestration and life cycle management scripts will automate monitoring and enforcement of operational policies for the CSC's service, such as when to reconfigure service components and user workloads to manage both normal operations and abnormal risk events.

■ **Alarms and manual CSC mechanisms**—CSC staff monitor performance and alarm status of the target service and take manual actions to correct issues that are not effectively addressed via automatic mechanisms.

■ **CSC georedundancy**—CSCs will arrange for sufficient user service capacity to be available from geographically distributed cloud data centers so that a disaster event will not cause service impact beyond the organization's RTO or cause permanent data loss for greater than the organization's RPO.

Practitioners can identify what risk controls are deployed in each layer of protection. LOPA can guide fault insertion, Chaos Monkey, disaster, or other adversarial testing that verifies robust performance of protection layers.

29.3.2 *Hazard Analysis and Critical Control Points*

Hazard analysis and critical control points (HACCP) analysis is covered in Annex B.7 of ISO/IEC 31010 (ISO/IEC, 2009-11). Originally developed in the context of food safety, this technique focuses on critical control points in the production chain to mitigate potential sources of harm. When applied to cloud-based applications, one considers all of the components in the user service delivery path to assure that sufficient quality monitoring and control points exist across the service delivery path to promptly detect and localize service quality problems.

HACCP is based on seven principles:

1. **Conduct a hazard analysis**—Figure III.1, "User service quality risks confronting cloud service customers," derived in Section III, "Cloud Service Quality Risk Inventory," is an excellent starting point for a hazard analysis of a cloud-based application service quality.
2. **Identify critical control points**—While cloud-based applications don't have traditional critical control points like the cooking phase in the farm-to-fork delivery chain, there are points in the application delivery chain where risk controls and monitoring mechanisms can be inserted. This step identifies appropriate monitoring and control points in the application service delivery path.
3. **Establish critical limits for each critical control point**—Control limits (e.g., maximum and/or minimum acceptable measured values) should be established at each critical control point.
4. **Establish critical control point monitoring**—Deploy monitoring and reporting mechanisms across the service delivery and control paths to measure quality at all critical control points and alarm when control limits are breached.
5. **Establish corrective actions**—Policies should dictate what action should be taken when a critical control point monitoring mechanism indicates that a control limit has been violated. For example, should the application configuration or user workload distribution automatically redirect traffic to another application instance, or should the impacted application instance shed traffic by activating its overload controls?
6. **Establish procedures to ensure that the HACCP system is working as intended**—Verify that the corrective actions actually mitigate the hazard and assure that user service quality is acceptable.
7. **Establish record keeping procedures**—HACCP records are useful input to drive continuous quality improvement.

29.3.3 Event Tree Analysis

Event tree analysis (ETA) is covered in Annex B.15 of ISO/IEC 31010 (ISO/IEC, 2009-11) and Annex A.4 of CEI/IEC 300-3-9 (IEC, 1995). According to ISO/IEC 31010 (ISO/IEC, 2009-11), "ETA is a graphical technique for representing the mutually exclusive sequences of events following an initiating event according to the functioning/not functioning of the various systems designed to mitigate its consequences." As shown in Figure 29.10, ETA offers a useful tool for understanding both the qualitative impact of user service risks as well as quantitatively

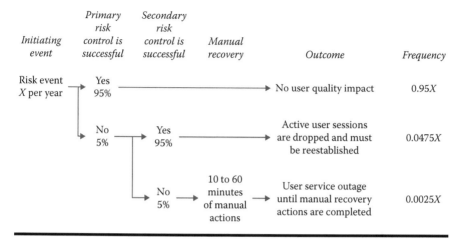

Figure 29.10   Sample event tree analysis.

estimating the likelihood of any particular risk control path. While at least some outcomes of controlled and uncontrolled risk events can be characterized during testing, the rate of initiating events and probabilities of successful controls must be estimated based on engineering judgment and test results, and can be revised as field data become available.

ETA can be applied to most risk controls identified by LOPA (Section 29.3.1) or HACCP (Section 29.3.2).

29.3.4 Bow-Tie Analysis

Bow-tie analysis is a visualization linking pathways from risk causes to their consequences; the technique is covered in Annex B.21 of ISO/IEC 31010 (ISO/IEC, 2009-11). Figure 29.11 gives a sample bow-tie analysis visualization.

1. A particular risk event is at the center of the diagram; sources of risk are to the left; consequences of the risk event are to the right.
2. Causes of the risk event are enumerated on the left edge side of the diagram, and prevention controls applicable to the risk cause are arranged between the risk cause and the risk event.
3. Factors that might cause a risk event to escalate can be shown, along with controls of those escalation factors.
4. Possible consequences of the risk event are laid out on the right side of the diagram, and applicable mitigation and recovery controls are arranged between the risk event and the possible consequence.

Figure 29.12 illustrates the risk types that might benefit from bow-tie analysis.

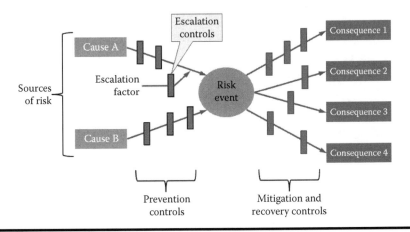

Figure 29.11 Sample bow-tie analysis.

29.4 Risk Evaluation Techniques

Having identified and assessed service quality risks via general risk identification and analysis techniques (Section 29.1), specialized risk identification and analysis techniques (Section 29.2) and risk control analysis techniques (Section 29.3), risks can be rated and ranked using one or more of the following techniques:

- Failure mode effect and criticality analysis (Section 29.4.1)
- Dose–response (toxicity) assessment (Section 29.4.2)
- Consequence–probability matrix (Section 29.4.3)
- *F–N* curves (Section 29.4.4)
- Risk indices (Section 29.4.5)
- Cost/benefit analysis (Section 29.4.6)

29.4.1 Failure Mode Effect and Criticality Analysis

Having completed a FMEA ("Failure Mode Effect Analysis," Section 29.1.3), one can overlay criticality information to produce a failure mode effect and criticality analysis (FMECA). FMECA is discussed in Annex B.13 of ISO/IEC 31010 (ISO/IEC, 2009-11).

Criticality is often considered in terms of the following:

- **Footprint of impact**—How many users are impacted by the failure?
- **Nature of impact**—Is impact to partial functionality, or is all functionality impacted?
- **Duration of impact**—For how long is user service impacted?

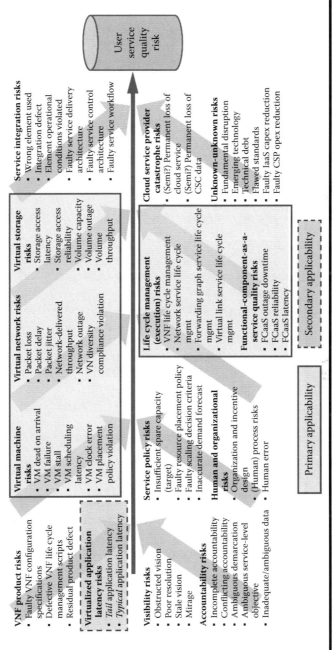

Figure 29.12 Applicability of bow-tie analysis of cloud user service quality risk types.

- **User inconvenience**—Can users simply retry the request (e.g., reload a web page) to clear failure impact, or must they take more dramatic action like explicitly reestablishing a session or restarting their application?

Note that criticality applies to both end-user service as well as visibility and controllability for operations, administration, maintenance, and provisioning of end-user service. For instance, "user inconvenience" can apply to both end users and the CSC's operations staff.

As explained in Section 28.4, "Risk Evaluation," risks are routinely partitioned into three categories:

- Generally acceptable risks—shaded green—such as for risks with no user service impact
- Tolerable risks—shaded amber—such as for risks with small and transient user service impact
- Unacceptable risks—shaded red—such as for outages and severe user service impairments (e.g., premature session termination)

Table 29.2 applies these criticality color ratings to the sample FMEA table (Table 29.1) from Section 29.1.3. Service architects and developers can initially focus on driving red cells to amber, and then on driving amber cells to green.

Table 29.2 Sample FMECA Table (Derived from Table 29.1)

Service Component	Impact of Component Failure		
	Service Quality A	*Service Quality B*	*Service Quality C*
Component 1	Active user sessions served by component are lost	No impact	No impact
Component 2	No impact	Function X unavailable to all users for 15 seconds during failover	No impact
Component 3	No impact	No impact	New user sessions (logins) unavailable for 5 seconds during failover

29.4.2 Dose–Response (Toxicity) Assessment

Sensitivity or dose–response testing is covered in Section 7.10, "Sensitivity (or Dose–Response) Testing."

29.4.3 Consequence–Probability Matrix

The consequence–probability matrix is covered in Annex B.29 of ISO/IEC 31010 (ISO/IEC, 2009-11). A consequence–probability matrix maps risk types onto a two-dimensional space with severity of consequences on the *x*-axis and likelihood on the *y*-axis.

- **Consequences** (*x*-axis) often can be quantitatively estimated, such as the portion of users impacted by a particular risk event or estimated duration of service outage downtime per event. If consequences cannot easily be quantified, then one can bucket risks by severity. Table 29.3 shows the TL 9000 problem classification definitions, and Table 29.4 shows the MIL-STD-882E safety risk classifications; one (or both) of these classification models might be useful when defining consequence categories for a target application service.
- **Probability** (*y*-axis) can be quantitatively estimated via absolute probability (e.g., annualized rate); alternately, likelihood can be bucketed, such as frequent, probable, occasional, remote, and improbable. Table 29.5 gives the six risk probability levels defined in MIL-STD-882E, which can be tailored for the target application service.

Figure 29.13 illustrates two sample risk types on a consequence–probability graph. Once all applicable risks are plotted on a single consequence–probability chart, one can see rate and rank risks based on the CSC's risk criteria and risk appetite.

Note that consequences for complex, distributed systems can be hard to predict due to emergent or chaotic behaviors triggered by failure events, so there is some inherent stochastic uncertainty in consequence–probability analyses.

29.4.4 F–N Curves

F–N curves (considered in ISO/IEC 31010 Annex B.27), like Figure 29.14, provide a straightforward risk evaluation for quantitative risk estimates when quantitative risk criteria are used.

A useful description of the *F–N* curve technique is given by the Dam Safety Office (2011), which differentiates between the following:

- *f-N chart*—"An *f-N* 'event' chart is composed of individual *f-N* pairs, where each pair typically represents one potential failure mode (or in the case of total risk, the summation of all potential failure modes). On the *f-N* chart,

Table 29.3   TL 9000 Problem Reporting Categories

TL 9000 Problem Category	Typical Severity	TL 9000 Definition (QuEST Forum, 2012-12-31)
Critical	1	"Conditions that severely affect the primary functionality of the product and because of the business impact to the customer require nonstop immediate corrective action, regardless of time of day or day of the week, as viewed by a customer on discussion with the organization, such as a. Product inoperability (total or partial outage) b. A reduction in the capacity capability, that is, traffic/data-handling capability, such that expected loads cannot be handled c. Any loss of emergency capability (for example, emergency 911 calls) d. Safety hazard or risk of security breach"
Major	2	"Product is usable, but a condition exists that seriously degrades the product operation, maintenance, or administration, etc., and requires attention during predefined standard hours to resolve the situation. The urgency is less than in critical situations because of a lesser immediate or impending effect on product performance, customers and the customer's operation, and revenue, such as a. Reduction in product's capacity (but still able to handle the expected load) b. Any loss of administrative or maintenance visibility of the product and/or diagnostic capability c. Repeated degradation of an essential component or function d. Degradation of the product's ability to provide any required notification of malfunction"
Minor	3	"Other problems of a lesser severity than 'critical' or 'major' such as conditions that have little or no impairment on the function of the system"

Source: QuEST Forum, TL 9000, *Measurements Handbook Release 5.0,* QuEST Forum, 2012-12-31.

Table 29.4 Safety Risk Severity Categories

Description	*Severity Category*	*Mishap Result Criteria (from MIL-STD-882E)*
Catastrophic	1	"Could result in one or more of the following: death, permanent total disability, irreversible significant environmental impact, or monetary loss equal to or exceeding $10M."
Critical	2	"Could result in one or more of the following: permanent partial disability, injuries or occupational illness that may result in hospitalization of at least three personnel, reversible significant environmental impact, or monetary loss equal to or exceeding $1M but less than $10M."
Marginal	3	"Could result in one or more of the following: injury or occupational illness resulting in one or more lost workday(s), reversible moderate environmental impact, or monetary loss equal to or exceeding $100K but less than $1M."
Negligible	4	"Could result in one or more of the following: injury or occupational illness not resulting in a lost workday, minimal environmental impact, or monetary loss less than $100K."

Source: Table I of Department of Defense, MIL-STD-882E, *System Safety*, Wright-Patterson Air Force Base: United States Department of Defense, 2012-05-11.

f represents the annualized failure probability over all loading ranges. N represents the estimated life loss or number of fatalities associated with an individual failure mode, or the weighted equivalent number of fatalities associated with the summation of failure modes" (Dam Safety Office, 2011).

■ *F–N chart*—"Some organizations that quantitatively assess risk use complementary cumulative distribution functions to portray risk; they plot the number of fatalities (N) on the horizontal axis versus the annual exceedance probability for causing 'N' lives or greater on the vertical axis. The $F–N$ curves typically show the cumulative frequency of fatalities for all loading events and failure modes" (Dam Safety Office, 2011).

As low as reasonably practicable (ALARP) is a common term in risk management. ISO/IEC 31010 (ISO/IEC, 2009-11) visualizes the notion of ALARP via

Table 29.5 Safety Risk Probability Levels

Description	Level	Specific Individual Item (from MIL-STD-882E)	Fleet or Inventory (from MIL-STD-882E)
Frequent	A	"Likely to occur often in the life of an item."	"Continuously experienced."
Probable	B	"Will occur several times in the life of an item."	"Will occur frequently."
Occasional	C	"Likely to occur sometime in the life of an item."	"Will occur several times."
Remote	D	"Unlikely, but possible to occur in the life of an item."	"Unlikely, but can reasonably be expected to occur."
Improbable	E	"So unlikely, it can be assumed occurrence may not be experienced in the life of an item."	"Unlikely to occur, but possible."
Eliminated	F	"Incapable of occurrence. This level is used when potential hazards are identified and later eliminated."	"Incapable of occurrence. This level is used when potential hazards are identified and later eliminated."

Source: Table II of Department of Defense, MIL-STD-882E, *System Safety*, Wright-Patterson Air Force Base: United States Department of Defense, 2012-05-11.

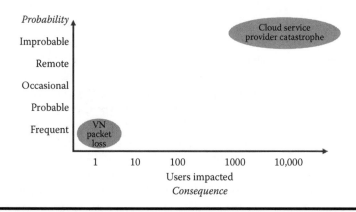

Figure 29.13 Sample consequence–probability visualization.

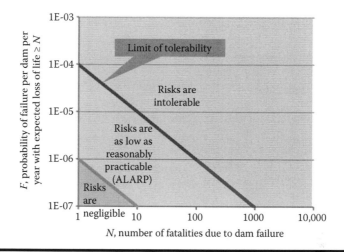

Figure 29.14 Sample *F-N* chart. (From Figure 2 of Dams Safety Committee, *Risk Management Policy Framework for Dam Safety,* New South Wales Government, 2006.)

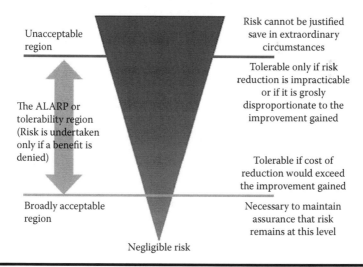

Figure 29.15 The ALARP concept. (From Figure B.12 of ISO/IEC, *31010—Risk Management—Risk Assessment Techniques,* Geneva, Switzerland: International Organization for Standardization & International Electrotechnical Committee, 2009-11.)

Figure 29.15 but does not offer a definition. A serviceable definition of ALARP is as follows:

> The "As-Low-As-Reasonably-Practicable" (ALARP) considerations provide a way to address efficiency in reducing risks. The concept for the use of ALARP considerations is that risk reduction beyond a certain level may not be justified if further risk reduction is impracticable or if the cost is grossly disproportional to the risk reduction. ALARP only has meaning in evaluating the justification for, or comparison of, risk reduction measures: it cannot be applied to an existing risk without considering the options to reduce that risk. (Dam Safety Office, 2011)

29.4.5 Risk Indices

Risk indices are covered in Annex B.28 of ISO/IEC 31010 (ISO/IEC, 2009-11). Risk indices normalize a range of risks onto an arbitrary scale (often from 1 for low risk to 5 for extreme risk) to compare levels of risk. Technically, risk indices score each component of risk based on likelihood, efficacy of controls, and consequences. The scores are normalized and aggregated, such as in the hypothetical risk indices visualization of Figure 29.16, in which risk type scores are rolled up by risk vector.

29.4.6 Cost/Benefit Analysis

Cost/benefit analysis is covered in Annex B.30 of ISO/IEC 31010 (ISO/IEC, 2009-11). Cost/benefit analysis monetizes and aggregates expected benefits and consequences so one can evaluate the net present value of competing risk treatment options. Real-option valuation (aka real-option analysis) techniques may be useful for analyzing broad, strategic risks of cloud-based applications, especially project initiation options and project abandonment options.

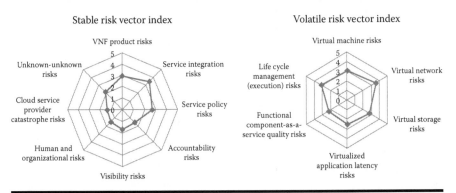

Figure 29.16   Hypothetical risk indices visualization.

29.5 Additional Techniques

The following are additional risk assessment techniques that can be considered:

- **Checklists**—Checklists are considered in ISO/IEC 31010 Annex B.4 (ISO/IEC, 2009-11). ISO/IEC 31010 Annex B.4.1 begins, "Check-lists are lists of hazards, risks or control failures that have been developed usually from experience, either as a result of a previous risk assessment or as a result of past failures." For example, preflight checklists used by pilots are a well-known way to manage safety risks associated with aircraft operations. Preflight-style checklists may eventually be developed and deployed as risks and mitigations become very well understood.
- **Delphi technique**—The Delphi technique (considered in Annex B.3 of ISO/IEC 31010 [ISO/IEC, 2009-11]) is a procedure to reach a reliable consensus opinion from a group of experts. As this technique takes more effort than structured interview and brainstorming (Section 29.1.4), it is less commonly used.
- **Cause–consequence analysis**—Cause–consequence analysis is a combination of fault tree and ETA, and is considered in Annex B.16 of ISO/IEC 31010 (ISO/IEC, 2009-11). This technique requires greater effort than either fault tree or ETA, so it is not often necessary for cloud-based application services.
- **Sneak analysis**—Sneak analysis is covered in Annex B.23 of ISO/IEC 31010 (ISO/IEC, 2009-11). According to ISO/IEC 31010 (ISO/IEC, 2009-11), this technique identifies four categories of sneak circuits (which could be software "circuits"):

  a) **sneak paths**: unexpected paths along which current, energy, or logical sequence flows in an unintended direction;
  b) **sneak timing**: events occurring in an unexpected or conflicting sequence;
  c) **sneak indications**: ambiguous or false displays of system operating conditions that may cause the system or an operator to take an undesired action;
  d) **sneak labels**: incorrect or imprecise labelling of system functions, e.g. system inputs, controls, display buses that may cause an operator to apply an incorrect stimulus to the system.

  Formal or informal sneak analysis of VNFs, infrastructure, management, and orchestration elements is useful but is often impractical across an application service delivery chain.

- **Markov analysis**—Markov analysis is covered in Annex B.24 of ISO/IEC 31010 (ISO/IEC, 2009-11). Architecture-based Markov models are routinely used to predict service outage downtime of repairable systems.
- **Monte Carlo analysis**—Monte Carlo analysis is covered in Annex B.25 of ISO/IEC 31010 (ISO/IEC, 2009-11). Monte Carlo analysis can be used to simulate service quality impairments, such application service latency degradation for stochastic impairments like packet loss, packet jitter, and scheduling latency. Fuzz testing, which provides random, unexpected, or invalid inputs, is a practical alternative to purely simulation-based Monte Carlo techniques.
- **Bayesian analysis**—Bayesian analysis is covered in Annex B.26 of ISO/IEC 31010 (ISO/IEC, 2009-11). Bayesian analysis can be used in diagnosing in situ root causes.
- **Root cause analysis**—Root cause analysis (RCA) is considered in Annex B.12 of ISO/IEC 31010 (ISO/IEC, 2009-11). RCA is performed after a failure event to determine the true root causes that drive corrective actions to appropriately treat the underlying risks and enable continuous improvement.
- **Decision tree**—Decision trees are covered in Annex B.19 of ISO/IEC 31010 (ISO/IEC, 2009-11). Decision trees may be useful when evaluating different treatment options for a particular risk.
- **Multicriteria decision analysis**—Multicriteria decision analysis (MCDA) is covered in Annex B.31 of ISO/IEC 31010 (ISO/IEC, 2009-11). MCDA is useful when potentially conflicting risks and treatment options must be balanced, but this is rarely the case when narrowly considering user service quality risks.

Chapter 30

Service Quality Risk Management Process

Section IV, "Cloud Service Quality Risk Assessment and Management," has methodically applied ISO 31000 risk management processes to user service quality of cloud-based application services. Chapter 11, "Service Strategy," especially Section 11.6, "Risk Thinking about Service Strategy," argues that risk management should be integrated into an organization's strategy and processes. To facilitate smooth integration of ISO 31000 into service strategy for cloud-based applications, this chapter offers the following:

- Risk management in a nutshell (Section 30.1)
- Risk assessment report overview (Section 30.2)
- Integrating risk management with service management (Section 30.3)

30.1 Risk Management in a Nutshell

The ISO 31000–based risk management process recommended in Section IV, "Cloud Service Quality Risk Assessment and Management," is visualized in Figure 30.1:

1. **Identify the key user service quality objectives**—Section 27.5, "Establish Service Quality Objectives," considers this activity in detail. Setting quality objectives is fundamentally a three-step process:
   a. Select quality objective metrics (Section 27.5.2)
   b. Select service quality measurement points (Section 27.5.3)
   c. Set performance targets for each key quality objective (Section 27.5.4)

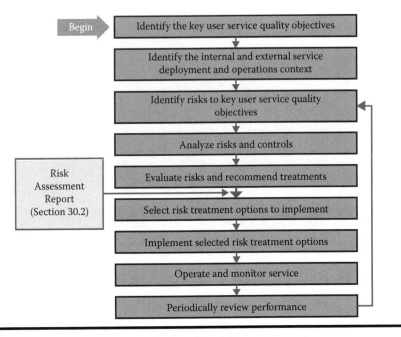

Figure 30.1 Canonical user service quality risk management process.

2. **Identify the internal and external service deployment and operations context** (Chapter 27, "Risk Context"), including the risk criteria used by the organization.

3. **Identify risks to key user service quality objectives**—Section III, "Cloud Service Quality Risk Inventory," reviewed a broad set of risk vectors and types that can challenge the user service quality of cloud-based application services. The activity of risk identification is considered in Section 28.2. Chapter 29, "Risk Assessment Techniques," reviews specific techniques for risk identification, especially Section 29.1, "General Risk Identification and Analysis Techniques," and Section 29.2, "Specialized Risk Identification and Analysis Techniques."

4. **Analyze risks and controls**—Risk analysis is considered in Section 28.3. Chapter 29, "Risk Assessment Techniques," reviews specific techniques for risk identification, especially Section 29.1, "General Risk Identification and Analysis Techniques," Section 29.2, "Specialized Risk Identification and Analysis Techniques," and Section 29.3, "Risk Controls Analysis Techniques."

5. **Evaluate risks and recommend treatments**—Risk evaluation is considered in Section 28.4, and Section 29.4, "Risk Evaluation Techniques," offers several methods for rigorously evaluating, rating, and ranking identified risks. This activity proposes appropriate risk treatment options and prepares supporting materials to enable cloud service customer (CSC) leaders to make risk treatment decisions.

6. **Select risk treatment options to implement**—As considered in Section 28.5, "Risk Treatment," CSC business leaders select risk treatments to implement from the recommended menu of treatment options. Treatments not selected for immediate implementation may be added to the project's work backlog or road-mapped for future releases.

7. **Implement selected risk treatment options**—Implementation of selected risk treatments by the designated treatment owner proceeds according to the treatment owner's processes. CSC project management processes should track progress and completion of each selected risk treatment.

8. **Operate and monitor service**—Key user service quality indicators and performance at all critical control points should be monitored, along with routine alarms and performance metrics, to assure that acceptable service quality is continuously delivered to end users. Corrective actions should be taken when performance exceeds control limits.

9. **Periodically review performance**—Continual service improvement (Chapter 9) is based on regular plan–do–check–act (PDCA) cycles to review and improve performance. Changing market conditions and other factors may prompt the CSC to reevaluate their business and user service quality objectives, and reassess risks based on those revised service quality objectives and risk context.

30.2 Risk Assessment Report Overview

Best practice is for the risk assessment activity to conclude a risk assessment report to openly communicate the identified, analyzed, and evaluated risks facing the organization, as well as recommended treatment options. Treatment options actually selected by the organization's decision makers should also be formally recorded, but that may appear in a separate artifact.

ISO 31010, *Risk Assessment Techniques*, (ISO/IEC, 2009-11) clause 5.5, "Documentation," offers the following outline for a written risk assessment report:

- ▪ Objectives and scope;
- ▪ Description of relevant parts of the system and their functions;
- ▪ A summary of the external and internal context of the organization and how it relates to the situation, system or circumstances being assessed;
- ▪ Risk criteria applied and their justification;
- ▪ Limitations, assumptions and justification of hypotheses;
- ▪ Assessment methodology;
- ▪ Risk identification results;
- ▪ Data, assumptions and their sources and validation;
- ▪ Risk analysis results and their evaluation;

- Sensitivity and uncertainty analysis;
- Critical assumptions and other factors which need to be monitored;
- Discussion of results;
- Conclusions and recommendations;
- References.

The following structure is often appropriate for risk assessment reports:

1. **Business objectives and context**—What are the CSC organization's business objectives for deploying the target application service? This section should include the organization's risk appetite statements related to the target service (Section 3.4, "Risk Appetite").
2. **Service architecture overview**—Overview of target service delivery architecture to be analyzed. This section includes a reliability block diagram of the user service delivery path.
3. **Service quality objectives**—Rigorously capture the organization's user service quality objectives, as discussed in Section 27.5, "Establish Service Quality Objectives."
4. **Risk context**—Frames the risk context, especially the following
   a. Internal context (Section 27.1) and external context (Section 27.2) guide risk ownership and influence risk criteria.
   b. Risk criteria (Section 27.3) guide risk rating and ranking of risks, and selection of risk treatments.
   c. Context of the risk management process (Section 27.4) guides both what treatment information is appropriate to enable a timely risk treatment decision and who the CSC decision maker(s) are.
5. **Assumptions**—Enumerate assumptions made regarding context, risk ownership, risk criteria, risk inventory, risk analysis, risk evaluation, and risk treatment.
6. **Risk inventory and analysis**—Risks are inventoried and analyzed using appropriate techniques from Section 29.1, "General Risk Identification and Analysis Techniques," and perhaps Section 29.2, "Specialized Risk Identification and Analysis Techniques." Diligence often includes the following:
   a. Influence diagrams (Section 29.1.1) and/or cause-and-effect analysis (Section 29.1.2)
   b. Failure mode effect analysis (FMEA, Section 29.1.3)
   c. Team-based technique with applicable experts: structured interview and brainstorming (Section 29.1.4) and/or structured "what-if" technique (SWIFT, Section 29.1.5)
7. **Risk controls assessment**—Risk controls for significant quality risks are identified and methodically analyzed via some techniques from Section 29.3, "Risk Controls Analysis Techniques."

8. **Risk rating and ranking**—Define tailored risk rating definitions that are consistent with the organization's risk criteria (Section 27.3). Apply at least one technique from Section 29.4, "Risk Evaluation Techniques," to rate and rank all identified risks.

9. **Recommended risk treatments**—Risk treatment options are proposed for all unacceptable risks. Appropriate supporting information is provided to enable effective decision making by CSC leaders, such as cost estimates and recommended implementation organizations.

10. **References, abbreviations, and acronyms**—As the risk assessment report will potentially reviewed by business leaders, staff in the office of the chief financial officer (CFO), or chief risk officer (CRO), it is important to expand abbreviations and acronyms that are not well known across the CSC's organization.

As CSC organizations focus on delivering new services and value fast with improved operational efficiency, the risk assessment report is likely to be a lightweight document that can be easily revised as the organization pivots from one market opportunity to another.

30.3 Integrating Risk Management with Service Management

ISO 31000 clause 3 (ISO, 2009-11-15) enumerates 11 principles for effective risk management; a CSC's service strategy should appropriately align with these principles.

a. **Risk management creates and protects value.** A CSC service strategy should explicitly create value for the organization; risk management should be an integral part of that service strategy to assure that the expected value is delivered.

b. **Risk management is an integral part of all organizational processes.** Risk management should explicitly be considered by the CSC's service strategy.

c. **Risk management is part of decision making.** Decision gates in the service strategy, design, transition, and operations processes should explicitly consider risks.

d. **Risk management explicitly addresses uncertainty.** Risks to both user service quality and achieving expected opex reductions and acceleration in the pace of service innovation should explicitly be considered.

e. **Risk management is systematic, structured, and timely.** The service strategy should assure that risk management is appropriate, considered in a systematic, structured, and timely way.

f. **Risk management is based on the best available information.** Obviously, the most accurate assessments and best decisions are based on the best available information.

g. **Risk management is tailored.** Section III, "Cloud Service Quality Risk Inventory," explicitly considers user service quality risks to cloud-based applications, and Section IV, "Cloud Service Quality Risk Assessment and Management," explicitly considers assessment and management of risks to user service quality of cloud-based applications.

h. **Risk management takes human and cultural factors into account.** Human and organizational risks are explicitly considered in Chapter 22 of Section III, "Cloud Service Quality Risk Inventory," and as part of the internal context discussed in Section 27.1.

i. **Risk management is transparent and inclusive.** CSCs should transparently and inclusively deploy risk management to their organization.

j. **Risk management is dynamic, iterative, and responsive to change.**

k. **Risk management facilitates continual improvement of the organization.** CSCs should methodically monitor service quality performance and periodically compare actual results to objectives to drive continual service improvement as discussed in Chapter 9.

30.4 Integrating Risk Management and Quality Management

Individuals who design, integrate, or operate cloud-based services should be familiar with their organization's quality management system (QMS). That QMS is presumably based on the ISO 9000 suite of quality management standards and probably based on a Deming PDCA cycle of continuous improvement. To minimize duplicative continual service improvement activities, organizations should align their PDCA cycles as discussed in Section 9.3, "Aligning PDCA Cycles." In particular, their information technology (IT) service management (e.g., ITIL or ISO 20000) continuous improvement cycle (Section 9.1.3), quality management improvement cycles (Section 9.1.1), risk management cycles (Section 9.1.2), and efficiency improvement cycles (Section 10.8) should be aligned and integrated to minimize overlapping and wasteful work.

DISCUSSION

V

We conclude our consideration of risk-based thinking for cloud-based application services with the following chapters:

- **Cloud and Creative Destruction** (Chapter 31) considers cloud computing as a wave of creative destruction that enables innovative organizations to deliver new services and value faster to grow their organization's top line, and to improve operational efficiency to grow their organization's bottom line. Organizations that effectively leverage these capabilities will achieve material advantage over their competitors.
- **Connecting the Dots** (Chapter 32) summarizes the key insights and recommendations of the book. The chapter includes extensive cross-references to previous chapters, so busy professionals can use this chapter as a gateway to the rest of the book.

Chapter 31

Cloud and Creative Destruction

Creative destruction is an ongoing process that drives innovation to better serve markets to gain business advantage and drive profitability. Economist Joseph Schumpeter (1883–1950) popularized the notion of creative destruction in his book *Capitalism, Socialism and Democracy*, which offers the following insight:

> The opening up of new markets, foreign or domestic, and the organizational development from the craft shop to such concerns as U.S. Steel illustrate the same process of industrial mutation...that incessantly revolutionizes the economic structure from within, incessantly destroying the old one, incessantly creating a new one. This process of Creative Destruction is the essential fact about capitalism. (Schumpeter, 1950)

Waves of innovation and creative destruction are easily recognized in the recorded music business:

- Vinyl record albums
- Eight-track tapes
- Cassette tapes
- Compact disks
- MP3 downloads
- Streaming music services

Cloud computing enables another wave of creative destruction to sweep across industry as enterprises reconfigure their information value chains to find new arrangements that give them advantages over their competitors. Innovative enterprises that leverage cloud computing to deliver new services and value faster to customers with greater operational efficiencies can take market share from slower and less effective organizations.

This chapter considers the cloud as a driver of creative destruction in the following sections:

- Containerization as an analog for cloud computing (Section 31.1)
- Strategic benefits of cloud computing (Section 31.2)
- Tactical benefits and strategic directions (Section 31.3)
- Other catalyzing factors (Section 31.4)
- Outlook (Section 31.5)

31.1 Containerization as an Analog for Cloud Computing

Containerized shipping is a useful analog for cloud computing. Marc Levinson explains in *The Box: How the Shipping Container Made the World Smaller and the World Economy Bigger* (Levinson, 2008) how the world evolved from slow and costly break bulk shipping (Figure 31.1) to highly efficient containerized shipping (Figure 31.2). Massive infrastructure-as-a-service providers like Amazon Web

Figure 31.1 Handling break bulk cargo circa 1912. (From Lewis Hine, courtesy of US Archives.)

Figure 31.2   Handling containerized cargo circa 2007. (Courtesy of Wikimedia.)

Services, Microsoft, IBM, and Google compete to offer virtualized resource services, automated life cycle management, and functional components offered as-a-service to enterprises as Maersk, MSC, CMA-CGM, and others compete to haul shipping containers across the globe for industrial, commercial, governmental, and nongovernmental organizations. Just as warehouse-scale data centers offer operational efficiencies unattainable with traditional data center architectures, ultralarge container vessels (ULCVs) carrying more than 14,500 twenty-foot-equivalent cargo containers offer unprecedented operational efficiencies transporting cargoes.

Beyond causing massive upheaval and wholesale job losses in the shipping industry itself, the cost savings and logistical changes enabled by containerization led to massive reengineering of manufacturing across the globe, which impacted business and employment patterns across a huge range of industries and geographies. Modern manufacturers now leverage global sourcing and shipping to deliver value to their customers fast and at the lowest cost to grow their businesses. Information technology (IT) and application service provider organizations that do not successfully embrace and leverage cloud-based virtual resources, automated life cycle management, and functional components offered as-a-service may turn out like manufacturers that failed to embrace global supply chains: low-volume producers of artisanal products…or bankrupt.

31.2 Strategic Benefits of Cloud Computing

Cloud computing offers the following potential strategic benefits to cloud service customer (CSC) organizations:

- Aggressive automation and pulling humans out of the loop (Section 31.2.1)
- From supply push to demand pull (Section 31.2.2)
- Perfect capacity management (Section 31.2.3)
- Aggressive cost management (Section 31.2.4)
- Rich and dynamic service value chains (Section 31.2.5)
- Shifting capital and risk (Section 31.2.6)

31.2.1 Aggressive Automation and Pulling Humans out of the Loop

While automated life cycle management, like self-healing of inevitable failure events, is a well-known benefit of cloud computing, often, folks fail to consider how the cloud might ultimately remove 90% or more of the human effort related to IT service management of cloud-based applications. Figure 31.3 visualizes the likely automation of service life cycle management activities over time. Early cloud deployments will likely automate execution of service life cycle management actions, like scripting application service start-up, shutdown, and repair actions. Later, automated planning and orchestration actions can coordinate automated

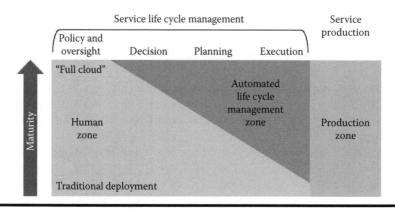

Figure 31.3 Service life cycle management maturity.

execution actions, like synchronizing tasks such as waiting for active traffic to drain from a service component before shutting it down. Eventually, decision making is fully automated; for example, determining exactly when to trigger a repair or capacity change action can be supported with cognitive analytics and machine learning. Humans will likely retain ultimate responsibility both for specifying the policies that are used by the decision engine and for general oversight. However, the staffing level required for policy and oversight is likely to be a tiny fraction of the staffing required for traditional application service management.

As a practical example, consider the automated bill-paying services offered by banks today: one specifies the name of the counterparty (e.g., your mortgage supplier, credit card company, local utility) and the day of the month to pay the bill along with relevant account identifiers, and the bank automatically pays the billed amount every month. The human account holder retains ultimate oversight responsibility to assure that his/her account is not overdrawn; however, additional automations can both automatically notify the account holder of low-balance conditions and provide automatic overdraft protection. The result is that users who embrace online banking hugely reduce the time and energy they spend on bill paying, thereby freeing up their time and effort for more productive endeavors and/or enjoyable pursuits. Ultimately, application service life cycle management may be as automated as online bill paying is today.

31.2.2 From Supply Push to Demand Pull

Traditionally deployed application capacity is similar to the assembly-line model of production in that organizations focus on deploying sufficient application capacity to produce a fixed level of service at the lowest per-unit cost. Figure 31.4 visualizes the cost model for this traditional deployment strategy by showing the numbers of users served on the *x*-axis and the total cost to serve on the *y*-axis. Note that in the traditional deployment model, a massive investment in capacity must be made before

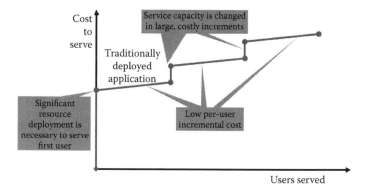

Figure 31.4   Traditionally deployed application cost model.

service can even be offered to the first user, but with that investment having been made, additional users can be served at very low incremental cost. At some point, user demand exceeds the deployed capacity, so another significant investment in additional capacity must be made to serve the next tier of demand at low incremental cost.

While the incremental per-user cost may be very small in most cases, the upfront, sunk cost for application capacity may never be recovered if the service is not popular. However, as fulfilling service capacity growth actions would often require weeks or months of lead time for planning, logistics, and so on, if a service was unexpectedly popular, then the organization might not be able to grow online service capacity before surging demand vanished. Thus, organizations offering traditionally deployed applications often carried significant business risks for capital invested in application capacity that might never be used if the application was less popular than expected. This often led to a supply-push business model where prices were discounted heavily in the hope of pushing aggregate demand and revenue to at least break even. Unfortunately, this supply-push business model discouraged businesses from rapidly adapting to market wants and needs because they had to push users to consume the sunk capacity that they had deployed rather than better serving new and evolving user needs and wants with some different application.

Decades ago, manufacturers overcame this fundamental limitation of supply-push assembly-line production models by moving to flexible and lean manufacturing systems, which focus on producing what is actually sold rather than stuffing their channel with mass-produced products that may not actually sell at a profit. For example, rather than buying 3 months' worth of parts at a rock-bottom price and hoping that forecast demand for finished goods materializes, lean manufacturers generally pay slightly more (e.g., a 5% premium) for the parts they need to serve demand *today* and let their supplier cover the risk of demand decreasing or increasing or otherwise changing over the coming weeks or months. As demand forecasts months into the future are often highly uncertain, there is significant business value in tying production costs more closely to actual demand even if per-unit production costs are slightly higher than if production had been optimized for the perfectly forecast level of demand.

Rapid elasticity and scalability (Section 1.4.5) enable CSC organizations to embrace a lean, just-in-time capacity management model that ties production costs much closer to actual demand than with traditional deployment. Figure 31.5 overlays costs for a hypothetical cloud-based application onto the traditional deployment cost model of Figure 31.4; key cost model differences for cloud-based applications are as follows:

- **Minimum viable service configuration cost to serve the first user is generally much lower** because
  - Rapid elasticity makes it more cost effective to scale from very, very small configurations to very, very large configuration in many small steps
  - Usage-based pricing of application capacity and functional components offered as-a-service enables a CSC's costs to track actual and exact usage

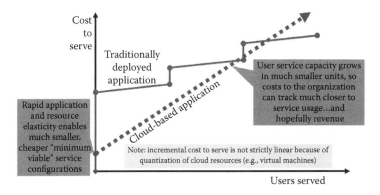

Figure 31.5   Cloud-based application cost model.

- Cost-per-user slope is likely to be somewhat steeper than for rapidly elastic applications than for traditionally deployed applications—Application suppliers and cloud service providers will likely charge slightly higher usage charges when CSCs pay for usage "retail" on basis (e.g., per actual individual user) rather than when they pay for usage on a "wholesale" basis (e.g., up to 1000 simultaneous users, up to 2000 simultaneous users, etc.).
- A CSC's cost to serve is likely to be more linear from the first user than for traditionally deployed applications. While some software and functional-component-as-a-service usage charges might track on exact, actual service usage (making incremental cost to serve linear), virtual machine and virtual storage volume instances are more granular, so one instance may be added for every N users. However, units of elastic capacity growth are likely to be smaller for cloud-based applications than for traditional deployments because the cloud makes it cost effective to automatically grow and shrink by much smaller increments of service capacity (e.g., one virtual machine instance). As user demand grows and expands into different geographies, the CSC may create additional application instances to better serve those users, and each application instantiation accrues a modest cost increment.

The cloud-based application cost model fundamentally derisks the organization's business case because a much smaller minimum viable block of capacity can be held online to offer service to users, so the organization's costs track closer to actual user demand with cloud-based applications than with traditionally deployed applications.

31.2.3 Perfect Capacity Management

Capacity growth actions have been rare, expensive, and risky for traditionally deployed applications, so organizations would engineer their hardware and software configurations to serve the peak demand forecast for several quarters into the future, plus a substantial safety margin. Traditional capacity change actions often required formal approvals of the organization's change management board and advance planning to order hardware components or equipment, schedule staff and maintenance windows, and so on, all of which pushed capacity change lead times to weeks or even months. Given the inconvenience and service quality risks of complex manual configuration change procedures, application capacity change actions were not frequent for traditionally deployed applications. Figure 31.6 illustrates the two fundamental business risks of traditional application capacity management:

- **Underprovisioning**—If actual user demand outstrips online application capacity, then some user demand will not be served, or will not be served with acceptable user service quality, which negatively impacts the quality of experience for some users.
- **Overprovisioning**—If online application capacity significantly exceeds actual user demand, then physical infrastructure resources, and perhaps software licenses, are wasted.

Figure 31.7 frames an application capacity management change as a delta-epsilon problem:

- Capacity change lead time is the x-axis δ_{Time}.
- Application capacity change is the y-axis $\varepsilon_{Capacity}$.

In the limit, driving both the capacity change lead time to be as short as possible and application capacity change increment to be as small as possible enables actual application capacity to track closer to any time-varying pattern of actual user demand.

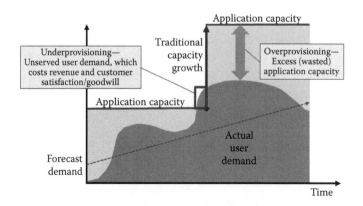

Figure 31.6   Traditional capacity management risks.

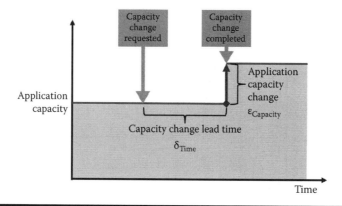

Figure 31.7   Application capacity as a delta-epsilon problem.

Figure 6.5 shows application demand for a sample application on a typical Thursday. Comparing Figure 6.5 to the traditional application capacity management risk figure (Figure 31.6), one sees that a single capacity setting across the day leads to significant resource wastage and/or significant unserved demand, depending upon exactly where the application capacity level is set. Considering the sample demand of Figure 6.5 as a delta-epsilon problem as shown in Figure 31.7, one sees that as δ_{Time} and $\varepsilon_{Capacity}$ shrink (i.e., faster capacity change lead times and smaller application capacity change increments), it should be possible for a CSC's online application capacity to track very closely to actual user demand, thereby minimizing both wasted resources and unserved user demand.

As explained in Section 6.2.1, there are inherent Capacity Fulfillment Uncertainties in that requested capacity changes ($\varepsilon_{Capacity}$) may not successfully be completed in the expected capacity change fulfillment time (δ_{Time}). As explained in Section 6.2.2, predicting future user demand, failures, and other events inevitably carries Capacity Decision Uncertainties. To treat these and other risks, organizations carry some online spare capacity beyond the working online capacity necessary to serve expected user demand. Figure 31.8 shows a cushion of reserve capacity above the level of working capacity necessary to serve actual user demand; perfect application capacity is the level of online application capacity necessary to serve user demand, plus the cushion of reserve capacity stipulated by the organization's policies. Chapter 6, "Lean Application Capacity Management," especially Section 6.8, considers Perfect Capacity Management in detail.

Figure 31.9 overlays perfect capacity management from Figure 31.8 with the traditional capacity management model of Figure 31.6. One immediately recognizes that the perfect capacity management model both eliminates significant wasted online application capacity and serves user demand that was previously not addressed with acceptable service quality. Reducing both wasted resources and unmet user demand improves operational efficiency and overall business results.

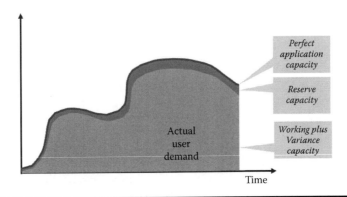

Figure 31.8 Perfect capacity management example.

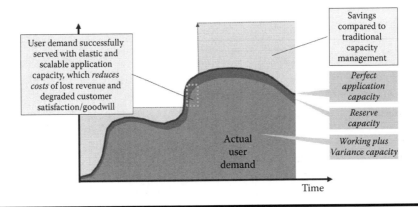

Figure 31.9 Perfect capacity management risks.

31.2.4 Aggressive Cost Management

Standardized product offerings, efficient markets, and powerful information systems have enabled airlines and many other industries to aggressively manage prices to maximize the value to the enterprise offering products to the market. The key cloud characteristic of resource pooling (Section 1.4.6) stipulates the following:

> From the customer's perspective, all they know is that the service works, while they generally have no control or knowledge over how the resources are being provided or where the resources are located. (ISO/IEC, 2014-10-15)

Coupled with the key cloud characteristics of measured service (Section 1.4.2) and broad network access (Section 1.4.1), one can foresee a range of dynamic

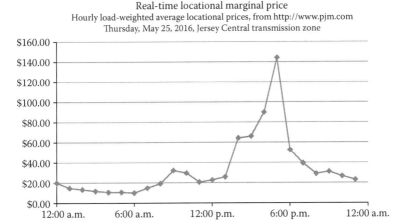

Real-time locational marginal price
Hourly load-weighted average locational prices, from http://www.pjm.com
Thursday, May 25, 2016, Jersey Central transmission zone

From http://www.pjm.com: "Please note that these load-weighted averages are ESTIMATES only, actual load-weighted averages used in PJM accounting may vary since the calculations of bus loads are not final until five days after the end of the month."

Figure 31.10 Wholesale electricity pricing example.

pricing arrangements that simultaneously enable cloud service providers to maximize the utilization and operational efficiency of their capital investment in cloud infrastructure equipment, software, and data centers, while CSCs can shop around for the most attractive service terms and pricing.

Like cloud computing, the wholesale market for electric power also features standardized product offerings, efficient markets, and powerful information systems. Figure 31.10 illustrates the average, load-weighted locational marginal price for wholesale electricity on a Thursday in the transmission zone that serves the author's home. For the week including the Thursday in Figure 31.10, wholesale electricity prices ranged from –$6.48* at 4 a.m. Monday morning to $170.10 at 6 p.m. Friday evening. While cloud resource pricing is unlikely to ever go negative, it certainly could be as volatile as electric power pricing for some resources (e.g., on-the-spot market) and thus encourage CSCs to deploy advanced techniques to minimize their resource costs to improve business results.

---

* Electricity prices can go negative when the supply of electric power production exceeds the current demand for electricity. Unlike electric lights, which can simply be switched off and on, large power plants must ramp power production up or down, often by a few megawatts per minute. Since electric power generally cannot be stored quickly in industrial quantities and the power has to go somewhere to avoid damaging equipment, utilities occasionally pay others to consume the excess electricity.

31.2.5 Rich and Dynamic Service Value Chains

CSCs operate in a rich and dynamic ecosystem. As discussed in Section 1.2, "Roles in Cloud Computing," CSCs can select from a variety of public cloud service providers—and perhaps private and/or community cloud service providers—offering infrastructure, automated life cycle management, and functional components offered as-a-service on demand in nominally unlimited quantity. A variety of traditional and new entrant software suppliers will offer myriad service components and applications that can be deployed onto the cloud. In addition, several cloud service partner roles are defined* to serve CSCs:

- The **cloud service developer** provides design, development, testing, and maintenance services to support a CSC's service implementation. This role also covers service integration and developing service components.
- The **cloud broker** negotiates relationships between CSCs and cloud service providers. Key activities of cloud brokers include optimal matching of CSCs' technical, business, and regulatory needs with cloud service provider offerings, and negotiating terms, conditions, and prices between matching customers and providers.
- The **cloud auditor** audits provision and use of cloud services, such as for the following:
  - Operations, including usage-based charges assessed by cloud service providers
  - Performance, such as adherence to service-level objectives stipulated in service-level agreements (SLAs) between cloud service providers and CSCs
  - Security, such as audits against ISO/IEC 27002:2013, *Code of Practice for Information Security Controls*
  - Service availability or reliability

Optimal arrangements of cloud service providers, software suppliers, cloud service developers, cloud brokers, and cloud auditors can reduce the risks of a CSC failing to achieve their objectives of delivering new service and value fast with improved operational efficiency and with acceptable user service quality. As enterprises learned over decades, contracting out a business process or service to another party carries risks if poorly executed but can provide material benefits to organizations that can exploit the expertise, budgetary flexibility, and control that come from well-executed outsourcing arrangements. Thus, CSCs will have more profound build-versus-buy decisions to make when constructing their cloud-based applications.

---

* These roles are defined in ISO/IEC 17788, *Cloud Computing Overview and Vocabulary* (ISO/IEC, 2014-10-15), and ISO/IEC 17789, *Cloud Computing Reference Architecture* (ISO/IEC, 2014-10-15).

31.2.6 Shifting Capital and Risk

As explained in Section 2.1, "Cloud Infrastructure Service Provider Business Models," cloud infrastructure service providers own and operate the physical equipment that enables on-demand self service (Section 1.4.4) with rapid elasticity and scalability (Section 1.4.5) via resource pooling (Section 1.4.6) and multitenancy (Section 1.4.3) to multiple CSCs. Ownership and operation of that physical infrastructure equipment, data centers, and enabling software means that the cloud service provider organization is responsible for necessary capital, as well as the operational complexities and risks associated with generating an acceptable business return on the invested capital. In order to generate acceptable returns on the capital that cloud infrastructure service providers must invest to offer virtualized compute, memory, storage, networking, automated life cycle management, and functional components offered as-a-service to CSCs, the cloud service providers will charge CSCs for their usage of measured service (Section 1.4.2). Shifting significant capital expense, complexity, and business risk from the CSC's business model to the cloud service provider's business model enables the CSC to better focus their scarce resources on creating their unique business value, especially via their cloud-based application services.

Beyond removing the capital and operational complexity associated with the compute, memory, storage, and networking resources from the CSC, the cloud materially reduces the business risks confronting an organization offering a new or improved service:

- **Rich and dynamic service value chains** (Section 31.2.5) enable CSCs rapid access to a broad range of service components, infrastructure, and professional services, many of which are offered on a pay-as-you-go basis.
- **Perfect capacity management** (Section 31.2.3) largely reduces risks related to demand forecasting because application capacity will scale to serve actual demand, and operating expenses will track with actual online application capacity.
- **Aggressive automation and pulling humans out of the loop** (Section 31.2.1) reduce the risk of hiring too many or too few operations engineers and customer support staff because automated mechanisms can scale up and down much faster and more cost effectively than human staff levels can be adjusted.

31.3 Tactical Benefits and Strategic Directions

Figure 31.11 visualizes the primary expected benefits of cloud computing that were considered in Chapter 2, "Desired Cloud Service Customer Benefits," and were captured in Figure 2.1.

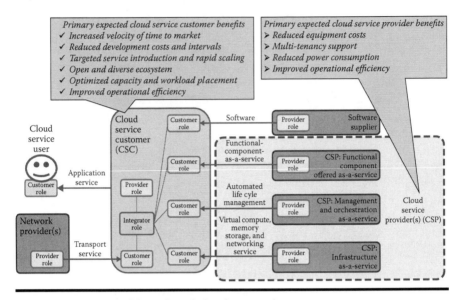

Figure 31.11   Tactical benefits of cloud computing.

The tactical benefits to the CSC in Figure 31.11 are certainly attractive, but they don't clearly connect to the broader Strategic Benefits of Cloud Computing considered in Section 31.2. Figure 31.12 illustrates how the tactical benefits of the cloud from Section 2.3, "Factoring Benefits of Cloud/Network Functions Virtualization," map to strategic directions from Section 31.2 "Strategic Benefits of

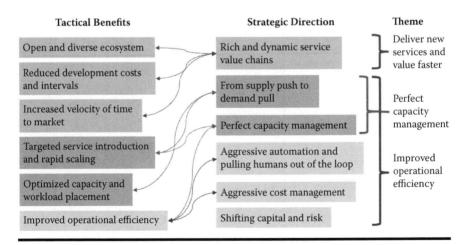

Figure 31.12   Evolving tactical benefits to strategic directions.

Cloud Computing." Both the tactical benefits and strategic directions for CSCs fit into three broad themes:

- **Deliver new services and value faster**—rich and dynamic service value chains (Section 31.2.5) enable CSCs to effectively leverage a wide range of off-the-shelf service components, service offerings, and expertise to deliver value to their customers faster. Competition between myriad players offering products and services throughout the value chain simultaneously drives prices to the CSC down while improving the features, qualities, and delivery intervals of those offerings. The network functions virtualization (NFV) white paper benefits of an open and diverse ecosystem (Section 2.3.5), reduced development costs and intervals (Section 2.3.3), and increased velocity of time to market (Section 2.3.2) fit into this theme of leveraging cloud-enabled value chains to deliver value to customers faster.

- **Perfect capacity management**—The key cloud characteristic of rapid elasticity and scalability (Section 1.4.5) enables CSCs to change their business model from supply push to demand pull (Section 31.2.2) like how manufacturers shifted from an economy-of-scale, supply-push operation to a lean, just-in-time demand-pull operation decades ago. Perfect capacity management (Section 31.2.3) is the goal of lean capacity management, in which the CSC holds just enough online application capacity at any instant to cover current actual cyclical demand and random variations, plus a small increment of reserve capacity to mitigate risks of failures, unforecast surges in demand, and other unforeseen circumstances. Online application capacity is adjusted every few minutes to assure that enough capacity is online to serve user demand with acceptable quality without wasting resources by holding excess online capacity. The broader theme of perfect capacity management covers two of the well-known benefits of cloud of targeted service introduction and rapid scaling (Section 2.3.4) and optimized capacity and workload placement (Section 2.3.6).

- **Improved operational efficiency**—The primary strategy for improving efficiency of CSC operations is aggressive automation and pulling humans out of the loop (Section 31.2.1). Perfect capacity management (previous bullet) is also an important part of improved CSC operational efficiency. In addition, aggressive cost management (Section 31.2.4) by the cloud service provider creates an opportunity for CSCs to capture further savings on cloud-based resources that may be available via exceptional market efficiencies available via thick and vibrant markets for cloud services. Shifting capital and risk (Section 31.2.6) enables CSCs to outsource ownership and operation of standard resources, automated life cycle management systems, and some service components so they can focus their scarce resources on creating differentiated value to improve business results. Improved operational efficiency (Section 2.3.9) has long been a recognized driver of technologies, processes, and practices, and was explicitly cited as one of the benefits of NFV.

31.4 Other Catalyzing Factors

Beyond the cloud-centric factors enumerated in Section 31.2, "Strategic Benefits of Cloud Computing," several other industry trends help catalyze the transformative capabilities of cloud computing:

- **Agile development techniques**—Agile principles (Beck, Beedle, and others) can be successfully adopted for traditionally deployed applications, but as explained in Section 11.2, "Agile Thinking about Service Strategy," the key characteristics of cloud computing make it easier to embrace Agile development.
- **DevOps**—As explained in Section 11.3, "DevOps Thinking about Service Strategy," the key cloud characteristics of on-demand self-service (Section 1.4.4) and rapid elasticity and scalability (Section 1.4.5) make DevOps easier when applications are deployed on the cloud compared to traditional deployment models.
- **Simplified customization**—The cloud characteristic of rapid elasticity and scalability (Section 1.4.5) makes it easier to create an application instance or service component that is configured precisely for a particular individual or group of users to offer them a tailored quality of experience.
- **Standardization and skilled workers**—Early technology systems (e.g., power looms in the early industrial revolution) were largely proprietary, which forced workers to develop firm-specific skills that were not portable. Firm-specific skills both depressed workers' wages (because they were not valuable to other employers) and limited growth potential for firms (because learning firm-specific skills took time). Standardization of open-source and commercially available technologies (e.g., OpenStack, Linux, Hadoop, Cassandra, etc.); programming languages and tools (e.g., Java, Python, HTML5, etc.); processes ([e.g., Information Technology Infrastructure Library [ITIL®]); and methodologies (e.g., Agile) means that the skills workers have developed on the job at one firm and via formal instruction are immediately valuable to expanding firms. Access to a broader and deeper pool of appropriately skilled workers enables enterprises to expand faster and drives up wages for workers with those appropriate skills.

31.5 Outlook

Enterprises constantly seek to both deliver value faster to their customers and deliver value more efficiently than their competitors. As discussed in Section 31.2, "Strategic Benefits of Cloud Computing," and Section 31.3, "Tactical Benefits and Strategic Directions," cloud computing offers organizations that effectively leverage the technology the opportunity to deliver value faster and cheaper to their customers than current market players, thereby creating an opening to gain market share. As a final example, consider the abridged history of in-home video entertainment:

- Terrestrial broadcast programming
- Cable and satellite broadcast programming
- VHS rental from local stores
- DVD rental from local stores
- DVD by mail
- Streaming video services

Today's streaming video services are a fine illustration of how enterprises effectively exploited the capabilities of the cloud to deliver in-home video entertainment to customers faster than via DVD by mail, DVD rental from local stores, or broadcast programming. The prospect of market rewards for the enterprises that most effectively exploit the ability to deliver value faster and cheaper assures that enterprises will experiment and innovate until optimal strategies are found to maximize the commercial benefits of cloud technology.

Chapter 32

Connecting the Dots

Organizations deploy their applications on the cloud instead of traditional, physical hardware expecting to

1. *Deliver new services and value faster* to grow their top line
2. *Improve operational efficiency* to boost their bottom line

As shown in Figure 3.12, those organizations apply risk management to maximize the likelihood of achieving the upside benefits of delivering new services and value faster with improved operational efficiency while minimizing the likelihood of unacceptable downside consequences like compromising user service quality, reliability, latency, or availability.

This chapter integrates and summarizes the key insights of Section I, "Framing the Cloud Service Customer's Problem," Section II, "Analyzing the Cloud Service Customer's Problem," Section III, "Cloud Service Quality Risk Inventory," and Section IV, "Cloud Service Quality Risk Assessment and Management," of this book in the following sections:

- Risk and risk management (Section 32.1)
- Context of cloud risk management (Section 32.2)
- CSC benefit 1: Deliver new services and value faster (Section 32.3)
- CSC benefit 2: Improved operational efficiency (Section 32.4)
- Potential downside service quality consequences (Section 32.5)
- Optimal cloud service customer risk management (Section 32.6)
- Cloud risk management process (Section 32.7)
- Concluding remarks (Section 32.8)

32.1 Risk and Risk Management

The standard definition of *risk* is "effect of uncertainty on objectives" (ISO, 2009). Entrepreneurs and investors take prudent risks, like investing in development of new products and services or expanding business operations, in pursuit of returns. There are also downside risks, such as factors that cause schedule slips, cost overruns, unacceptable quality, and other adverse outcomes.

Risk appetite is defined as "amount and type of risk that an organization is willing to pursue or retain" (ISO, 2009). Organizations and individual inevitably have different risk appetites. Risks are often visualized on a risk map like Figure 32.1, with probability of impact on the *x*-axis and magnitude of impact on the *y*-axis. A particular organization's risk appetite determines the boundaries between acceptable (green), tolerable (yellow), and unacceptable (red) regions on a risk map. Sophisticated organizations recognize that extremely low risks can be opportunities to accept greater risk in pursuit of returns. For example, holding substantial cash in a government insured, non-interest-bearing checking account carries negligible risk of loss but offers no possibility of a return; many individuals would see that situation as an opportunity to move their cash into a money market account or other investment instrument that offered some return with a downside risk that they consider acceptable.

The standard definition of *risk management* is "coordinated activities to direct and control an organization with regard to risk" (ISO, 2009). Figure 3.10 illustrates the ISO 31000 process for risk management; Section 32.7, "Cloud Risk Management Process," gives a summary, and Section IV, "Cloud Service Quality Risk Assessment and Management," considers the process in detail.

As explained in Section 3.3, "Risk Treatment Options," one has several fundamental options for treating any risk:

1. **Replace or remove the risk source** (Section 3.3.1), such as replacing a disappointing supplier with a more promising supplier.

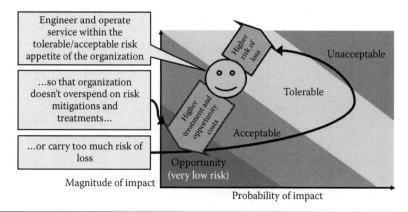

Figure 32.1   Sample risk map.

2. **Change the risk likelihood** (Section 3.3.2), such as by deploying quality improvement measures.
3. **Change the risk consequences** (Section 3.3.3), such as by deploying redundant or spare capacity to mitigate the impact of inevitable failures.
4. **Share the risk with an external party** (Section 3.3.4), such as by purchasing insurance.
5. **Retain the risk** (Section 3.3.5)—Organizations generally retain accountability for fundamental risks of their core business, like the desirability of their product and service offerings.
6. **Reject accountability** (Section 3.3.6) by politely declining accountabilities that should be held by other parties. For example, users are accountable for keeping their mobile devices charged, so if a user's session is abruptly terminated because he/she enjoys the cloud service customer's (CSC's) application service on his/her mobile device to the point of battery exhaustion, then the CSC can politely reject accountability for the user's unfortunate experience.
7. **Avoid the risk** (Section 3.3.7), such as by carefully timing market entry to avoid entering a market too early or too late.

Better risk management practices enable entrepreneurs, investors and enterprises to prudently take greater risk in pursuit of rewards.

32.2 Context of Cloud Risk Management

As discussed in Section I, "Framing the Cloud Service Customer's Problem," there are two primary types of cloud service organizations:

- ■ **Cloud Service Providers (CSPs)**, which own and operate physical infrastructure equipment and enabling software that serves virtual resources, automated life cycle management, and functional components offered as-a-service to CSC organizations. CSPs primarily operate either public clouds in which service is available to any CSC on a commercial basis (e.g., Elastic Compute Cloud from Amazon Web Services) or private clouds in which service is offered exclusively to organizations in a single enterprise.
- ■ **Cloud Service Customers (CSCs)**, which operate applications supported by the virtual resources, automated life cycle management, and functional-component-as-a-service offerings of cloud service providers.

Chapter 2, "Desired Cloud Service Customer Benefits" considered the purported benefits of cloud computing. Figure 32.2 shows how the highest-level benefits of the cloud offered in the first European Telecommunications Standards Institute (ETSI) network functions virtualization (NFV) white paper accrue differently to both cloud infrastructure service provider organizations and CSC organizations.

Purported NFV benefit from first ETSI White Paper (ETSI, 2012-10-22)	Directly Benefits Cloud Infrastructure Service *Provider*	Directly Benefits Cloud Service *Customer*	Risk to User Service Quality
Reduced equipment costs	✓✓✓	No	💣
Increased velocity of time to market	No	✓✓✓	💣
Reduced development costs and intervals	No	✓✓	💣
Targeted service introduction and rapid scaling	No	✓✓✓	💣💣💣💣
Open and diverse ecosystem	No	✓✓	💣💣
Optimized capacity and workload placement	No	✓✓	💣💣
Multitenancy support	✓✓✓	No	💣💣💣💣
Reduced power consumption	✓✓	No	💣💣
Improved operational efficiency	✓✓✓	✓✓	💣💣

Figure 32.2   Summary of NFV benefits by role.

Chapter 31, "The Cloud and Creative Destruction," considered the benefits to CSC organizations more deeply and derived Figure 32.3. The six tactical benefits to CSCs in Figure 32.2 ultimately support six strategic benefit directions for CSCs:

■ Aggressive automation and pulling humans out of the loop (Section 31.2.1)
■ From supply push to demand pull (Section 31.2.2)
■ Perfect capacity management (Section 31.2.3)
■ Aggressive cost management (Section 31.2.4)
■ Rich and dynamic service value chains (Section 31.2.5)
■ Shifting capital and risk (Section 31.2.6)

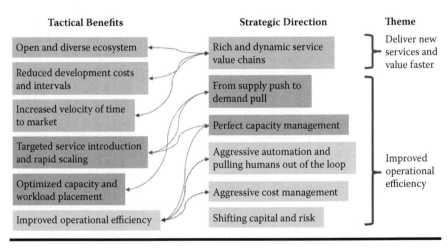

Figure 32.3   Cloud service customer benefits of cloud computing.

As shown in Figure 32.3, these six strategic directions for CSCs support two broad themes:

- **CSC benefit 1: Deliver new services and value faster** (Section 32.3) to grow the CSC organization's top line
- **CSC benefit 2: Improved operational efficiency** (Section 32.4), which includes perfect capacity management (Section 32.4.2), to boost the CSC's bottom line

32.3 CSC Benefit 1: Deliver New Services and Value Faster

The cloud enables organizations to deliver new services and value faster via

- Enhanced CSC service value chains (Section 32.3.1)
- Accelerated application service life cycle (Section 32.3.2)
- Agile service strategy (Section 32.3.3)

32.3.1 Enhanced CSC Service Value Chains

As explained in Section 31.2.5, "Rich and Dynamic Service Value Chains," CSCs have a wide range of off-the-shelf service components available both as software, which they can host directly on cloud infrastructure, and as functional components offered as-a-service that they can include in their service delivery chains. In addition to high-functionality—and likely high-quality—service components that are available off the shelf, CSCs will leverage automated life cycle management services offered by cloud service providers and may also leverage value from cloud service partners like cloud service developers, cloud service integrators, and cloud service auditors. Leveraging off-the-shelf service components and professional services enables one to deliver new services and value much faster than building service components or expertise on the fly.

32.3.2 Accelerated Application Service Life Cycle

A big part of delivering new services faster is streamlining an organization's service design and transition processes. Chapter 5, "Application Service Life Cycle," considered how application life cycle processes change with the cloud, especially when more high-functionality service components are available off the shelf. As explained in Chapter 11, "Service Strategy," Agile development and DevOps methodologies can enable this acceleration. Figure 5.4 illustrates which of the technical processes of the ISO/IEC/IEEE 15288 system life cycle process are likely to change to accelerate the pace of delivering new services and value when applications are engineered to run on cloud platforms. Table 32.1 summarizes the key application life cycle

Table 32.1   Changes to Business or Mission Analysis Processes to Deliver Value Faster (from Table 5.1)

ISO/IEC/IEEE 15288, Business or Mission Analysis Process Activity	*Accelerates Innovation*
System requirements definition process (Section 5.2.3)	✓
B: Define system requirements	✓
C: Analyze system requirements	✓
Agile development with continuous integration and continuous deployment provides timely user feedback to support agile definition and analysis of system requirements.	
Architecture definition process (Section 5.2.4)	✓
B: Develop architecture viewpoints	✓
C: Develop models and views of candidate architectures	✓
D: Relate the architecture to design	✓
Greater standardization of interfaces, functionality, assumptions, and so on across the cloud ecosystem creates a foundation for somewhat faster, cheaper architecture definition activities.	
Design definition process (Section 5.2.5)	✓
B: Establish design characteristics and design enablers related to each system element	✓
C: Assess alternatives for obtaining system elements	✓
Off-the-shelf service components such as functional components offered as-a-service and virtualized network functions (VNFs) featuring standardized interfaces are likely to be available for consideration, along with standard service architecture and workflow templates, which accelerates service design.	
System analysis process (Section 5.2.6)	✓
B: Perform system analysis	✓
System analysis results are likely to get better and faster as advanced analysis tools (e.g., formal method checkers, Monte Carlo simulators, etc.) become available for popular cloud environments.	
Implementation process (Section 5.2.7)	✓✓
B: Perform operation	✓✓

(Continued)

Table 32.1 (Continued)   Changes to Business or Mission Analysis Processes to Deliver Value Faster (from Table 5.1)

ISO/IEC/IEEE 15288, Business or Mission Analysis Process Activity	*Accelerates Innovation*
Standardized interfaces and off-the-shelf service components, as well as standard service architecture and workflow templates, simplify implementation.	
Integration process (Section 5.2.8)	✓✓✓
B: Perform integration—successively integrate system element configurations until the complete system is synthesized	✓✓✓
Off-the-shelf functional components offered as-a-service and software components, coupled with standardized interfaces and on-demand resource capacity supported with automated allocation and configuration of resources, applications, and services, enable materially faster and cheaper integration processes.	
Verification process (Section 5.2.9)	✓✓✓
B: Perform verification	✓✓✓
Arbitrarily large test beds are created on demand to automate parallel execution of test cases.	
Transition process (Section 5.2.10)	✓✓✓
B: Perform the transition	✓✓✓
Automated life cycle management enables greater service agility (faster service transitions) and reduces costs.	
Validation process (Section 5.2.11)	✓✓✓
B: Perform operation	✓✓✓
Automated validation testing enables greater service agility (faster service transitions) and reduces costs.	
Maintenance process (Section 5.2.13)	✓
B: Perform maintenance	✓
C: Perform logistics support	✓
Cloud management and orchestration permits life cycle management actions to be automated so that human operators are mostly *on* the maintenance process loop rather than *in* the maintenance process loop.	

(Continued)

Table 32.1 (Continued) Changes to Business or Mission Analysis Processes to Deliver Value Faster (from Table 5.1)

ISO/IEC/IEEE 15288, Business or Mission Analysis Process Activity	*Accelerates Innovation*
Disposal process (Section 5.2.14)	✓✓✓
B: Perform disposal	✓✓✓
C: Finalize the disposal	✓✓✓
Retiring or disposing of older and/or unsuccessful releases of cloud-based application services is much faster and simpler than for traditionally deployed application services. These differences underpin support for "failing fast, failing cheap."	

process changes that are likely to enable faster delivery of new services and value by CSC organizations.

Chapter 7, "Testing Cloud-Based Application Services," considered how cloud impacts application testing to both accelerate the pace of service innovation and reduce costs. Figure 7.7 links testing to several application service life cycle processes that will change for cloud-based applications. Standardized interfaces, automation mechanisms, technology components, and other factors enable formal methods like model checking and proof of correctness as well as simulation to be used to verify service architectures and high-level designs in the analysis stage of service design, as well as advanced static testing techniques like inspections, reviews, model verification, and static analysis. Rapid elasticity and scalability (Section 1.4.5) makes dynamic specification-, structure-, and experience-based testing cheaper and faster during integration, verification, transition, and validation. The overall result is shortening the verification and validation intervals in both service design and service transition phases to CSC benefit 1: Deliver new services and value faster.

32.3.3 Agile Service Strategy

As explained in Section 11.2, "Agile Thinking about Service Strategy," the key characteristics of cloud computing encourage agile software development. The first Agile principle ("our highest priority is to satisfy the customer through early and continuous delivery of valuable software" [Beck, Beedle, and others]) is focused on delivering new service and value fast. The cloud's key characteristic of rapid elasticity and scalability (Section 1.4.5) simplifies implementation of Agile's third principle ("deliver working software frequently, from a couple of weeks to a couple of months, with a preference for the shorter timescale" [Beck, Beedle, and others]), and if the software release becomes popular or goes viral, then online capacity can rapidly scale to serve user demand. Rapid elasticity and scalability also simplifies retiring a previous software release when a new software release becomes available.

32.4 CSC Benefit 2: Improved Operational Efficiency

As explained in Chapter 31, "Cloud and Creative Destruction," and visualized in Figure 32.4, the theme of improved operational efficiency for organizations that own and operate cloud-based applications is enabled via aggressive automation and pulling humans out of the loop (Section 31.2.1), aggressive cost management (Section 31.2.4), and shifting capital and risk (Section 31.2.6), as well as moving from supply push to demand pull (Section 31.2.2) and perfect capacity management (Section 31.2.3).

Chapter 10 considered improving operational efficiency of cloud-based applications. The primary business benefit of improved operational efficiency is lower service production costs for the CSC. Figure 32.5 visualizes a CSC's service production costs as the sum of the following:

- Usage-based charges for application and software components, infrastructure services, functional-component-as-a-service offerings, cloud management, and orchestration services
- Labor costs for CSC staff
- Maintenance and support fees
- CSC support systems costs
- General and administrative overhead costs

Figure 32.5 also illustrates the fundamental strategies to improve operational efficiencies of a CSC's service production:

1. **Aggressive automation** (Section 32.4.1)
2. **Perfect capacity management** (Section 32.4.2)

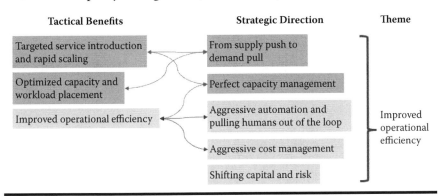

Figure 32.4 Improved operational efficiency theme.

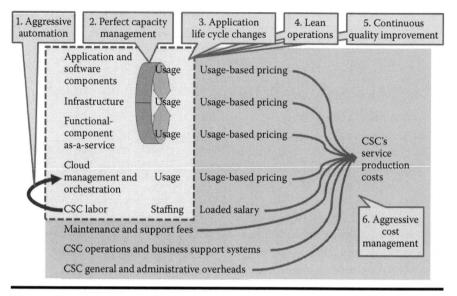

Figure 32.5 Strategies to improve CSC operational efficiency.

3. **Application life cycle changes to improve operational efficiency** (Section 32.4.3)
4. **Lean operations** (Section 32.4.4)
5. **Continuous quality improvement** (Section 32.4.5)
6. **Aggressive cost management** (Section 32.4.6)

32.4.1 Aggressive Automation

As discussed in Section 31.2.1, "Aggressive Automation and Pulling Humans out of the Loop," service operations of application service provider organizations are likely to mature. With traditional deployments, human operations staff establish service life cycle management policy, as well as making all decisions and plans and performing configuration management and other execution tasks. As CSC organizations leverage more powerful management and orchestration capabilities, they first rely on automated life cycle management mechanisms to execute some configuration management and basic changes (e.g., replacing a failed component), then allow automated life cycle management to plan and manage execution of more sophisticated life cycle management tasks (e.g., onboarding an application instance), and finally allow automated mechanisms to make autonomous decisions, like initiating scaling actions. Even with "full cloud," humans will make the policies that cloud management and orchestrations will use to drive automated decision, planning, and execution.

Chapter 8, "Service Design, Transition, and Operations Processes," considered how CSCs' information technology (IT) service management processes would likely be impacted by cloud computing. Figure 8.7 visualizes the processes likely to be most aggressively automated to improve operational efficiency.

32.4.2 Perfect Capacity Management

As explained in Section 31.2.3, "Perfect Capacity Management," the key cloud characteristic of rapid elasticity and scalability (Section 1.4.5) enables CSCs to transform their business model from supply push to demand pull (Section 31.2.2) and capture the benefits of targeted service introduction and rapid scaling (Section 2.3.4) and optimized capacity and workload placement (Section 2.3.6).

Chapter 6 considered lean application capacity management and explained that the notion of perfect capacity is derived from the application capacity model of Figure 6.10:

- **Working (or productive) capacity** is held online by CSCs to serve current user workload. Working capacity is engineered to serve the combination of
  - Cyclical load based on time of day, day of week, and so on
  - Random workload load variations, including inevitable minute-to-minute and second-to-send variations
- **Reserve (or spare online) capacity** is held above working capacity to mitigate nonforecast demand events, serve lead time demand when additional application capacity is being elastically grown, and mitigate occasional failures that render some online application capacity inoperable. Continuous quality, process, and architectural improvements enable the overhead of reserve capacity to be reduced.
- **Excess capacity** is online capacity beyond the sum of working and reserve capacities, and thus represents waste to be eliminated.

Application capacity management can be seen as two linked processes:

- **Capacity management decision processes**—Every few moments, application capacity management processes evaluate whether it is necessary initiate any changes to online application capacity. These processes apply the CSC's capacity policy and decision criteria to
  - Current, historic, and forecast user demand
  - Lead times for capacity fulfillment actions
  - Resource usage
  - Alarms and failure conditions
  - CSC target reserve level, service-level agreements, and other policies
  - Cloud resource pricing
  - Etc.

  The result of this process is a decision on what, if any, capacity change orders must be executed to keep application capacity within the CSC's capacity management policy. If no capacity change is necessary, then the process sleeps until the next time it reevaluates online application capacity (e.g., 5 minutes later). If a capacity change is necessary, then a capacity change order is dispatched to the configuration change process.

■ **Configuration change processes**—Capacity change orders (nominally service transitions) from the capacity decision process are dispatched to automated life cycle management mechanisms for execution.

Figure 32.6 illustrates how automated capacity management decision processes and automated capacity fulfillment processes fit into the service operation and service transition phases of the Information Technology Infrastructure Library (ITIL®) service management model.

Section 31.2.3, "Perfect Capacity Management," explained how as both application capacity change lead times and application capacity change increments get smaller, it becomes possible for online application capacity to track closer to the CSC's instantaneous application capacity target. Figure 31.8 illustrates the following:

■ How actual user demand can vary over time
■ How the level of reserve capacity varies over time based on forecast user demand, online application configuration, and other factors
■ How perfect application capacity is logically the sum of these two

With the right reserve capacity target and operational policies, perfect application capacity management can optimize a CSC's online application capacity

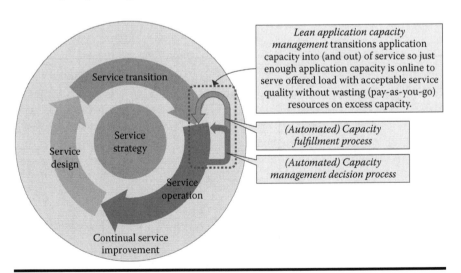

Figure 32.6 Automated application capacity management.

similar to how an inventory management system helps a retailer keep the optimal stock level in their shops that balances inventory costs against stockout probability. Operationally, perfect application capacity simultaneously minimizes costs of carrying excess online capacity against costs (analogous to overstock) of having insufficient online capacity to serve demand (analogous to stockout).

32.4.3 Application Life Cycle Changes to Improve Operational Efficiency

Chapter 5, "Application Service Life Cycle," considered how application life cycle processes change with the cloud; Figure 5.5 visualizes key process changes to improve CSC's operational efficiency, and Table 32.2 summarizes the key application life cycle process changes that are likely to reduce a CSC's operating expenses.

32.4.4 Lean Operations

Chapter 10 considered improved operational efficiency of cloud-based applications and offered the lean computing goal to sustainably achieve the shortest lead time, best quality and value, and highest customer delight at the lowest cost. The lean computing strategy is supported by the pillars of respect (Section 10.7) and continuous improvement (Section 10.8), and enabled by a handful of key principles and methodical recognition and reduction of waste (Section 10.6).

Lean cloud capacity management drives organizations away from traditional, capacity-driven operations to demand-driven, just-in-time operations. This transformation enables capital and operating expense improvements compared to traditional models via two themes:

1. **Demand-driven capacity decision, planning, and fulfillment cycles are very frequent**, routine, and reliable, so excess online application capacity is minimized.
2. **Waste is methodically squeezed out** of the end-to-end service/value delivery chain.

The lean transformation is achieved through partnership across the service delivery chain of cloud-based application services to optimize and streamline the whole process. The partners collaborate to identify the essential and core value-adding functions that must be performed, and work to minimize or eliminate non-value-adding activities. Transparent, usage-based pricing encourages parties to monitor and appropriately manage their resource consumption. Keep in mind that the business goal is to maximize overall efficiency rather than minimize any single waste category, and implementing efficient resource management adds some

Table 32.2 Changes to Business or Mission Analysis Processes to Improve Operational Efficiency (from Table 5.1)

ISO/IEC/IEEE 15288, Business or Mission Analysis Process Activity	Reduces CSC Costs
Architecture definition process (Section 5.2.4)	✓
B: Develop architecture viewpoints	✓
C: Develop models and views of candidate architectures	✓
D: Relate the architecture to design	✓
Greater standardization of interfaces, functionality, assumptions, and so on across the cloud ecosystem creates a foundation for somewhat faster, cheaper architecture definition activities.	
System analysis process (Section 5.2.6)	✓
B: Perform system analysis	✓
More effective system analysis processes find problems earlier in the application life cycle, when it is cheaper to fix.	
Implementation process (Section 5.2.7)	✓✓
B: Perform operation	✓✓
Standardized interfaces and off-the-shelf service components, as well as standard service architecture and workflow templates, simply implementation.	
Integration process (Section 5.2.8)	✓✓
B: Perform integration—successively integrate system element configurations until the complete system is synthesized	✓✓
Off-the-shelf software components, coupled with standardized interfaces and on-demand resource capacity supported with automated allocation and configuration of resources, applications, and services, enable materially faster and cheaper integration processes.	
Verification process (Section 5.2.9)	✓✓✓
B: Perform verification	✓✓✓
Using appropriately sized test beds to execute test cases in parallel can be more efficient than serializing test case execution.	

(Continued)

Table 32.2 (Continued)   Changes to Business or Mission Analysis Processes to Improve Operational Efficiency (from Table 5.1)

ISO/IEC/IEEE 15288, Business or Mission Analysis Process Activity	*Reduces CSC Costs*
Transition process (Section 5.2.10)	✓✓✓
B: Perform the transition	✓✓✓
Automated life cycle management enables greater service agility (faster service transitions) and reduces costs.	
Validation process (Section 5.2.11)	✓✓✓
B: Perform operation	✓✓✓
Automated validation testing enables greater service agility (faster service transitions) and reduces costs.	
Operation process (Section 5.2.12)	✓✓✓
B: Perform operation	✓✓✓
D: Support the customer	✓✓✓
Cloud management and orchestration enables powerful service monitoring and analytics to automate and improve operations activities.	
Maintenance process (Section 5.2.13)	✓✓✓
B: Perform maintenance	✓✓
C: Perform logistics support	✓✓✓
Cloud management and orchestration permits life cycle management actions to be automated so that human operators are mostly *on* the maintenance process loop rather than *in* the maintenance process loop.	
Disposal process (Section 5.2.14)	✓✓✓
B: Perform disposal	✓✓✓
C: Finalize the disposal	✓✓✓
Retiring or disposing of prior (and unsuccessful) releases of cloud-based application services is much faster and simpler than for traditionally deployed application services. These differences underpin support for "failing fast, failing cheap."	

overhead. Thus, one typically applies Pareto analysis to focus on the biggest waste items and accept modest overhead to manage those items as a necessary cost of doing business.

32.4.5 Continuous Quality Improvement

Figure 32.7 visualizes the canonical software failure cascade in which a residual defect is activated to become an error, which produces a failure, which results in a user service–impacting incident. Detecting and localizing failures and incidents, as well as subsequent service restoral, consumes resources and impacts user satisfaction, which squanders customer goodwill. Root cause analysis, defect correction, and deployment of a patched software release to correct the underlying problem also consume resources, which degrades an organization's operational efficiency. Thus, quality improvement activities that eliminate residual defects and other quality-impacting risks can improve both operational efficiency and user satisfaction.

Figure 4.8 visualizes the data–information–knowledge–wisdom (DIKW, Section 4.5) hierarchy, which is at the heart of continuous improvement. One must analyze *data* to extract clean and useful *information* about the *who, what, when,* and *where* of adverse and suboptimal outcomes. Analysis of that information produces *knowledge* about how those suboptimal outcomes occurred. Deeper consideration of that knowledge produces *wisdom* such as *why* the suboptimal outcomes occurred. Understanding why a suboptimal outcome occurred enables one to craft effective corrective actions to improve future outcomes.

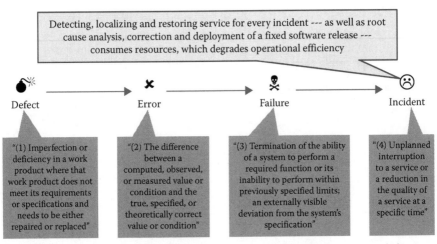

Figure 32.7 General failure cascade.

ITIL's seven improvement steps onto the DIKW hierarchy are as follows:

1. Define what should be measured.
2. Define what can be measured.
3. Gather data.
4. Process data.
5. Analyze the data.
6. Use the information.
7. Implement corrective actions.
   ...and repeat

Note that the decision of what *should* be measured (step 1) and recognition of what can practically be measured (step 2) are based on the wisdom of skilled human professionals. Thus, the seven improvement steps do not begin at the base of the DIKW hierarchy.

Implementation considerations appear on the right side of Figure 32.8:

■ **Automated data collection** mechanisms deployed by the cloud service provider and CSC, as well as data collection mechanisms implemented in application software components, provide the bulk of the raw data for continuous improvements.
■ **Automated data analysis**, such as advanced analytics tools, distill the vast pool of raw data into useful information and basic knowledge of the who, what, when, where, and how of suboptimal outcomes.
■ **Skilled professionals** further analyze the data, information, and knowledge into wisdom about why, which drives corrective actions.

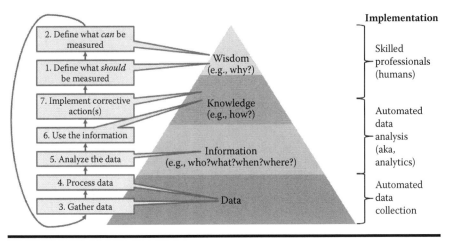

Figure 32.8 Seven improvement steps and DIKW.

As a single risk event can impact both IT service management (e.g., service operations) and user service quality, as well as adversely impacting the organization's costs and perhaps altering the best-estimate probability of future risk events, it is useful to appropriately align the continuous-improvement plan–do–check–act cycles for IT service management (e.g., ITIL, ISO/IEC 20000), quality management (e.g., ISO 9001), risk management (e.g., ISO 31000), and lean, efficient operations. Operationally, this means the following:

- Collect sufficient data for deep analysis of IT service management, user quality, risk management, and lean, efficient operations.
- Service management, quality management, risk management, and efficiency experts share their root cause analyses to assure that true root causes of poor performance are fully understood.
- Agree on corrective actions that improve outcomes for all stakeholders.

Rapidly and reliably determining the true root cause of poor performance and then implementing robust corrective actions directly supports the lean operations goal to sustainably achieve the shortest lead time, best quality and value, and highest customer delight at the lowest cost.

32.4.6 Aggressive Cost Management

Aggressive management of an organization's costs is the foundation of improved operational efficiency. Beyond controlling general and administrative overheads and costs, the CSC should look carefully at all of their actual costs. For example, CSCs may consider time-of-day and other discounts when making capacity fulfillment decisions to minimize costs, or shift some workloads across space (i.e., to cheaper data centers) and time (i.e., execute when resources cost less) to reduce their costs. In addition to leveraging perfect capacity management (Section 32.4.2) to improve efficiency, CSCs may still wish to reserve or prepurchase some cloud capacity to lower the cost they pay for at least some cloud resource capacity.

32.5 Potential Downside Service Quality Consequences

Chapter 4 considered cloud service qualities. ISO/IEC 25010 offers the following fundamental definition of quality:

> The *quality* of a system is the degree to which the system satisfies the stated and implied needs of its various stakeholders, and thus provides value. (ISO/IEC, 2011-03-01)

The ISO/IEC 25000 Software product Quality Requirements and Evaluation (SQuaRE) family of standards offers the following:

- **Quality in use** (Section 4.2.3), which includes *effectiveness* for "accuracy and completeness with which users achieve specific goals" (ISO/IEC, 2011-03-01) and *satisfaction* for "degree to which user needs are satisfied when a product or system is used in a specified context of use" (ISO/IEC, 2011-03-01), as well as *efficiency, freedom from, risk* and *context coverage.*
- **Product quality** (Section 4.3), which includes *reliability, security, maintainability,* and so on.
- **Data quality** (Section 4.4), which includes *accuracy, completeness, consistency,* and so on.

Section III, "Cloud Service Quality Risk Inventory," focused on the risks to user service qualities, especially

- **Reliability**—probability that a correct service response is returned for any user request
- **Latency**—elapsed time for service offering to return a response to any user request
- **Availability**—probability that service is online and available to serve user requests

These user service qualities drive the satisfaction attribute of quality in use, which directly impacts users' quality of experience and indirectly impacts the popularity and success of an organization's service offering.

Figure 32.9 visualizes the fundamental risk vectors and risk items challenging user service quality of cloud-based applications; Table 32.3 gives cross-references to detailed risk discussions in Section III, "Cloud Service Quality Risk Inventory."

32.6 Optimal Cloud Service Customer Risk Management

As shown in Figure 7.2, the service quality delivered to the CSC's users from a cloud-based application is fundamentally subject to two types of uncertainties:

- **Knowledge-based (or epistemic) uncertainties** are theoretically knowable facts, like the details of an as-yet-unknown residual software defect that can be activated and cascade into a service-impacting incident. Testing, analysis, and experience can reduce knowledge-based uncertainties.

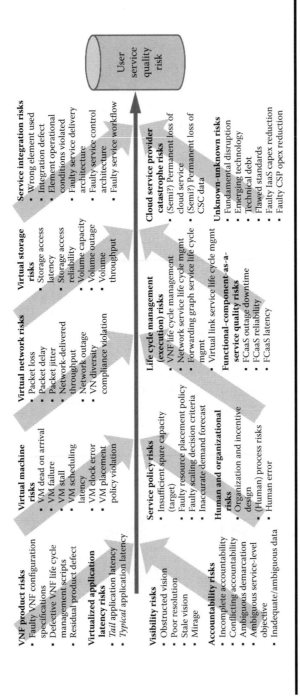

Figure 32.9 Cloud user service quality risk inventory. FCaaS, functional-component-as-a-service; IaaS, infrastructure-as-a-service; VM, virtual machine; VN, virtual networking; VNF, virtualized network function.

Table 32.3   Inventory of Cloud User Service Risks

Risk Item	Reference	Page
VNF Product Risks	**Chapter 13**	**249**
Faulty VNF configuration specification risk	Table 13.1	251
Residual defect in VNF life cycle management script risk	Table 13.2	252
Residual product defect risk	Table 13.3	252
Virtual Machine (VM) Risks	**Chapter 14**	**257**
VM dead-on-arrival (DOA) risk	Table 14.1	259
VM premature release (failure) risk	Table 14.2	260
VM stall risk	Table 14.3	261
VM scheduling latency risk	Table 14.4	262
VM clock error risk	Table 14.5	263
VM placement policy violation risk	Table 14.6	264
Virtual Networking Risks	**Chapter 15**	**269**
Packet loss risk	Table 15.1	271
Packet delay risk	Table 15.2	271
Packet jitter (delay variation) risk	Table 15.3	272
Network-delivered throughput risk	Table 15.4	272
Network outage risk	Table 15.5	273
VN diversity compliance violation risk	Table 15.6	273
Virtual Storage Risks	**Chapter 16**	**277**
Storage access reliability risk	Table 16.1	279
Storage access latency risk	Table 16.2	279
Volume capacity risk	Table 16.3	280
Volume outage risk	Table 16.4	280
Volume throughput risk	Table 16.5	281

(Continued)

Table 32.3 (Continued)   Inventory of Cloud User Service Risks

Risk Item	Reference	Page
Virtualized Application Latency Risks	**Chapter 17**	**283**
Tail application latency risk	Table 17.1	284
Typical application latency risk	Table 17.2	285
Service Integration Risks	**Chapter 18**	**289**
Wrong-element-used risk	Table 18.1	292
System/service integration defect	Table 18.2	292
Element operational conditions violated	Table 18.3	293
Faulty service delivery architecture risk	Table 18.4	293
Faulty service control architecture risk	Table 18.5	294
Faulty service workflow risk	Table 18.6	294
Visibility Risks	**Chapter 19**	**295**
Obstructed vision risk	Table 19.1	297
Blurred vision risk	Table 19.2	298
Stale vision risk	Table 19.3	299
Mirage risk	Table 19.4	300
Service Policy Risks	**Chapter 20**	**303**
Insufficient spare capacity (target) risk	Table 20.1	306
Faulty resource placement policy risk	Table 20.2	307
Faulty scaling decision criteria risk	Table 20.3	307
Inaccurate demand forecast risk	Table 20.4	308
Accountability Risks	**Chapter 21**	**309**
Incomplete accountability risk	Table 21.1	310
Conflicting accountability risk	Table 21.2	311
Ambiguous demarcation risk	Table 21.3	312
Ambiguous service-level objective risk	Table 21.4	313
Inadequate/ambiguous data risk	Table 21.5	313

(Continued)

Table 32.3 (Continued)   Inventory of Cloud User Service Risks

Risk Item	Reference	Page
Human and Organizational Risks	**Chapter 22**	**317**
Organization and incentive design risk	Table 22.2	320
Human process risk	Table 22.3	321
Human error risk	Table 22.4	321
Life Cycle Management (Execution) Risks	**Chapter 23**	**325**
VNF life cycle management (execution) risks	Table 23.2	330
Network service life cycle management (execution) risks	Table 23.3	331
Forwarding graph service life cycle management (execution) risks	Table 23.4	332
Virtual link service life cycle management (execution) risks	Table 23.5	333
Functional-Component-as-a-Service Quality Risks	**Chapter 24**	**335**
Functional-component-as-a-service outage downtime risk	Table 24.2	336
Functional-component-as-a-service reliability risk	Table 24.3	336
Functional-component-as-a-service latency risk	Table 24.4	338
Cloud Service Provider Catastrophe Risks	**Chapter 25**	**339**
(Semi?) Permanent loss of cloud service risk	Table 25.1	340
(Semi?) Permanent loss of CSC data risk	Table 25.2	340
Unknown-Unknown Risks	**Chapter 26**	**343**
Fundamental business/operations disruption risk	Table 26.1	345
Emerging technology risk	Table 26.2	346
Technical debt risk	Table 26.3	346
Flawed standards risk	Table 26.4	347
Faulty infrastructure capex reduction risk	Table 26.5	347
Faulty CSP opex reduction risk	Table 26.6	348

- **Stochastic (or aleatoric) uncertainties** are fundamentally uncertain characteristics, like the queuing delay or jitter for a single network packet. Applications deployed on the cloud inherently carry more stochastic uncertainties than traditionally deployed applications due to resource pooling (Section 1.4.6) and multitenancy (Section 1.4.3). On-demand self-service (Section 1.4.4) and rapid elasticity and scalability (Section 1.4.5) also increase the stochastic uncertainties to user service quality. Stochastic uncertainties can cause tardy or inconsistent service latency and unacceptably slow operations, and otherwise impact users' quality of experience. Testing, analysis, and experience can better characterize, but not remove, stochastic uncertainties. For example, flipping a coin more times can better characterize probable outcomes but does not materially increase the certainty of outcome of any particular coin toss.

The user service quality risks of Section III, "Cloud Service Quality Risk Inventory," like other risks, are potentially addressed via one or more treatment approaches:

- Replace or remove the risk source (Section 3.3.1)
- Change the risk likelihood (Section 3.3.2)
- Change the risk consequences (Section 3.3.3)
- Share the risk with an external party (Section 3.3.4)
- Retain the risk (Section 3.3.5)
- Reject accountability (Section 3.3.6)
- Avoid the risk (Section 3.3.7)

Many treatments address multiple risks, and some risks warrant multiple treatments. Careful risk identification, analysis, and evaluation enable one to select a suite of risk treatments to suit the organization's risk appetite. Unfortunately, those treatment options often increase costs (thereby undermining CSC benefit 2: Improved operational efficiency) and/or increase schedule intervals (thereby undermining CSC benefit 1: Deliver new services and value faster). Thus, the CSC's risk management challenge is to reduce the uncertainty of the organization achieving the upside benefits of faster delivery of new services and value and improved operational efficiency without the downside consequences of unacceptably service quality, reliability, latency, or availability. Chapter 30 considered the service quality risk management process.

Optimal risk management for CSCs means balancing uncertainties regarding achieving desired benefits—CSC benefit 1: Deliver new services and value faster and CSC benefit 2: Improved operational efficiency—against potential downside consequences of unacceptable user service quality. The key characteristics of the cloud, especially rapid elasticity and scalability (Section 1.4.5), open up new opportunities to better manage risks to improve business outcomes. For example, if users expect "five 9s" of service reliability and availability, then delivering "seven 9s" or more of service reliability and availability means that an organization has overengineered their service and potentially has an opportunity to reduce resource consumption and boost operational efficiency. This notion is best understood via an example: Figure 32.10 illustrates how optimal risk-map concepts of Figure 32.3 can be usefully applied to a dose–response curve (Section 7.10 "Sensitivity [or Dose–Response] Testing").

- *X*-axis—level of cloud service impairment—Gives the "dose" of cloud infrastructure service impairment applied to the application, such as packet loss, which would be measured as 10^{-6}, 10^{-5}, etc., packet loss rates.
- *Y*-axis—user service quality, in defective operations per million—Gives the user service quality "response" to the dose of infrastructure impairment.
- Opportunity/acceptable/tolerable/unacceptable bands—These horizontal bands reflect the CSC's user service quality expectations. This example assumes that 0.1 DPM to 1 DPM is the CSC's target (*acceptable*) quality level, and greater than 10 DPM is *unacceptable*. Thus, quality levels between 1 DPM and 10 DPM are tolerable, and service quality better than (i.e., less than) 0.1 DPM is much better than target and is *super*acceptable, and thus is an opportunity to directly or indirectly soften cloud service-level objectives to reduce operating expenses for the CSC. For example, one might release some resources allocated to the application to reduce the organization's usage-based costs for cloud infrastructure.
- Service performance—Shows results of dose–response testing for some cloud service impairment of interest (e.g., virtual network packet loss).

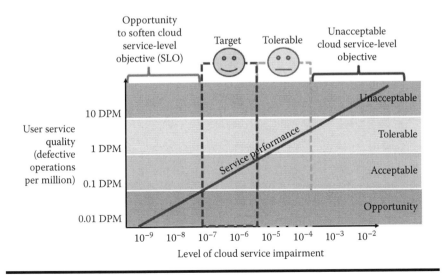

Figure 32.10 Sample dose–response curve.

Performance targets for the cloud service impairment of interest are often based on where the service performance curve crosses both the *opportunity–acceptable* and *tolerable–unacceptable* user service quality thresholds. CSC organizations will adjust their targets based on the following:

- **Organization's risk appetite**—Organizations with a higher appetite for risk (e.g., accepting more user service quality risk in exchange for less costly cloud resources) may push to set more aggressive service-level objectives.
- **Overall sensitivity of user service quality behavior**—Each user service is likely to be sensitive to a number of chronic cloud service impairments (e.g., lost virtual network packets) as well as acute events (e.g., virtual network outage events). Thus, the cloud service provider must decide what portion of the user service quality impairment budget (e.g., how many DPM) to allocate to a target cloud service impairment.
- **Experience and engineering judgment**—Measured dose–response test results will inevitably differ from actual behavior of production systems. Based on both previous experience and engineering judgment, CSCs may derate the measured test results when selecting service-level objectives.

Optimal cloud risk management compares an organization's overall risk position to the organization's risk appetite so that appropriate actions (e.g., risk treatments) can be taken to maximize the expected business outcome.

32.7 Cloud Risk Management Process

Section IV, "Cloud Service Quality Risk Assessment and Management," applied ISO 31000 risk management processes to the CSC's risk management problem (Figure 32.4). For pedagogical reasons, Section IV focused on downside user service quality risks associated with the vectors and items of Section III, "Cloud Service Quality Risk Inventory," but in practice, organizations will balance their desired benefits (e.g., CSC benefit 1: Deliver new services and value faster and CSC benefit 2: Improved operational efficiency) against the downside quality risk vectors of Section III in the context of their organization's service design, service transition, and service operation processes and practices. The typical CSC's core risk management challenge is likely to be to reduce the uncertainty of the organization achieving the upside benefits of delivering new services and value faster with improved operational efficiency without the downside consequences of unacceptable service quality, reliability, latency, or availability. CSCs will manage this risk in the broader context of their organization's enterprise risk management, project risk management, security risk management, and business process frameworks.

While computer-based applications have always been vulnerable to knowledge-based (epistemic) uncertainties like unknown residual defects, cloud-based applications are vulnerable to a broad range of additional stochastic (aleatoric) uncertainties associated with enabling service components and operations of cloud service providers and others in the service delivery chain. Tornadoes offer a useful analogy for the stochastic uncertainties facing CSCs: although one can't prevent tornadoes from occurring, we have studied tornadoes enough to understand the weather patterns that spawn them and the damage caused by them enough to know how to harden structures as well as policies and practices to minimize risks to people and property. While the stochastic uncertainties facing CSCs are certainly less dramatic than tornadoes, diligent analysis and hardening of cloud-based applications, appropriate service design, transition and operation processes, and prudent operational policies can reduce the risk of unacceptable user service impact.

Figure 32.11 generalizes the user quality–centric risk management process of Figure 30.1 to consider expected upside benefits as well as avoiding downside consequences. Each of the generalized process steps are considered individually:

- Identify the key objectives (Section 32.7.1)
- Identify the internal and external service deployment and operations context (Section 32.7.2)
- Identify risks to key objectives (Section 32.7.3)
- Analyze risks and controls (Section 32.7.4)
- Evaluate risks and recommend treatments (Section 32.7.5)
- Select risk treatment options to implement (Section 32.7.6)

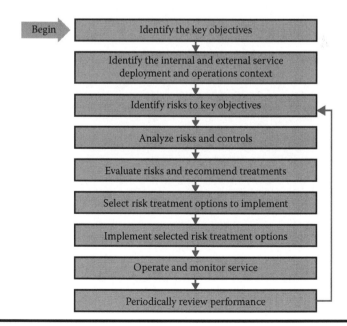

Figure 32.11   Simplified risk management flowchart.

- Implement selected risk treatment options (Section 32.7.7)
- Operate and monitor service (Section 32.7.8)
- Periodically review performance (Section 32.7.9)

32.7.1 Identify the Key Objectives

Quantitatively defining measurable objectives for an organization's desired benefits is the sensible first step in achieving those objectives. Section 27.5, "Establish Service Quality Objectives" considered measurable objectives for acceptable user service quality via a three-step process:

- Select quality objective metrics (Section 27.5.2)
- Select service quality measurement point(s) (Section 27.5.3)
- Set performance targets for each key quality objective (Section 27.5.4)

As a practical matter, services offered to captive users—like proprietary systems that an organization's employees are required to use to complete their job—can have lower quality objectives because those captive users can be compelled to use the service regardless of the service quality delivered. Services offered to general users must offer both a compelling service and good quality of experience to discourage users from fleeing to competitors. Setting quality objectives too low produces a service that users may not tolerate, and setting quality objectives too high will drive up the organization's service design, transition, and operations costs.

Quantitative and measurable objectives for delivering new services and value faster, improving operational efficiency, and other key business goals should also be captured.

32.7.2 Identify the Internal and External Service Deployment and Operations Context

Chapter 27 considers risk context. A CSC's risk management process—especially risk assessment—operates within a context with three broad aspects:

- **Organizational context**—It is essential to understand the roles, responsibilities, and accountabilities of both parties within the organization (aka Internal Context, Section 27.1) that are directly controlled by the organization and parties outside the organization (aka External Context, Section 27.2) that are indirectly controlled.
- **Process context**—CSC organizations undoubtedly have processes for service design, service transition, service operation, project management, continual improvement/quality management, and so on. Risk management activities should be appropriately integrated with these routine processes.

■ **Organization's risk appetite**—As explained in Section 3.4, risk appetite is the "amount and type of risk that an organization is willing to pursue or retain." An organization's appetite for risk drives what risks are considered unacceptable, tolerable, and acceptable, and what represents opportunities to take greater risk in pursuit of business value.

32.7.3 Identify Risks to Key Objectives

Figure 32.12 summarizes the purpose of this activity:

1. **Identify risk events** that can impact key objectives from Section 32.7.1, "Identify the Key Objectives"
2. **Identify the deployed and planned risk controls** for those events that treat the identified risk events

Methods from general risk identification and analysis techniques (Section 29.1) and specialized risk identification and analysis technique (Section 29.2) are useful for identifying risks:

1. **Influence diagrams** (Section 29.1.1), such as Figure 29.1
2. **Cause-and-effect analysis** (Section 29.1.2), such as Figure 29.2
3. **Failure mode effect analysis** (Section 29.1.3)
4. **Structured interview and brainstorming** (Section 29.1.4)
5. **SWIFT—structured "what-if" technique** (Section 29.1.5)
6. **Fault tree analysis** (Section 29.1.6)

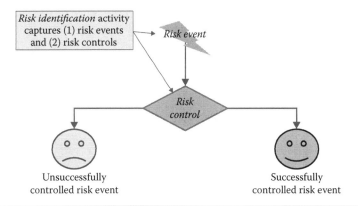

Figure 32.12   Risk identification.

Section 28.2, "Risk Identification," suggested using a table to document user service quality risks with one row per risk type capturing

- Risk condition(s) given
- Risk causes for each condition
- Planned risk controls for each risk
- Risk owner
- Impact on key objective if risk is unsuccessfully controlled

32.7.4 Analyze Risks and Controls

Figure 32.13 summarizes primary risk and control analysis activities:

1. Estimate the frequency of identified risk events
2. Estimate the probability of successful control of risk events
3. Estimate impact of successful control of risk events
4. Estimate the probability of *un*successful control of risk events
5. Estimate the impact of *un*successful control of risk events

Likelihood of a risk event occurring is analyzed by considering relevant past performance, input of experts (e.g., Section 29.1.4, "Structured Interview and Brainstorming," Delphi method, etc.), and engineering judgment.

Section 29.3 reviewed the following generally useful risk control analysis techniques:

1. **Layers-of-protection analysis (LOPA)** (Section 29.3.1)
2. **Hazard analysis and critical control points (HACCP)** (Section 29.3.2)

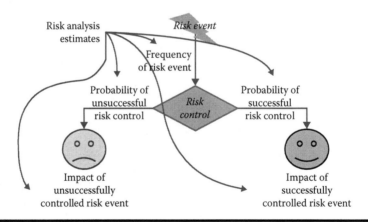

Figure 32.13 Canonical risk analysis model.

3. **Event tree analysis** (Section 29.3.3), such as Figure 29.10
4. **Bow tie analysis** (Section 29.3.4), such as Figure 29.11

As discussed in Section 28.3, results of risk analysis can be captured via columns in the risk assessment table.

32.7.5 Evaluate Risks and Recommend Treatments

Risk evaluation involves rating and ranking risks; risk treatments are proposed to drive unacceptable risks to become tolerable or better. Conceptually, risk evaluation begins by rating all risks after deployed and planned risk treatments as acceptable (green), tolerable (yellow), or unacceptable (red). Methodical risk rating and ranking is performed via techniques like the following:

■ Failure mode effect and criticality analysis (Section 29.4.1)
■ Dose–response (toxicity) assessment (Section 29.4.2)
■ Consequence/probability matrix (Section 29.4.3)
■ *F–N curves* (Section 29.4.4)
■ Risk indices (Section 29.4.5)
■ Cost/benefit analysis (Section 29.4.6)

Risk IT (ISACA, 2009) suggests considering five parameters when evaluating and recommending a risk treatment:

■ **Cost of treatment** to reduce risk to tolerable levels. Each risk treatment option carries a cost, which can be estimated.
■ **Importance of risk**, indicated by position on the probability-of-impact/magnitude-of-impact risk map.
■ **Capability to implement risk treatment**—Organizations may not have the maturity or capability to successfully plan, implement, deploy, and operate some advanced risk treatments, so simpler risk treatments may be more appropriate choices. Ideally, the recommended risk treatment is routine and simple (as in "keep it simple, stupid") for the organization to execute because exotic and unique treatments introduce additional risks.
■ **Effectiveness of risk treatment**—How likely the treatment is to reduce the frequency and impact of the particular risk.
■ **Efficiency of risk treatment**—The benefits of the risk treatment compared to the costs of the treatment.

As explained in Section 32.1, sophisticated organizations may also identify opportunities (blue) where the organization might accept somewhat greater risk (e.g., soften requirements or objectives) and still keep the risk acceptable. A risk map (Figure 32.3), consequence-probability chart (Figure 29.13), *F–N* chart

(Figure 29.14), or similar two-dimensional visualization of risk impact versus probability of impact simplifies rating of dissimilar risks. Typically, risks in the lower left corner near the *x,y* origin are acceptable (green) or even opportunities (blue), and risks in the upper right corner with large *x* and *y* values are unacceptable (red). Relative positioning of risks across the risk map are driven by good judgment of the professionals executing the risk assessment.

After rating the risks, one ranks the unacceptable risks in descending order of overall risk to the organization, so the second risk is less important to treat than the first ranked risk, and so on. Risk treatment options are proposed for all unacceptable risks, and the cost of each treatment option should be estimated. The professionals executing the risk assessment and the project team may recommend specific treatment options to CSC decision makers, and those recommendations might be captured via a "Project Team Recommendation" column with a "yes" or "no" entry for each treatment option.

32.7.6 Select Risk Treatment Options to Implement

Ultimately, a decision maker in the CSC organization must consider how much risk the organization can afford to take in pursuit of its business goals and will make a go/no-go decision on each of the recommended risk treatment options. The risk rating, ranking, treatment options, estimated cost of each option, and project team's recommendations provide information necessary for the leader to appropriately balance costs and benefits to the organization when making go/no-go decisions for each option...or perhaps decide that the aggregate risk is unacceptable and abandon the entire project. Along with each *go* decision, the leader might also assign an organization or individual to lead implementation of each selected treatment.

32.7.7 Implement Selected Risk Treatment Options

Risk treatments selected by CSC decision makers should be implemented by the assigned treatment owner according to the treatment owner's processes. CSC project management processes should track progress and completion of each selected risk treatment.

32.7.8 Operate and Monitor Service

Service operation and monitoring are covered by the CSC's IT service management processes, especially their service operation processes (Chapter 8, "Service Design, Transition, and Operations Processes"). Key user service quality indicators and performance at all critical control points should be monitored, along with routine alarms and performance metrics, to assure that acceptable service quality is continuously delivered to end users. Corrective actions should be taken when performance exceeds control limits.

32.7.9 Periodically Review Performance

Actual service performance should be reviewed regularly (e.g., monthly or quarterly). Root cause analysis should be conducted on both acute and chronic problems, and appropriate corrective actions deployed. Chapter 9, "Continual Service Improvement," considered this topic.

32.8 Concluding Remarks

As discussed in Chapter 31, "The Cloud and Creative Destruction," organizations effectively embracing cloud technology can deliver value faster and operate with greater efficiency, thereby creating competitive advantage. When considering any new technology, including cloud computing, organizations should thoughtfully consider

- Benefits of the new technology
- Organizational and technical impacts of adopting the new technology
- Risks associated with operating the new technology
- Consequences of not adopting the new technology

Beyond merely leveraging cloud computing to deliver new services and value to the market with improved operational efficiency, successful organizations must assure that acceptable quality of experience is delivered to their customers. Risk thinking better manages these factors so organizations can prudently take more risk in pursuit of returns.

Works Cited

Axelos Limited. (2011). *ITIL® Glossary and Abbreviations*. AXELOS Limited: https://www.axelos.com/Corporate/media/Files/Glossaries/ITIL_2011_Glossary_GB-v1-0.pdf.

B. Gisin, Q. G. (2010). "Perfect dispatch"—As the measure of PJM real time grid operational performance. *Power and Energy Society General Meeting, 2010 IEEE* (pp. 1–8). Minneapolis: IEEE.

Bauer, E. (2016). *Lean Computing for the Cloud*. Piscataway, NJ: Wiley-IEEE Press.

Bauer, E., & Adams, R. (2012). *Reliability and Availability of Cloud Computing*. Piscataway, NJ: Wiley-IEEE Press.

Bauer, E., & Adams, R. (2013). *Service Quality of Cloud-Based Applications*. Hoboken: Wiley-IEEE Press.

Beck, K., Beedle, M., van Bennekum, A. et al. (n.d.). Principles behind the Agile Manifesto. Retrieved May 17, 2016, from Manifesto for Agile Software Development: http://agilemanifesto.org/principles.html.

Cannon, D. (2011-07-29). *ITIL Service Strategy*. Norwich: The Stationary Office.

Dam Safety Office. (2011). *Interim Dam Safety Public Protection Guidelines—A Risk Framework to Support Dam Safety Decision-Making*. Denver, Colorado: U.S. Department of the Interior.

Dams Safety Committee. (2006). *Risk Management Policy Framework for Dam Safety*. New South Wales Government.

Department of Defense. (2012-05-11). *MIL-STD-882E System Safety*. Wright-Patterson Air Force Base: United States Department of Defense.

Enterprise Risk Management Committee. (2003). *Overview of Enterprise Risk Management*. Casualty Actuarial Society: http://mgt.ncsu.edu/erm/documents/CasualtyActuarialSocietyOverviewofERM.pdf.

ETSI. (2007-01). *EG 202 009-1 V1.2.1 Quality of Telecom Services; Part 1: Methodology for Identification of Parameters Relevant to the Users*. Sophia Antipolis Cedex: European Telecommunications Standards Institute.

ETSI. (2012-10-22). *Network Functions Virtualisation—Introductory White Paper*. Sophia Antipolis, France: European Telecommunications Standardization Institute.

ETSI. (2014-12). *INF 010 NFV Service Quality Metrics*. Sophia Antipolis, France: European Telecommunications Standard Institute.

ETSI. (2014-12). *NFV-MAN 001 Management and Orchestration*. Sophia Antipolis, France: European Telecommunications Standardization Institute: http://www.etsi.org/deliver/etsi_gs/NFV-MAN/001_099/001/01.01.01_60/gs_NFV-MAN001v010101p.pdf.

ETSI. (2016-01). *NFV-REL 005—Network Function Virtualisation Report on Quality Accountability Framework.* Sophia Antipolis Cedex, France: European Telecommunication Standardization Institute.

FAA. (2008-01-08). *Reliability, Maintainability and Availability (RMA) Handbook.* Federal Aviation Administration, US Government.

Hayek, F. (1944). *The Road to Serfdom.* Chicago: University of Chicago Press.

Hunnebeck, L. (2011-07-29). *ITIL Service Design.* Norwich: The Stationary Office.

IEC. (1995). *CEI/IEC 300-3-9—Dependability Management—Part 3: Application Guide— Section 9: Risk Analysis of Technological Systems.* Geneva, Switzerland: International Electrotechnical Commission.

ISACA. (2009). *The Risk IT Framework.* Rolling Meadows, IL: ISACA: http://www.isaca .org.

ISO. (2009). *Guide 73—Risk Management—Vocabulary.* Geneva, Switzerland: International Organization for Standardization.

ISO. (2009-11-15). *31000—Risk Management Principles and Guidelines.* Geneva, Switzerland: International Organization for Standardization.

ISO. (2015-09-15). *9000—Quality Management Systems—Fundamentals and Vocabulary.* Geneva, Switzerland: International Organization for Standardization.

ISO. (2015-09-15). *9001—Quality Management Systems—Requirements.* Geneva, Switzerland: International Organization for Standardization.

ISO/IEC. (2005-08-01). *25000—Software Product Quality Requirements and Evaluation (SQuaRE)—Guide to SQuaRE.* Geneva, Switzerland: ISO/IEC.

ISO/IEC. (2008-12-15). *25012—Software Engineering—Data Quality Model.* Geneva, Switzerland: International Organization for Standardization and International Electrotechnical Commission.

ISO/IEC. (2009-10-01). *15939—Systems and Software Engineering—Measurement Process.* Geneva: International Organization for Standardization and International Electrotechnical Commission.

ISO/IEC. (2009-11). *31010—Risk Management—Risk Assessment Techniques.* Geneva, Switzerland: International Organization for Standardization and International Electrotechnical Committee.

ISO/IEC. (2011). *27005—Information Security Risk Management.* Geneva, Switzerland: International Organization for Standardization and International Electrotechnical Committee.

ISO/IEC. (2011-03-01). *25010—System and Software Quality Models.* Geneva, Switzerland: ISO/IEC.

ISO/IEC. (2011-04-15). *20000-1—IT Service Management System Requirements.* Geneva, Switzerland: International Organization for Standardization and International Electrotechnical Commission.

ISO/IEC. (2012). *25041—Systems and Software Quality Requirements and Evaluation (SQuaRE)—Evaluation Guide for Developers, Acquirers and Independent Evaluators.* Geneva: International Organization for Standardization and International Electrotechnical Commission.

ISO/IEC. (2012-02-15). *20000-2:2012—Guidance on the Application of Service Management Systems.* Geneva: International Organization for Standardization and International Electrotechnical Commission.

ISO/IEC. (2014-04-01). *Guide 51—Safety Aspects—Guidelines for Their Inclusion in Standards*. Geneva, Switzerland: International Organization for Standardization and International Electrotechnical Committee.

ISO/IEC. (2014-10-15). *17788—Cloud Computing—Overview and Vocabulary*. International Organization for Standardization and International Electrotechnical Committee.

ISO/IEC. (2014-10-15). *17789—Cloud Computing—Reference Architecture*. International Organization for Standardization and International Electrotechnical Committee.

ISO/IEC. (2015-09-15). *20243—Open Trusted Technology Provider™ Standards (O-TTPS)—Mitigating Maliciously Tainted and Counterfeit Products*. Geneva: International Organization for Standardization.

ISO/IEC/IEEE. (2006-12-15). *16085-2006—Systems and Software Engineering—Risk Management*. Geneva, Switzerland: International Organization for Standardization.

ISO/IEC/IEEE. (2010-12-15). *24765—Systems and Software Engineering Vocabulary*. Geneva: ISO, IEC, IEEE.

ISO/IEC/IEEE. (2013-09-01). *29119-1—Software Testing—Part 1: Concepts and Definitions*. Geneva, Switzerland: ISO/IEC/IEEE.

ISO/IEC/IEEE. (2013-09-01). *29119-2—Software Testing Part II Test Processes*. Geneva: ISO/IEC/IEEE.

ISO/IEC/IEEE. (2015-05-15). *15288—Systems and Software Engineering—System Life Cycle Processes*. Geneva: International Organization for Standardization et al.

ITU-T. (2008-09). *E.800 Definitions of Terms Related to Quality of Service*. Geneva: International Telecommunications Union.

Levinson, M. (2008). *The Box: How the Shipping Container Made the World*. Princeton: Princeton University Press.

Lloyd, V. (2011-07-29). *ITIL Continual Service Improvement (Best Management Practices)*. Norwich: The Stationary Office.

Mell, P., & Grance, T. (2011-09). *The NIST Definition of Cloud Computing*. Gaithersburg, MD: National Institute of Standards and Technology, US Government.

Musa, J. (1999). *Software Reliability Engineering*. New York: McGraw-Hill.

PJM Interconnection. (2014-02-06). Perfect dispatch fact sheet. Retrieved March 28, 2016, from Perfect Dispatch Fact Sheet: http://www.pjm.com/documents/~/media/about-pjm/newsroom/fact-sheets/perfect-dispatch-fact-sheet.ashx.

QuEST Forum. (2015-08). *Quality Measurement of Automated Lifecycle Management Actions*. tl9000.org: Quality Excellence for Suppliers of Telecommunications Forum. QuEST Forum: web resource included in QuEST Forum's TL 9000 supplemental measurements library: http://www.tl9000.org/resources/sup_measurements.html; document URL: http://www.tl9000.org/resources/documents/QuEST_Forum_ALMA_Quality_Measurement_150819.pdf.

QuEST Forum. (2012-12-31). *TL 9000 Measurements Handbook Release 5.0*. QuEST Forum: http://www.tl9000.org/handbooks/measurements_handbook.html.

Rance, S. (2011-07-29). *ITIL Service Transition (Best Management Practices)*. Norwich: The Stationery Office.

Schumpeter, J. (1950). *Capitalism, Socialism and Democracy*. New York: Harper Perennial Modern Classics.

Smith, M. L., & Erwin, J. (n.d.). Role & responsibility charting (RACI). Retrieved May 12, 2016, from https://pmicie.starchapter.com/images/downloads/raci_r_web3_1.pdf.

Snedaker, S. (2013). *Business Continuity and Disaster Recovery Planning for IT Professionals, Second Edition.* Rockland: Syngress.

Steinberg, R. A. (2011-07-29). *ITIL Service Operation (Best Management Practices).* Norwich: The Stationery Office.

Taleb, N. N. (2010). The Impact of the Highly Improbable: With a new section: "On Robustness and Fragility." *The Black Swan,* 2nd edition. Incerto.

TM Forum. (2012-11). *GB 917 SLA Management Handbook.* Morristown, New Jersey: Telemanagement Forum.

Index

Page numbers followed by f and t indicate figures and tables, respectively.

Printed and bound by CPI Group (UK) Ltd, Croydon, CR0 4YY

28/10/2024

01780263-0002